a killer chess opening repertoire

by Aaron Summerscale

EVERYMAN CHESS

Everyman Chess, formerly Cadogan Chess, is published by Everyman Publishers, London

First published in 1998 by Everyman Publishers plc, formerly Cadogan Books plc, Gloucester Mansions, 140A Shaftesbury Avenue, London WC2H 8HD in association with Gambit Publications Ltd, P.O. Box 32640, London W14 0JN.
Reprinted 2002

British Library Cataloguing in Publication Data
A CIP catalogue record for this book is available from the British Library.
ISBN 1 85744 519 8

Distributed in North America by The Globe Pequot Press, P.O. Box 480, 246 Goose Lane, Guilford, CT 06437-0480
Telephone 1-800 243 0495 (toll free)

All other sales enquiries should be directed to Everyman Chess, Gloucester Mansions, 140A Shaftesbury Avenue, London WC2H 8HD
tel: 020 7539 7600 fax: 020 7379 4060
email: chess@everymanbooks.com
website: www.everymanbooks.com

For Claire

EVERYMAN CHESS SERIES (formerly Cadogan Chess)
Chief Advisor: Garry Kasparov
Series Editor: Murray Chandler

Edited by Graham Burgess and Chris Baker and typeset by Petra Nunn for Gambit Publications Ltd.

Printed in Great Britain by The Bath Press, Bath, Somerset.

Contents

Symbols

+	check
++	double check
#	checkmate
!!	brilliant move
!	good move
!?	interesting move
?!	dubious move
?	bad move
??	blunder
+–	White is winning
±	White is much better
⩲	White is slightly better
=	equal position
⩱	Black is slightly better
∓	Black is much better
–+	Black is winning
Ch	championship
Cht	team championship
Wch	world championship
Ech	European championship
Wcht	World Team Championship
ECC	European Clubs Cup
Ct	candidates event
IZ	interzonal event
Z	zonal event
OL	olympiad
jr	junior event
wom	women's event
mem	memorial event
rpd	rapidplay game
corr	correspondence game
1-0	the game ends in a win for White
½-½	the game ends in a draw
0-1	the game ends in a win for Black
(*n*)	*n*th match game
(D)	see next diagram

Introduction

This book is aimed primarily at club-level players with a playing strength of up to about 2200 Elo (or 200 BCF). When I was a young player at school I was always looking out for new repertoire books. I wanted something which would give me all I needed to know about the opening, without being too time-consuming, as I had plenty of other things to do with my time. I guess you could say I was not a very serious chess student and in fact I delighted in getting my opponents on unfamiliar ground, when my natural ability would get a chance to shine through.

The problem I found with the repertoire books of the time was they attempted to cover too much material. Main-line variations would be covered in just a few pages, so justice was never done to the lines recommended. In the end I would have to consult a more specialized work on one of the suggested variations to find out the true story behind it and waste valuable time in the process. Meanwhile, I would suffer a few painful reverses, as my lack of understanding was exposed on the board.

The aim of this book is to provide a complete repertoire for the boy I used to be. The variations chosen are a little offbeat, but they fit together very nicely. The three main systems, the Barry Attack, the 150 Attack and the Colle-Zukertort, can be used against virtually any defence Black plays against to 1 d4. These contain the meat and bones of the book and once mastered will provide a complete repertoire for White against most defences. I have used all three successfully myself.

I have chosen systems that I believe will have the greatest psychological impact. There is a school of thought that says "you should play the man, not the board". If you accept this, then you can learn a lot about an opponent from their choice of opening variation. For example, King's Indian players tend to be well booked-up. They often accept structural weaknesses in return for attacking chances. The Barry Attack is likely to annoy King's Indian players, who will be thrown on to their own resources from an early stage in unfamiliar positions where the usual plans just don't work.

With reference to the material itself, wherever possible, I have tried to place the emphasis on understanding what is occurring through explanation, rather than by weighty variations. This is because, for the most part, the variations I recommend are flexible and the move-orders are often quite interchangeable. In such situations, understanding what you are trying to achieve is of far greater importance than remembering specific moves.

I have included a number of non-grandmaster games in the material. This is because I feel it will be useful for the reader to have a number of examples where Black defended less than perfectly, just as might happen in your average weekend tournament or local club match. These variations, although not objectively critical, should help to build your confidence in the recommended openings and aid you in understanding the various tactical motifs. Having confidence in your opening repertoire is in many ways as important as memorizing theory, because if you hit a snag, believing in your pet line will give you the self-assurance to solve any problems your opponent might set for you.

The astute reader will notice that Black has possibilities of achieving greater flexibility and therefore perhaps better chances of equality by utilizing a clever move-order, for instance, after 1 d4 ♘f6 2 ♘f3 c5 or 1 d4 d5 2 ♘f3 ♘f6 3 e3 and then 3...♗g4 or 3...c5. While it is possible to play a Colle-Zukertort system against these moves, Black has better chances than normal. Therefore, to make the repertoire more effective, I have included chapters on the Anti-Benoni, Classical Queen's Indian and Black's alternatives after 1 d4 d5 2 ♘f3. These variations give White the best chance of an opening advantage and can be added to the repertoire, as and when the reader feels ready, thus giving maximum flexibility. To save the reader time, I have tried to give only one recommendation per move for White, unless I felt it was prudent to give other examples of play to help you understand the main ideas. When I have given two possible continuations, they are usually of equal merit and it is up to you to decide which suits your personal style. Above all, I have offered variations that are likely to lead to the most fun for White as, after all, apart from for hard-nosed professionals, that is what playing chess is all about!

Aaron Summerscale
London, November 1998

1 The Barry Attack

Introduction

Why does the average club player as White need something offbeat against the King's Indian? Aren't the main lines good enough? To answer this, let us look at a main-line variation of the King's Indian.

1 d4 ♘f6 2 ♘f3 g6 3 c4 ♗g7 4 ♘c3 0-0 5 e4 d6 6 ♗e2 e5 7 0-0 ♘c6 8 d5 ♘e7 9 ♘e1 ♘d7 10 ♗e3 f5 11 f3 f4 12 ♗f2 g5 *(D)*

W

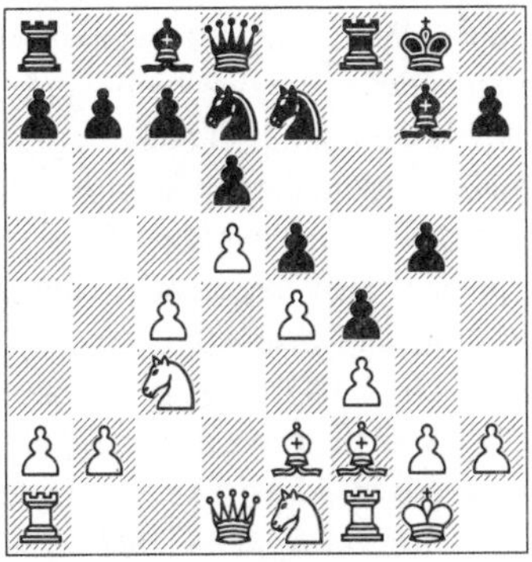

This is one of the critical main lines of the Classical King's Indian after 12 moves. For many players, White's position will represent a chess nightmare. Black has an automatic and very powerful long-term kingside attack. As if this weren't enough, there are plenty of books telling Black exactly how to proceed, either to deliver mate or create enough chaos to make the issue completely unclear. Perhaps the worst thing is that Black seems to have all the fun. If you haven't got hours, days or maybe even weeks to study this one line then you could be in trouble.

Why should White have to subject himself to this sort of onslaught in the search for an opening advantage? Isn't it time to put the ball back in Black's court? The Barry Attack avoids not only the King's Indian, but the Grünfeld as well. It is a 'plug in and play' opening which can be learnt in a few hours. The basic idea is simple, if a little crude. No more mister nice guy; it's time for blood!

For those who need a little reminder of just how much fun it can be to take White in the above diagram, I include the rest of the short and (for White) very painful game Perruchoud-Tischer, Biel 1990:

13 ♘b5 b6 14 b4 a6 15 ♘c3 ♘g6 16 a4 ♖b8 17 ♘d3 ♘f6 18 a5 bxa5 19 ♖xa5 h5 20 c5 g4 21 b5 g3 22 hxg3 fxg3 23 ♗xg3 h4 24 ♗f2 ♘h5 25 bxa6 ♕g5 26 ♗e1 ♘gf4 27 ♘xf4 ♘xf4 28 ♖f2 ♖b2 29 a7 ♕g3 30 a8♕ h3 31 ♗d2 ♖xd2 32 ♕xd2 h2+ 33 ♔h1 ♕xf2 0-1

Absolutely typical! Just as White was busying himself taking his opponent's queenside pieces and queening his passed pawn, Black launches a lethal mating attack. Enough of this pain and suffering! It's time for the Killer Barry Attack.

Game 1
Pira – Hebden
Seville 1987

1	**d4**	**♘f6**
2	**♘f3**	**g6**
3	**♘c3**	**d5**
4	**♗f4**	**♗g7**
5	**e3**	**0-0**
6	**♗e2** *(D)*	

B

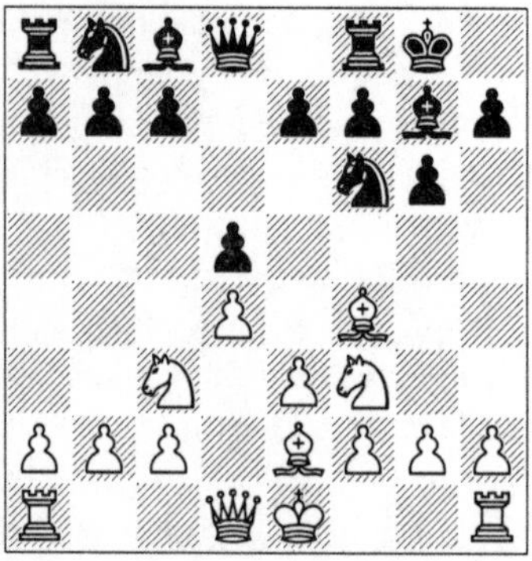

Welcome to the wonderful world of the Barry Attack. The outlook for the moment is calm and there is not a pawn-storm in sight! Well, certainly not against the white king anyway. White has a crude, almost barbaric plan from this position: shove the h-pawn up the board and attempt to tear the black king limb from limb! There are a few circumstances when, as you might expect, this is not justified: specifically, when Black plays 6...c5 and continues to attack the centre and queenside aggressively. Then it is time to show your opponent that you are not just a mad hacker and hone those endgame skills to exploit the small but persistent advantages that arise. One of the main plus-points of the Barry Attack is that this time there are almost no books for Black to go running back to check.

6 ... c5

The year 1987 was a particularly important one for the Barry Attack, for it was the year that Mark Hebden was introduced, somewhat painfully, to its delights. After his defeat in this game, Hebden, a renowned King's Indian specialist, went home and had a long, hard look at the opening. As we will see, today he is one of the world's leading exponents of the Barry Attack – he obviously came to the conclusion "if you can't beat them, join them!"

6...c6 7 h4, 6...♗g4 7 ♘e5 and 6...b6 7 ♘e5 are all important alternatives, which we will examine later.

7 ♘e5 b6?!

7...♘c6 is critical – it is important for Black to put as much pressure on the white centre as possible, so as to dissuade White from his kingside attack.

8 h4 ♗a6
9 ♗f3

The light-squared bishop plays a very important part in supporting

White's kingside attack, so naturally White avoids its exchange.

9 ... ♗b7
10 h5 ♘bd7
11 hxg6 fxg6

This gives Black some central light-squared weaknesses (particularly e6) but is safer than the other recapture, which is extremely dangerous for the health of the black king.

If 11...hxg6 then 12 ♗g4 with the idea of ♕f3-h3.

12 ♗g4 ♘xg4
13 ♕xg4 *(D)*

B

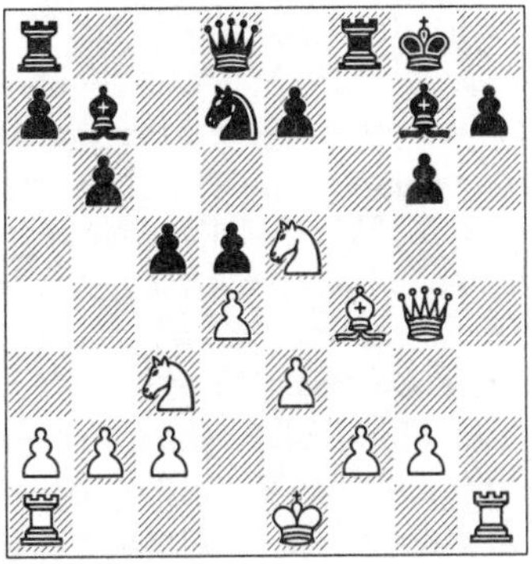

One thing you will often notice about the Barry Attack is that although White tends to build up a powerful attacking position, like here, he leaves no real weaknesses for Black to exploit. Indeed, if you look at the diagram you will see that it is Black who has the weak points for White to target.

13 ... ♖f5
14 ♕h3 ♘f8
15 g4 ♖xf4

Sometimes Black will have to sacrifice in order to get meaningful counterplay and to stem the tide of the white attack. Here, this proves to be insufficient, but the alternatives were not much more attractive. If 15...♖f6 then 16 ♗h6 gives White a strong kingside attack, at no risk.

16 exf4 cxd4
17 ♘e2 g5
18 ♕h5 ♕d6
19 ♕f7+ ♔h8
20 0-0-0 ♗xe5
21 fxe5 ♕xe5
22 ♘xd4 ♕g7
23 ♕xg7+ ♔xg7 *(D)*

W

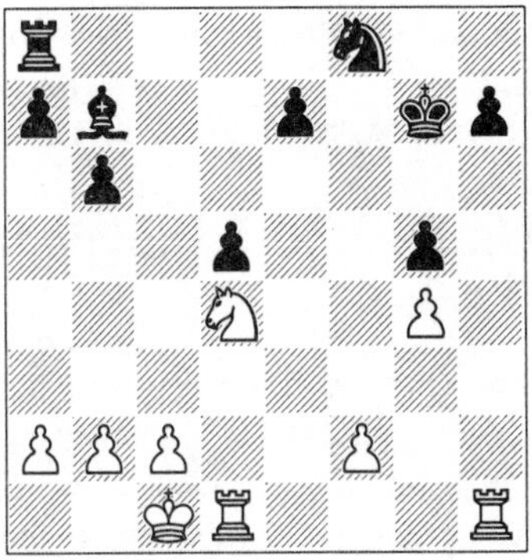

Black struggles on from here valiantly, but is ultimately lost, not only because of the material disadvantage, but also due to the passivity of his pieces.

24 ♖de1 ♖e8 25 ♖h5 ♔g6 26 ♘f3 h6 27 ♘e5+ ♔g7 28 ♖eh1 d4 29 ♖1h2 ♖c8 30 f4 gxf4 31 ♖f5 ♘g6 32 ♘xg6 ♔xg6 33 ♖xf4 e5 34 ♖f5 ♖c5 35 ♖fh5 ♗e4

Black has done a great deal to improve the positioning of his pieces, but has not been able to redress the weakness of his pawn-structure.

36 ♖xh6+ ♔g5 37 ♖h8 ♔xg4 38 ♖f8 ♗f3 39 ♔d2 e4 40 ♖d8 ♖c4 41 b3 ♖c7 42 ♖xd4 ♔g3 43 ♖h8 ♔f2 44 ♖e8 ♖g7 45 ♖dxe4

White simplifies to a won rook and pawn endgame.

45...♗xe4 46 ♖xe4 ♖d7+ 47 ♔c3 ♔f3 48 ♖e8 ♖c7+ 49 ♔b2 ♔f4 50 c4 ♔f5 51 ♔c3 b5 52 ♖e2 ♔f4 53 ♔d4 bxc4 54 bxc4 ♖d7+ 55 ♔c5 ♔f3 56 ♖e6 ♖c7+ 57 ♔d5 ♔f4 58 c5 ♔f5 59 ♖e2 ♖d7+ 60 ♔c6 ♖h7 61 ♔d6 1-0

Again, it is no coincidence that shortly after this game, Hebden became one of the Barry Attack's strongest advocates.

Unusual fifth moves for Black

The Barry Attack is a somewhat unusual opening and as such, may encourage irregular responses from Black. As we shall see in this section, this approach by no means guarantees Black success.

Game 2

R. Scherbakov – Hoang Thang

Cheliabinsk 1989

1	**d4**	**♘f6**
2	**♘f3**	**g6**
3	**♘c3**	**d5**
4	**♗f4**	**♗g7**

5 e3 *(D)*

B

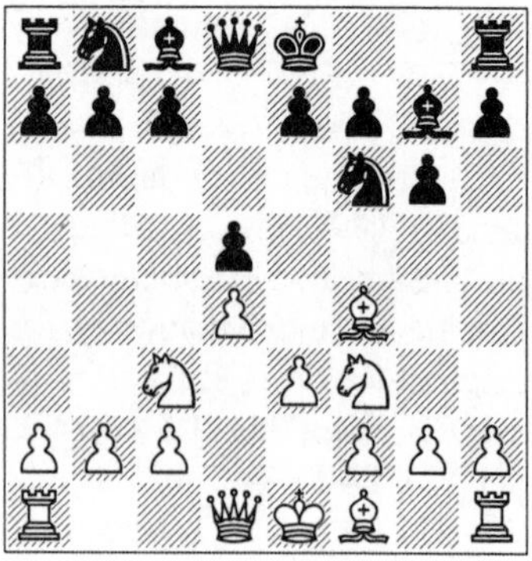

5 ... a6

The alternatives are:

a) 5...♘bd7?? 6 ♘b5 +– has been a quick point-collector on the British tournament circuit.

b) 5...♘h5? is an attempt to harass the white bishop but wastes too much time. 6 ♗g5 h6 7 ♗h4 g5 (the most logical continuation of Black's somewhat dubious plan, which he began on move 5, to bag the bishop-pair; with accurate moves, White is able to exploit Black's loss of tempi) 8 ♘e5!. Now Black has a choice:

b1) 8...♘f6 is a little illogical, because the whole point of Black's play has been to exchange off White's dark-squared bishop. If Black fails to achieve this, he has simply weakened his kingside for no apparent reason. White has a clear edge after 9 ♗g3 ♗f5 10 ♗d3 ♗xd3 11 ♕xd3 c6 12 h4 g4 13 h5 ♘bd7 14 ♕e2 ♕a5 15 ♘xd7 ♔xd7 16 0-0-0, Wirthensohn-Bloessel, Lenk 1992.

b2) 8...♗xe5 9 dxe5 ♘g7 (after 9...gxh4 10 ♕xh5 Black has no compensation for his kingside pawn weaknesses) 10 ♗g3 ♗e6 11 h4! (the most incisive – Black is made to pay for his over-ambitious kingside pawn advances) 11...♖g8 12 hxg5 hxg5 13 e4 ± (Black is given no respite and now faces the unenviable choice of opening the centre for White's better placed forces, or closing it, and leaving his knight on g7 woefully misplaced) 13...dxe4 (13...d4 14 ♘a4 b6 15 ♕d2 f6 16 exf6 exf6 17 0-0-0 c5 18 ♘c3 ♕e7 leads to a large advantage for White after 19 ♘b5) 14 ♕xd8+ ♔xd8 15 ♘xe4 ♘f5 16 0-0-0+ ♔e8 17 ♘xg5 ♘xg3 18 ♘xe6 ♘xh1? 19 ♖d8# (1-0) J.Přibyl-Penzold, 2nd Bundesliga 1992. An unusual mating position!

c) 5...♗f5 6 ♗e2 c6. Black often has difficulties in the Barry Attack with the development of his light-squared bishop. On g4 it can be attacked by ♘e5, while on f5, as here, it can be a target for White's kingside pawn advances. The awkward positioning of Black's bishop led to an advantage for White in Suetin-Borisenko, USSR Ch (Kiev) 1954 after 7 ♘e5 ♘fd7 8 g4 ♗e6 9 ♘d3 c5 10 0-0 0-0 11 ♘b5 ♘a6 12 ♗g3 ♘f6 13 ♘f4 ♗d7 14 ♘c3 cxd4 15 exd4 ♘c7 16 ♗f3 ♗c6 17 ♖e1 b6 18 ♘d3 ♗b7 19 ♗e5 ♘e6 20 ♗g2 ♖c8 21 ♕e2 ♘e4 22 ♘xe4 dxe4 23 ♗xe4 ♗xe4 24 ♕xe4 ♘xd4 25 ♗xg7 ♔xg7 26 ♖ad1 ♘c6 27 ♘c5 ♕e8 28 ♘d7 ♖h8 29 b4 b5 30 a4. White has kept the initiative.

6 ♗e2 **♘bd7**
7 ♘e5 **c6**
8 h4 *(D)*

B

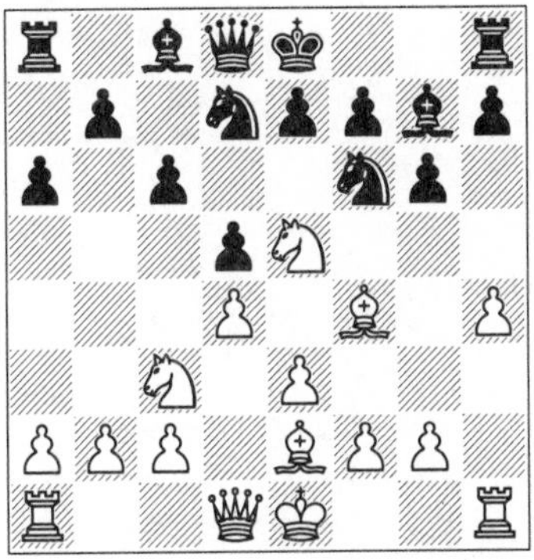

This is the basic attacking set-up in the Barry Attack. The advance of the h-pawn works best if Black adopts a slow plan, typically when he avoids the advance ...c5.

8 ... **♘e4**

Black tries to defuse the oncoming attack using the accepted method of piece exchanges, but he suffers a lack of coordination since his king is still in the centre. Although the black king is safer in the middle, White nevertheless finds a clever way to create problems on the kingside.

9 ♘xe4 **dxe4**
10 h5 **♘xe5**
11 h6! *(D)*

A nice intermezzo. The move h6 can be a major irritant to Black if he has not castled kingside, and justifies White's early kingside pawn advance.

11 ... **♕a5+**
12 ♕d2 **♕xd2+**

B

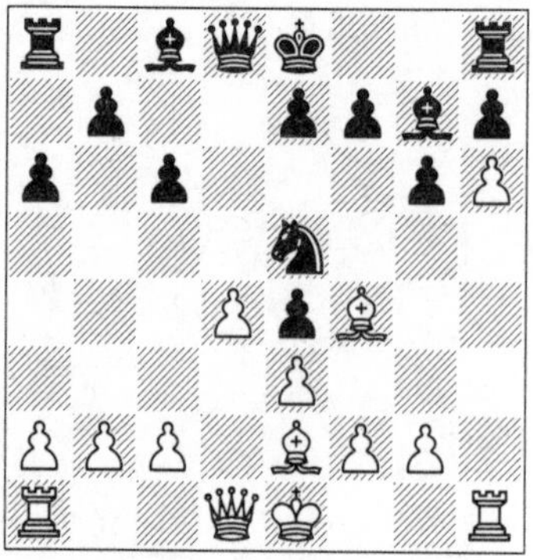

13	♔xd2	♗xh6
14	♗xe5	f6
15	♖xh6	fxe5
16	♖ah1	♗e6
17	♖xg6	

The dust has settled and material equality has been restored. Black is saddled with the worse bishop and, more importantly, a damaged pawn-structure. At grandmaster level, Black is simply lost, with no way to defend his weaknesses in the long term. To his credit, Black struggles on valiantly for 30 moves, but the result is never in doubt.

17...♔d7 18 ♖g7 ♖ag8 19 ♖xg8 ♖xg8 20 g3 exd4 21 exd4 ♖f8 22 ♔e3 ♗f5 23 ♔d2 ♔d6 24 ♔e3 ♗g6 25 ♗h5 ♗f5 26 ♖h4 e5 27 dxe5+ ♔xe5 28 ♖f4 ♖d8 29 g4 ♗g6 30 ♗xg6 hxg6 31 ♖xe4+ ♔f6 32 f4 ♖d1 33 ♖d4 ♖b1 34 ♖d6+ ♔e7 35 ♖xg6 ♖xb2 36 ♔d3 ♖xa2 37 ♖g7+ ♔f6 38 ♖xb7 ♖a4 39 c4 ♖a3+ 40 ♔d4 ♖f3 41 ♔e4 ♖c3 42 g5+ ♔g6 43 ♔d4 ♖f3 44 ♔e5 ♖e3+ 45 ♔d6 ♖e4 46 c5 ♖xf4 47 ♔xc6 ♔xg5 48 ♖e7 ♔f6 49 ♖e3 ♖c4 50 ♔d5 ♖c1 51 ♖e6+ 1-0

5...♗g4

Game 3
Blatny – Fette
Vienna 1991

1	**d4**	**♘f6**
2	**♘f3**	**g6**
3	**♘c3**	**d5**
4	**♗f4**	**♗g7**
5	**e3**	**♗g4** *(D)*

W

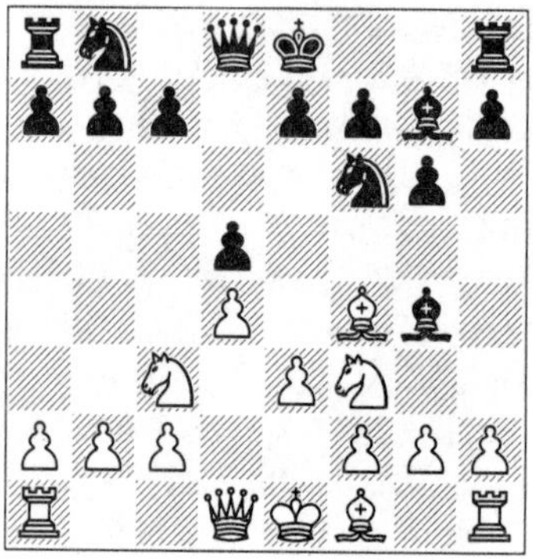

6 ♗e2

This move is standard, but Mark Hebden introduced an important new idea at the 1997 British Championship, viz. 6 ♕d3, by which White attempts to take advantage of the fact that Black has not yet castled. 6...c6 (6...♗xf3 7 ♕b5+ ♘bd7 8 gxf3 wins a pawn for White) 7 ♘e5 ♗f5 8 ♕d2 ♘bd7 9 h4 h5 10 f3 ♖c8 11 ♗e2 b5 12 ♘d1 (White shows that he too does not yet need to commit his king; the c3-knight, which was possibly White's worst-placed piece, manoeuvres to f2, from where it will assist with the kingside attack) 12...0-0 (Black decides he has run out of useful waiting moves, but in any case, he cannot put off castling indefinitely) 13 c3 ♘e8 14 ♘f2 ♘d6 15 g4 hxg4 16 ♘exg4 ♗xg4 17 ♘xg4 (this is the culmination of White's plan which he began on move 12; the g4-knight is a key attacking piece) 17...f5 18 ♘e5 ♘xe5 19 dxe5 ♘c4 20 ♗xc4 dxc4 (despite Black's piece exchanges, his kingside remains chronically weak; White now mops up with ease) 21 ♕g2 ♕d5 (21...♕e8 22 h5 gxh5 23 ♗h6 ♕f7 24 ♖g1) 22 ♕xg6 ♖cd8 (22...♕xf3 23 ♖g1 ♖f7 24 e6) 23 ♖g1 ♕d2+ 24 ♔f1 ♕d3+ 25 ♔g2 ♖f7 26 ♔h3 e6 27 ♕xe6 ♔f8 28 ♖ad1 ♖e8 29 ♕xc6 ♕e2 30 ♕d6+ ♔g8 31 ♕d5 1-0 Hebden-Bates, British Ch (Hove) 1997.

6	**...**	**c6**
7	**♘e5**	**♗xe2**
8	**♕xe2**	**♘bd7**
9	**0-0-0**	**0-0**

Alternatively, 9...♕a5 is a more logical continuation of Black's plan to delay castling for as long as possible. In practice, play has continued 10 ♘xd7 ♘xd7 11 e4 dxe4 12 ♕xe4 e6 13 h4 ♘f6 14 ♕e5 (White aims for a small endgame advantage, but could also play for a kingside attack with ♕e2, g4, h4-h5) 14...♕xe5 15 ♗xe5 0-0 16 f3 ♖fd8 17 g4 ♘d5 18 ♘e4 b5 19 g5 ± Blatny-Lutz, Altensteig 1991. White's advantage lies in his control of the dark squares and the difficulty Black has in striking back at White's centre.

10	**h4**	**♕a5**
11	**h5** *(D)*	

B

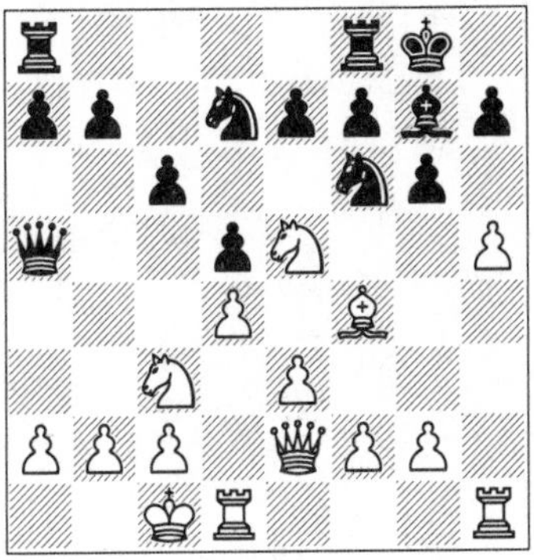

White's idea is very simple: prise open the h-file and mate!

11	**...**	**♘xe5**
12	**dxe5**	**♘e4**
13	**hxg6**	**♘xc3** *(D)*

Instead:

a) 13...fxg6 gives White another avenue of attack: 14 ♘xe4 dxe4 15 ♕c4+ ♖f7 (15...♔h8 16 ♖xh7+ ♔xh7 17 ♖h1+ ♗h6 18 ♗xh6 +–) 16 ♖xh7 +–.

b) 13...hxg6 14 ♕g4 ♘xc3 15 bxc3 ♖fd8 16 ♕h4 ♔f8 17 ♕h7 e6 18 ♖d3 (White safeguards his king before beginning the final attacking phase) 18...♕xa2 19 ♔d2 ♕a3 20 ♖h3 a5 21 ♖f3 (White has a brutal plan in mind: transfer the bishop to f6 and mate!) 21...♖d7 (21...♕e7 22 ♗h6 ♗xh6 23 ♕h8#) 22 ♗g5 a4 (Black's plan of pushing the a-pawn looks a little slow, but he is at a loss for any meaningful counterplay) 23 ♗f6 ♗xf6 24 exf6 ♔e8 25 ♕h8+ ♕f8 26 ♖h3 1-0 Blatny-Peek, Groningen 1990.

W

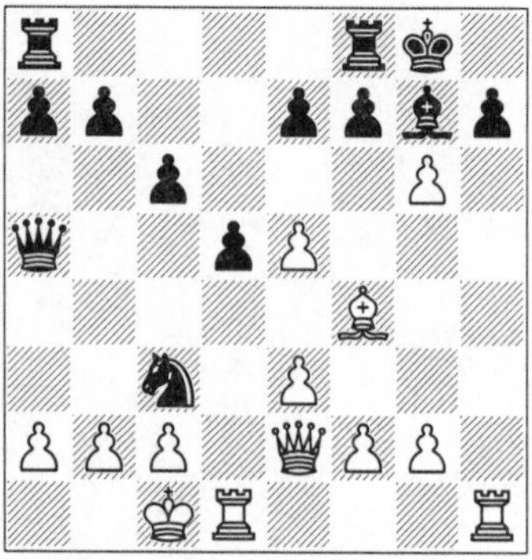

14 ♕h5

Quite amusingly, White is just ignoring Black and getting on with the business in hand.

14 ... ♘xa2+
15 ♔b1 fxg6
16 ♕xh7+ ♔f7
17 ♗h6 ♖g8
18 ♖h4 g5
19 ♗xg7 gxh4

19...♖xg7 loses to 20 ♕f5+ ♔g8 21 ♕e6+ ♖f7 22 ♖h7.

20 ♗f6+ ♔e6
21 ♕xe7+ ♔f5 *(D)*

W

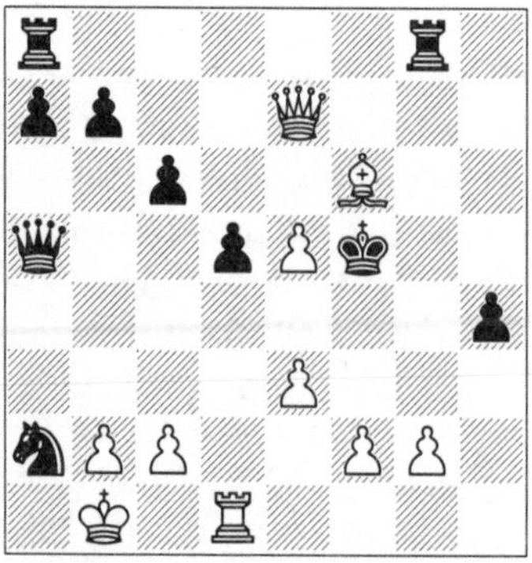

22 ♕h7+ ♔e6
23 e4 1-0

Black is defenceless against the threats of ♕e7# and ♕f5+.

5...c6: Black delays ...0-0

Game 4
Hodgson – Wolff
New York 1990

1 d4 ♘f6
2 ♘f3 g6
3 ♘c3 d5
4 ♗f4 ♗g7
5 e3 c6
6 ♗e2 *(D)*

B

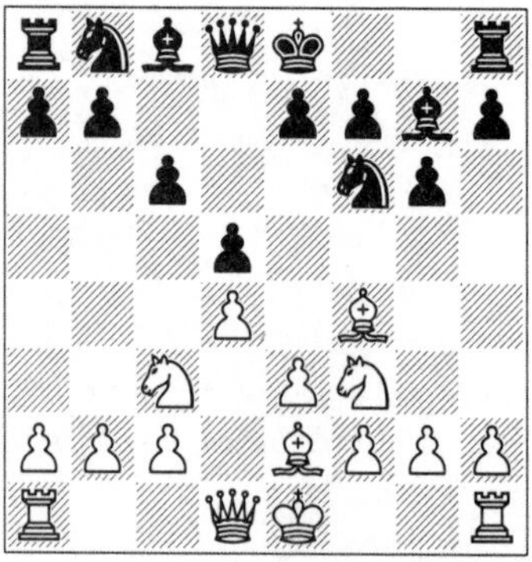

6 ... ♕b6

If Black is trying to delay castling kingside, then this is probably his most logical choice. By attacking the pawn on b2, Black more or less forces a weakening of White's queenside, which makes long castling less attractive and more difficult to achieve. Nevertheless, as White shows in this game, the queen is misplaced on b6 if White switches plans and instead decides to attack on the queenside.

The other main option is 6...♘bd7, by which Black seeks to delay castling and at the same time exchange off one of White's most influential pieces. 7 ♘e5 ♘xe5 8 ♗xe5 ♗e6 9 g4 h6 10 ♕d2 ♕d7 11 f3 0-0 *(D)* and now:

W

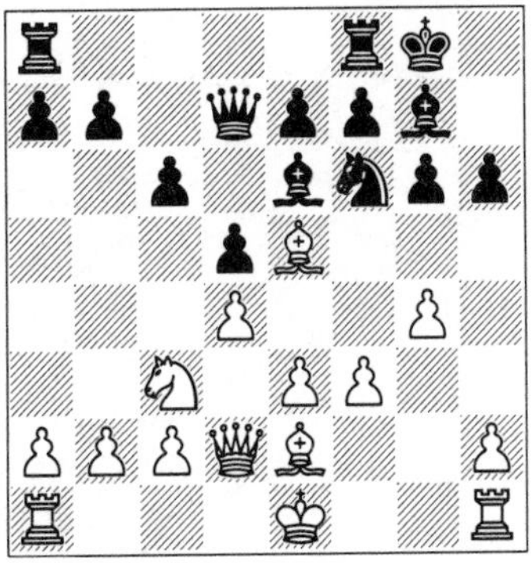

a) 12 0-0-0 leads to a real bloodbath, with both sides going all-out for the kill, and is certainly the most uncompromising approach. 12...b5 13 h4 a5 14 g5 gives rise to a typical scenario when players have castled on opposite sides. Each colour has quickly advancing pawn storms on both flanks. This type of position is not for the faint-hearted, as winning or losing often depends on a single tempo. 14...♘h5 15 ♗xg7 ♔xg7 16 ♖dg1 hxg5 17 hxg5 ♖h8 18 ♕e1 (18 f4 ♘g3!?) 18...♕d6 19 f4 a4 20 ♘d1 b4 21 ♖h4 c5 22 dxc5 ♕xc5 23 ♗d3 ♖ac8 24 ♖g2 d4 25 f5 (it is essential for both sides to open lines against the enemy king as soon as possible, even at the cost of material) 25...gxf5 (25...♗xf5 26 exd4 ♕d5 27 ♗xf5 ♕xf5 28 ♕xe7 is unclear) 26 exd4 ♕d5 27 ♘e3 ♕xa2 28 ♘xf5+ ♗xf5 29 ♕e5+ (a clever intermezzo, forcing the king to an inferior square, before recapturing the bishop) 29...♔g8 30 ♗xf5 a3 31 bxa3 e6 (31...♕xa3+ 32 ♔d2 ♕c3+ 33 ♔e2 ♕c4+ 34 ♔f2) 32 g6 exf5 33 gxf7+ ♔xf7 34 ♕xf5+ (it is fair to say that White has won the race to expose the enemy king; the black monarch is caught in no man's land, with nowhere safe to run) 34...♔e7 (the other attempt at defence, 34...♘f6 35 ♕g6+ ♔e7 36 ♖e2+ ♔d7 37 ♕g7+ ♔c6 38 ♕xf6+, is no better for Black) 35 ♖e4+ ♔d8 36 ♕g5+ ♔c7 37 ♕e7+ ♔b8 38 ♕xb4+ ♔a8 39 ♕a4+ ♔b8 40 ♕b5+ ♔a8 41 ♕a5+ ♔b8 42 ♕b4+ (White has been teasing Black for the last few moves, letting him know who's boss, and now comes in for the kill!) 42...♔a8 43 ♖e5 (although more complicated, 43 ♖e7 is perhaps a quicker way to finish Black off: 43...♕a1+ 44 ♔d2 ♖xc2+ 45 ♔xc2 ♕a2+ {45...♖c8+ 46 ♔b3 ♕d1+ 47 ♔a2 ♖c2+ 48 ♖xc2 ♕xc2+ 49 ♕b2 ♕c4+ 50 ♕b3 +−} 46 ♔d1 ♕a1+ 47 ♔d2 ♕a2+ 48 ♔e3 +−) 43...♖h7 44 ♖ge2 ♖a7 45 ♖xh5 ♖xa3 46 ♕b2 ♕xb2+ 47 ♔xb2 (Black has managed to survive to the endgame, but unfortunately for him, it is completely lost) 47...♖ac3 48 ♖b5 ♖3c4 49 ♖d2 ♖8c7 50 ♖b3 ♖b7 51 ♖dd3 1-0 Hebden-Ernst, London Lloyds Bank 1991.

b) 12 ♘d1 b5 13 ♘f2 is perhaps a more circumspect way to attack the black king, without giving Black such a large target to aim at. The plan is h4 and business as usual. In this position, White would continue to delay castling, since, for the moment, his king is undoubtedly safer in the centre than on the queenside.

7 a3! ♗g4 *(D)*

After 7...♕xb2?? 8 ♘a4 Black loses his queen.

W

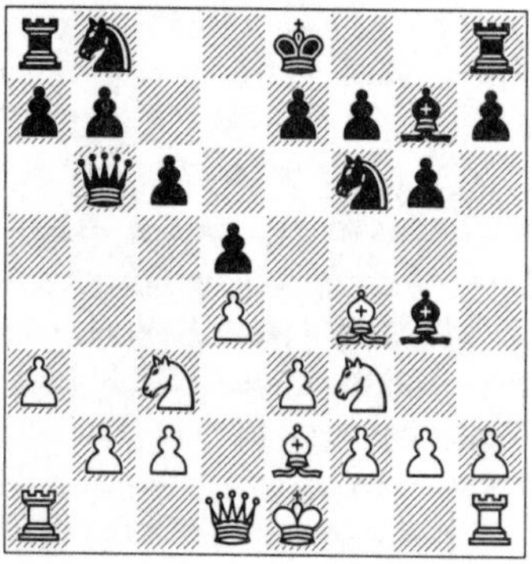

8 b4

White attempts to set up a bind on the queenside, making it harder for Black to achieve the freeing advance ...c5. This more or less obliges Black to seek counterplay in the centre via ...e5. If White can prevent this, he will have a positional advantage.

8 ... ♘bd7

9 0-0

9 h3 is interesting, aiming to avoid the problems White is presented with in the main line.

9 ... ♘h5

10 ♗g5 h6

10...e5? is a move Black would like to play, but it has a tactical drawback: 11 ♘xe5 ♗xe2 12 ♘xd7 ♗xd1 13 ♘xb6 axb6 14 ♖fxd1 wins a pawn for White.

11 ♗h4 g5

12 h3 *(D)*

B

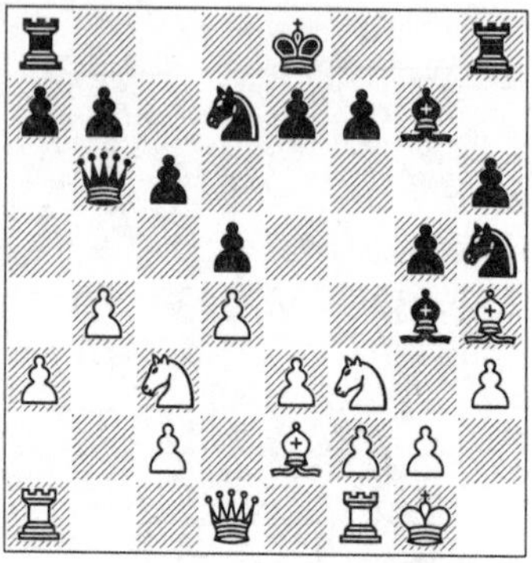

This is an intelligent way for White to keep his dark-squared bishop, a key piece in the fight for control of e5.

12 ... ♗e6

White meets 12...gxh4 by 13 hxg4 ♘hf6 14 ♘xh4 and 12...♗xh3!? by 13 gxh3 gxh4 14 ♘xh4 ♘hf6 15 ♘f5.

13 ♘d2 ♘f4

14 ♗g3 ♘xe2+

15 ♕xe2 f5

Black discourages e4 in the long term and prepares counterplay on the kingside.

16 ♘b3 ♕d8

17 ♘a5

White is slightly better because of his bind on the queenside and the awkwardly placed bishop on e6.

17 ... ♕c8
18 ♘a4 b6

Black feels compelled to evict the knight from e5, but creates a potential weakness on c6 in the process.

19 ♘b3 0-0
20 ♖ac1 ♗f7
21 f4

White prevents ...e5 and fixes a possible weakness on f5.

21 ... ♘f6
22 fxg5 hxg5
23 ♘d2 *(D)*

B

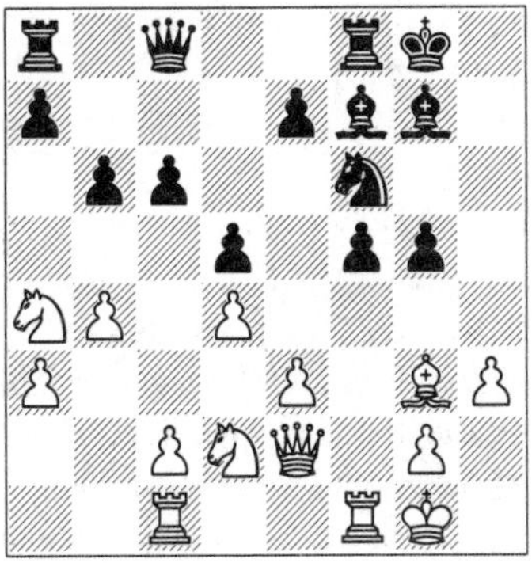

Play is now concentrated on the battle for control of e5.

23 ... ♕e6
24 ♖ce1 ♘d7
25 ♘f3 ♗h5
26 ♘b2 a5

Because Black cannot realistically achieve the freeing advance ...e5, he instead opts for queenside counterplay.

27 ♘d3 axb4
28 axb4 ♖a2
29 ♕d1 ♕h6

As White controls the centre, Black must seek counterplay on the flanks.

30 ♕b1 ♖a3
31 ♘fe5 ♘xe5
32 ♗xe5 ♗xe5
33 ♘xe5 *(D)*

B

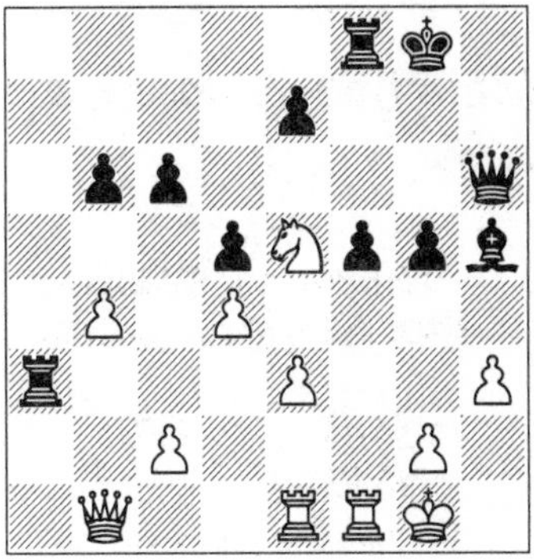

This is the culmination of White's plan: he has complete control of the e5-square, and his knight is superbly placed.

33 ... g4

Black has lost the strategic battle and so tries to muddy the waters.

34 hxg4 ♗xg4
35 c4 ♖fa8

35...♖xe3 36 ♕c1 +–.

36 cxd5 ♖a2

36...cxd5 37 ♘xg4 fxg4 38 ♕f5 ±.

37 ♘xg4

White trades in his positional advantage for a material one.

37 ... fxg4
38 ♕e4 g3
39 ♕g4+ ♔h8
40 ♕xg3 ♖g8
41 ♕e5+ ♕g7

42	♕xg7+	♖xg7
43	♖f2	♖xf2
44	♔xf2	cxd5
45	♖h1+	♔g8

1-0

After ♖h6 White is completely winning.

Main line: 5...0-0 6 ♗e2 ♗g4

Game 5
Hebden – L. Williams
British Ch (Swansea) 1995

1	d4	♘f6
2	♘f3	g6
3	♘c3	d5
4	♗f4	♗g7
5	e3	0-0
6	♗e2	♗g4 *(D)*

W

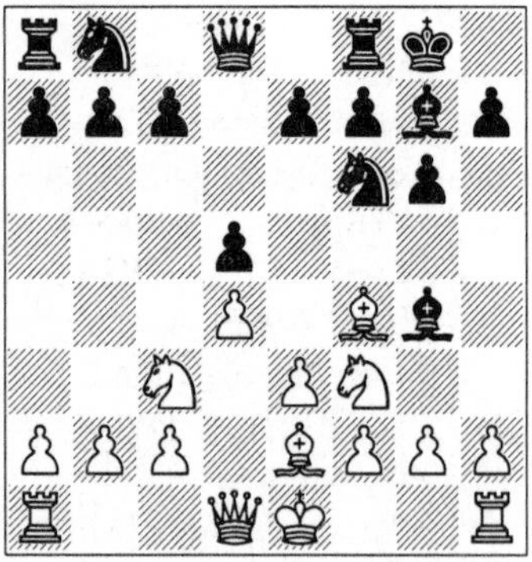

As Black often has a problem with his light-squared bishop, it may seem logical to solve this by exchanging it, the drawback being the acceleration of White's attack.

7	♘e5	♗xe2
8	♕xe2	c6

Black's other main option is 8...c5. This is an interesting hybrid of the ...♗g4 and ...c5 systems, which White should seek to exploit immediately by 9 ♕b5 cxd4 10 exd4, when Black has a fairly wide choice:

a) 10...♕b6 11 ♕xb6 axb6 leaves Black with permanently weak pawns, and White with at least a small advantage.

b) 10...b6 weakens Black's control of the light squares on the queenside. For example: 11 0-0 ♘bd7? 12 ♘c6 ♕e8 13 ♖fe1 ±.

c) 10...♕c8 11 ♘xd5 ♘xd5 12 ♕xd5 ±.

d) 10...♘c6 is critical, but is not ultimately sufficient for equality. 11 ♕xb7 ♘xd4 12 0-0-0 ♖b8 (12...♘h5 13 ♖xd4 ♘xf4 14 ♘c6 ±) 13 ♕xa7 (although it may appear dangerous for White to open lines towards his own king, he has a material advantage and Black is hard-pressed to keep the queens on) 13...♘b5 14 ♘xb5 ♖xb5 15 ♘c6 ♕a8 (avoiding the endgame is no better: 15...♕e8 16 ♘xe7+ {16 a4!?} 16...♔h8 17 ♗e5 +–) 16 ♘xe7+ ♔h8 17 ♕xa8 ♖xa8 18 ♗e5 ♖xa2 19 c4 ♖b7 (19...dxc4 20 ♖d8+; 19...♖c5 20 ♔b1 +–) 20 ♔b1 ♖axb2+ (the last throw of the dice) 21 ♗xb2 ♘e4 22 ♖xd5 ♘c3+ (22...♖xb2+ 23 ♔c1 +–) 23 ♔c1 ♘a2+ 24 ♔d1 ♗xb2 25 ♖a5 ♗d4 26 ♖xa2 ♖b1+ 27 ♔e2 ♖xh1 28 ♘c6 ♗f6 29 h3 ♖c1 30 ♘a5 ♔g7 31 ♔d3 h5 32 ♖c2 +– Hebden-McDonald,

British Ch (Eastbourne) 1991. The bishop versus knight endgame is won for White, while if Black keeps the rook, then he simply pushes his c-pawn.

9 h4 *(D)*

This is the prescribed medicine whenever Black adopts a slow system.

Instead 9 0-0-0 led to a nice attacking win for White in the game Vescovi-O.Jakobsen, Copenhagen 1995: 9...♘h5 10 g4 ♘xf4 11 exf4 e6 12 ♘a4 ♘d7 13 h4 ♘xe5 14 fxe5 ♕a5 15 b3 c5 16 dxc5 b5 17 ♘b2 ♕xa2 18 ♘d3 ♖fc8 19 f4 ♗f8 20 ♔d2 ♕a5+ 21 b4 ♕c7 22 h5 a5 23 hxg6 fxg6 24 f5 axb4 25 fxg6 ♗xc5 26 ♖xh7 ♗e7 27 ♕e3 ♕xc2+ 28 ♔e1 ♕c3+ 29 ♖d2 ♖c4 30 ♖h8+ 1-0.

B

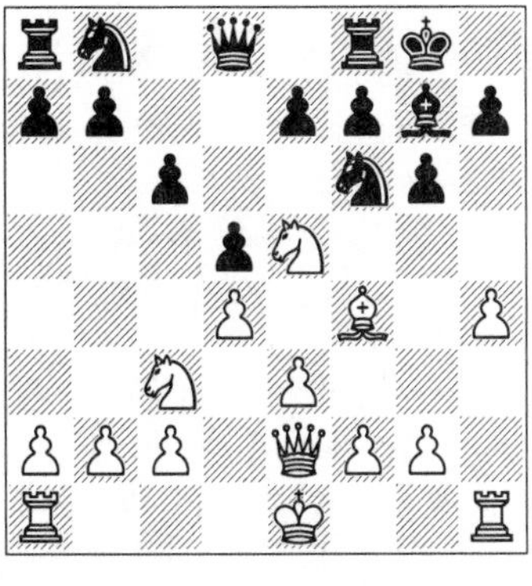

9 ... ♘bd7

The active 9...♕a5 resulted in the usual bloodfest in Blatny-Trapl, Cham 1991: 10 h5 c5 11 hxg6 fxg6 12 ♕f3 ♘c6 13 ♕h3 ♘xe5 14 dxe5 ♘h5 15 0-0-0 d4 16 ♕e6+ ♔h8 17 ♘e4 c4 18 g4 dxe3 19 fxe3 ♕xa2 20 gxh5 ♕a1+ 21 ♔d2 ♖ad8+ 22 ♔e2 ♖xd1 23 ♖xd1 ♕xb2 24 ♘g5 ♕xc2+ 25 ♖d2 ♕f5 26 ♕xf5 ♖xf5 27 ♘e6 ♔g8 28 ♖d8+ ♔f7 29 ♘g5+ ♖xg5 30 ♗xg5 ♗xe5 31 ♖d7 ♗d6 32 hxg6+ hxg6 33 ♖xb7 a5 34 ♗f4 ♗b4 35 ♖c7 c3 36 ♗e5 1-0.

10 0-0-0 ♘h5

This move is necessary in order for Black to slow down White's attack. However, as the course of the game shows, while White's dark-squared bishop is useful, it is not essential in the attack against the black king.

Black has two alternatives:

a) 10...♕a5 has already been considered in Game 3.

b) 10...♖c8 will be discussed in Game 9.

11 g4 ♘xf4

12 exf4 e6

13 h5 f6?

Black panics in a difficult position. After 13...♕e7, White still has a strong attack, but Black is by no means completely lost.

14 ♘xg6! *(D)*

B

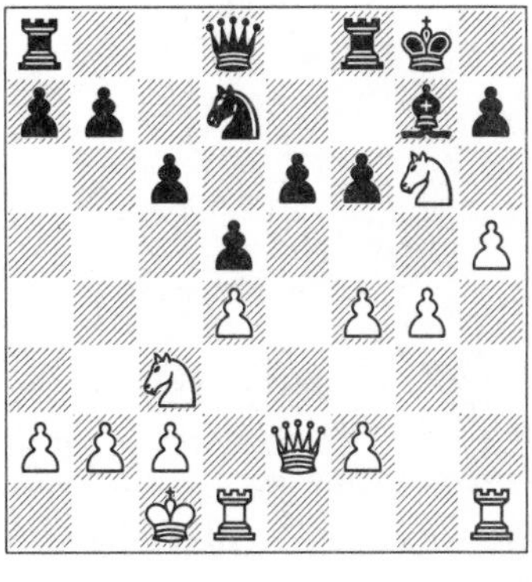

14 ... ♖e8

If 14...hxg6 White cleans up as follows: 15 ♕xe6+ ♔h7 16 hxg6+ ♔xg6 17 f5+ ♔g5 18 ♕e3+ ♔xg4 19 ♕h3+ ♔f4 20 ♘e2+ ♔e4 21 ♕d3#.

15 h6

15 ♘h4 is a more materialistic approach, but is not in keeping with the demands of the position.

15 ... hxg6
16 hxg7 ♔xg7
17 ♕e3 f5
18 g5

Black has fought off the first wave of the white attack, but can do little about the weakness of his king in the long term.

18 ... ♕e7

18...♖h8 is met by 19 ♕xe6.

19 ♖h3 ♖h8
20 ♖dh1 ♖ag8
21 ♘e2 ♕e8
22 ♕a3! *(D)*

B

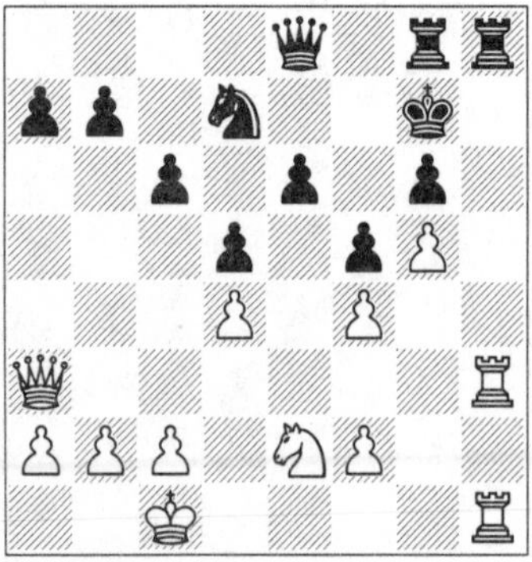

A masterful switch-over in order to bring the queen into the centre of the action.

22 ... ♖xh3
23 ♖xh3 a6
24 ♕d6

The white queen rules supreme in the heart of the black position.

24 ... ♕f7
25 ♕c7 ♕e7

25...♘f8 fails to 26 ♕e5+.

26 ♘g1

The black queenside pawns are going nowhere, so White can afford the time to improve the position of his worst placed piece.

26 ... ♖e8
27 ♘f3 ♔g8
28 ♕xb7 ♖b8
29 ♕xc6 1-0

White is two pawns to the good and Black has no hope!

Main Line: Black plays ...b6

Game 6
Murshed – Rogers
Hong Kong 1984

1 ♘f3 ♘f6
2 d4 g6
3 ♘c3 d5
4 ♗f4 ♗g7
5 e3 0-0
6 ♗e2 b6 *(D)*

In the 1980s, 6...b6 was a popular way to meet the Barry Attack. However, it was soon discovered that this method was flawed, as White is given too free a hand on the kingside.

7 ♘e5 c5

W

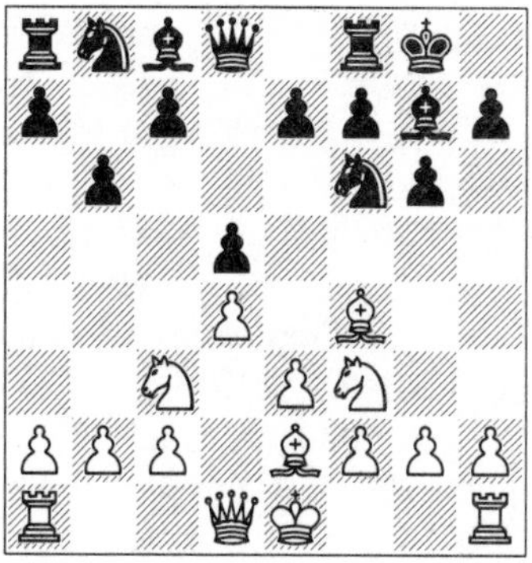

Black has another important option in 7...♗b7, which is dealt with in the next two games.

8 h4 ♗b7

9 h5 ♘c6

The alternative is 9...♘bd7, by which Black puts less pressure on the white centre, but hopes that the knight will be better placed to protect the black king. White's chances are to be preferred after 10 hxg6 hxg6 11 ♕d2 (11 ♗b5 will most likely transpose into the 9...♘c6 line) 11...♘e4 (as mentioned before, the c3-knight is often White's worst placed piece, so he has no objections to exchanging it) 12 ♘xe4 dxe4 13 ♘g4! *(D)*.

B

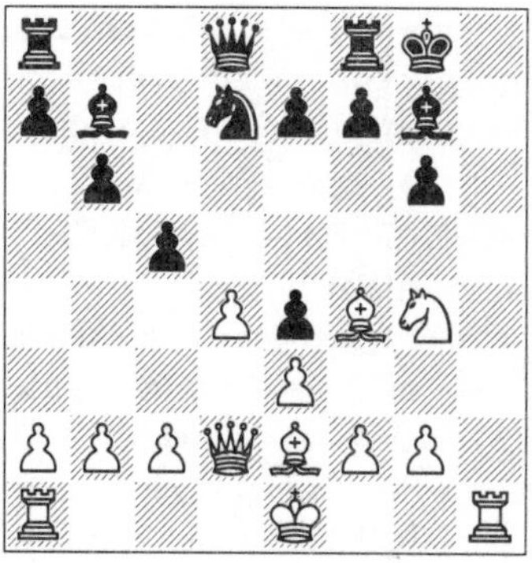

This manoeuvre is well worth remembering. The arrival of the knight on h6 will often cost Black his dark-squared protector. 13...♖e8 14 ♘h6+ ♗xh6 (14...♔f8 15 ♗c4) 15 ♖xh6 e5 16 dxe5 ♘xe5 17 ♕c3 (as can clearly be seen, Black is ruing the loss of his king's bishop) 17...♕d6 18 ♗b5 ♖e7 19 ♖d1 (in this position, it only remains for White to arrange the transfer of his queen's rook to the h-file for his attack to be decisive) 19...♕f6 20 ♔e2 ♗c8 21 ♖dh1 ♗g4+ 22 ♔f1 (Black is utterly defenceless against the threat of ♖h8+) 22...♕d6 23 ♖h8+ ♔g7 24 ♖1h7+ ♔f6 25 ♖xa8 c4 26 ♕d4 ♕b4 27 ♗xe5+ ♖xe5 28 ♖xf7+ 1-0 Izeta-Barbera, Spanish Ch 1992.

10 hxg6 *(D)*

B

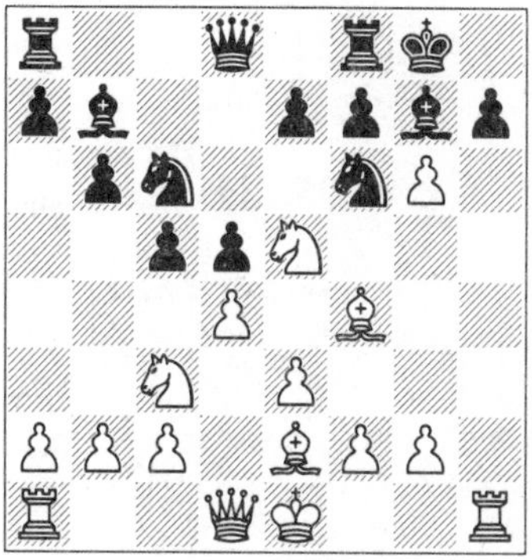

10 ... hxg6

10...fxg6 is probably the better recapture, but White still enjoys an advantage after 11 ♗b5 ♘xe5 12 dxe5 ♘d7 13 ♕g4 ♖f5 14 0-0-0 ♘xe5 15

♕h3 h5 16 ♗xe5 ♖xe5 17 f4 ♖f5 18 e4, with a dangerous initiative, Rogers-Zsu.Polgar, Dortmund 1985.

11 ♗b5 ♕c8

One of the main choices that Black has to make in the Barry Attack is whether to exchange on e5. This exchange removes one of White's attacking pieces but, at the same time, often forces Black's best defensive piece to give way. For example, 11...♘xe5 12 dxe5 ♘h5 (other knight moves are met by ♕g4-h4, with a devastating attack) 13 ♖xh5! *(D)*.

B

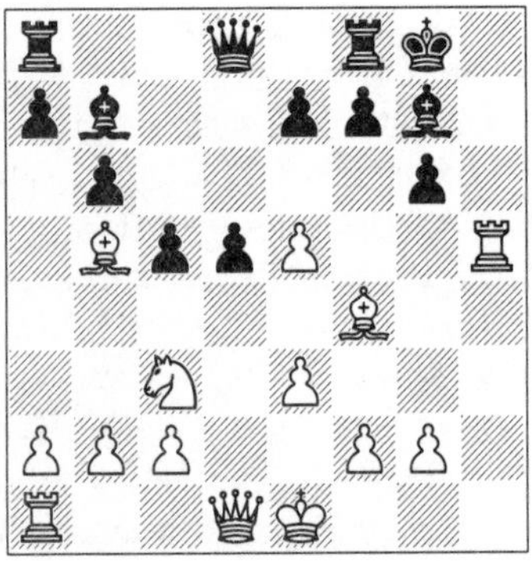

A thematic exchange sacrifice, to blow open the black king's defences. After 13...gxh5 14 ♕xh5 f5 White has two promising continuations:

a) 15 ♕g6 e6 (more or less forced, due to the threat of ♗h6, e.g. 15...a6 16 ♗h6 ♖f7 17 e6) 16 ♕xe6+ ♖f7 17 0-0-0 ♕e7 18 ♕xe7 ♖xe7 ± (Black has reached an endgame the exchange up, but White has collected more than enough extra pawns) 19 ♘xd5 ♖xe5 (19...♗xd5 20 ♖xd5 ♔f7 21 ♗d7 +–) 20 ♗xe5 ♗xe5 21 f4 ♗h8 22 ♘e7+ ♔f7 23 ♘xf5 ♗xg2 24 ♖d6 ♖f8 25 ♗c4+ ♔e8 1-0 Murshed-P.Thipsay, 1984.

b) 15 exf6 ♖xf6 (Black also experiences significant problems in defending his king in this variation) 16 0-0-0 e6 17 ♗g5 ♖f5 18 f4 ♕f6 19 ♖h1 ♖xg5 (the black rook on f5 is out on a limb, for example: 19...♕f7 20 ♕h7+ ♔f8 21 g4) 20 fxg5 ♕f5 21 ♖f1 ♕h7 22 ♕f7+ ♔h8 23 ♕xb7 1-0 Rogers-Canfell, Utrecht 1988.

12 ♗xc6 ♗xc6
13 ♕f3 cxd4 *(D)*

W

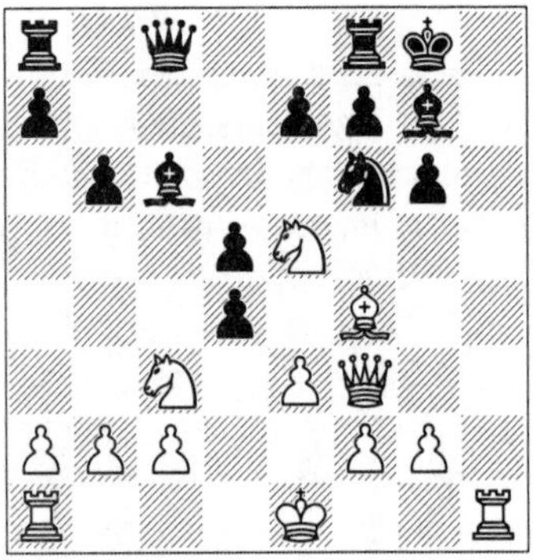

14 exd4 b5

Black's bid for counterplay seems pathetically slow, but it is hard to suggest a decent alternative, or a way of preventing White's usual attacking plan.

15 g4 ♗b7
16 0-0-0 ♕e6
17 ♕h3 ♗c8
18 ♗h6 ♘h5

Taking advantage of the pin, but only delaying the inevitable.

19	**♗xg7**	**♔xg7**
20	**♕h4**	**f6**
21	**♘xg6**	**♕xg4**
22	**♘xf8**	**♕f4+**
23	**♔b1**	**1-0**

Black is losing a whole rook. It is no coincidence that Ian Rogers started to play the Barry Attack himself shortly after this storming game!

Game 7
Hebden – Birnboim
Rishon le Zion 1992

1	**d4**	**♘f6**
2	**♘f3**	**g6**
3	**♘c3**	**d5**
4	**♗f4**	**♗g7**
5	**e3**	**0-0**
6	**♗e2**	**b6**
7	**♘e5**	**♗b7**
8	**h4** *(D)*	

B

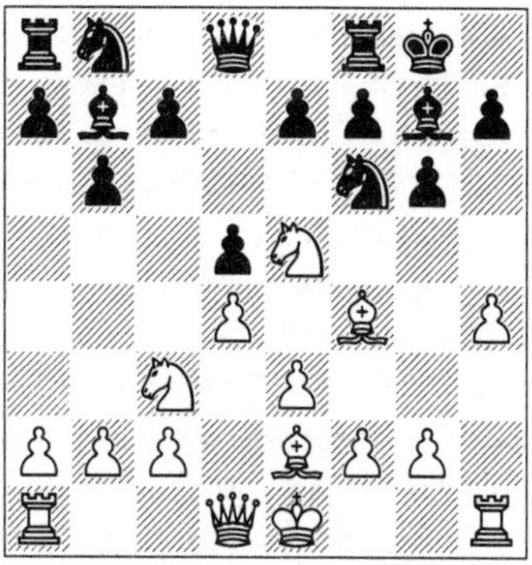

8	**...**	**h6**

For 8...♘bd7 see the next game.

8...♘fd7 (Black's main problem in this line is that he finds himself unable to put enough pressure on White's centre to deflect him from his kingside assault) 9 h5 ♘xe5 *(D)*.

W

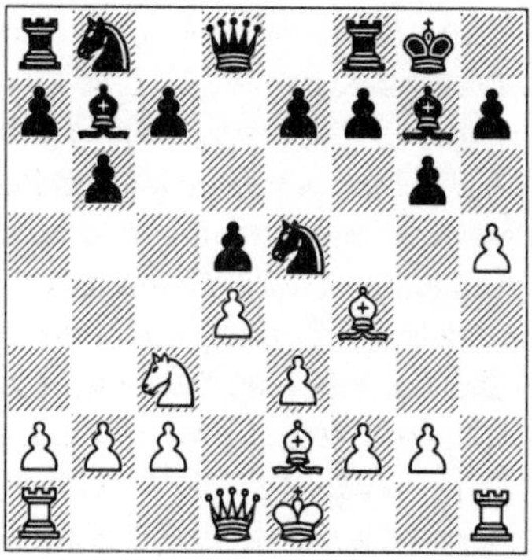

Now both recaptures give White a pleasant attacking position:

a) 10 dxe5 e6 11 hxg6 fxg6 12 ♗d3 (the beauty of White's plan in this type of position is despite its crude simplicity {queen to the h-file and mate!}, Black has an arduous task to prevent it) 12...♘d7 13 ♕g4 ♘c5 14 ♕h3. White has completed his plan and Black is faced with insurmountable problems, although he struggled admirably for the remainder of the game: 14...♘xd3+ 15 cxd3 ♔f7 16 ♘b5 (White conceives a clever idea to bring his knight to g5, via d4 and f3) 16...♕e7 17 ♖c1 ♖fc8 (17...♕b4+ 18 ♔f1 ♕xb5 19 ♖xc7+ winning) 18 ♔e2 ♗a6 19 ♘d4 c5 20 ♘f3 (with the knight's arrival, Black's position collapses) 20...h6 21 ♗xh6 ♖h8 22 ♘g5+ ♔e8 23 ♕xe6 ♕xe6 24 ♘xe6 ♗xe5 25 ♗f4 ♔f7 26 ♖xh8 1-0 Rogers-J.Přibyl, Tallinn 1985.

b) 10 ♗xe5 with a further split:

b1) 10...♘d7 11 ♗xg7 ♔xg7 12 ♕d2 (with the removal of Black's dark-squared bishop, White can now lay siege to the very squares that this piece defended) 12...♘f6 13 f4 c5 14 g4 ♕c8 15 g5 ♘xh5 16 ♗xh5 gxh5 17 0-0-0 (as so often happens in the Barry Attack, Black is left with a permanent weakness on the h-file, and an insecure king) 17...♕f5 18 ♖xh5 ♖h8 19 ♖dh1 ♖ac8 20 ♘e2 (one of the recurrent themes in the Barry Attack is the improvement of White's worst-placed piece, usually the knight on c3; when this unit is included in the attack, it is often too hot to handle) 20...cxd4 21 ♘g3 ♕g4 22 ♕xd4+ ♔g8 23 ♕xh8+! ♔xh8 24 ♖xh7+ ♔g8 25 ♖h8+ ♔g7 26 ♖1h7+ ♔g6 27 ♖h6+ ♔g7 28 ♘h5+ ♕xh5 29 ♖8h7+ 1-0 J.Přibyl-Mi.Horvath, Prague 1987.

b2) 10...♗xe5 11 dxe5 c5 12 ♕d2 e6 13 hxg6 fxg6 14 ♗g4 ♖e8 15 f4 (White has a very straightforward and effective plan: to mount pressure on Black's kingside by doubling on the h-file; Black was possibly feeling the tension, as he goes completely off the rails over the next couple of moves) 15...♕d7? 16 0-0-0 ♘c6?? 17 ♘e4 1-0 Hebden-Likavsky, Cappelle la Grande 1992. Black must lose material after ♘f6.

9 h5 g5

10 ♗xg5 *(D)*

David Norwood originally suggested this sacrificial sequence as an improvement on his game, from the British

B

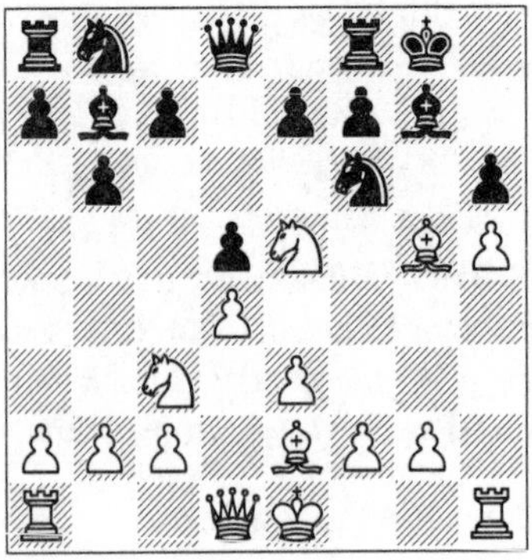

Championship 1988, against Jonathan Mestel, where he played the inferior 9 g4. Certainly, practical results have heavily favoured White from the above diagram.

10 ... hxg5

11 h6

Now Black has to decide whether to retreat or to stand and fight!

11 ... ♗h8

Black tries to hang on to his extra material, but his avarice will lead to his demise. It is more sensible to return the extra material with 11...♗xh6 12 ♖xh6 ♔g7 13 ♖h3. This has fared poorly in practice, but may not be as bad as its reputation. The analysis is as follows:

a) 13...♘e4 14 ♘xe4 dxe4 15 ♗c4 ♗c8 1-0 Laszlo-Kanyadi, Debrecen Ch 1994. Black did not want to wait for ♕h5, with a devastating attack.

b) 13...♘bd7 14 ♖g3 ♘h7 15 ♗d3 f5 (15...f6 16 ♕h5) 16 ♘f3 g4 17 ♘h2 ♔h8 18 ♘e2 e6 19 ♘f4 ♕f6 20 ♘xg4 fxg4 21 ♕xg4 ♖f7 22 ♘g6+ ♔g7 23 ♘e5+ ♔f8 24 ♘xd7+ ♖xd7 25 ♖f3

1-0 J.Christensen-Mo.Hansen, Århus 1990.

c) 13...♖h8! 14 ♖g3 ♖h1+ 15 ♗f1 ♘h7 16 ♕f3 f6 17 ♘d3 ♘d7 18 0-0-0 ♘df8 is given as 'unclear' by Norwood, but surely Black's more exposed king and weakened pawn-structure must give White some advantage.

12 h7+ ♔g7

This is critical, but White gets more than sufficient compensation for the piece.

The alternative is to capture the annoying h-pawn by 12...♘xh7 but this move is simply unplayable. 13 ♗a6! is the refutation: 13...♗c8 (13...♗xa6 14 ♕h5 +–) 14 ♗xc8 ♕xc8 (14...♗xe5 15 ♕h5 ♖e8 16 dxe5 e6 17 ♕xh7+ ♔f8 18 ♕h8+ ♔e7 19 ♕f6+ ♔f8 20 ♖h8#) 15 ♕h5 ♕f5 16 g4 ♕xc2 17 e4 +–. This analysis is all new and 13 ♗a6! is a trap just waiting to be sprung.

13 ♗d3

White's attack is quite slow-burning, although incredibly difficult to stop. As usual, White's plan is to bring his queen to the h-file and go for the kill!

13 ... ♗a6
14 ♕f3 ♗xd3
15 cxd3 ♕d6

15...e6 16 ♕h3 +–; 15...♕c8 16 ♘xd5 ♘xd5 17 ♕h5 +–.

16 ♕f5 ♖d8
17 ♕xg5+ ♔f8
18 ♔e2

Despite Black's extra piece, he is in a hopeless position. The pawn on h7 is a monster and the black king has no effective escape route.

18 ... a6
19 ♖h6 ♘bd7
20 ♖ah1 ♕e6
21 ♖1h4 *(D)*

B

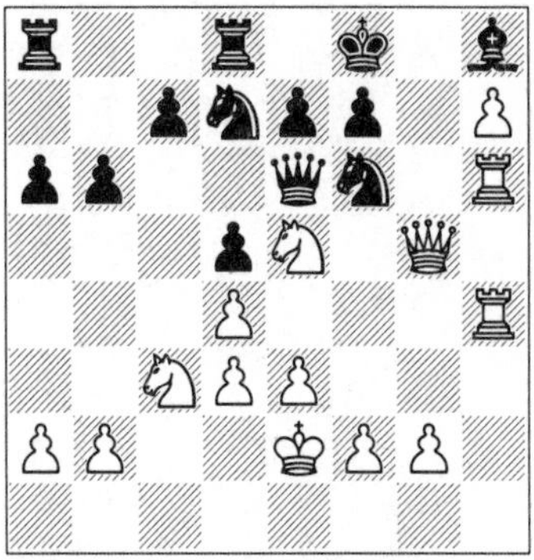

White is winning.

21 ... ♘xe5

22 ♖g4 was the threat.

22 dxe5 ♔e8
23 exf6 exf6
24 ♕g3 ♔e7
25 ♕xc7+ ♖d7
26 ♕g3 ♖c8
1-0

White has regained his sacrificed material with interest, whilst all of Black's problems remain.

Game 8
Hebden – Donchev
Cappelle la Grande 1994

1 d4 ♘f6
2 ♘f3 g6
3 ♘c3 d5
4 ♗f4 ♗g7
5 e3 0-0

6 ♗e2 b6
7 ♘e5 ♗b7
8 h4 ♘bd7
9 h5 *(D)*

B

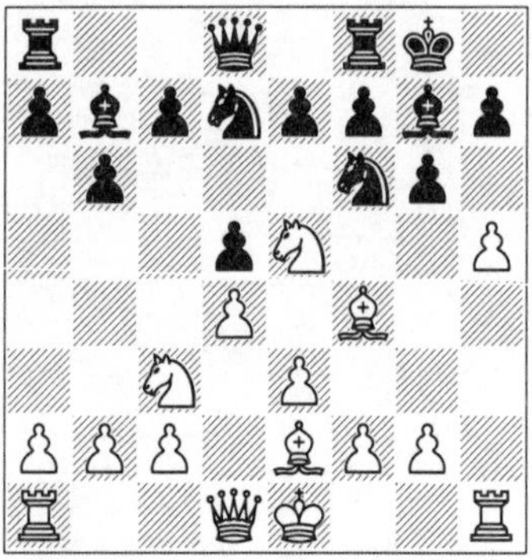

9 ... ♘xe5

Black has also tried 9...♘e4, but this was dealt a death-blow in the game Hodgson-W.Schmidt, Haifa Echt 1989, which went 10 hxg6 hxg6 11 ♘xe4 dxe4 12 ♘g4 (this is the crucial difference: the white knight proves to be an awesome attacking piece) 12...♖e8 13 ♘h6+ ♔f8 14 ♗c4 e6 15 ♕g4 ♗d5 (Black attempts to relieve the tension by swapping bishops; however, White skilfully negotiates the exchange of his light-squared bishop under his own terms) 16 ♗b5 a6 17 ♗g5 f6 18 ♗xd7 ♕xd7 19 ♗xf6! ♗xf6 20 ♕f4 ♔e7 21 ♘g4 ♗g7 22 ♘e5! ♕a4 (22...♗xe5 23 ♖h7+) 23 ♕f7+ ♔d8 24 ♕xg7 ♔c8 25 0-0 (I really like this calm move after all the preceding tactics – White makes his king safe before commencing the final assault on the black king) 25...♔b8 26 c4 ♗b7 27 c5 1-0. White has an extra pawn, a strong attack and the better placed pieces, so Black understandably called it a day.

10 dxe5

10 ♗xe5 has also been played successfully, but the text-move is more forcing.

10 ... ♘e4

10...♘d7 is the other move to have been used in practice, but it was very roughly treated in Hermlin-Kiltti, Tampere 1996: 11 e6! *(D)*.

B

A thematic sacrifice – at the cost of a pawn White critically weakens the black kingside. The game concluded 11...fxe6 12 hxg6 hxg6 13 ♗d3 ♖f6 14 ♕g4 ♔f7 15 0-0-0 ♘c5 16 ♖h7 ♘xd3+ 17 cxd3 ♔g8 18 ♖dh1 ♕d7 19 ♕h3 1-0. Black is defenceless against the threat of ♖xg7+.

11 hxg6 hxg6
12 ♗d3 ♕c8

The capture on c3, 12...♘xc3 13 bxc3, doesn't seem to significantly change Black's chances. Here is a sample variation: 13...♕d7 14 ♕f3

♕e6 15 ♕g3 (with the idea of ♕h2) 15...f5 16 exf6 ♕xf6 17 0-0-0 e5 (17...e6 18 ♗e5 ♕xe5 19 ♕xg6 ♖f5 20 g4 +–) 18 ♗xe5 ♕xe5 19 ♕xg6 +– ♕xc3 20 ♖h8+ ♔xh8 21 ♕h7#.

13 ♕f3 ♕e6
14 ♘b5

As the text-move doesn't lead to much for White, I recommend taking the pawn here with 14 ♘xe4 dxe4 15 ♗xe4 ♗xe4 16 ♕xe4 ±. White is a pawn to the good and retains attacking chances against the black king, e.g. 16...♖fd8 (16...f5 17 ♕f3 ♗xe5 18 ♕h3 ♖f7 19 ♗xe5 ♕xe5 20 0-0-0 ± with the idea of tripling on the h-file) 17 ♗g5 ♕xe5 (17...♗xe5 18 ♕h4 ♔f8 19 ♕h7 ±) 18 ♕xe5 ♗xe5 19 ♗xe7 ♗xb2 20 ♗xd8 ♗xa1 21 ♗xc7 ±.

14 ... ♗xe5
15 ♘xc7 ♗xc7
16 ♗xc7 ♔g7

As Black has a firm stance in the centre, the loss of his dark-squared bishop is not a serious problem and he is able to neutralize White's kingside initiative.

17 0-0-0 ♖h8
18 ♗xe4 dxe4
19 ♕f4 f6
20 ♖xh8 ♖xh8
21 ♗d8 ♕xa2
22 ♕c7 ♕a1+
23 ♔d2 ♕a5+
24 c3 ♕e5

The game is now equal.

25 ♕xe5 fxe5 26 ♗xe7 ♔f7 27 ♗g5 ♔e6 28 c4 ♖h2 29 ♔e2 ♖h5 30 ♗d8 ♖h7 31 b4 ♖d7 32 ♖xd7 ♔xd7 33 ♗f6 ♔e6 34 ♗g7 a6 35 ♔d2 b5 36 cxb5 axb5 ½-½

Game 9

Hebden – Fox

Hastings 1994/5

1 d4 ♘f6
2 ♘f3 g6
3 ♘c3 d5
4 ♗f4 ♗g7
5 e3 0-0
6 ♗e2 c6

This is a flexible system for Black, who keeps his options open. Black retains the option of queenside expansion and of developing his bishop to g4. Meanwhile 7 ♘e5 can be answered by 7...♘fd7!. The main drawback is Black's lack of pressure on the centre, so a flank attack becomes a more attractive option for White.

7 h4 *(D)*

B

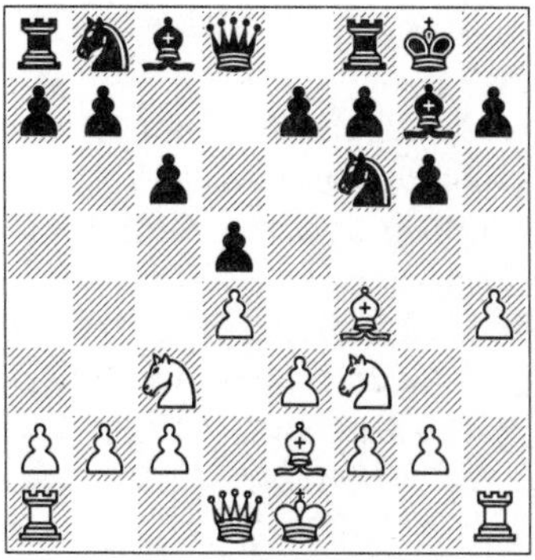

7 ... ♗g4

This really doesn't help Black, as it leads to the type of position we have seen before under 6...♗g4. I have given it detailed coverage, as it is the sort of move that for many players will be an automatic response, and besides, having suffered myself as White in so many classical King's Indian mating attacks, it is always nice to see Black getting a taste of his own medicine! The other possibilities are:

a) 7...b5 is an attempt to take the game down unexplored channels. 8 ♘e5 b4 9 ♘a4 ♘fd7 10 h5 ♘xe5 11 ♗xe5 f6 and now *(D)*:

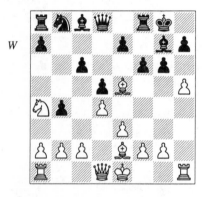

W

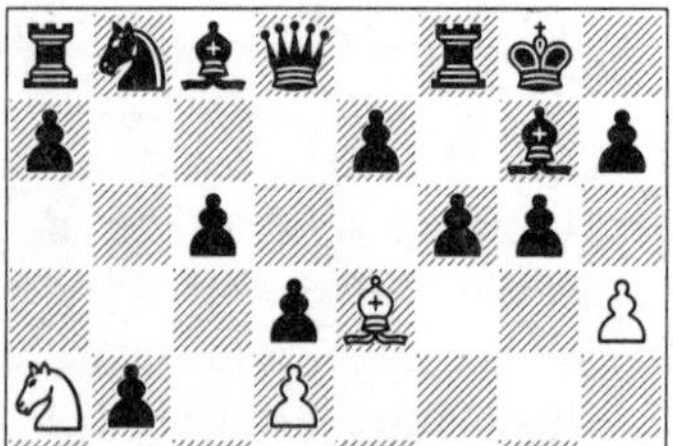

a1) 12 ♗g3?! was chosen when this position was seen in practice, but I feel Black equalizes comfortably with 12...e5, viz. 13 hxg6 hxg6 14 ♘c5 ♕e7 15 ♕d2 a5 16 0-0-0 ♘d7 17 ♘xd7 ♗xd7 18 e4 ♗e6 19 ♗d3 ♗f7 20 ♖h2 dxe4 21 ♗xe4 ♖fd8 22 ♖dh1 ♖xd4 23 ♕e3 ♖ad8 24 ♗xc6 ♕d6 25 ♗f3 a4 26 ♖h7 g5 27 ♗e2 ♗g6 28 ♖7h3 ♖c8 29 ♔b1 ♖xc2 30 ♔a1 a3 31 b3 ♖dd2 32 ♗c4+ ♖xc4 33 bxc4 ♖d1+ 0-1 G.Buckley-Fogarasi, Guildford 1991.

a2) 12 ♗xb8 is my recommended improvement. It may seem strange to give up the bishop-pair and take an undeveloped knight. The key point is that White has an outpost on c5 and therefore taking on b8 removes a possible defender of that square and provides the extra tempo that White needs to induce additional weakness on the black kingside. 12...♖xb8 13 hxg6 hxg6 14 ♗d3 ♕e8 (14...f5 15 f4 gives White a clear positional advantage; White's minor pieces are evidently superior to their black counterparts) 15 ♕f3 e5 16 ♕g3 ±. White has the upper hand due to his outpost on c5 and kingside attacking chances. A sample continuation is 16...f5 17 0-0-0 ♗d7 18 ♘c5 exd4 19 exd4 ♗xd4? 20 ♕h4 ±.

b) 7...c5!? is a rare and provocative move. Black argues he can spend a tempo playing ...c5, since h4 achieves little for White if he castles kingside. 8 ♘e5 ♘c6 9 h5 (9 ♕d2!?) 9...cxd4 10 exd4 ♕b6 11 ♘xc6 bxc6 12 ♘a4 ♕d8 13 ♔f1 led to a mess in Mitkov-Kovačević, Cetinje 1991 – I'm afraid I will use the old standby for once and call this position completely unclear. 13 c3!? and 13 0-0!? are playable continuations for the less bloodthirsty.

c) After 7...♕b6 8 a3 play can develop along the same lines as in Game 4, Hodgson-Wolff, except this time it will be harder for Black to harass the white bishop.

8 ♘e5 ♗xe2
9 ♕xe2

We have now transposed to Game 5.

9 ... ♘bd7
10 0-0-0 ♖c8

All other moves were discussed in Game 5.

11 h5 ♖e8
12 hxg6 fxg6
13 ♕f3 ♘f8
14 g4 b5
15 ♗h6

And from a seemingly clear sky, lightning is about to strike. Black is hard-pressed to meet the threat of 16 g5.

15 ... ♘8d7
16 ♗xg7 ♔xg7
17 g5 ♘xe5
18 gxf6+ exf6
19 dxe5 fxe5
20 ♖xh7+ *(D)*

B

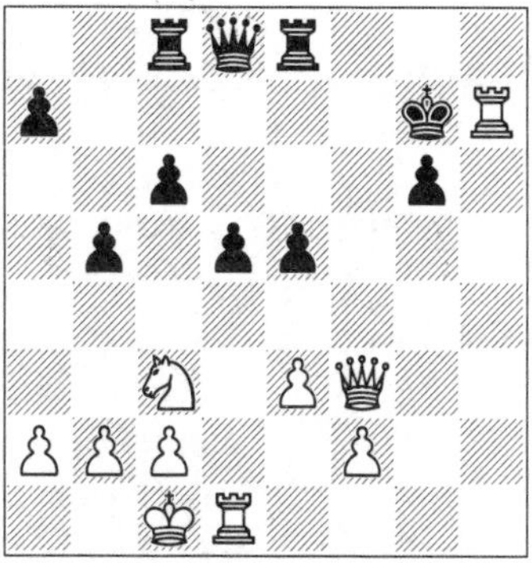

Many players would take their material advantage and run, but Hebden is a real killer!

20 ... ♔xh7
21 ♕f7+ ♔h6
22 ♖h1+ ♔g5
23 ♖g1+ 1-0

Main Line: Black plays ...c5 – Introduction

Game 10
P. Bank – J. Jensen
Århus 1993

1 d4 ♘f6
2 ♘f3 g6
3 ♘c3 d5
4 ♗f4 ♗g7
5 e3 0-0
6 ♗e2 c5 *(D)*

W

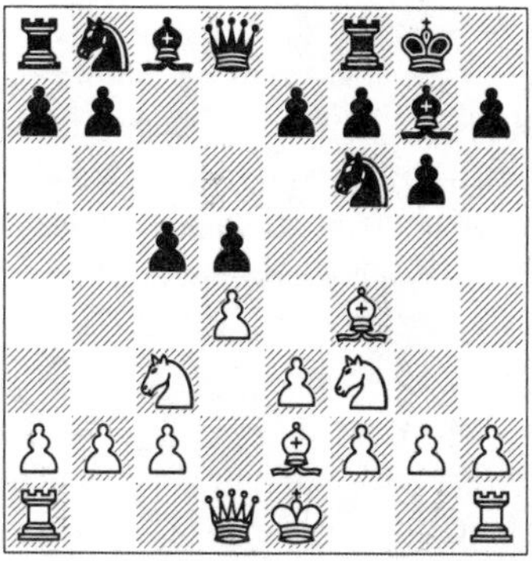

This is widely believed to be Black's best answer to the Barry Attack. Barry exponent Mark Hebden plays it himself as Black, Joe Gallagher recommended it in his book *Beating the Anti-King's Indians* and John Nunn, a highly respected theoretician, also uses this line.

7 ♘e5 ♘c6
8 ♕d2

I have included this game to serve as a warning to any blood-thirsty hackers who insist on trying to mate their opponent's king no matter what! Unfortunately, this tunnel-visioned approach just does not work when Black counterattacks vigorously in the centre and on the queenside.

8 ... ♕a5
9 h4 ♘d7
10 0-0-0 ♘dxe5
11 dxe5 d4

It is Black's ability to play disruptive central breaks like this, in conjunction with a queenside attack, which makes over-aggression by White less viable.

12 exd4 cxd4
13 ♘b1 ♕xa2

This is a very sad sight for any Barry player. Black's queenside attack looks far stronger than the white kingside effort, the pawn on e5 is weak and Black is a pawn up, to boot.

14 h5 ♗f5
15 ♗d3

This time, it is White who attempts to relieve the mounting pressure on his position with exchanges. In this example, it is a case of too little, too late!

15 ... ♗xd3
16 ♕xd3 ♖ac8

The black attack more or less plays itself.

17 hxg6 fxg6
18 ♗d2

This grovelling retreat, while preventing the threat of ...♘b4, blocks the last escape square of the white king. Instead, 18 ♕h3 is met by 18...h5 ∓.

18 ... ♘xe5
19 ♕b5 a6 *(D)*

0-1

W

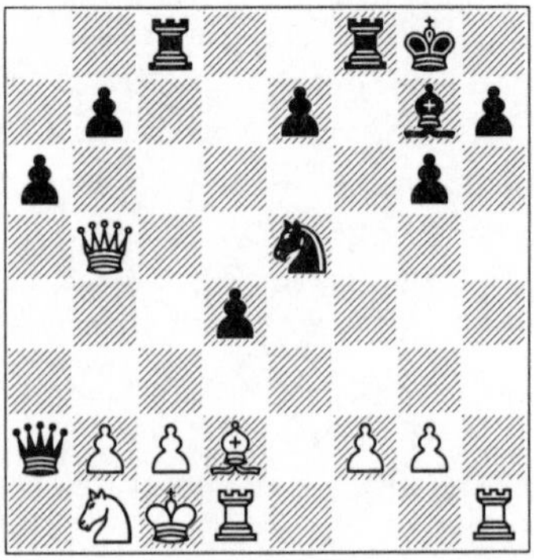

White had seen enough. Black has threats of ...♘c4 and ...d3 to name but two, and for once, the kingside counterattack is going nowhere. The factors which differentiate this game from those preceding are an increased danger to the white king and greater influence for Black in the centre.

Main Line: 6...c5 7 ♘e5

Game 11
Hebden – Nunn
Hastings 1997/8

1 d4 ♘f6
2 ♘f3 g6
3 ♘c3 d5
4 ♗f4 ♗g7
5 e3 0-0
6 ♗e2 c5
7 ♘e5 *(D)*

By sinking his knight into e5, White keeps his options open, waiting to see whether Black can develop his counterplay.

7 ... cxd4

B

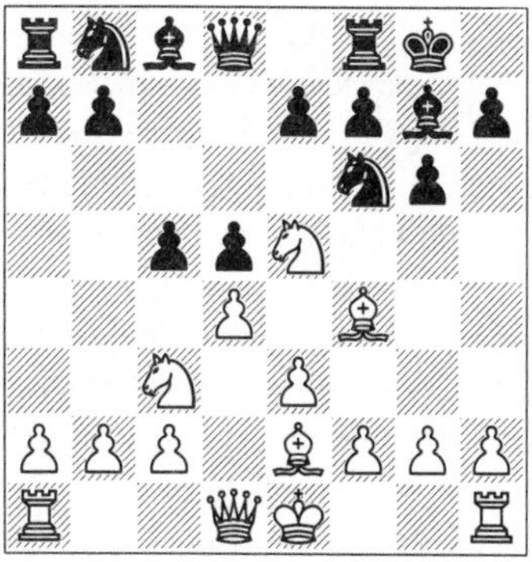

Black has a wide range of alternatives to this capture:

a) 7...♘c6 8 0-0 is a more sensible approach than we saw in the previous game, if a little sedate. Instead of wielding the axe, White plays for a small positional advantage. Black now has a further choice:

a1) 8...♗f5 is Joe Gallagher's recommendation in *Beating the Anti-King's Indians*. Indeed, it is a very solid option, although uninspiring for Black. After 9 ♕d2 cxd4 10 exd4 *(D)* Black has:

B

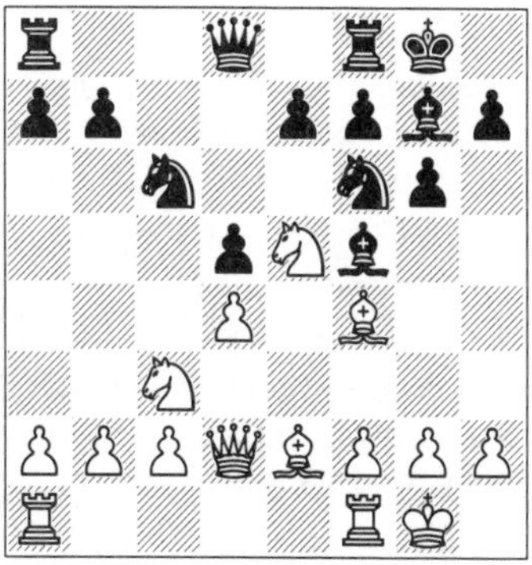

a11) 10...♕b6 11 ♘xc6 leads to similar positions as those seen in line 'a3'.

a12) 10...♘e4 11 ♘xe4 ♗xe4 (if 11...dxe4, then 12 ♘xc6 bxc6 13 c3 ±) is an attempt by Black to benefit from the fact that White has no knight to land on c5, and so reach an improved version of the 7...♘c6 line. However, there is a tactical drawback, in that the bishop on e4 is woefully short of squares after 12 ♘xc6 bxc6 13 g4! ♕b6 14 c3, when Black must lose material due to the threat of f3.

a13) 10...♘d7 11 ♘xd5 ♘dxe5 12 dxe5 ♗xc2 (12...♘xe5 13 ♖ad1 e6 14 ♘e3 ♕xd2 15 ♖xd2 ♗e4 16 ♖fd1 is slightly better for White due to his control of the d-file) 13 ♗f3 ♗f5 14 ♕e3 ♗e6 15 ♖fd1 ♗xd5 16 ♖xd5 ♕b6 17 ♕xb6 axb6 18 ♖b5 ± Hebden-Fernandez Garcia, Linares Z 1995. In conjunction with Black's queenside pawn weaknesses, White enjoys the advantage of the bishop-pair.

a2) 8...♕b6 loses a pawn to 9 ♘a4.

a3) 8...cxd4 9 exd4 ♕b6 10 ♘xc6 bxc6 (10...♕xc6 11 ♗b5 ♕b6 12 a4 ±; White threatens to simply gain space on the queenside with a5, when the black queen is embarrassed for decent squares) 11 ♘a4 ♕a5 12 c3. White's advantage here is due to his ability to clamp down on the pawn-break that would most improve Black's position, namely ...c5. This only gives Black one other meaningful pawn-break, ...e5. However, even when Black achieves this, he is still left with the worse pawn-structure. 12...♘d7 13 b4 ♕d8 *(D)* and now:

W

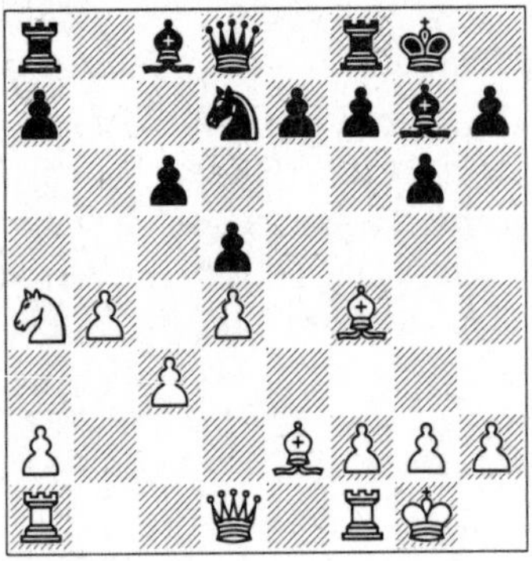

a31) 14 ♕d2 e5 15 ♗h6 (this is an important theme, because White assures himself of the better bishop; this game illustrates how accumulating small advantages, *à la* Steinitz, is an effective way of increasing a positional edge) 15...♗xh6 16 ♕xh6 ♖e8 17 ♖fe1 ♖b8 18 dxe5 ♖xe5 19 ♕d2 a5 20 ♗f1 axb4 21 cxb4 ♕f6 22 ♖xe5 ♘xe5 23 ♖e1 ♔g7 24 ♘c5 (White has transformed the nature of his advantage; the knight on c5 has an excellent outpost and the passed a-pawn is of much greater significance than the black d-pawn) 24...♗f5 25 a3 d4?! (Black understandably goes for counterplay, but the pawn simply lacks enough support for this to be successful) 26 f4 ♘d7 27 ♘xd7 ♗xd7 28 ♖e5 (this is the problem: Black must lose a pawn) 28...c5 29 ♖xc5 ♗f5 30 ♖d5 d3 31 ♗xd3 ± ♕a1+ 32 ♗f1 ♕xa3 33 ♕d4+ f6 34 ♖d6 ♕xb4 35 ♕xf6+ ♔h6 36 h3 ♕xf4? 37 ♖d4 +– ♕e3+ 38 ♔h2 1-0 Hebden-Nunn, Hastings 1996/7. Black has no good way to prevent ♖h4+, with disastrous consequences. An important victory against a leading King's Indian theoretician.

a32) 14 ♗g5 is an alternative approach to the position. White entices the black kingside pawns forward in an attempt to exploit the resulting weaknesses. 14...f6 15 ♗h4 ♘b6 16 ♘c5 g5 17 ♗g3 e5 18 a4 ♕e7 19 dxe5 fxe5 (although the black pawn-structure in the centre is solid, his kingside weaknesses give cause for concern) 20 ♖e1 ♘d7 21 ♘xd7 ♗xd7 22 c4 ♕e6 23 ♖c1 d4 24 c5 (White prepares a light-squared bind) 24...♔h8 25 ♗c4 ♕f5 26 ♗d3 ♕f7 (White has a clear positional advantage; as so often happens in such cases, the clearest way to exploit this is tactical) 27 ♖xe5! ♗xe5 28 ♗xe5+ ♔g8 29 ♕d2 h6 30 ♗xd4 (there is not much Black can do about the coming invasion on the dark squares) 30...♗f5 31 ♗c4 ♗e6 32 ♗f1 ♖fe8 33 ♗b2 ± as ♕c3 will follow, Antoshin-Balashov, Moscow 1967.

b) 7...♕a5 (this active move avoids the problems of the main line, but the queen can be slightly more exposed here) 8 0-0 ♘c6 9 ♕d2 ♗f5 10 ♖fd1 (with a threat) 10...cxd4 (10...♖ad8? 11 ♘xc6 bxc6 12 ♘xd5 +–) 11 exd4 ♘d7 12 ♘xd7 ♗xd7 13 ♗h6 ♖ad8 14 ♗xg7 ♔xg7 (a subtle positional struggle now ensues, where White exploits the small superiority gained from having the better bishop) 15 ♗b5 ♘b8 16 ♗d3 ♘c6 17 a3 ♕b6 18 ♗b5 ♘a5 19

♗f1 ♝g4 20 ♘a4 ♛c7 21 ♖e1 ♝f5 (this bishop is the root of Black's problems – although it is actively posted here, Black has difficulties negotiating White's pressure on the e-file; Black would like to play ...e6, but this would leave the bishop out on a limb) 22 ♖ac1 ♞c6 23 ♗b5 ♞a5 24 ♘c5 ♜d6 25 ♕f4 ♜c6 26 ♕e3 ♜b6 (White's central pressure has induced Black to misplace his rook) 27 ♕c3 ♞c6 (27...♜xb5 28 ♘e6+ +–) 28 a4 ♜c8 29 ♕d2 ♞xd4 (Black unsuccessfully resorts to tactics in a difficult position) 30 ♘d7! (this wins the exchange and the game) 30...♞xc2 (30...♞f3+ 31 gxf3 ♝xd7 32 ♖xe7 ♜d6 33 ♕d4+ ♚g8 34 ♕f4 +–) 31 ♘xb6 ♛xb6 32 ♖xe7 ♛f6 33 ♖xb7 ♛xb2 34 ♗a6 ♛a3 35 ♖xf7+ ♚xf7 36 ♗xc8 ♞d4 37 ♖c7+ 1-0 Hebden-Rõtšagov, Cappelle la Grande 1995.

c) 7...b6 transposes to the 6...b6 variation covered previously.

d) 7...♛b6 8 ♘a4 ♛a5+ 9 c3 cxd4 10 b4 ♛d8 11 cxd4 ±. White has a queenside space advantage and the better bishops.

8 exd4 *(D)*

8 ... ♞fd7

B

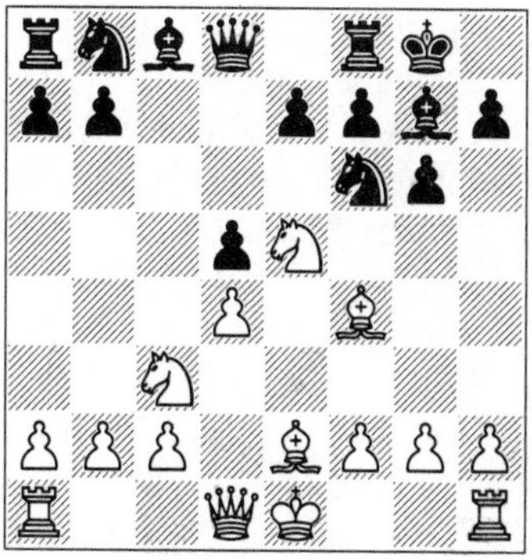

This was Nunn's attempted improvement on his earlier game with Hebden. Practice has seen two other approaches for Black here, apart from moves transposing to variations we have already examined:

a) 8...♞bd7 puts insufficient pressure on White's centre and again allows White to pursue a more aggressive plan. After 9 h4 ♞xe5 10 ♗xe5 a6 11 h5 b5 12 a3 ♝e6 13 ♕d2 ♛d7 14 f3 ♛b7 15 ♔f2 ♜ac8 (although Black has played natural moves, his queenside counterplay simply lacks bite; meanwhile, White can build up at his own leisure on the kingside) 16 ♗d3 ♛d7 17 ♖h4 ♝f5 18 ♗xf5 ♛xf5 19 g4 ♛d7 20 ♖ah1 *(D)*. White has established an impressive attacking position and starts to move in for the kill; the daunting task facing Black can be shown through the following sample variations, illustrating White's attacking plan:

B

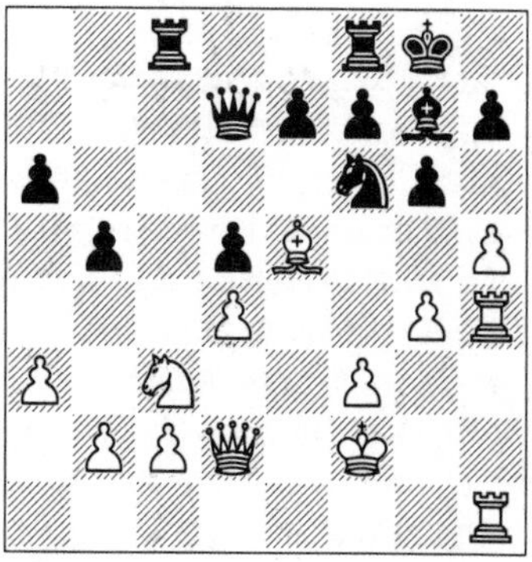

a1) 20...a5 21 hxg6 hxg6 (21...fxg6 22 ♗xf6 ♖xf6 23 ♖xh7 ♕xg4 24 ♖xg7+ ♔xg7 25 ♕h6+ ♔f7 26 ♕h7+ ♔e8 27 ♕g8+ ♔d7 28 ♕xd5+ ♔c7 29 ♕e5+ ♔b6 30 ♕xf6+ +–) 22 ♕f4 b4 23 ♗xf6 ♗xf6 24 ♕xf6 exf6 25 ♖h8+ ♔g7 26 ♖1h7#.

a2) 20...gxh5 (Black cracks under the pressure of White's attack) 21 ♗xf6 ♗xf6 22 ♖xh5 ♖fd8 23 ♖xh7 ♗g7 24 ♖xg7+ 1-0 M.Přibyl-Přibylova, Prague 1989. After 24...♔xg7 25 ♕g5+ it's mate next move.

b) 8...e6 seems unnecessarily passive *(D)*:

W

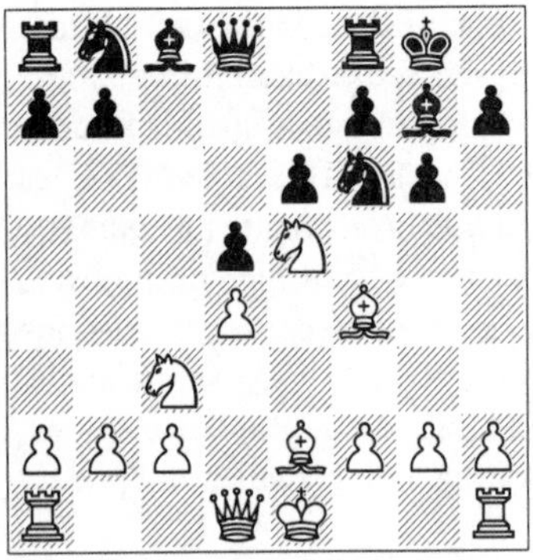

b1) 9 0-0 is a quiet approach, promising White a small advantage. 9...♘fd7 10 ♖e1 ♘xe5 11 ♗xe5 ♗h6 (Black tries to retain his best bishop) 12 ♘b5 ♘c6 13 ♗d6 ♖e8 14 ♗g3 and White is a little better due to the control of his dark squares, one of the consequences of Black's 7th move, Balashov-Gufeld, Moscow 1969.

b2) 9 ♕d2 ♘fd7 10 ♘f3 ♘c6 11 ♗h6 ♘f6 12 ♗xg7 ♔xg7 13 0-0-0 (this is a fully viable, sharp approach to the position: White aims for a quick slaughter) 13...♗d7 14 ♘e5 ♖c8 15 h4 ♘b4 16 ♔b1 (a useful precautionary move) 16...b5 17 h5 ♕e7 18 hxg6 fxg6 19 ♕h6+ ♔g8 20 g4 (White summons the reserves) 20...♗e8 21 g5 ♘d7 22 ♗g4 ♘xe5 23 ♗xe6+! ♔h8 24 ♗xc8 ♘c4 25 ♖he1 ♕f7 26 ♗e6 ♕xf2 27 ♖e2 ♕f4 28 ♖h2 ♕c7 29 ♕xf8# (1-0) G.Mohr-Rotshtein, Maribor Pirc mem 1994. Note how Black's counterplay never really got going in this game.

9	**♘f3**	**♘f6**
10	**♘e5**	**♘fd7**
11	**♘f3**	

When asked afterwards why he had repeated moves like this, Hebden replied "I was just teasing him". Psychological warfare is part and parcel of any killer's chess repertoire.

11	**...**	**♘f6**
12	**♕d2** *(D)*	

B

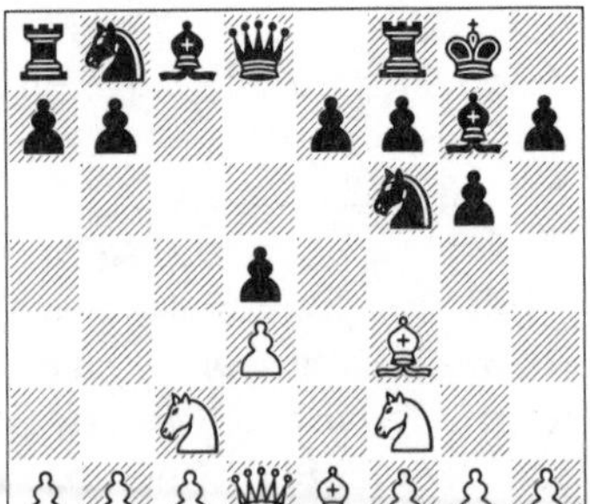

12	**...**	**♗g4**
13	**♘e5**	**♗xe2**

14 ♕xe2

As per usual, the drawback Black faces with the exchange of his problem bishop is the acceleration of White's attack.

14 ... ♘h5

14...♘c6!? 15 0-0-0.

15 ♗e3 ♘c6

16 0-0-0 ♖c8

17 f4

White cements his knight on e5.

17 ... ♘f6

18 g4 ♕a5

19 a3

This is a clever prophylactic move, which anticipates Black's following exchange sacrifice.

19 ... ♘xe5?

20 fxe5 ♖xc3

21 exf6 ♖fc8 *(D)*

22 ♔b1!

W

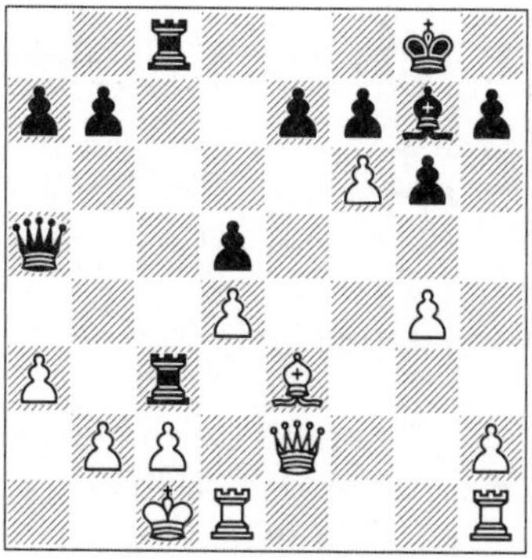

If Black was dreaming of 22 bxc3 ♕xa3+ 23 ♔d2 ♕xc3+ 24 ♔c1 ♕a1+ with a draw, he was certainly in for a rude awakening. Perhaps the earlier repetition had lulled him into a peaceful frame of mind.

22 ... ♖xc2

23 ♖d2 1-0

White will win a piece.

2 The 150 Attack

Introduction

The 150 Attack is a system for White against all Modern and Pirc Defence players. We will examine all the ways Black can reach his desired set up, whether it be from a Barry Attack move-order (1 d4 ♘f6 2 ♘f3 g6 3 ♘c3 ♗g7 4 e4 d6 5 ♗e3), or otherwise. I used to play the Pirc Defence in order to lure White onto unfamiliar territory from an early stage. I suspect that, like myself, the majority of club players who try the Pirc or Modern Defence do so because they are intimidated by the more usual main-line openings. By opting out, Black has greater opportunities to confuse White with his various move-orders, which are hard to pin down.

What White needs is a simple, yet effective response, which can be used against any black system. The 150 Attack fits the bill perfectly. White negotiates the course of events under his own terms. I feel the 150 Attack is putting Black off playing the Pirc/Modern Defences at all levels. It has been successfully adopted by the world's elite, such as Adams, Khalifman, Nunn and Leko, to name just a few. To whet your appetite, here is an attractive white victory, from a recent super-grandmaster clash.

Game 12
Leko – Beliavsky
Madrid 1998

1	**d4**	**d6**
2	**e4**	**♘f6**
3	**♘c3**	**g6**
4	**♘f3**	**♗g7**
5	**♗e3** *(D)*	

B

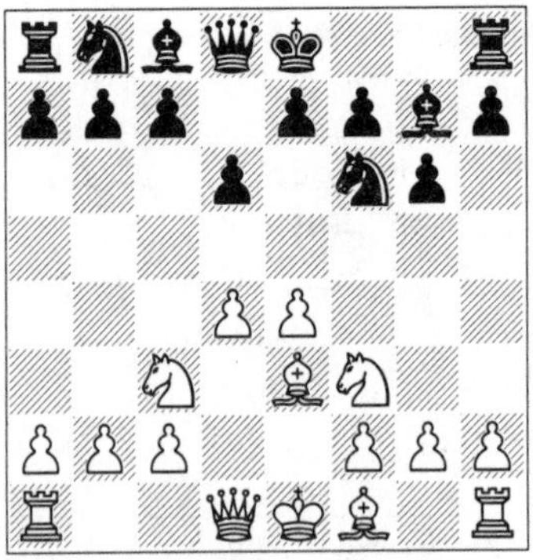

This is White's basic set-up in the 150 Attack. The 150 Attack supposedly got its name because it was widely used by a lot of medium-strength club and tournament players in Britain (a British grading of 150 is approximately equivalent to 1800 Elo). The basic idea was to exchange the dark-squared bishops and play for a mating attack on the black king. Since then, it has become much more refined, but we still have the unusual case of the world's grandmasters and super-grandmasters borrowing the ideas of lesser players!

5 ... c6

5...0-0 is an important possibility, which we will consider at a later stage.

6 ♕d2 b5

Even positional players like to use the 150 Attack, although in their case it is sometimes a bluff. White sets up an attacking formation pointing towards Black's kingside. The automatic response for Black is this counterstroke on the queenside. However, then White can suddenly change tack, castle on the kingside, and set about exploiting the queenside weaknesses left by Black's pawn advances. This time it is Black who is left bewildered and confused!

7 ♗d3 ♗g4

8 e5 *(D)*

8 ♘h4 is also possible, but the text-move is obviously more potent. The advance e5 often plays a key part in White's victories in the 150 Attack.

B

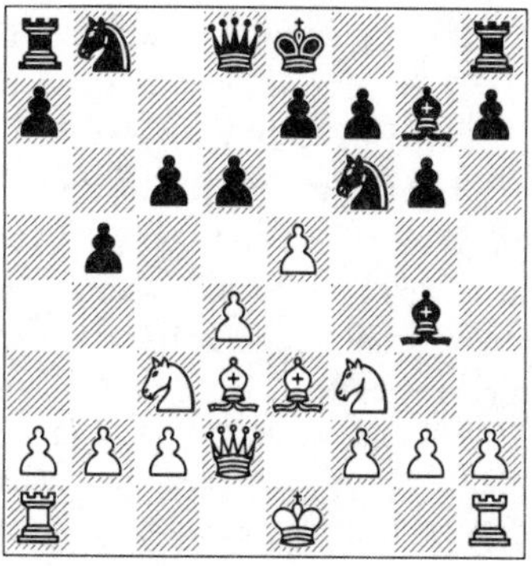

8 ... b4

9 ♘e4 ♘xe4

10 ♗xe4 d5

11 ♗d3 ♗xf3

12 gxf3

White's pawn-structure has been compromised, but he has definite attacking chances on the kingside.

12 ... a5

13 h4 ♘d7

13...h5 is well met by the disruptive 14 e6.

14 h5 ♕b6

15 c4

White opens up a second front for the attack.

15 ... bxc3

16 bxc3 e6

17 ♖b1 ♕c7

18 ♗h6 ♗f8

Obviously now was not the right time for Black to castle!

19 ♗g5 ♖g8

20 hxg6 hxg6

21 ♔e2 ♗e7

22 ♗xe7 ♔xe7

23 ♕g5+ ♔e8

24 f4

White has a truly dominating position and only needs to find the final breakthrough. The text-move threatens exactly this through f5.

24 ... ♕d8

25 ♕g3 ♔f8

26 ♖bg1 ♖b8

27 f5 ♖b2+

Black lands a check, but one piece does not constitute an attack.

28 ♔e3 exf5

29 ♗xf5 ♘b6

30	**♗d3**	**♘c4+**
31	**♗xc4**	**dxc4**
32	**♕f4**	**♕e7**
33	**♖b1**	**♕a3**
34	**♔f3**	**g5**

34...♕xc3+ 35 ♔g2 g5 36 ♕f5 ♕xd4 37 e6 wins for White.

35	**♕c1!**	**1-0**

150 Attack vs the Modern Defence (Black delays or omits ...♘f6)

Game 13

Pein – Swanson

British League (4NCL) 1996/7

1	**d4**	**d6**
2	**e4**	**g6**
3	**♘c3**	**♗g7**
4	**♗e3** *(D)*	

B

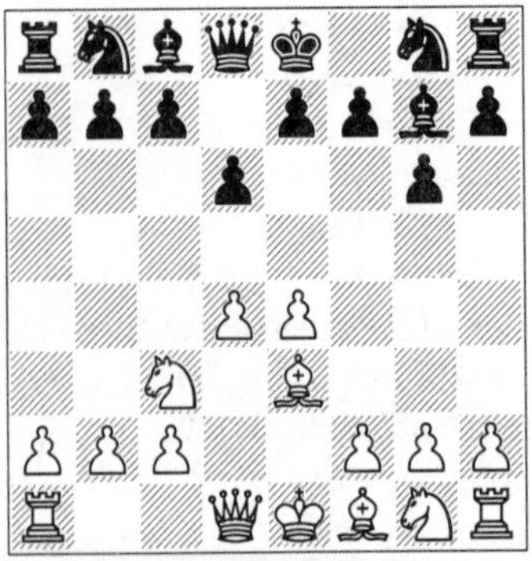

4	**...**	**c6**

The main alternative is 4...a6. After 5 ♘f3 Black has a choice:

a) 5...♗g4 is an attempt by Black to take the game back to the realms of the Classical Variation, but the loss of tempo should give White at least a small advantage; for example, 6 ♗e2 ♘c6 7 d5 ♗xf3 8 ♗xf3 ♘e5 9 ♗e2 ♘f6 10 0-0 0-0 11 a4 (Black has difficulty organizing counterplay without moving his c-pawn, which enables White to prepare to fix a weakness on b6, and simultaneously gain space on the queenside) 11...c5 12 a5 b5 13 axb6 ♕xb6 14 ♗c1 ♖fb8 15 ♔h1 ♘ed7 16 f4 (White is slightly better here, due to his bishop-pair, Black's structural weakness on a6 and the possibility of a central breakthrough, involving some combination of e5 and/or f5) 16...♕c7?? (unfortunately, this blunder makes the rest of the game relatively irrelevant, as White now gains a winning material advantage) 17 ♖xa6 ♖xa6 18 ♗xa6 c4 19 ♕e2 ♘b6 20 ♗b5 (any hopes Black had of trapping the white bishop are now well and truly destroyed) 20...♘fd7 21 ♗c6 ♕a7 22 h3 ♕a1?! (although this looks threatening, all Black has achieved is the loss of another pawn) 23 ♗xd7 ♘xd7 24 ♕xc4 ♖xb2 (desperation!) 25 ♗xb2 ♕xb2 26 ♕c8+ ♘f8 27 ♘e2 h5 28 ♕c4 ♘d7 29 ♕c8+ ♘f8 30 ♕c4 and White went on to convert his material advantage into victory in the game Dunnington-Carlier, Hafnarfjördur Arason mem 1996.

b) 5...b5 (this is the logical continuation of Black's previous move) 6 ♕d2 ♗b7 7 ♗d3 ♘d7 8 a4 *(D)*.

This is an extremely important pawn lever in the 150 Attack. Black is

B

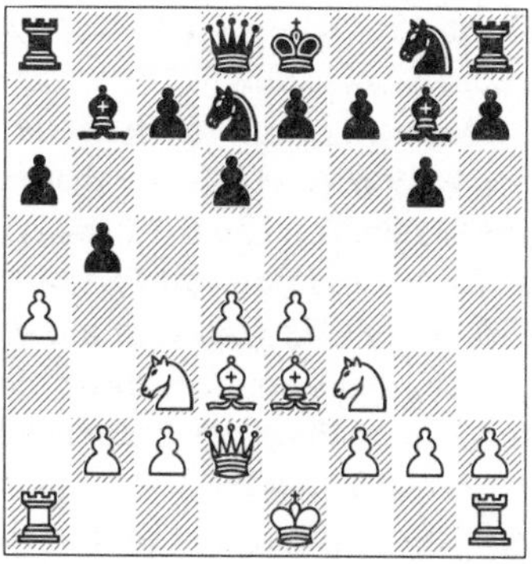

faced with the unpleasant choice of capturing on a4, or protecting his b-pawn with ...c6 or else advancing to b4.

b1) 8...bxa4 just leaves Black saddled with a permanently weak a-pawn.

b2) 8...c6 makes more sense, but blocks in the light-squared bishop and leaves Black potentially vulnerable to a capture on b5, followed by d5.

b3) 8...b4 (the most popular, driving the knight away from c3, but it still leaves Black with queenside weaknesses, which White can seek to exploit) 9 ♘e2 ♘gf6 10 ♘g3. Although the knight may not seem particularly well placed here, it is actually a key piece in many kingside attacks. Black can now choose to defend his b-pawn in two ways:

b31) 10...a5 11 ♗h6 0-0 (11...♗xh6 12 ♕xh6 is the lesser evil, but makes life hard for the black king, who will not feel comfortable on the queenside) 12 h4 with a looming kingside attack.

b32) 10...c5 11 dxc5 ♘xc5 (this is far too ambitious; 11...dxc5 12 ♗h6 0-0 is a better option for Black, although White retains the better position) 12 ♕xb4 ♖b8 13 ♗xc5 dxc5 14 ♕xc5 ♘d7 15 ♕a3 ♗c6 16 c3 (Black has clearly insufficient compensation for the two-pawn deficit) 16...h5 17 0-0 h4 18 ♘e2 e5 19 ♗xa6 ♖a8 20 ♗c4 ♖xa4 21 ♗xf7+ (Black's pawns just seem to fall off the board) 21...♔xf7 22 ♕b3+ ♔f6 23 ♖xa4 ♘c5 24 ♕c4 ♗xa4 25 ♕xc5 ♖e8 26 ♘xh4 ♗f8 27 ♕e3 ♗b5 28 ♘f3 ♔g7 29 ♖a1 ♖e6 30 h4 ♗e7 31 h5 ♕f8 32 ♘g3 ♗c5 33 ♕g5 ♔h7 34 hxg6+ ♖xg6 35 ♕h5+ ♔g7 36 ♕xe5+ ♔g8 (Black must either have been very short of time, or an amazing believer in the power of the two bishops to keep going now, five pawns down!) 37 b4 1-0 Krasenkov-Vokač, Pardubice 1994.

5 ♕d2 ♘d7

5...b5 is a popular move, seeking to initiate immediate counterplay on the queenside. After 6 ♗d3 Black has two approaches that have independent significance:

a) 6...a6 and now:

a1) Cautious players might consider 7 h3, preventing ...♗g4.

a2) 7 a4 is interesting, immediately putting the question to the black queenside. After 7...b4 8 ♘ce2 a5 9 c3 (White is very consistent in his attempts to clarify the structure on the queenside) 9...♗a6 10 cxb4 ♗xd3 11 ♕xd3 axb4 12 ♘f3 ♘f6 13 0-0 0-0 14 ♕c2 with a small advantage, Sion-Garcia Blazquez, Spanish Ch (Linares) 1993. The c6-pawn is weak and under surveillance and the a-pawn will be an asset in the endgame.

a3) 7 ♘f3 would be my choice, completing development. 7...♗g4 8 h4 h5 (I don't feel this move is very consistent; although the white attack is certainly dangerous, Black should try 8...♗xf3 here) 9 ♘g5 (now White builds up a powerful attack without making any positional concessions) 9...♘h6 10 f3 ♗c8 11 0-0-0 ♘d7 12 g4! *(D)*.

B

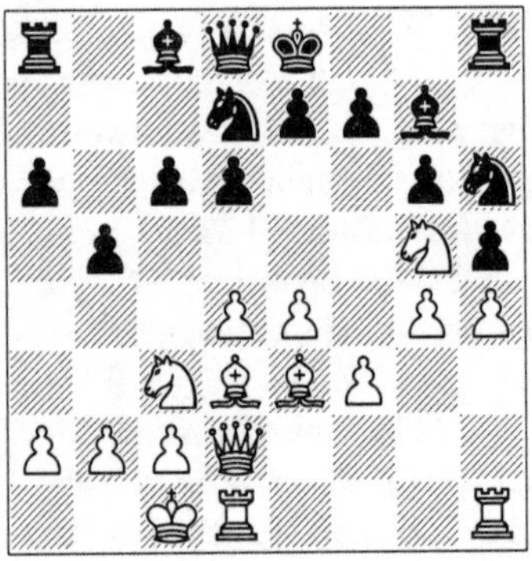

Continuing the theme, White opens the kingside. 12...c5 (12...hxg4 13 h5) 13 dxc5 dxc5 14 gxh5 gxh5 15 ♖hg1 ± (White has a large lead in development and can attack on any sector of the board) 15...♗d4 16 ♘d5 ♗xe3 17 ♘xe3 ♗b7 18 ♕c3 e5 19 ♗xb5! (it is not surprising that White has a combinative finish, with so many attacking pieces) 19...axb5 20 ♖xd7 ♔xd7 (20...♕xd7 21 ♕xe5+ also wins for White) 21 ♖d1+ ♔c6 22 ♖xd8 ♖hxd8 23 b4 +– f6 24 ♕xc5+ ♔d7 25 ♘d5 ♗xd5 (25...fxg5 26 ♕e7+ ♔c6 27 ♕c7#) 26 ♕xd5+ 1-0 Kupreichik-Lutikov, Sochi 1970.

b) 6...b4 (this move must be considered inaccurate, given that White often expends a tempo with a4 in order to get Black to do just this) 7 ♘ce2 ♕b6 8 ♘f3 d5 (Black is mixing up systems in order to confuse White; however, he is lagging behind with development) 9 e5 ♕b7 10 c4 (the side with better-developed pieces should normally attempt to open the position) 10...dxc4 11 ♗xc4 e6 12 ♘g5 ♘e7 13 ♘e4 (Black's somewhat eccentric opening play has left him with critically weak dark squares) 13...0-0 14 ♗h6 (playing against a weak colour complex, it usually makes sense to exchange any pieces that can guard the crucial squares) 14...♘d7 15 ♗xg7 ♔xg7 16 h4 c5 (faced with an awesome kingside attack, Black is compelled to strike back) 17 ♕f4 f6 18 exf6+ ♘xf6 19 ♘xc5 ♕xg2 20 ♖g1 ♕c6 21 ♕e5 ♘ed5 22 ♘g3 ♕c7 23 ♘h5+ (placing Black on the critical list) 23...♔g8 24 ♘xf6+ ♖xf6 25 ♗xd5 and Black could easily have resigned in J.Schneider-Stassen, Wallertheim 1994.

6 ♘f3 b5

7 ♗d3 *(D)*

7 ... a6

Apart from this, Black has two other options:

a) 7...♘b6 (this early attempt at queenside counterplay seems set to rebound on Black if White castles kingside) 8 0-0 a5?! 9 h3 ♘c4?! (consistent,

B

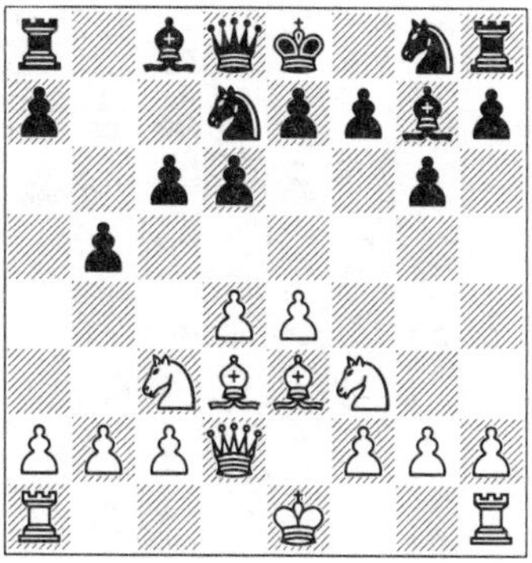

B

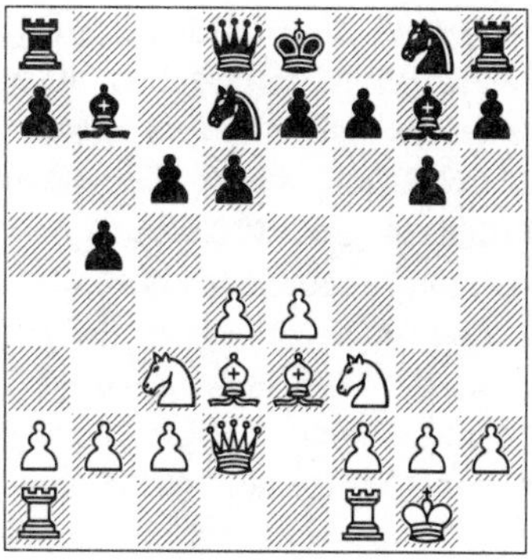

but again Black is neglecting his development) 10 ♗xc4 bxc4 11 d5! ♗b7 (after 11...c5 12 e5 dxe5 13 ♗xc5 White is clearly better, as Black will find it hard to complete his development) 12 ♗d4 ♘f6 13 dxc6 ♗xc6 14 e5! dxe5 15 ♘xe5 ♗b7?! (15...♗d5 16 ♖ad1 0-0 17 ♕e2 ±) 16 ♖fd1 (16 ♘xc4 ♘e4 17 ♘xe4 ♕xd4 18 ♘ed6+ exd6 19 ♘xd6+ ♔d7 20 ♕xd4 ♗xd4 21 ♘xb7 ±) 16...0-0 (16...♖c8 17 ♕e2, 16...♕c8 17 ♕e2 and 16...♕c7 17 ♕e2 ♖c8 18 ♘b5 are all ±) 17 ♘xc4 (Black has survived the opening, but at the cost of a pawn, for which the two bishops are insufficient compensation) 17...♕c7 18 b3 ♖fd8 19 ♕e3 a4 20 ♗e5 ♕c6 21 f3 ♗a6 22 ♘b6 ♖ab8 23 ♗xb8 ♖xb8 +– 24 ♘bxa4 ♖e8 25 ♕b6 ♕c8 26 ♘c5 ♘h5 27 ♘d5 ♗e2 28 c3 ♗xd1 29 ♖xd1 ♕f5 30 ♕c6 ♔f8 31 ♕xe8+ 1-0 Palac-Minasian, Pula Echt 1997.

b) 7...♗b7 8 0-0 *(D)* with another division:

b1) 8...a6 9 a4 b4 10 ♘e2 a5 11 c3 (this is nearly always the correct response to Black's queenside pawn advance) 11...bxc3 12 bxc3 e5 13 ♖ab1 ♕c7 14 dxe5 dxe5 15 ♗c4 (although Black has an equal share of space, White's actively placed pieces give him a slight advantage) 15...♗a6 16 ♗xa6 ♖xa6 17 ♖b2 ♘gf6 18 ♖fb1 0-0 19 ♖b7 (White now has complete control of the position) 19...♕d8 20 ♕d3 (or 20 ♖d1 ±) 20...♖a8 21 ♕c4 ♕c8 22 ♘g3 h6 23 h3 ♔h7 24 ♗c1 c5 25 ♕b5 ♕xb7 26 ♕xb7 ♖ab8 27 ♗a3 ♖xb7 28 ♖xb7 (despite the exchange of two sets of major pieces, White's advantage has not diminished) 28...♖a8 29 ♘d2 ♗f8 30 ♘c4 ♖a6 31 ♘f1 ♔g7 32 ♘fe3 ♖a8 33 f3 ♗e7 34 ♘d5 (White converts his positional advantage into a material one) 34...♗f8 35 ♘xf6 ♘xf6 36 ♘xe5 ♗d6 37 ♘xf7 ♗g3 38 ♗xc5 g5 39 ♗d6 1-0 Norri-Salmensuu, Tampere 1996.

b2) 8...♕c7 9 a4 (immediately challenging the b5-pawn is a logical approach) 9...b4 10 ♘e2 a5 11 ♖fe1 ♘gf6 12 ♗h6 0-0 13 ♘g3 c5 14 c3 (as usual, White simply strengthens his centre, leaving Black biting on granite)

14...e6 15 ♕g5 (with control of the centre, White can switch his attentions to the kingside) 15...bxc3 16 bxc3 cxd4 17 cxd4 ♖fc8 18 h4 (business as usual; I think the fact that White can castle short and continue his kingside attack attracts many players to the 150 Attack) 18...♕d8 19 ♗xg7 ♔xg7 20 h5 (White is simply piling on the pressure, waiting until Black reaches breaking point; meanwhile, because of White's rock-solid centre, Black lacks meaningful counterplay) 20...♘g8 21 ♕g4 ♗a6 22 ♗b1 ♖ab8 23 hxg6 hxg6 24 ♘h5+ ♔f8 25 ♘f4 (White feints at a sacrifice on e6 or g6, after perhaps playing e5; Black avoids the issue, but gives White a nice outpost on d5 as a result) 25...e5 26 ♘d5 ♘df6 27 ♕g3 ♘xd5 (Black had to try 27...exd4) 28 exd5 exd4 29 ♗xg6! fxg6 30 ♘g5 +– ♕d7 31 ♘e6+ ♔f7 32 ♕f4+ 1-0 Hodgson-Webster, Dublin 1993.

8 h3

Although very sensible and safe, this isn't really necessary yet and I would recommend an immediate strike against the black queenside. The move that really fits the bill is 8 a4. This is the classic response to Black's queenside pawn advance. White seeks to gain ground on the queenside to increase his manoeuvring space and has done rather well in practice following 8...♗b7 9 0-0 *(D)*:

a) 9...♘b6 10 ♖fe1 ♘f6 11 a5 ♘c8 (11...♘c4 is well met by 12 ♗xc4 bxc4 13 e5 ±) 12 e5 dxe5 13 dxe5 ♘d5 14 ♗h6 ♗xh6 (Black had to try 14...0-0

B

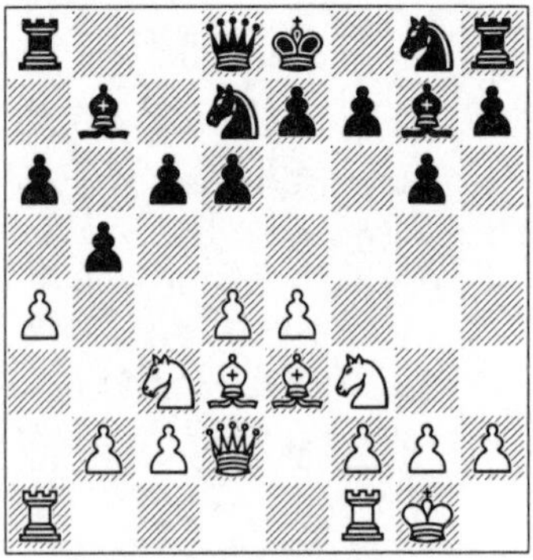

although after 15 ♘e4 White has a clear advantage) 15 ♕xh6 ♘xc3 16 bxc3 ♔d7 17 ♘g5 ♕f8 18 ♕xf8 ♖xf8 19 ♘xf7 ♖xf7 20 e6+ ♔e8 21 exf7+ gave White a winning material advantage in the game Miles-Wohl, Linares 1998.

b) 9...♕c7 10 axb5 cxb5 (10...axb5 11 ♖xa8+ ♗xa8 12 d5 b4 13 dxc6 ±) 11 ♘d5 ♕d8 12 ♕a5 (White's clear strategic plan is to gang up on the a6-pawn, a plan which Black is hard-pressed to meet) 12...♖c8 13 ♕xd8+ ♔xd8 14 ♘b4 ± ♘gf6 15 e5 dxe5 16 ♘xe5 ♘xe5 17 dxe5 ♘d7 18 f4 g5 (Black desperately tries to find counterplay, but it is too late) 19 ♖fd1 gxf4 20 ♗xf4 ♖c5 21 ♘xa6 ♖d5 22 ♘b4 ♖d4 23 c3 ♖xf4 24 ♗xb5 ♗xe5 25 ♖xd7+ ♔c8 26 ♖a7 1-0 Adams-Dunnington, Hastings Masters 1995.

8 ... ♕c7
9 0-0 ♘gf6
10 ♗h6 0-0
11 ♘e2

Interestingly, White re-routes his knight without being asked.

11 ... ♖e8
12 ♗xg7 ♔xg7
13 ♘g3 ♘f8

13...e5 was essential to prevent White's next, although even then 14 ♕g5 is a little better for White.

14 e5

If allowed, this is a key part of White's armoury in the 150 Attack.

14 ... dxe5
15 dxe5 ♘g8
16 ♖fe1 c5
17 h4

White sounds the charge.

17 ... ♘e6
18 ♘g5 ♕b6
19 h5 c4
20 hxg6 fxg6
21 ♗e4 ♖a7 *(D)*

W

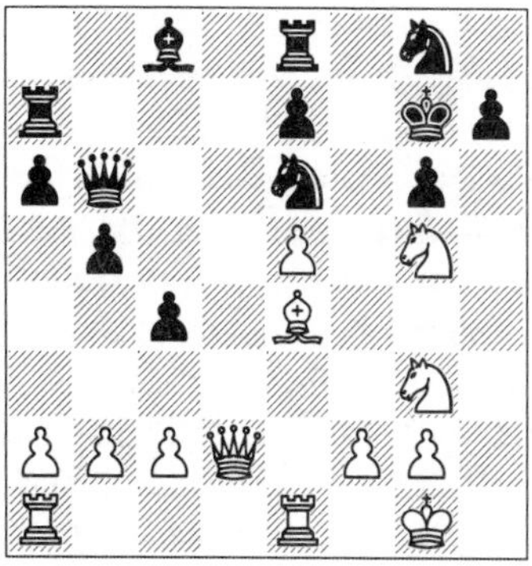

22 ♘h5+! gxh5

22...♔h8 23 ♘f7#.

23 ♘xe6+ ♕xe6
24 ♕g5+ ♔f8

After 24...♔h8 25 ♕xh5 ♘f6 26 exf6 exf6 27 ♖e3 White has a huge attack.

25 ♖e3 ♕g4
26 ♖f3+ ♘f6
27 ♕h6+ ♕g7
28 ♕e3 ♗g4

Black decides to keep his knight for defence.

29 ♕xa7 ♗xf3
30 ♗xf3 ♘g4
31 ♖e1 ♘xe5
32 ♗xh5 ♘g6
33 ♕xa6

Black has had to pay a high price for the safety of his king, with all the black pieces huddled on the kingside. Now White threatens simply to Hoover the queenside pawns.

33 ... ♘f4
34 ♗f3 ♕g5
35 ♕b6 ♔g7
36 ♕e3 e5
37 g3 1-0

150 Attack vs the Pirc Defence: Black delays ...0-0

Game 14
Hebden – Felecan
Cappelle la Grande 1993

1 d4 ♘f6
2 ♘f3 g6
3 ♘c3 ♗g7
4 e4 d6
5 ♗e3 *(D)*
5 ... ♘g4

This attempt to harass the white bishop badly backfires. Black should stick to the main alternative 5...c6 when after 6 ♕d2 Black has a choice:

B

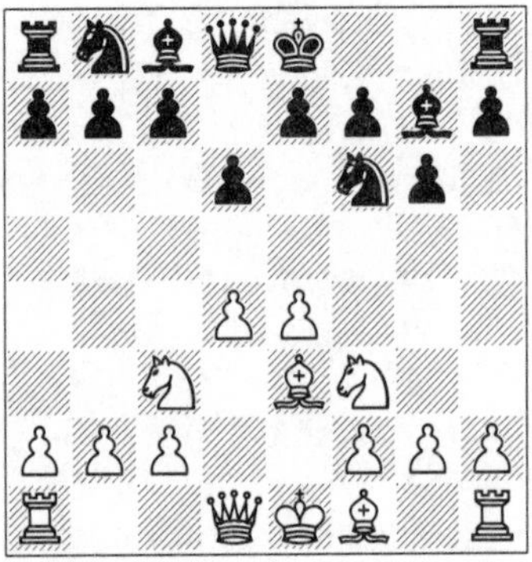

a) 6...b5 7 ♗d3 with the following options for Black:

a1) After 7...♗b7 a recent miniature continued 8 ♗h6 ♗xh6 9 ♕xh6 b4 10 ♘e2 ♕b6 11 0-0 c5 12 e5 dxe5 13 dxe5 ♗xf3 14 ♕g7 ♖f8 15 exf6 ♗xe2 16 fxe7 ♔xe7 17 ♗xe2 ♘d7 18 ♗g4 1-0 Yagupov-Zakharevich, St Petersburg Petrov mem 1998.

a2) 7...a6, supporting b5, is not the most active of alternatives, but Black bolsters his queenside, giving White the following promising choices:

a21) 8 ♗h6 0-0 9 e5 (as a general rule, a flank attack is often most successfully parried by a counter in the centre) 9...dxe5 10 dxe5 ♗xh6 11 ♕xh6 ♘g4 12 ♕f4 f6 (this is forced, due to the threat of h3) 13 h3 ♘xe5 (13...fxe5 14 ♕g5 ±) 14 ♘xe5 fxe5 15 ♕xe5 ♕d6 16 ♕e2 ♘d7 17 0-0-0 ± Gallagher-Todorčević, Biel 1991. White is better structurally, and has a lead in development.

a22) 8 a4 (striking at the black queenside to try to create a weakness) 8...b4?! (this pawn thrust is illogical in conjunction with Black's previous play; better is 8...♗b7 9 0-0 ±) 9 ♘e2 a5 10 ♘g3 0-0 (if Black does not castle, ♗h6 will be hard to meet) 11 ♗h6 ♕c7 (Black prepares ...e5 but is beaten to the punch) 12 ♗xg7 ♔xg7 13 e5 dxe5 14 dxe5 ♘g4 (14...♘d5 15 ♘h5+ gxh5 {15...♔h8 16 ♕h6 ♖g8 17 ♘g5 +–} 16 ♕g5+ ♔h8 17 ♕h6 +–) 15 ♕f4 +– f6 (this loses on the spot, but there was nothing much better, for example 15...♘a6 16 h3 ♘h6 17 ♘h5+ +–) 16 exf6+ 1-0 Summerscale-Weeramantry, Las Vegas 1998. Black lost here because he simply wasted too much time with pawn moves on the queenside.

a3) 7...♗g4 (aiming to disrupt White's normal plan by threatening to double his pawns) 8 ♘h4 (White could consider 8 0-0-0 or 8 e5!, as in Game 12) 8...e5 9 dxe5 dxe5 10 h3 (White's point is that ♘h4 is not really a waste of time, as the bishop lacks a good retreat-square, since on e6 it could be harassed by a later ♘g5, and on d7 it seems to hamper the progress of Black's development after 11 a4!). 10...♗c8 11 ♘f3 ♘bd7 12 a4 b4 13 ♘e2 a5 14 c3 (this is a common idea, to open lines on the queenside in order to exploit the holes left by Black's pawn moves) 14...c5 15 cxb4 cxb4 16 0-0 0-0 17 ♖fd1 (the knight on d7 is a serious cause of concern for Black) 17...♗b7 18 ♗b5 *(D)* and now:

a31) 18...♕e7 19 ♕xd7! (imaginative; perhaps Black was only expecting 19 ♗xd7 ♖fd8) 19...♘xd7 20

B

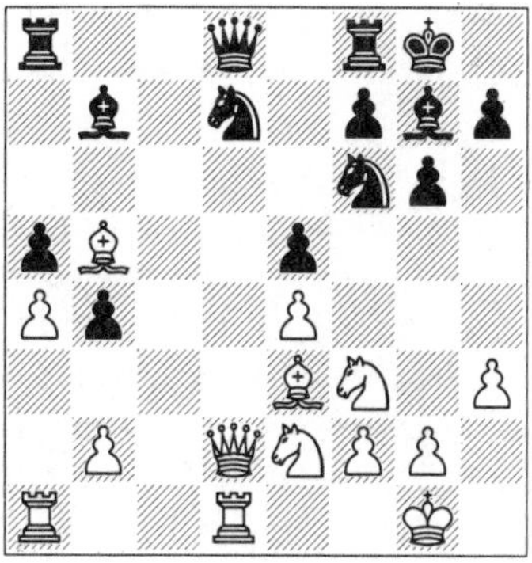

♖xd7 ♕e6 21 ♖xb7 (White has a clear advantage, with three well-organized pieces for the queen) 21...♕b3 22 ♘d2 ♕xb2 23 ♖b1 ♕a2 24 ♘c1 ♕e6 25 ♘cb3 ♕c8 26 ♖b6 ♕d8 27 ♖c6 (the black queen is kept under lock and key) 27...f5 28 ♗c5 (this forces Black to part with material, without any compensation) 28...♗h6 (28...♖e8 29 ♖d6; 28...♖f7 29 ♗c4) 29 ♗xf8 ♕xf8 30 exf5 ♗xd2 31 ♘xd2 gxf5 32 ♘c4 +– e4 33 ♘d6 ♖d8 34 ♖d1 ♕h6 35 ♖d5 ♕f6 36 ♖xf5 ♕a1+ 37 ♔h2 ♕d4 38 ♗c4+ ♔g7 39 ♖d5 ♖xd6 (39...♕xf2 40 ♘f5+) 40 ♖xd4 ♖xd4 41 ♖c5 1-0 Izeta-Striković, Elgoibar 1994.

a32) 18...♕b8 (a better try than 18...♕e7; Black exploits the tactical trick that 19 ♗xd7 can be met by 19...♖d8) 19 ♘g3 ♖c8 (19...♖d8 20 ♗c4 ♕c7 21 ♕c2 ♖ac8 22 ♖ac1 ♔f8 23 ♘g5 ♗a6 24 ♘xf7 ♗xc4 25 ♘d6 +– is given by Nunn) 20 ♖ac1 ♖xc1 21 ♖xc1 ♘f8 22 ♗c4 (just as Black solves one problem, a new one arises) 22...♘e6 (this amounts to positional suicide, but in any case Black lacks a satisfactory way to stop ♘g5) 23 ♗xe6 fxe6 24 ♘g5 ♖a6 25 ♖d1 h6 26 ♕d8+ ♕xd8 27 ♖xd8+ ♗f8 28 ♖b8! +– hxg5 29 ♖xb7 (Black's pawn-structure is horrific!) 29...♖d6 30 ♖b5 ♖d1+ 31 ♔h2 ♖b1 32 ♖xe5 ♗d6 33 ♖xe6 ♗xg3+ 34 ♔xg3 ♔f7 35 ♖a6 ♘xe4+ 36 ♔f3 ♘f6 37 ♗d4 1-0 Nunn-Gelfand, Munich 1991. This game actually arose via a wholly different move-order, with the result that the move-numbers in the game were actually two less than those given. The opening is of interest, as it demonstrates the other significant possibility for Black of holding back on ...♗g7 (I suspect at club level this will be something of a rarity): 1 e4 d6 2 d4 ♘f6 3 ♘c3 g6 4 ♗e3 c6 5 ♕d2 (it is important to know the response if Black should delay developing the f8-bishop in order to gain a move when White plays ♗h6) 5...b5 6 ♗d3 ♘bd7 7 ♘f3 e5 (Black does well to play this straight away, as waiting moves allow White to play a4 with advantage, as the following shows: 7...♕c7 8 0-0 e5 9 a4 b4 10 ♘e2 exd4 11 ♘exd4 c5 12 ♘b5 ♕c6 13 ♗c4 ♗b7 14 ♗f4 a6 15 ♗d5 ♘xd5 16 exd5 ♕b6 17 ♖fe1+ ♔d8 18 ♘g5 axb5 19 ♘xf7+ ♔c7 20 ♘xh8 winning, Nunn-McNab, Walsall 1992) 8 dxe5 dxe5 9 h3 ♗g7 (although this move is very natural, Black would probably do better to delay it) 10 a4 b4 11 ♘e2 a5 12 c3 c5 (White was aiming to capture on b4 and target c6) 13 cxb4 cxb4 14 0-0 0-0

15 ♖fd1 ♗b7 16 ♗b5 and we have arrived at the position after White's 18th move in Izeta-Striković.

a4) 7...0-0 (Black puts king-safety as his highest priority, although, as we shall see, often his majesty wishes he had remained in the centre) 8 ♗h6 *(D)* and now:

B

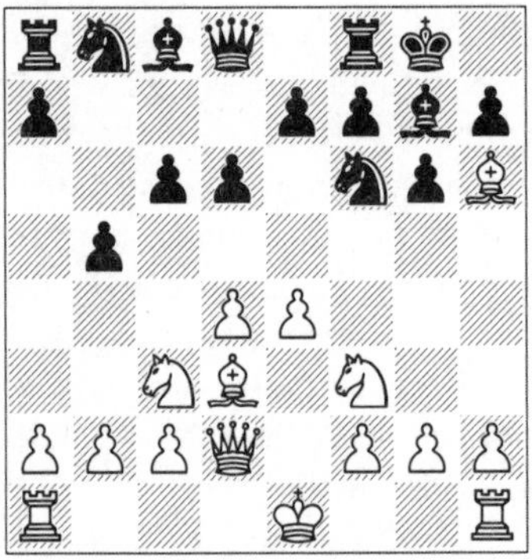

a41) 8...b4 (again with hindsight this looks like a mistake, as White is often prepared to expend a tempo with a4 to provoke this) 9 ♘e2 ♘a6 10 ♘g3 (the pleasant thing about this manoeuvre after Black has played ...b4 is it probably appears non-threatening; Black may even feel he has driven the knight to a worse square and cost White two tempi, while furthering his queenside options, but nothing could be further from the truth!) 10...c5 11 e5 (this central breakthrough is the prelude to a kingside attack) 11...♘g4 (11...♗xh6 12 ♕xh6 ♘g4 13 ♕f4 dxe5 14 dxe5 f6 15 h3 is Black's only chance, although clearly better for White) 12 ♗xg7 ♔xg7 13 h3 ♘h6 14 ♘h5+ gxh5 15 ♕g5+ ♔h8 16 ♕xh6 1-0 Hebden-P.Littlewood, Walsall 1992. A total rout!

a42) 8...♗g4 (at least with this move Black keeps a firm hand on the h5-square) 9 a4 (White could consider 9 ♘h4 here) 9...b4 10 ♘e2 a5 11 ♘g3 ♘bd7 12 h4 e5 13 dxe5 dxe5 14 h5 ♗xh5 15 0-0-0 with an exciting attacking position, Zapata-Schüssler, Santa Clara 1996.

b) 6...♗g4 7 ♗h6 ♗xh6 (this is always an option for Black, but it makes the position of his king more precarious; 7...0-0 8 ♗xg7 ♔xg7 9 ♘g5, with the idea of h3 and f4, gave White a small advantage in the game Baklan-Pe.Schmidt, Passau 1997) 8 ♕xh6 ♕a5 9 ♕e3 (a very solid move, recentralizing the queen and hinting at a central breakthrough) 9...♗xf3 10 gxf3 b5 11 a4 (it looks strange to advance on the queenside when that seems a likely resting place for White's king, but White has a devilishly clever idea!) 11...♘bd7?! (despite leaving light-squared weaknesses, 11...b4 had to be tried) 12 b4! ♕xb4 (12...♕a6 13 ♖b1 ±) 13 axb5 ♖c8 14 ♖a4 ♕b2 15 ♖a2 ♕b4 16 ♖a4 ♕b2 17 ♔d2 ± Kinsman-Watson, London ECC 1996. White threatens simply to bring the h-rook to b1.

c) 6...♕a5 (in my opinion, this is the most flexible move for Black, as he holds back from giving White a target with ...b5) 7 h3 (the most accurate response; since Black is keeping his options open, it would seem best to play quietly and look for an opportunity to exploit the sometimes shaky position of the black queen) and now Black has tried:

c1) 7...0-0 8 ♗d3 e5 9 0-0 ♘bd7 10 a4 ♖e8 11 ♖fd1 (White is well placed for the inevitable opening of the centre, after which he will be better, thanks to his slight space advantage) 11...♕c7 (11...exd4 12 ♗xd4 {it is usually more accurate to recapture with the bishop for tactical reasons} 12...♘c5? 13 b4 ♕xb4 14 ♗xf6 ♗xf6 15 ♘d5 ♕b2 16 c3 +– is given by Burgess/Pedersen in *Beating the Indian Defences*) 12 a5 (a useful move, gaining space) 12...exd4 13 ♗xd4 ♘c5 14 e5 (this is another reason for recapturing with the bishop on d4) 14...♘fd7 15 exd6 ♕xd6 16 ♗f1 ± Nunn-Azmaiparashvili, Wijk aan Zee 1993.

c2) 7...♘bd7 8 a3 (I believe that this move is unnecessary; White would do better with 8 ♗d3) 8...0-0 9 ♗d3 e5 10 0-0 ♕c7 11 a4 (this is the problem with the inaccuracy on move 8: White has a similar position to Nunn-Azmaiparashvili, above, with one tempo less) 11...b6 12 a5 b5 13 dxe5 dxe5 14 ♘e2 a6 15 c4 (White has played energetically since move 8 and now takes the initiative on the queenside) 15...bxc4 16 ♗b1 ♖b8 17 ♘c3 ♘h5 18 ♖a4 ♖d8 19 ♖d1 ♗b7 20 ♕e2 ± Hebden-McNab, London Lloyds Bank 1994. White will regain his pawn and then take aim at Black's structural weaknesses.

6	**♗g5**	**h6**
7	**♗h4**	**c6**
8	**♕d2**	**g5** *(D)*

W

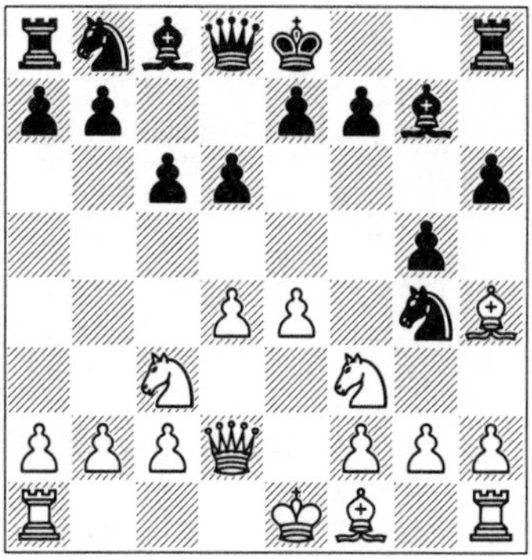

This is consistent with Black's previous moves, but frankly does not impress. All Black has achieved is to weaken his kingside.

9	**♗g3**	**♘d7**
10	**0-0-0**	**b5**
11	**e5**	

The usual remedy to a flank attack.

11	**...**	**b4**
12	**♘b1**	

Not 12 ♘e4? due to 12...d5.

12	**...**	**dxe5**
13	**dxe5**	**♕a5**
14	**h4**	

Making Black pay for his previous aggression.

14	**...**	**♘gxe5**

14...gxh4 15 ♖xh4 ♘gxe5 16 ♘xe5 ♘xe5 17 ♗xe5 ♗xe5 18 ♖xh6 ♖xh6 19 ♕xh6 ±.

15	**♘xe5**	**♘xe5**
16	**hxg5**	**hxg5**
17	**♖xh8+**	**♗xh8**

18 ♗b5!! *(D)*

B

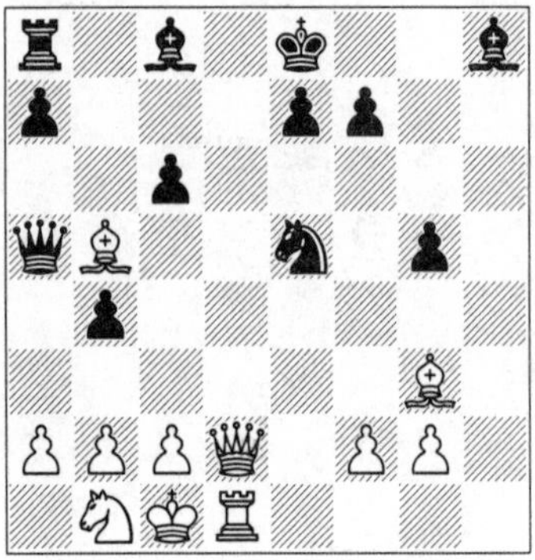

A thunderbolt.

18 ... ♗g4

18...♕xb5 19 ♕d8#; 18...cxb5 19 ♕xg5 ♘g6 20 ♕d5 +–.

19 ♖h1 ♗f6

20 ♗xe5 ♖d8

21 ♗xc6+ 1-0

White wins material after 21...♔f8 22 ♗xf6.

5...0-0

Game 15

Khalifman – Adams

Lucerne Wcht 1997

1 d4 d6

2 e4 ♘f6

3 ♘c3 g6

4 ♘f3 ♗g7

5 ♗e3 0-0

I suspect that the majority of Pirc players will reach this position as a matter of course.

6 ♕d2 ♗g4

Black continues to treat the position in the same manner, as a Classical Pirc, but is in for a rude awakening. 6...♘c6 is the major alternative, but again, White can go an independent way:

a) 7 0-0-0 ♗g4 8 ♗e2 (owing to my poor tournament standing in the competition from which this game is taken, I was trying to combine solidity with aggression) 8...♖e8 9 h3 ♗xf3 10 ♗xf3 e5 11 dxe5 (11 d5 ♘d4!?) 11...dxe5 12 ♕xd8 ♘xd8 13 ♗e2 (this is perhaps inaccurate, as a major idea for White is to relocate the knight on c3, in order to play c3 and control d4) 13...c6 (in turn Black slips; an improvement would be an immediate 13...♘e6) 14 g4 ♘e6 (and here, 14...h6 was definitely called for) 15 g5 ♘h5 16 ♗xh5 gxh5 17 ♘e2 (White now has a definite advantage, due to the weakness of the black h-pawns and kingside) 17...h4 18 ♘g1 f6 19 ♘f3 fxg5 20 ♘xg5 ♘d4 21 c3 ♘e2+ 22 ♔c2 ♘f4 23 ♖d7 +– b6 24 ♗xf4 exf4 25 ♖g1 1-0 Summerscale-B.Jacobsen, Århus 1993.

b) 7 d5 deserves consideration.

c) 7 ♗b5 (Hebden goes his own way) 7...a6 8 ♗xc6 bxc6 9 ♗h6 (White's approach is fairly unambitious: he hopes to exploit the weakened black queenside later on in the game; obviously, such an idea requires a great deal of technique, but with little counterplay available for Black, White hopes to grind down his weaker opponent) 9...♗g4 10 ♗xg7 ♔xg7 11

♕f4 ♗xf3 12 ♕xf3 ♘d7 13 0-0 (many players would be tempted to castle queenside and attack the black king; this would, however, simply help Black organize more effective counterplay) 13...e5 14 ♖ad1 exd4 15 ♖xd4 ♖e8 16 ♕d1 ♕b8 17 b3 ♕b6 18 ♔h1 (preparing to push the f-pawn, taking away a natural square for the black knight) 18...♕a5 19 ♕a1 ♕e5 (Black's queen has been going all round the houses without having any real effect; this demonstrates Black's problems coming up with an active plan) 20 ♖c4 c5 21 f4 ♕f6 22 e5 dxe5 23 ♘e4 ♕e7 24 f5 *(D)*.

B

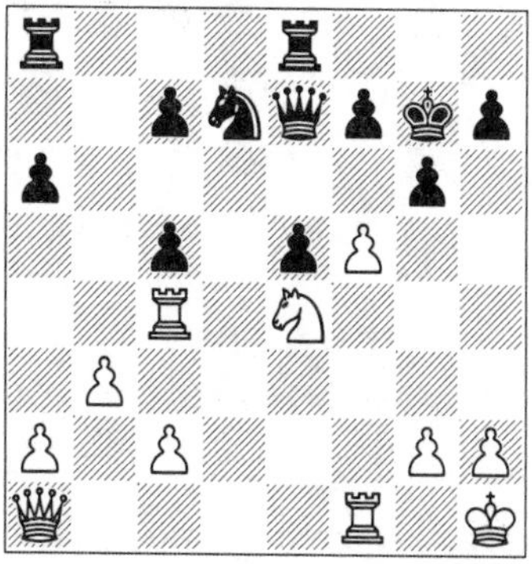

This thematic pawn sacrifice occurs in similar positions from the Benoni. The black pieces become more and more tied up, leaving Black with a long, arduous defence ahead. 24...f6 25 ♕c3 ♖ad8 26 h3 ♖f8 27 ♖a4 gxf5 28 ♘g3 ♕e6 29 ♘xf5+ ♔h8 30 ♕c4 (White realizes his positional advantage will be more pronounced in an endgame) 30...♕xc4 31 ♖xc4 ♔g8 32 ♖g4+ ♔h8 33 ♖g7 (the white pieces are like bones in Black's throat) 33...♖g8 34 ♖e7 ♘b6 (Black is helpless against the threat of ♖d1 so returns the material with interest in a bid for activity) 35 ♖xc7 ♘d5 36 ♖xc5 ♘f4 37 ♖f2 ♖g5 38 ♘e3 ♖dg8 39 ♔h2 (Black is enticed into the white position like a fly into a spider's web...) 39...♖g3 40 ♘g4 (...and the rook is caught) 40...♖xg2+ 41 ♖xg2 ♘xg2 42 ♘xf6 1-0 Hebden-Beikert, France 1993.

7 ♘g5! *(D)*

B

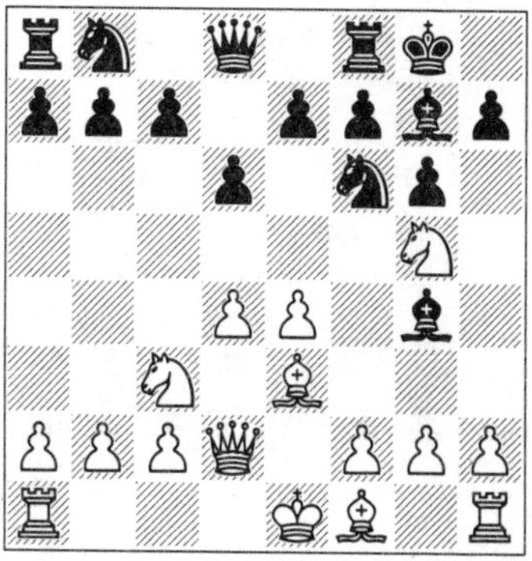

It was the discovery of this move that enhanced the popularity of the 150 Attack. White side-steps the bishop's attack and prepares his own on the kingside.

7 ... ♘c6

7...h6 8 h3 ♗h5 (8...♗d7 9 ♘f3 ♔h7 10 g4 with the initiative) 9 g4 hxg5 10 ♗e2 (a clever move, designed to put maximum pressure on h5, before taking there) 10...c5 (Black in turn tries to find counterplay on the queenside, but is simply too far behind in the race) 11 gxh5 cxd4 12 ♗xd4 ♘c6 13 ♗e3 ♘h7 14 h4 (White's strategy is simple: open as many lines as possible) 14...g4 15 hxg6 fxg6 16 h5 gxh5 17 ♖xh5 ± ♘e5 18 0-0-0 ♘f6 19 ♖g5 ♖c8 20 ♗d4 ♔f7 (20...♕a5 21 ♗xe5 dxe5 22 ♗xg4 +–) 21 ♗xe5 dxe5 22 ♖xg7+ 1-0 Kosten-Seret, Auxerre 1991. Black loses his queen after 22...♔xg7 23 ♕g5+.

8 d5 ♘b8

8...♘e5 9 f4 ♘ed7 10 h3 ±.

9 f3

This is the point: White can use Black's bishop as a target, in order to gain time for his attack.

9 ... ♗d7

10 h4 h5

11 g4! *(D)*

B

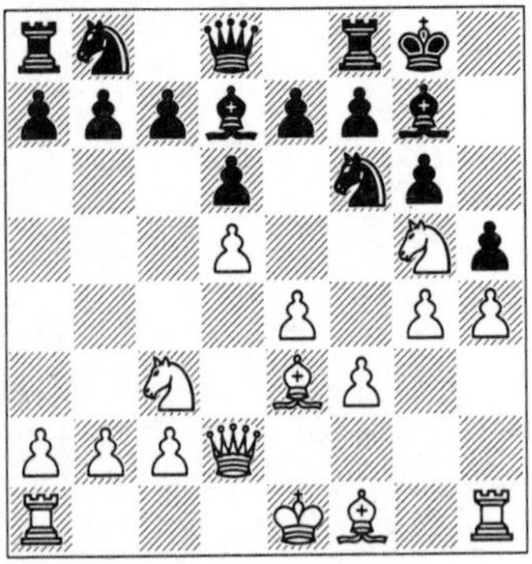

With Black's queenside pieces so poorly placed, White thinks nothing of offering a pawn to open lines against Black's king.

11 ... c6

Or 11...hxg4 12 ♗e2.

12 gxh5 ♘xh5

13 0-0-0 ♕a5

Black is trying hard to create some counterplay before White's kingside attack becomes too dangerous.

14 ♗d4 ♗xd4

15 ♕xd4 b5

16 ♔b1 b4

17 ♘e2

But now the counterattack seems to have reached a dead end.

17 ... ♖c8

18 ♕d2 cxd5

19 ♘f4 *(D)*

B

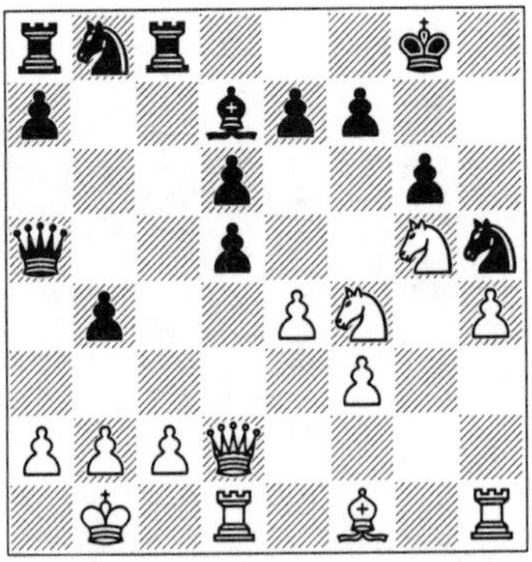

Black's position is critical, faced with the inevitable collapse of his kingside defences and with most of his queenside still undeveloped.

19 ... b3!?

Adams decides to go down fighting. Unfortunately for him, he never even gets close to reasonable compensation for his queen.

20 ♕xa5 bxc2+

21 ♔c1 cxd1♕++

22 ♔xd1 ♘xf4

23 exd5 ♗f5
24 ♕d2 ♘h5
25 ♕e3 ♖c7
26 ♗b5! *(D)*

B

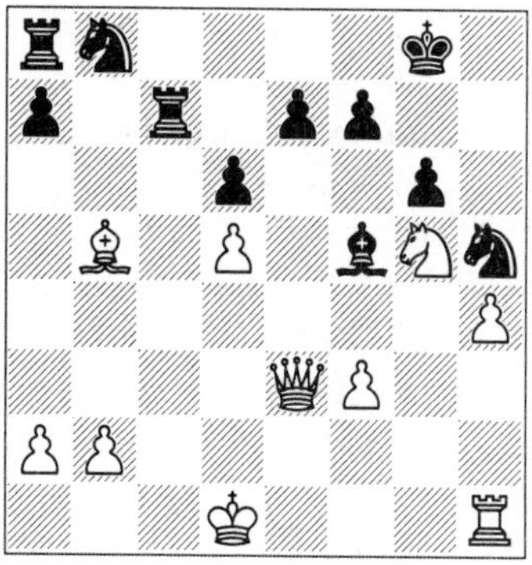

White goes back on the offensive, the clearest way to realize his advantage before Black can get organized. White ties Black up on the queenside and introduces the threat of ♗e8.

26 ... ♔f8
27 ♕d4

Black is given no rest, as White creates a threat with each move.

27 ... ♘f6
28 ♘h7+ ♔g7
29 ♘xf6 exf6
30 h5 gxh5
31 ♖xh5 1-0

Leaving Black defenceless against an invasion on the h-file.

3 The Colle-Zukertort System

Introduction

The Colle-Zukertort System is a flexible alternative to offering the Queen's Gambit. Through our recommended method of development, we take away many of Black's exciting options, such as the Botvinnik Variation of the Semi-Slav. Hopefully, we again lure Black onto unfamiliar ground. When I used to play a lot of amateur league chess, the majority of club players who defended the Queen's Gambit were fairly solid characters. They were happy to play slightly inferior positions for hours on end, waiting patiently for a mistake from their opponent (often caused by outright boredom). If this is true about your opponents, then they are in for a surprise!

On the surface, White's opening appears quite unassuming. However, with just a couple of inaccuracies, Black is often left facing a frontal attack against his king. For a normally stodgy opponent, the message will be clear: kill or be killed! The question is, will Black find things too hot to handle? To begin, let's take a look at the game where Zukertort, who generally played his opening in more positional fashion than I will be advocating, unleashed his novelty on an unsuspecting Englishman.

Game 16
Zukertort – Blackburne
London 1883

1 d4 d5
2 ♘f3 ♘f6
3 e3 e6
4 ♗d3 c5
5 b3

Please note that I have adjusted the move-order for the purpose of our discussion (the actual sequence was 1 d4 e6 2 ♘f3 ♘f6 3 e3 d5 4 ♗d3 ♗e7 5 0-0 0-0 6 b3 c5). Johannes Zukertort was the inventor of this system for White. The idea is to make the dark-squared bishop a more dangerous piece than in the sister variation (the Colle) where White plays c3. The beauty of the Colle-Zukertort is that the theory is easy to remember. White can set up the same attacking formation against whatever defensive regime Black chooses.

5 ... ♗e7

This passive development of the bishop may seem unduly cautious, but as we shall see, with the bishop on d6 White sometimes gets to release his dark-squared bishop with tempo, with devastating effect.

6 0-0 0-0
7 ♗b2 *(D)*

7 ... ♘c6

B

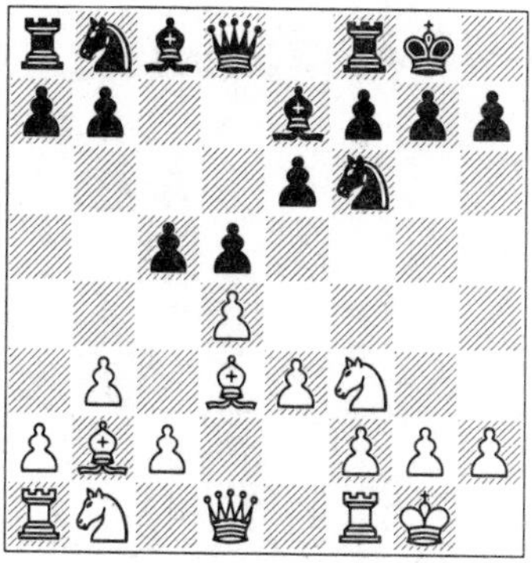

8 ♘bd2 cxd4
9 exd4 b6
10 c4

With this move, White begins an unusual plan of playing almost solely on the queenside and in the centre. More normal is 10 ♘e5 ♗b7 11 f4 followed by swinging a major piece over to h3 and bringing in the kingside attack. This idea will be discussed to a much fuller extent later on.

10 ... ♗a6
11 ♖e1 ♖c8
12 ♖c1 ♘a5
13 ♘e5

White is getting ready for the c5 push.

13 ... ♗b4

13...dxc4 is another idea, giving White the dynamic hanging pawn centre after 14 bxc4.

14 c5 *(D)*

With this move, White creates a powerful queenside passed pawn. Meanwhile, White's pieces are ideally placed to stop Black making anything of his central pawn majority.

B

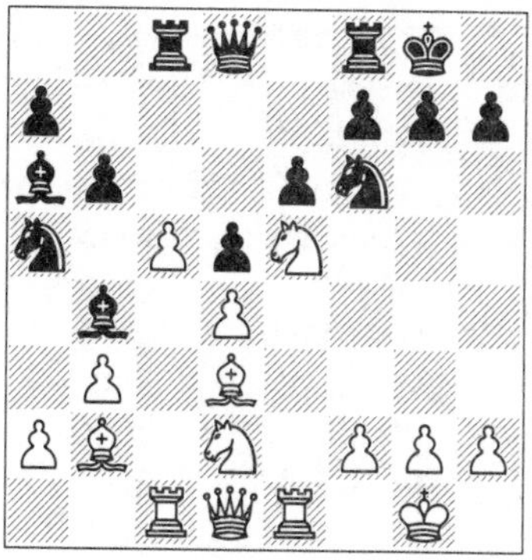

14 ... ♗xd3
15 ♘xd3 ♗xd2
16 ♕xd2 ♘e4
17 ♕e3 ♖e8
18 f3 ♘f6
19 ♖c2

White builds up slowly, which is very important even in the more attacking lines. Black's choice of active counterplay is limited, so White can afford to improve his position gradually.

19 ... ♘d7
20 ♖ec1 bxc5
21 dxc5 ♘b8
22 ♘e5 f6
23 c6

The c-pawn is a monster – White already has a clear advantage.

23 ... ♖c7

23...fxe5 24 c7 ♕d7 25 cxb8♕ ♖xb8 26 ♖c7 +–.

24 ♕d2 fxe5
25 ♕xa5 ♕c8
26 ♗xe5 ♖f7

26...♖xc6 27 ♕xa7 +–.

27 ♗xb8 ♕xb8
28 c7 ♕c8

29 ♕xa7 e5
30 ♖c5 e4
31 ♖b5

To convert his advantage White needs to exchange major pieces.

31 ... ♖ef8
32 ♖b8 ♕d7
33 ♖xf8+ ♖xf8
34 ♕a4 ♕xa4
35 bxa4 ♖c8
36 fxe4 dxe4
37 ♔f2 ♔f7
38 ♔e3 ♔e6
39 ♔xe4 g6
40 ♖c6+ ♔d7
41 ♔d5 1-0

Main Line: Black plays ...♘c6 & ...♗d6

Game 17
Summerscale – Sadler
Crewe 1991

1 ♘f3 d5
2 d4 e6
3 e3 ♘f6
4 ♗d3 c5
5 b3 *(D)*

This is the basic starting position for the Colle-Zukertort System. It would be reached through our repertoire move-order of 1 d4 d5 2 ♘f3 ♘f6 3 e3 e6 4 ♗d3 c5 5 b3. It is less frequently played than the Colle proper and this makes it less likely that your opponent will be ready for it. White aims to combine speedy development with kingside attacking chances.

B

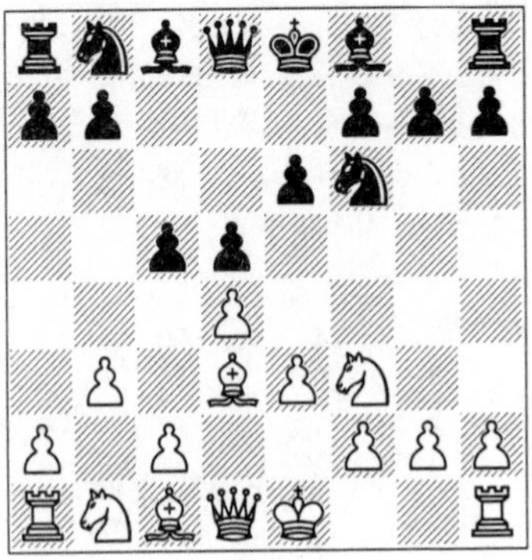

5 ... ♘c6

The systems where Black plays ...♗e7 or ...♘bd7 are covered later, so here I am only concerned with alternatives which do not easily transpose. The attempt to simplify by 5...cxd4 is possibly a mistake. By clarifying the central tension, Black makes it easier for White to access the key e5-square. 6 exd4 ♘c6 7 0-0 ♗d6 8 a3 (White often decides it is worth a tempo to avoid an annoying ...♘b4 at some stage) 8...0-0 9 ♖e1 h6?! (this move is clearly not necessary yet; Black should be completing his development with ...b6 and ...♗b7) 10 ♗b2 a5? (a misguided attempt at queenside counterplay; in reality, Black is simply wasting precious time) 11 c4 (this is a major option in the Colle-Zukertort; White gives Black the option of 'inflicting' hanging pawns in exchange for dynamic counter-chances) 11...♖e8 12 ♘bd2 ♗f8 13 ♖c1 ♗d7 14 ♗b1 ♕b8 (it must be said that Black's play leaves a lot to be desired – he seems content to shuffle his pieces around and await developments, but this type of planless play is usually severely punished) 15 ♘e5 ♖d8 16 ♕c2 ♗e8 17 ♘g4 1-0 J.Bellin-Moen, Gausdal 1992.

6 0-0 *(D)*

B

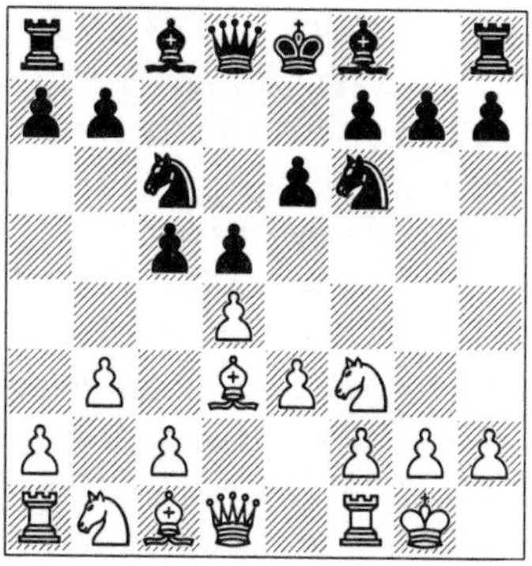

6 ... ♗d6

Alternatively Black has tried 6...a6, hinting at queenside expansion, but by 7 ♗b2! White sees that this will be to his advantage. Now:

a) 7...b5 is met by 8 a4 c4 (8...♖b8 9 axb5 axb5 10 dxc5 ±) 9 axb5 cxd3 10 bxc6 dxc2 11 ♕xc2 ±.

b) 7...cxd4 8 exd4 (the net effect of White calling Black's bluff is that he has gained a tempo on normal lines; as you would expect, this grants White the advantage with accurate play) 8...♗d6 9 ♘bd2 0-0 10 ♖e1 ♗d7 11 ♘e5 ♖c8 12 a3 (as this is a move White often has to play, it may be useful to introduce it much earlier in order not to worry about ...♘b4 at any stage; as the position is relatively closed, a3 is not a significant loss of tempo) 12...♘e7 13 ♘df3 ♘g6 14 g3 ♗e8 15 ♘g5 (White has built up a dream attacking position in the Colle-Zukertort) 15...♗e7 16 h4 (16 ♗xg6 hxg6 17 ♘xg6 fxg6 18 ♘xe6 is possible but passes the initiative to Black, which in the current position would be a crime) 16...♘h8 17 a4 (White takes away any possibility of ...♗b5, which hitherto would have been met by c4) 17...h6 18 ♘h3 ♘d7 19 ♘f4 ♗b4 20 c3 ♗d6 (20...♗xc3 21 ♕c2) 21 ♕c2 g6 22 ♕d2 (this game is impressive, as White is remarkably restrained about his various sacrificial possibilities and instead systematically increases the pressure with each move) 22...g5 (Black can stand the tension no longer and lashes out; this move serves only to weaken further his already loose kingside) 23 ♘h3 ♘xe5 24 dxe5 ♗e7 25 hxg5 hxg5 26 ♕e2 ♘g6 27 ♕g4 (the upshot of Black's 22nd move is that the g5-pawn is irrevocably weak and ultimately lost) 27...♔g7 28 ♖ad1 b5 29 axb5 axb5 30 c4 bxc4 31 bxc4 ♗c6 32 ♗c1 ♖h8 (Black introduces the idea of mate on h1, but it is easily dealt with – it is the black king that is in serious trouble) 33 ♘xg5 ♕e8 (33...dxc4 34 ♗e4 ±) 34 ♗xg6 fxg6 35 ♘xe6+ ♔g8 36 cxd5 ♗b7 37 ♗g5 ♗xg5 38 ♘xg5 ♖c5 39 ♘e4 1-0 Rubinstein-Chigorin, Lodz 1906.

7 ♗b2 *(D)*

7 ... 0-0

Black has plenty of other options here:

a) 7...♕e7 8 c4 (White goes his own way, but 8 ♘e5, with a likely

B

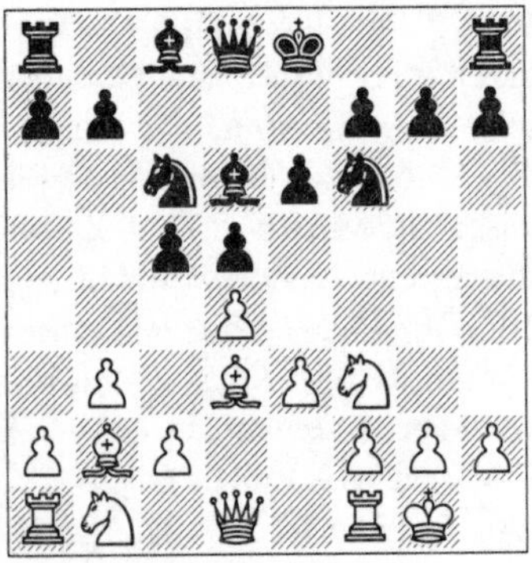

transposition to the main line, is also possible) 8...cxd4 9 exd4 dxc4 10 bxc4 (Black has inflicted hanging pawns on White, but as this game shows, the pawns have a great deal of dynamic strength; the push d4-d5, in particular, is likely to worry Black) 10...♘b4 11 ♗e2 ♗d7 12 ♖e1 ♖c8 13 a3 ♘c6 14 ♗d3 0-0 15 ♕d2 (this is an interesting attempt by White to stop ...♗f4 at some point, which might interfere with his attack) 15...♕d8 16 ♘e5 ♘a5 17 ♕e3 a6 18 ♘d2 b5 (Black's approach has been quite positional; here he seeks to exchange the c4-pawn, in order to leave White with a more static IQP) 19 ♘xd7 ♕xd7 (19...♘xd7 20 cxb5 axb5 21 ♘e4 ± is a more sensible approach by Black) 20 d5 ± (just look at those two raking bishops!) 20...♘xc4 21 ♘xc4 bxc4 22 ♗xf6 gxf6 23 ♗xh7+ +– ♔xh7 24 ♕h3+ ♔g7 25 ♕g4+ ♔h7 26 ♖e3 ♗f4 27 ♖h3+ 1-0 Sieg-Beckhuis, 2nd Bundesliga 1989/90.

b) 7...♕c7 8 c4 (with the black queen committed to c7, this advance is even more attractive) and now:

b1) 8...dxc4 9 bxc4 ♕b6 (this is the idea behind ...dxc4, but two early queen moves just to harass a bishop can't be right) 10 ♕c1 ♘b4 11 ♗e2 ♗d7 12 ♘bd2 ♕c7 13 dxc5 ♗e7 (13...♗xc5 14 ♗xf6 gxf6 15 ♘e4 ♗e7 16 ♕b2 ±) 14 ♘b3 ♘c6 15 ♗c3 0-0 16 ♕b2 ♖fd8 17 ♖ab1 ♘e8 18 ♘fd4 a5 19 ♘b5 ♕b8 20 a4 ± Dizdar-Sax, Vinkovci 1993.

b2) The other capture is also interesting: 8...cxd4 9 exd4 0-0 (Black tries a less ambitious approach, restricting himself to one pawn exchange, so as to reduce White's dynamic potential) 10 ♘bd2 b6 11 ♖c1 ♗b7 12 ♕e2 ♖fd8 13 ♘e5 ♗xe5 (if Black wants to take on e5, this would normally be a good time to do it, as White would otherwise play f4 and be able to recapture with the f-pawn; however, now the slightly awkward placing of the black queen becomes a factor) 14 dxe5 ♘d7 15 cxd5 exd5 16 b4 a6 17 e6 fxe6 18 ♕xe6+ ♔h8 19 ♕f7 (Black is bound hand and foot) 19...d4 20 ♗xd4 ♘ce5 21 ♕f5 1-0 Fuhrmann-D.Pedersen, German open U-20 Ch (Hamburg) 1993.

c) 7...cxd4 8 exd4 0-0 9 a3 ♕c7 10 ♘bd2 (White builds up slowly, as usual preparing ♕e2 and ♘e5) 10...♘g4 (Black tries to interfere with White's plan, but this early attack is bound to fail against such a solid position – one of the advantages of the Colle-Zukertort is that White is well-placed to withstand any early aggression by Black) 11 h3 (11 ♗xh7+ ♔xh7 12

♘g5+ ♔g6 13 ♕xg4 ♗xh2+ 14 ♔h1 ♕f4 is unclear) 11...♘h2 12 ♖e1 ♘xf3+ 13 ♘xf3 ♘a5 14 ♕e2 b6 15 ♘g5 (White does well not to be tempted by the unsound Greek Gift sacrifice 15 ♗xh7+ ♔xh7 16 ♘g5+ ♔g8 17 ♕h5 ♕xc2 ∓) 15...h6 16 ♘f3 ♗b7 17 ♘e5 ♘c6 18 f4 ♖ac8 19 ♖f1 (despite Black's best efforts, White has built up the ideal attacking position) 19...♖fd8 20 ♖ae1 ♕e7 21 ♘xc6 ♖xc6 22 f5 (White has prepared this breakthrough carefully) 22...♗g3 23 f6 ♕f8 24 ♖d1 ♖c7 25 ♕g4 ♗d6 26 ♗c1 g6 27 ♗xg6 fxg6 28 ♕xg6+ ♔h8 29 ♗xh6 ♕g8 30 ♕h5 1-0 Hawkins-MacLaughlin, British corr. Ch 1993.

Returning to the position after 7...0-0 *(D)*:

W

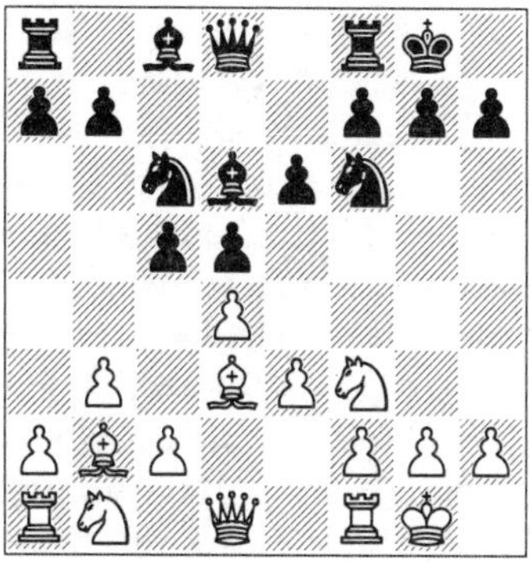

8 ♘bd2

Alternatively, White can try to create a dynamic imbalance with 8 c4 or set a trap with 8 ♘e5. Both variations contain plenty of useful motifs of the Colle-Zukertort, so we should examine them carefully:

a) 8 c4 (this makes slightly less sense when the black queen isn't on the c-file, but White has an original plan in mind) 8...b6 9 ♘c3 (this development of the queen's knight is more familiar to the Classical Queen's Indian) 9...cxd4 10 exd4 dxc4 11 bxc4 e5 (Black shows he is equal to the task and reduces White's dynamic potential at the expense of allowing a protected passed pawn) 12 d5 ♘a5 13 ♖e1 ♗g4 14 h3 ♗xf3 15 ♕xf3 ♖c8 16 ♘b5 (this is one possibility normally denied to White and indeed the knight proves to be a real workhorse) 16...♗b8 17 d6 a6 18 ♘c7 e4 19 ♖xe4! ♕xd6 (19...♘xe4 20 ♕xe4 ±) 20 ♗e5 ♕c6 21 ♗xf6 ♕xf6 22 ♕xf6 gxf6 23 ♘d5 (from meagre beginnings, the knight is now master of all he surveys) 23...f5 24 ♖h4 ♗e5 25 ♖b1 ♖ce8 26 ♖xb6 and White realized his material advantage in Ryan-Engqvist, Isle of Man 1995.

b) 8 ♘e5 (this early deployment of the knight is unusual, but involves a particularly nasty trap) 8...♕c7? (Black is trying to fianchetto on the queenside, but falls in with White's plans; 8...cxd4 9 exd4 ♕c7 is an improvement) 9 f4 b6 10 ♘xc6 ♕xc6 11 dxc5 ♗xc5 (11...♗e7 12 cxb6 ±) 12 ♗xf6 gxf6 13 ♗xh7+! ♔xh7 14 ♕h5+ ♔g7 15 ♕g4+ ♔h7 16 ♖f3 ♗xe3+ 17 ♔h1 1-0 Krabbé-*Dappet*, AEGON (The Hague) 1992.

Returning to 8 ♘bd2 *(D)*:

8 ... cxd4

Black has a number of other moves:

B

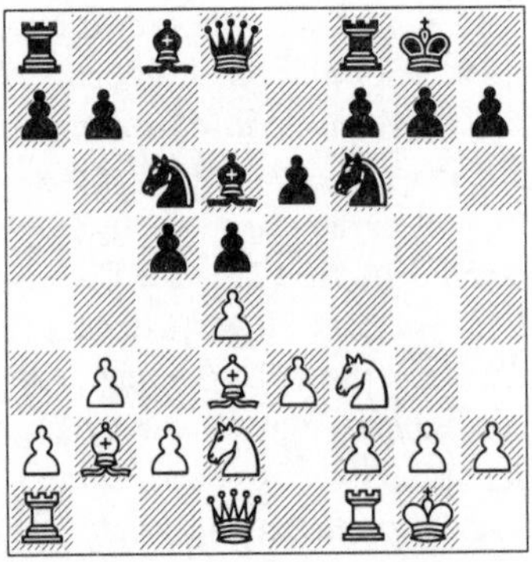

a) 8...♘b4 (this is intended to harass White's important bishop on d3, but as we shall see, Black gains no time by doing so) 9 ♗e2 b6 10 a3 ♘c6 11 ♘e5 ♘e7 12 ♗d3 ♗b7 13 ♕f3 ♘g6 14 ♕h3 (I must admit to being a fan of this queen manoeuvre, which puts pressure on h7 and e6 simultaneously) 14...cxd4 15 ♘xg6 hxg6 16 exd4 ♖c8 17 ♖fe1 ♖c7 18 ♘f3 ♘e4 (this is one of Black's most solid defensive tries, aiming to blunt the power of White's light-squared bishop; the game now becomes more positional, as outright attacking lines for White don't seem to work) 19 ♘e5 (19 ♗c1!? ♗e7) 19...♗xe5 20 dxe5 ♘c5 21 ♗d4 (a clever idea as after 21...♘xd3 22 ♕xd3 ♕c8 23 c3 it would be difficult for Black to get any serious counterplay without sacrificing material) 21...♕d7 22 b4 ♘e4 23 ♖e3 ♖fc8 24 ♖ae1 ♗c6 25 ♕g4 ♗b5 26 ♗xe4 dxe4 27 c3 ♗c6 28 h4 (with the c-file firmly covered, White has a free hand to attack) 28...♕e8 29 ♕f4 ♗d5 30 ♖g3 ♔h7 31 ♖ee3 ♕a4 (Black makes a break for freedom with his queen, but his king begins to feel the heat) 32 ♕g4 ♖h8 33 h5 ♔g8 34 hxg6 fxg6 35 ♖h3 ♖xh3 36 ♖xh3 e3 (36...♔f7 37 ♖h8) 37 ♕xg6 exf2+ (37...e2 38 ♕h7+ ♔f7 39 ♕h5+ ♔g8 40 ♕xe2 ±) 38 ♗xf2 ♕d1+ 39 ♔h2 ♖e7 40 c4 ♗c6 41 b5 ♕e2 42 bxc6 1-0 Rubinstein-Bogoljubow, Gothenburg 1920.

b) 8...♖e8 (this and line 'c' are attempts to achieve the freeing ...e5 advance, but it is easy for White to thwart this) 9 ♘e5 ♕c7 10 f4 cxd4 11 exd4 ♘b4 (the combination of ...♕c7 and ...♘b4 is one thing White needs to be wary of and I would advise the reader to prepare to meet ...♕c7 with either c4 or a3; in this particular position White is OK because he can attack the rook on e8 – but be careful!) 12 ♗b5 ♖e7 13 c3 ♘c6 14 ♕f3 ♗d7 15 ♗d3 ♗e8 16 ♕h3 g6 17 ♕h4 ♘d7 (Black seems to have defended himself with great care, whereas in reality, his pieces are in a bit of a tangle, mostly due to the rook on e7; White is quick to exploit this fact) 18 c4 (White opens up a second front on the queenside) 18...♘f8? (Black folds under the increasing pressure; 18...♘dxe5 19 fxe5 ♗b4 20 ♘f3 ♖d7 saves the piece but is hardly appetizing for Black) 19 ♘xc6 ♕xc6 20 c5 ♗xc5 21 ♖ac1 ♘d7 22 dxc5 1-0 Euwe-Kroone, Amsterdam 1921.

c) 8...♕e7 9 ♘e5 cxd4 10 exd4 ♗a3 11 ♗xa3 ♕xa3 12 c3 *(D)*.

This variation could perhaps be considered the most critical line of the

B

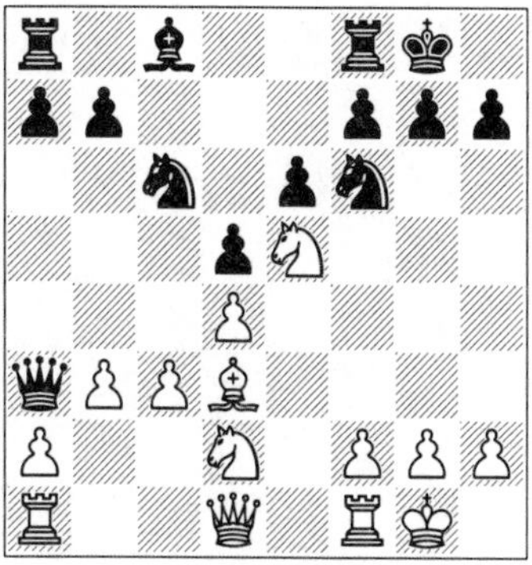

B

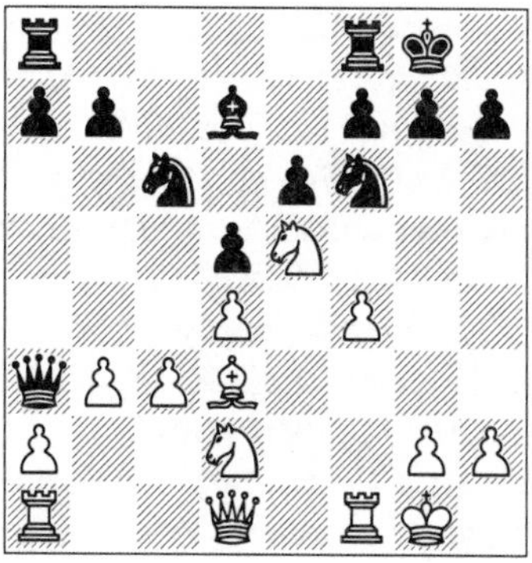

Colle-Zukertort. The good news is that White has been scoring well from this position. We consider three tries for Black:

c1) 12...♕d6 13 f4 (this is the basic idea: White sets up a Stonewall formation without the drawback of a dark-squared bishop) 13...♗d7 14 ♕f3 ♘e7 15 ♕h3 (as I have mentioned, this is one of my favourite manoeuvres) 15...♘g6 16 ♖f3 ♗c6 17 ♖e1 ♖fe8 18 g4 (I decided this pawn-push was worth the risk, since I could remove Black's light-squared bishop at will) 18...♖ac8 19 g5 ♘e4 (Black is more or less forced to part with a pawn, in order to relieve the tension as 19...♘d7 20 ♕h5 leaves White with a massive attack) 20 ♘xe4 dxe4 21 ♗xe4 ♗xe4 22 ♖xe4 ♕a3 23 ♘xg6 hxg6 24 ♖e2 ♖ed8 25 ♕f1 ± Summerscale-I.Thompson, Hastings 1994/5.

c2) 12...♗d7 13 f4 *(D)* and now:

c21) 13...♖fc8 does not make a great deal of difference, viz. 14 g4 (again White chooses this attacking lunge to gain space on the kingside and drive back the f6-knight) 14...♗e8 15 g5 ♘d7 16 ♖f3 (Black now has to contend with possible bishop sacrifices on h7) 16...♘cxe5 17 fxe5 g6 18 ♖c1 (in this variation White is much more concerned with keeping his central supporting c-pawn than his a-pawn) 18...♕a5 19 ♗b1 b5 20 ♘f1 (the knight is *en route* to g4, enticing Black to strike back on the queenside) 20...b4 21 c4 dxc4 22 bxc4 (White now enjoys a clear advantage, with a mobile central pawn majority, and clear weaknesses to exploit, in the form of Black's weak dark squares on the kingside and a target on f7) 22...♖d8 23 ♕e1 ♘f8 24 ♕f2 (with his centre stable, White can start to think about establishing a knight on f6 or h6, trebling on the f-file and loosening Black further with h4-h5) 24...♗c6 (faced with an extremely difficult defence, Black self-destructs) 25 ♖xf7 ♖xd4 26 ♕f6 ♖g4+ 27 ♘g3 1-0 Danner-Beim, Vienna 1996.

c22) 13...♖ac8 14 ♖f3 g6 15 ♕e1 ♔g7 16 ♖h3 ♗e8 17 ♘df3 ♖h8 18

♕d2 ♘e7 19 g4 (after a slower build-up, White again pushes his g-pawn towards goal) 19...♕a5 20 ♖c1 ♗b5 21 ♗b1 h5 (having defended well so far, Black falters and weakens his kingside) 22 ♘g5 ♖cf8 23 f5 (the upshot is that g6 is now critically weak) 23...♕a6 24 ♖e1 exf5 25 gxf5 ♕d6 26 ♖ee3 ♘fg8 27 fxg6 ♕f6 1-0 Høi-Danielsen, Ringsted 1995. It may seem strange to resign when you are threatening mate in one but after 28 ♖ef3 Black is totally lost.

c3) 12...♕a5 13 ♖c1 (this would be the response to 12...♕b2 as well) 13...♗d7 (we have already seen that White can quietly build up an awesome attack through natural moves and that the a-pawn is fairly irrelevant in the general scheme of things) 14 f4 ♖ac8 15 ♖f3 ♕c7 (Black introduces the threat of ...♘xd4, but it is easily dealt with) 16 ♖c2 ♘e7 17 ♖h3 g6 18 g4 ♔g7 19 g5 ♘fg8 (19...♘h5 20 ♖xh5) 20 ♕e1 (Black's position is marked by an obvious lack of counterplay) 20...♘f5 21 ♗xf5 exf5 22 ♕h4 h5 23 gxh6+ ♔h7 24 ♘df3 (White has excellent 'compensation' for his extra pawn!) 24...♗e8 25 ♘g5+ ♔h8 26 h7 ♘f6 27 ♘gxf7+ 1-0 Hoffmeyer-Krause, 2nd Bundesliga 1993.

9 exd4 *(D)*

9 ... b6

B

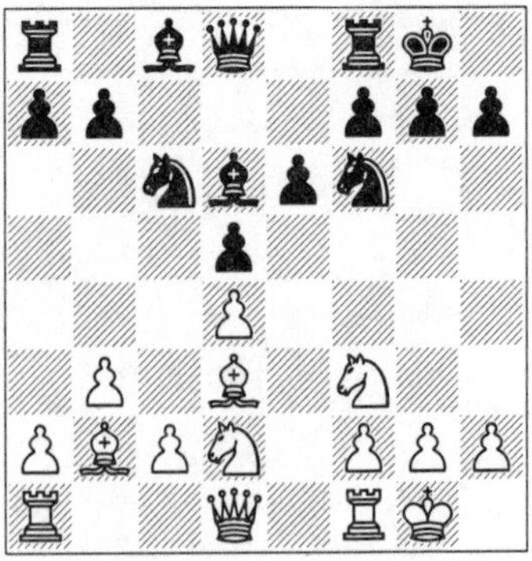

Here 9...♘b4 costs both sides the same amount of tempi, e.g. 10 ♗e2 ♗d7 11 a3 ♘c6 12 ♗d3 (back to square one!) 12...♕c7 13 ♕e2 ♘e7 14 ♘e5 ♘f5 15 g4 (this is a key idea at White's disposal in the Colle-Zukertort – the g-pawn advances so as to drive back Black's defenders on the kingside; this leaves some weaknesses on the white kingside but White counts on his initiative to see him through) 15...♘e7 16 g5 ♘e8 (the g4-g5 pawn-thrust is especially effective when Black has positioned his bishop on d7 rather than b7; on d7 the bishop takes away a retreat-square from the knight on f6 and there is less danger of an accident on the h1-a8 diagonal) 17 f4 ♘f5 18 ♘df3 f6 19 gxf6 ♘xf6 20 ♘g5 ♗c8 21 ♖ae1 h6 22 ♘h3 (the knight finds a route to g4) 22...a6 23 ♔h1 b6 24 ♖g1 ♗b7 25 ♖g2 ♘h4 26 ♖gg1 ♘f5 27 ♘f2 ♖ae8 28 ♘fg4 ♘xg4 29 ♕xg4 ♗xe5 30 fxe5 ♔h8 31 ♖ef1 ♕d7 (Black is defending himself quite well, but as usual finds it hard to develop counterplay) 32 ♖f3 ♖f7 33 ♕g6 ♖ef8 34 ♗c1 ♕e7 35 ♖h3 (White has completed the mobilization of his forces and Black is helpless against the following breakthrough) 35...a5 36 ♗xh6 gxh6 37 ♗xf5 exf5 38 ♕xh6+

1-0 Walmisley-Samworth, Connecticut 1994.

10 a3 ♗b7 *(D)*

W

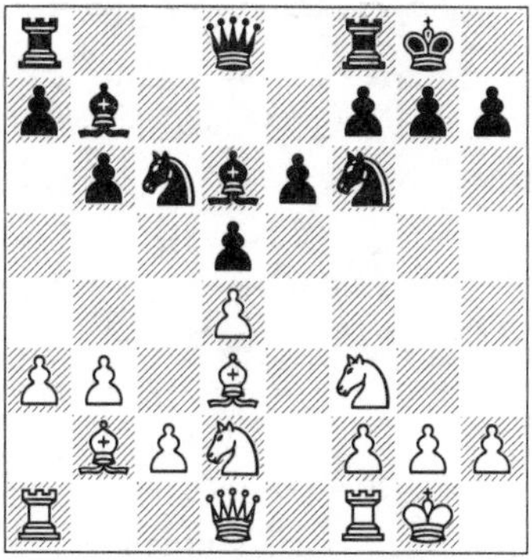

11 ♖e1

A different option to experiment with is 11 ♕e2 (if you like the idea of putting your rook on h3 then this is the move for you) 11...♖c8 12 ♘e5 ♕e7 13 f4 ♖fe8 14 ♖f3 ♕f8 15 ♖h3 g6 16 g4 ♕g7 17 ♖f1 ♘e7 18 ♖f2 (the main thing is for White not to rush the attack but to build up slowly; it is often harder to defend against vague threats than concrete ones you can calculate) 18...♔h8 19 ♖g2 ♖c7 20 ♘df3 ♘eg8 21 ♘g5 h6 (21...♖ec8 22 ♘gxf7+ ♖xf7 23 ♘xg6+ is winning for White) 22 ♘gxf7+ ♖xf7 23 ♘xg6+ ♔h7 24 ♘f8+ ♔h8 25 ♘g6+ ♔h7 26 ♘e5+ ♔h8 27 g5 (after toying with his opponent, White goes straight for the jugular) 27...♗xe5 28 gxf6 ♗xf6 29 ♖xg7 ♖xg7+ 30 ♖g3 ♗c8 31 c4 ♘e7 32 ♕h5 ♗d7 33 ♕xh6+ 1-0 Maroczy-Blake, Hastings 1923.

11 ... ♗f4

As we saw in the previous note, if White can establish knights on g5 and e5 then Black is in serious trouble. The text-move is an attempt to hinder this, but it is ultimately unsuccessful.

12 ♘e5 ♖c8
13 ♘df3 ♘e7
14 ♕e2 ♖c7
15 g3 ♗h6
16 h4 g6
17 ♘g5 ♕c8
18 a4

I wanted to show that Black has problems on both wings.

18 ... ♘f5
19 ♕f3 ♘e4

Black falls into a devious trap.

20 ♘xe4 dxe4
21 ♗xe4 ♗xe4
22 ♕xe4 ♖xc2
23 ♘c4 *(D)*

B

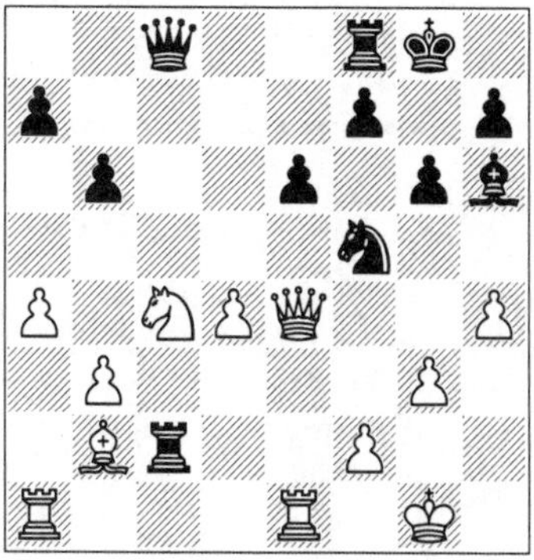

Trapping Black's rook! It has to be said that despite this, Sadler outplays me over the next few moves.

23 ... ♖xb2
24 ♘xb2 ♕c3

25 ♘d3 ♕xb3
26 ♘e5 ♗d2
27 ♖eb1 ♕c3
28 ♖d1

28 ♘c6 would keep an edge.

28 ... ♘xd4
29 ♖a2 f5
30 ♕d3 ♕xd3
31 ♘xd3 ♗h6
32 ♘e5 ♖d8
33 ♔g2 f4

33...♗g7 would give Black equal chances.

34 ♘f3 e5
35 ♘xe5 fxg3
36 ♘f3 ♘c6
37 ♖xd8+ ♘xd8
38 fxg3 ♘b7
39 ♘d4 ♗f8
40 ♘c6 a5
41 ♘e5

Although White has an advantage, the win is technically quite difficult and was made much easier by the mutual time-shortage common to weekend tournaments.

41 ... ♘d6
42 ♖c2 b5
43 axb5 ♘xb5
44 ♖c8 ♔g7
45 ♖a8 ♗d6
46 ♘c4 ♗b4
47 ♘xa5 ♗c3
48 ♘c4 ♗f6
49 ♖b8 ♘d4
50 ♖b7+ ♔g8
51 ♘d6

I now saw the potential to weave a mating net.

51 ... ♗e5
52 ♘f7 ♗f6
53 ♘h6+ ♔h8
54 ♘g4 ♗d8
55 ♖d7 ♗b6
56 ♘f6 1-0

A very satisfying win against one of Britain's best players.

Black Plays ...♘bd7/...♗e7

Game 18
Summerscale – Gimenez
Andorra 1991

1 ♘f3 c5
2 e3 e6
3 d4 ♘f6
4 ♗d3 d5
5 b3 *(D)*

B

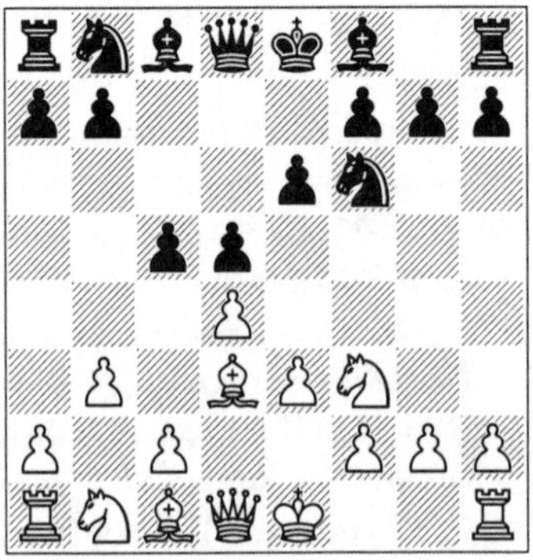

5 ... ♗e7

Black has several other ways to handle the position, and can choose between various placements of his f8-bishop and b8-knight. Obviously there are a lot of transpositional possibilities. White's attacking idea remains the same: slowly building up with natural moves and punishing any over-optimistic aggression.

a) 5...♗d6 (this attacks the e5-square but makes the bishop vulnerable to dxc5 in certain lines) 6 ♘bd2 ♘bd7 7 ♗b2 0-0 8 0-0 ♕c7 (I feel the knight is misplaced on d7; if Black continues normally with 8...b6 or 8...♕e7 then he will undoubtedly get an inferior version of the main line after 9 ♘e5, as taking on e5 becomes less attractive since the f6-knight lacks a decent retreat square; these disadvantages outweigh the fact that the knight on f6 is given some extra support in some lines) 9 c4 (the queen on c7 is even more exposed without a knight on c6 and Black tries to atone for this by striking back in the centre) 9...e5 10 cxd5 ♘xd5? (Black falls into the trap; 10...cxd4 11 exd4 exd4 12 ♖c1 ♕b8 13 ♗xd4 ♘xd5 14 ♕c2 is only slightly better for White, who enjoys a lead in development and the better placed pieces) 11 dxe5 ♘xe5 12 ♘xe5 ♗xe5 13 ♗xh7+ (this simple combination nets a clear pawn and effectively wins the game) 13...♔xh7 14 ♕h5+ ♔g8 15 ♗xe5 ♕c6 16 ♘c4 ♗e6 17 ♖ac1 (it seems as though White is just building up pressure on the c5-pawn, but in reality he is preparing a thunderbolt) 17...b6 18 ♗xg7! *(D)*.

A brave decision, as White is completely winning without any need for fireworks, but this sacrifice is highly

B

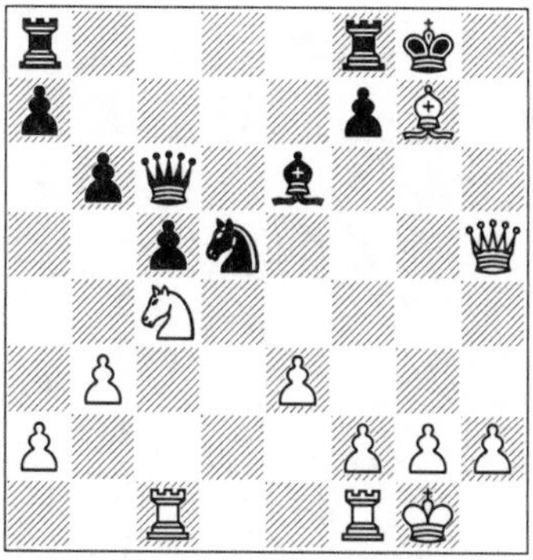

thematic and a classic example of the dangers Black must always watch out for. 18...♔xg7 19 ♕g5+ ♔h8 20 ♘e5 ♕c8 21 ♖c4 ♗f5 22 ♖h4+ ♗h7 23 ♕h6 1-0 Minarelli-Pastorini, Forli 1989. 23...♕f5 would be met by 24 e4 winning the queen.

b) 5...♘bd7 (this bolsters the f6-knight but is a little passive) 6 ♗b2 b6 7 0-0 ♗b7 8 ♘e5 a6 (Black is hoping for ...b5 and ...c4 to lock out White's bishops, but this plan is easily countered and wastes too much time) 9 ♘d2 b5 10 ♘xd7 ♕xd7 11 dxc5 ♗xc5 12 ♕f3 (Black has developed successfully but has unleashed the full fury of the two raking bishops on d3 and b2) 12...♗e7 13 ♕g3 0-0 14 ♘f3 ♖ac8 (Black is developing normally but without any real purpose, and White's next move puts him on the critical list) 15 ♘g5 g6 (forced due to the threat of ♘xh7) 16 ♕h4 h5 17 ♖ad1 (calmly bringing up the reserves and introducing ideas of e4 or c4) 17...♘h7 (Black cracks under the pressure) 18 ♕xh5! *(D)*.

B

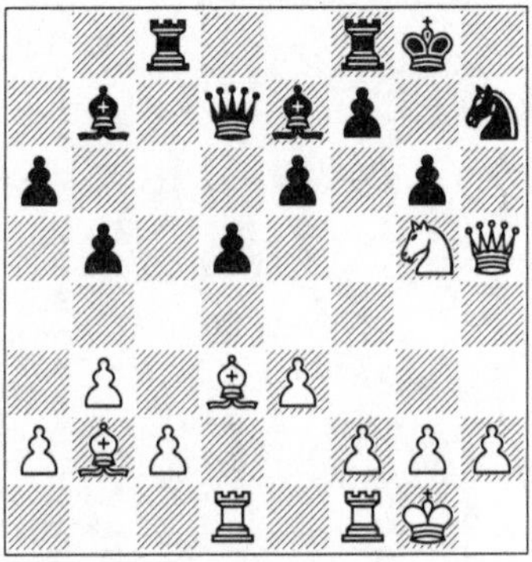

18...♗xg5 (18...gxh5 19 ♗xh7#) 19 ♗xg6 (White rips away the black king's pawn-cover and forces the return of the piece) 19...f6 20 f4 ♕g7 21 fxg5 ♘xg5 22 h4 ♘e4 (if 22...♘h7 then 23 ♖d4 is very persuasive – the idea is ♖g4) 23 ♗xe4 dxe4 24 ♖f4 1-0 Yusupov-Scheeren, Plovdiv Echt 1983.

c) 5...♘c6 (the most natural development of the knight) 6 ♗b2 ♗e7 7 0-0 0-0 8 ♘bd2 b6 9 ♘e5 (White could of course consider 9 a3 first, but there is nothing wrong with the text-move) 9...♘b4 10 ♗e2 ♗b7 and now White can choose between kicking back the black knight with normal play, or ignoring it, arguing that the knight has no real future on b4; the first choice is the usual answer but as Yusupov shows in line 'c2', creative play has its own rewards:

c1) 11 a3 ♘c6 12 f4 ♖c8 13 ♗d3 (again the two lost tempi ...♘c6-b4-c6 by Black and ♗d3-e2-d3 by White cancel each other out) 13...♕c7 14 ♕e2 ♗d6? (Black should play 14...cxd4 first, although White is still slightly better) 15 ♘xc6 ♕xc6 16 dxc5 (this device should be becoming familiar by now) 16...♗e7 (16...♗xc5 17 ♗xf6 gxf6 18 ♗xh7+ ♔xh7 19 ♕h5+ ♔g7 20 ♕g4+ ♔h7 21 ♖f3 +–) 17 cxb6 axb6 18 ♘f3 (White is winning, as he is a clear pawn up, but impressively continues to build up his attack rather than rest on his laurels) 18...♘e4 19 ♘d4 ♕c5 20 ♖f3 ♗f6 21 ♖d1 ♖fd8 22 g4 (as long as White can keep the light squares under control he can get away with this move) 22...♘c3 23 ♗xc3 ♕xc3 24 ♕f2 g6 25 g5 ♗e7 (the bishop would be better placed defensively on g7) 26 a4 ♕b2 27 h4 (White starts the second wave of the assault) 27...♗c5 28 h5 ♖e8 29 hxg6 hxg6 30 ♖h3 ♔g7 31 f5! exf5 32 ♗xf5 1-0 Donnelly-Gray, British corr. Ch 1993. Black is defenceless against the threat of ♗d7 with the idea of ♕f6+.

c2) 11 f4 ♘e4 (Black tries to take advantage of White's omission of a3 and the game takes an original course) 12 ♘xe4 dxe4 13 a3 ♘d5 (although the knight seems well placed here, it is not secure and can be kicked away easily) 14 ♕d2 ♖c8 15 c4 ♘f6 16 ♖ad1 ♗d6 17 dxc5 ♗xc5 18 ♕c3 ♕e7 19 f5 (a key pawn-lever to open lines against the black king) 19...exf5 20 ♖xf5 ♗xa3 (greedy, but Black was in trouble in any case) 21 ♗xa3 ♕xa3 22 ♖xf6! gxf6 23 ♘g4 ♖c6 24 ♘xf6+ ♖xf6 25 ♕xf6 ♕xb3 26 ♔f2 (calmly protecting everything before closing in for the kill) 26...♕a4 27 ♕g5+ ♔h8 28 ♕e7 1-0 Yusupov-Spiridonov,

Plovdiv Echt 1983. A powerful double attack as 28...♜b8 is met by 29 ♛e5+, winning the house.

6 ♗b2 0-0
7 0-0 *(D)*

B

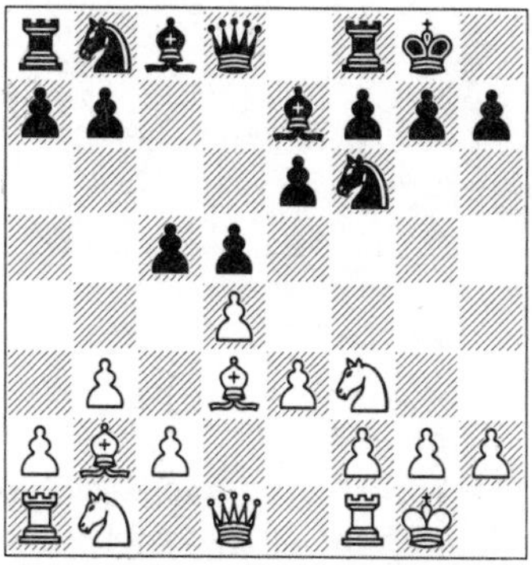

7 ... ♘bd7

After this move, White's f-pawn plays a pivotal role in the attack. Instead, after 7...b6 White attacks for a long time without the use of the f-pawn. 8 ♘e5 ♗b7 9 ♘d2 ♘bd7 10 ♕f3 ♖c8 and now White has been successful in practice with two approaches:

a) 11 ♖ad1 ♕c7 12 ♕h3 h6 (this is a different way of defending against the kingside threats, but it has fared no better in practice) 13 f4 ♘e4 (Black feels she can get away with this, now that White no longer has f3 at her disposal, but walks straight into a tactic) 14 ♘xd7 ♕xd7 15 ♗xe4 dxe4 16 dxc5 ♕b5 (16...♗xc5 17 ♘xe4 +–) 17 ♘c4 ♗xc5 18 ♕g4 f6 19 ♕xe6+ ♔h8 20 ♖d7 (through natural moves White has built up an overwhelming position) 20...♖c6 21 ♕g4 1-0 Zsu.Polgar-Mai Thi, Novi Sad wom OL 1990.

b) 11 ♕h3 and now:

b1) 11...♕c7 12 ♖ad1 transposes to 'a'.

b2) 11...♘e4 (trying to blunt the attack by blocking lines, but this knight sally is easily repulsed) 12 f3 ♘g5 13 ♕g3 f6 (Black takes measures to close the a1-h8 diagonal) 14 ♘xd7 ♕xd7 15 ♖ad1 (again White mobilizes his last piece before proceeding with the attack) 15...b5 16 dxc5 ♗xc5 17 f4 (now the knight can't go to e4) 17...♗d6 18 ♕g4 ♘e4? (the knight had to retreat with 18...♘f7 but then 19 e4 is slightly better for White) 19 ♘xe4 dxe4 20 ♗xb5 ♕xb5 21 ♕xe6+ ♔h8 22 ♕xd6 ♕e2 23 ♖f2 1-0 V.Kovačević-Nickoloff, Mississauga 1990. Black will lose yet more material after 23...♕xe3 24 ♗d4.

b3) 11...cxd4 12 exd4 ♕c7 13 a3 followed by ♖ae1 and f4 gives White the usual attack.

b4) 11...♘xe5 (Black seeks relief by means of exchanges) 12 dxe5 ♘e4 13 ♖ad1 ♘g5 14 ♕h5 g6 15 ♕e2 (having created a weakness, the queen returns to a more central position) 15...♕c7 16 c4 (White chips away at the black centre) 16...f5 17 f4 ♘e4 (this natural-looking move is in fact the decisive mistake; however miserable it may be, the knight had to retreat) 18 cxd5 exd5 19 ♘xe4 fxe4 20 ♗xe4! ♖fd8 (20...dxe4 21 ♕c4+ ♔h8 {21...♖f7 22 e6 ♖f6 23 ♖d7 ±} 22 ♖d7 ±) 21 f5! (rather than taking his pawn and running, White insists on crashing through on the kingside – Black is left to regret his pawn advances there) 21...dxe4 22 ♕c4+ ♔g7 23 f6+ ♗xf6 24 exf6+ ♔f8 25 ♖xd8+ ♕xd8 26 f7 (White prepares a dark-squared invasion; the pawn on f7 is a monster) 26...♕d2 27 ♕e6 ♕xe3+ 28 ♔h1 ♕d3 29 ♕xc8+ ♗xc8 30 ♗g7+ 1-0 Hartston-Upton, London 1984.

8 ♘bd2 b6

9 ♘e5 ♘xe5

Black takes on e5 before White has a chance to recapture with the f-pawn.

10 dxe5 ♘d7

11 f4 ♗b7

12 ♕h5

Provoking a weakness.

12 ... g6

12...h6 just encourages g4-g5.

13 ♕h3

My plan was to break through on the kingside with the pawn-lever f5.

13 ... b5

Black offers a pawn, which White is more or less obliged to accept, in the hope that the white bishop will become misplaced, thus blunting White's attack.

14 ♗xb5 ♕a5

15 ♗xd7 ♕xd2

16 ♖f2 ♕b4

17 a3 ♕b6

18 f5! *(D)*

The thematic breakthrough.

18 ... gxf5

19 ♖xf5!

A rook sacrifice that Black really has to accept, due to the threat of ♖h5.

B

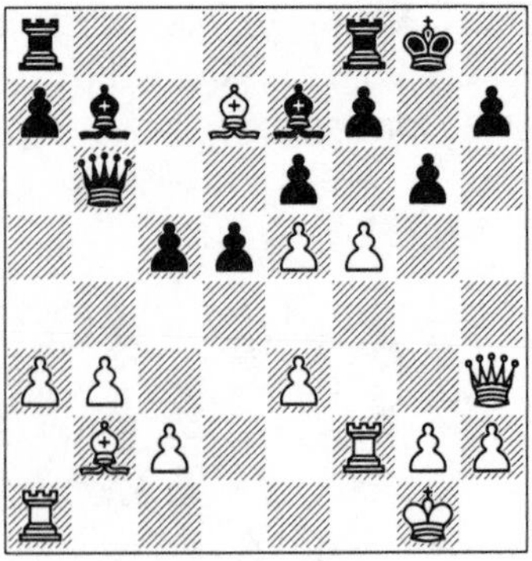

19 ... exf5

20 ♗xf5 h6

21 e6!

This great move brings the bishop on b2 into the attack and breaks the lines of communication between the black queen and the kingside.

21 ... ♗g5

22 ♗f6! *(D)*

B

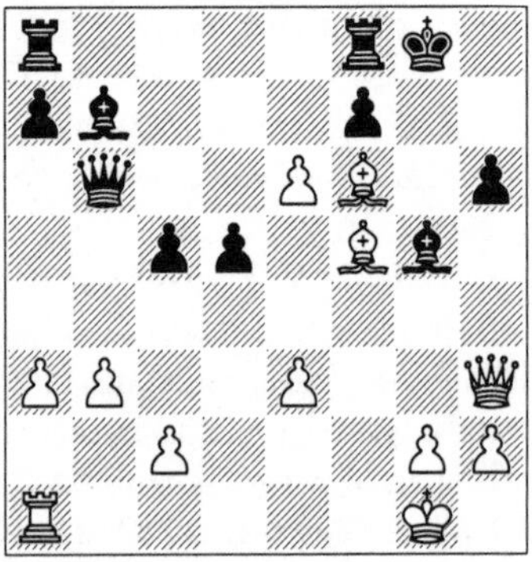

22 ... fxe6

22...♗xf6 23 ♕xh6 ♖fd8 24 ♗h7+ ♔h8 25 ♗g6+ ♔g8 26 ♕h7+ ♔f8 27 ♕xf7#.

23 ♗xe6+ ♖f7

24	♗xg5	hxg5
25	♖f1	♖af8
26	♖f6!	1-0

5...♕a5+

Game 19
Yusupov – Short
Dortmund 1997

1	d4	♘f6
2	♘f3	e6
3	e3	c5
4	♗d3	d5
5	b3	♕a5+ *(D)*

W

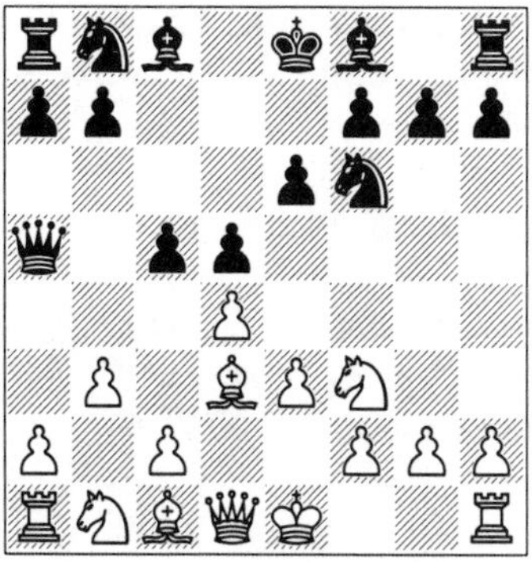

This attempt to disrupt White's development is a double-edged plan. White is more or less forced to play c3, which will restrict the mobility of his dark-squared bishop. On the other hand, the black queen is misplaced on a5 and if she returns to a more natural square, such as c7, then c4 will, as usual, become a major option for White.

6 c3

This is the only try for an advantage. 6 ♘bd2 cxd4 7 exd4 ♗b4 8 0-0 ♗c3 9 b4 ♕c7 10 ♖b1 ♘c6 11 ♗b5 a5 12 bxa5 0-0 13 ♗a3 ♖d8 14 ♗c5 was unclear in Yusupov-Miles, London USSR-RoW 1984.

6 ... cxd4?

If Black is playing to restrict White's dark-squared bishop then this move must be all wrong. It is surely better to keep the central tension, e.g. 6...♘c6 7 0-0 *(D)* and now:

B

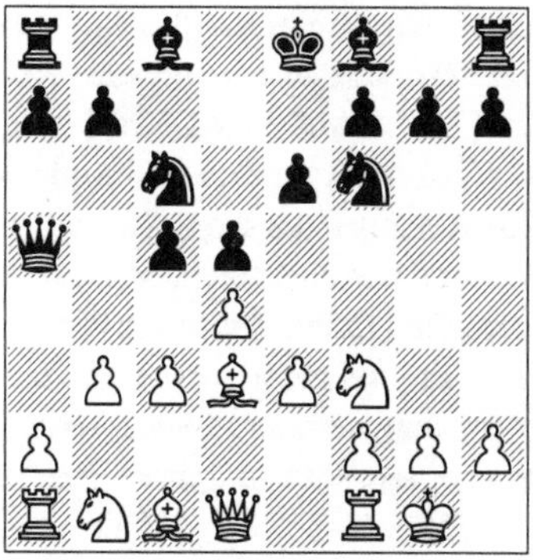

a) 7...♕c7 (withdrawing the queen to a less exposed square now that she has done her job) and then:

a1) 8 ♗b2 is a slower approach than 'a2', but White can still count on an edge with a timely c4: 8...cxd4 9 exd4 ♗e7 10 ♘bd2 0-0 11 ♕e2 b6 12 ♘e5 ♘xe5 (again Black makes this exchange before White can play f4) 13 dxe5 ♘d7 14 c4 ♘c5 15 cxd5 exd5 16 ♖ac1 ♕d8 17 ♘f3 and White is slightly better on account of Black's IQP, Høi-Inkiov, Gausdal International 1990.

a2) 8 c4 dxc4 9 bxc4 ♗e7 10 ♗b2 cxd4 11 exd4 (White will accept hanging pawns, as is usual in the Colle-Zukertort, after he has played c4; the only difference from the examples we have seen before is that the black bishop is on e7, which lends extra support to the knight on f6 but on the other hand the bishop could become a target on the e-file) 11...0-0 12 ♘bd2 b6 13 ♖c1 ♗b7 14 ♖e1 (again White improves his position as much as possible before doing anything active; 14 d5!? ♘b4 15 ♗b1 exd5 16 a3 ♘a6 17 cxd5 ♕d8 18 ♖e1 is unclear – Kovačević) 14...♖ad8 15 ♗b1 ♕f4 (this is a useful defensive move as the queen removes itself from the c-file and heads toward the vulnerable kingside) 16 d5 (even though this doesn't lead by force to a win, this game is a good example of the long-term pressure White enjoys for the price of a pawn) 16...exd5 17 cxd5 ♘xd5 18 ♖c4 ♕d6 19 ♘e4 ♕h6 20 ♗c1 ♕g6 21 ♗d2 (White's compensation is in the form of his active pieces and his ability to combine threats to the black queen with a kingside attack) 21...f5 22 ♘g3 ♔h8 23 ♕b3 ♗a8 24 h3 (this is a nice creeping move, combining safety, by removing the faint possibility of a back-rank mate, with aggression due to the possibilities of ♖g4 and ♘xf5) 24...♗c5 25 ♘xf5 (this combination regains the sacrificed pawn and leaves White with a clear edge) 25...♖xf5 26 ♖xc5 bxc5 27 ♘h4 ♕f6 28 ♘xf5 ♘d4 29 ♘xd4 cxd4 30 ♕d3 (the two bishops are more than a match for Black's passed d-pawn) 30...g6 31 ♕g3 (White prepares an attack on the dark squares weakened by Black's last move) 31...♕g7 32 ♕h4 ♖c8 33 ♗d3 h5 (this is a panic reaction to the threat of ♗h6 but Black was in trouble anyway) 34 ♖e6 ♕b7 1-0 V.Kovačević-P.Popović, Zagreb 1985.

b) 7...♗e7 (continuing development) 8 ♗b2 0-0 9 ♘bd2 ♕c7 10 c4 ♖d8 11 ♖c1 cxd4 12 ♘xd4 (unwisely giving up the centre; 12 exd4 would bring us to a familiar position with the usual attacking chances for White) 12...♘xd4 13 ♗xd4 e5 14 cxd5 ♕b8 15 ♗a1 ♖xd5 16 ♕e2 ♗g4 17 f3 ♕d8 ∓ McDonald-Piket, Groningen jr Ech 1986.

7 exd4

White now has an edge.

7 ... ♘c6

8 0-0 ♗e7

Perhaps Black should try to transpose back with 8...♕c7.

9 ♘e5 ♘xe5

10 dxe5 ♘d7

11 ♕g4 *(D)*

11 ... g6

12 ♖e1 h5

12...0-0 13 ♗g5 ♗xg5 14 ♕xg5 gives White a clear plan of attack on the h-file.

13 ♕e2 ♔f8

14 ♗e3?

In his notes Yusupov claims a clear edge for White after 14 ♗b2 ♕c7 15 ♘d2 (15 c4!?) 15...b6 16 c4 dxc4 17 ♘xc4. I see no reason to disagree with

B

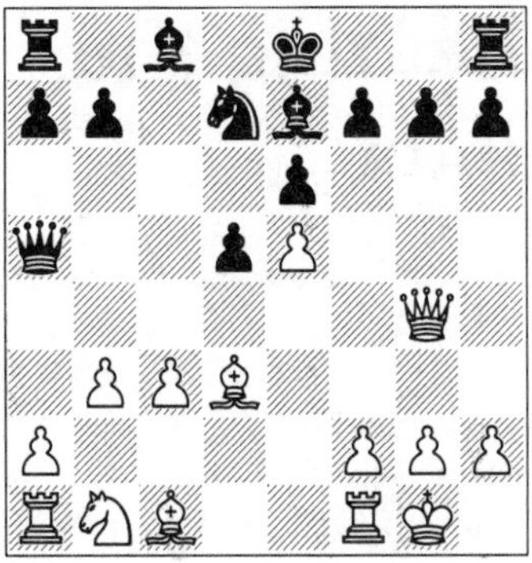

Yusupov's assessment, with the idea of ♘d6 looming.

14 ... ♘xe5
15 ♗d4 ♘xd3
16 ♕xd3

Now, however, White has enough compensation for the pawn but no more.

16 ... ♖g8
17 ♘d2 ♗d7

17...f6!? 18 c4! is unclear.

18 ♕e3

White prepares an invasion on the dark squares but Short defends himself well.

18 ... f6!
19 ♕h6+ ♖g7

After 19...♔f7? Yusupov gives 20 ♘f3 with the idea 20...♖h8 21 ♘g5+! +−.

20 ♕h8+

Yusupov shows why more ambitious alternatives don't bring home the bacon: 20 ♗xf6?! ♗xf6 21 ♕h8+ ♔e7 22 ♕xa8 ♗xc3 23 ♘f3 ♖f7 ∓ or 20 ♘f3?! ♔g8 21 ♘g5 ♕a6 ∓ (but not 21...e5 22 ♖xe5 fxe5 23 ♗xe5 ♗f8 24 ♗xg7 ♗xg7 25 ♕h7+ ♔f8 26 ♕xg6, when White wins).

20 ... ♖g8
21 ♕h6+ ♖g7
22 ♕h8+ ½-½

White has nothing better than to take the draw.

4 1 d4 d5 2 ♘f3: Beating the Anti-Colle Systems

1 d4 d5 2 ♘f3 Miscellaneous

Game 20
Steinitz – Chigorin
Havana Wch (2) 1889

1 d4 d5
2 ♘f3 *(D)*

B

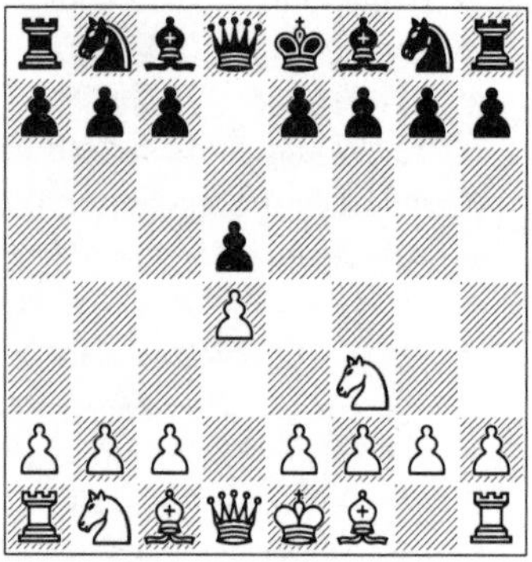

2 ... ♗g4

This reversed Trompowsky failed to impress even back in 1889! There are a number of other options for Black here:

a) 2...♗f5 is considered in the next game.

b) 2...c5 (Black immediately strikes at the white centre; this is a very challenging move as Black attempts to play a Queen's Gambit with colours reversed) 3 dxc5 (taking up the challenge; now 3...♘f6 and 3...♕a5+ are likely to transpose to Game 22) 3...e6 4 c4 ♗xc5 (4...dxc4 5 ♕xd8+ ♔xd8 6 e4 leads to a small endgame advantage for White) 5 cxd5 exd5 6 e3 ♘f6 7 a3 0-0 (7...a5 8 b3 with similar play but with White having control of b5) 8 b4 ♗d6 9 ♗b2 ♖e8 10 ♗e2 a6 11 0-0 ♘c6 12 ♘bd2 (White has a firm grip on the blockading square d4 in this IQP position) 12...♗c7 13 ♕b3 ♕d6 14 ♖fd1 ♗g4 15 ♘f1 (an unusual square for the knight in such positions; normally you would want it on d4, but on f1 it is useful defensively as it guards both h2 and e3) 15...♖ad8 16 ♖ac1 ♘e4 17 a4 ♗b6 (17...♘xb4 18 ♖xc7 ♕xc7 19 ♕xb4 ±) 18 b5 (driving away the well-placed knight on c6) 18...♘a5 19 ♕a2 axb5 20 axb5 (with most of White's kingside squares well defended and a clear plan of action – to blockade d4 and exchange pieces – White is slightly better) 20...♕g6? (this tactical oversight effectively loses the game) 21 ♘e5 ♖xe5 22 ♗xe5 ♘xf2 23 ♗xg4 (perhaps this is what Black missed: White keeps a material advantage and Black's attack shortly runs out of steam) 23...♘xd1 24 ♗xd1 ♕g5 25 ♕a1 and White converted his extra piece in Burmakin-Meszaros, Szeged 1993.

c) 2...♘c6 (Black indicates his willingness to play a Chigorin Defence) 3 ♗f4 (while this is not the most challenging reply, it is easier to play and remember than most of the complex main lines of the Chigorin Defence, and is definitely not as innocuous as it may look) 3...♗g4 4 e3 e6 5 c4 ♘f6 6 ♘c3 ♗b4 (Black has achieved a strange type of Queen's Gambit with his normally passive queen's bishop active but his queen's knight misplaced in front of his c-pawn) 7 ♗g5 (played to avoid any problems after ...dxc4 and ...♘d5) 7...dxc4 8 ♗xc4 h6 9 ♗h4 0-0 10 ♗e2 (again White shows caution and guards against the possibility of ...e5) 10...♗e7 11 0-0 ♘d5 12 ♗g3 ♗d6 13 ♖c1 (having completed his development, White begins to probe the drawbacks to Black's game and targets the c-pawn) 13...♗xg3 (Black, for his part, seeks relief through exchanges) 14 hxg3 ♘xc3 15 ♖xc3 ♘e7 16 ♕b3 ♕b8 17 ♗c4 (planning ♘e5) 17...♗xf3 18 gxf3 c6 19 ♔g2 ♘d5 20 ♖cc1 ♖d8 21 f4 and White, with bishop against knight and kingside attacking chances (with preparation White can pursue ideas of f5, ♖h1, g4-g5), was better in Garcia Ilundain-Narciso, Saragossa 1995.

3 ♘e5 ♗h5

4 ♕d3 *(D)*

B

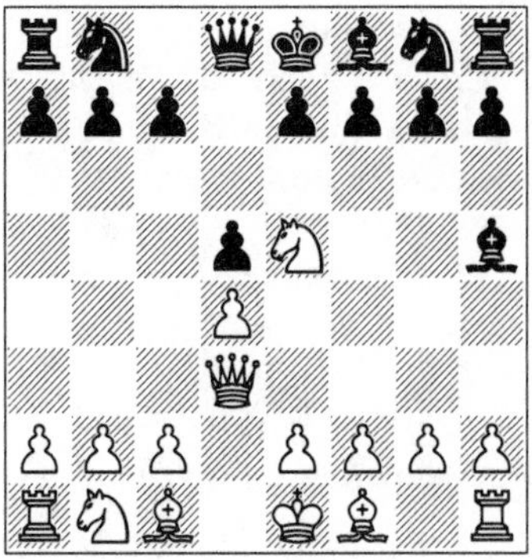

I like this move, which shows good imagination. The obvious threat is ♕b5+ winning a pawn. What is not so obvious is the positional threat of 5 ♕h3, when after 5...♗g6 6 ♘xg6 Black would be forced to capture anti-positionally with the f-pawn.

4 ... ♕c8

The only way to meet both threats.

5 c4

This is nearly always the way to take advantage of the early development of Black's queen's bishop.

5 ... f6

6 ♘f3 e6

7 ♘c3 ♗g6

8 ♕d1 c6

9 e3

A peculiar kind of Semi-Slav structure has arisen, However, it is significantly worse for Black than usual: Black's queen is misplaced on c8 and his pawn-structure has been weakened by ...f6, which hinders the natural development of the g8-knight.

9 ... ♗d6

10 ♗d2 ♘e7

11 ♖c1

Creating a concealed attack against the black queen and highlighting her awkward position.

11 ... ♘d7

12 ♘h4 *(D)*

B

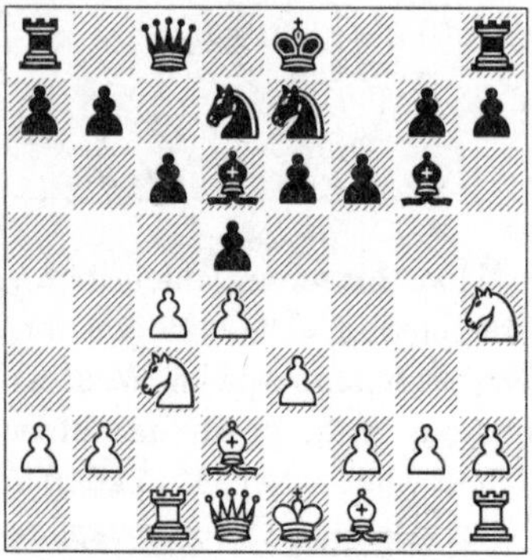

White tries to bag the bishops.

12 ... f5

Turning the position into a Dutch. Although passive, 12...♗f7 is better.

13 g4

A standard pawn lever (nowadays) to open up the kingside.

13 ... ♘f6

14 h3 ♘e4

15 ♗d3 fxg4?

Allowing his centre to collapse. Black had to castle, when White only has a small advantage.

16 ♘xg6 ♘xg6

17 ♗xe4 dxe4

18 ♘xe4 ♗e7

19 hxg4

White has a clear advantage.

19 ... e5

20 d5 ♕d7

21 ♗c3 ♖d8

22 ♖h5 cxd5

23 cxd5 0-0

24 d6 ♕e6

24...♗xd6 25 ♘xd6 ♕xd6 26 ♕xd6 ♖xd6 27 ♗b4 +-.

25 ♕b3 ♕xb3

26 axb3 ♗xd6

27 ♘xd6 ♖xd6

28 ♗b4 +- ♖b6

29 ♗xf8 ♔xf8

Black could have already resigned.

30 ♖c8+ ♔f7 31 ♖c7+ ♔f6 32 ♖f5+ ♔e6 33 ♖ff7 ♖b4 34 ♖xb7 ♖xg4 35 ♖xg7 h5 36 ♖xa7 ♔f5 37 f3 ♖g2 38 ♖a6 1-0

Game 21

Krallmann – Drill

Kassel 1994

1 d4 d5

2 ♘f3 ♗f5

Developing the bishop outside Black's intended pawn-chain.

3 c4 e6

4 ♕b3 *(D)*

B

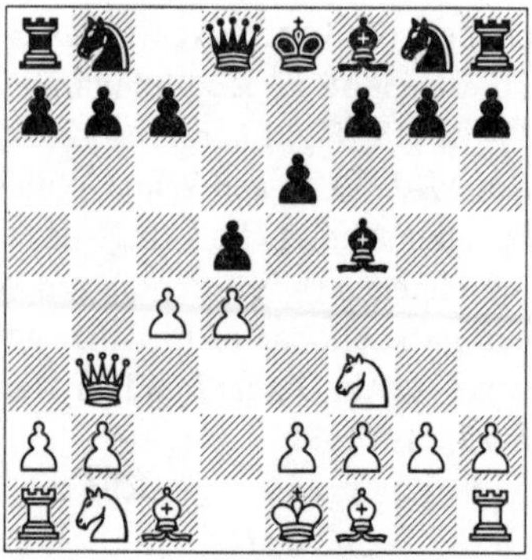

This is the most logical way to take advantage of Black's early bishop sortie. The b7-square is no longer defended, so White immediately goes about attacking it and the queenside light squares in general.

4 ... ♘c6

This is the most active move, by which White is prevented from taking on b7 due to ...♘b4. The main alternative here is 4...♕c8 but after 5 ♘c3 White has the idea of quick development and attack on the queenside, i.e. ♗f4, ♖c1, cxd5 and an eventual b4-b5, while 4...b6 is exactly the sort of light-squared weakness White was trying to provoke.

5 c5

This excellent response renews the threat of taking on b7 and shuts out Black's king's bishop.

5 ... ♖b8
6 ♗f4

Another good move. White has a long-term plan of advancing on the queenside, which will give him a clear plus. Meanwhile he completes his development, while restricting Black's possibilities. Black has two ways to break against White's pawns. The first, ...b6, is ill-advised since it critically weakens the black knight on c6 after ♕a4; the second, more realistic, option is to play for ...e5. Thus White intensifies his grip on this square.

6 ... ♘f6
7 ♘c3 a6

Black takes away the b5-square from White's knight.

8 e3 ♗e7
9 ♗e2 ♘e4
10 ♘xe4 ♗xe4
11 ♕a4 0-0
12 0-0 ♗f6
13 ♖fd1

Played to pressurize d5 in the event that Black manages to play ...e5.

13 ... ♖a8
14 b4

White has a space advantage on the queenside and clearly should attack there.

14 ... ♕e7
15 ♖ac1 ♖fd8

15...e5 16 dxe5 ♘xe5 17 ♘xe5 ♗xe5 18 ♗xe5 ♕xe5 19 c6 b5 20 ♕b3 gives White the long-term plan of attacking the weak pawn on d5.

16 ♕b3 ♖a7
17 a4 *(D)*

B

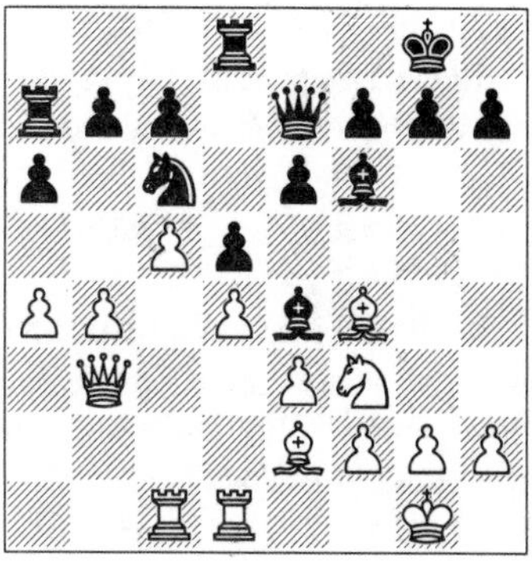

17 ... ♖da8

Black is being very prophylactic in his aim to discourage White's natural plan of b5. However, if White delays this, the two rooks look strange doubled up on a file that can only open if White chooses to play b5.

18 ♖d2

The game now enters a phase of positional manoeuvring, where both sides try to achieve their strategic goals without allowing the opponent to achieve his; it's a clear case of cat and mouse.

18 ... h6
19 h3 ♔h8
20 ♖a2 ♘d8
21 ♖ca1

White plays the same game and, because he has more space, can even think about trebling on the a-file.

21 ... ♗xf3
22 ♗xf3 c6
23 ♕c3

The queen keeps a firm eye on the critical e5-square.

23 ... ♕d7
24 ♗e2 ♗e7
25 ♖a3 f6

Black again hints at playing ...e5 one day but critically weakens the light squares on his kingside.

26 ♗h5 ♗f8
27 ♗g6 *(D)*

With the bishop on g6, the b5 thrust becomes a more realistic possibility as the opening of lines will highlight the weakness of Black's back rank.

27 ... a5

Therefore Black strikes out.

28 b5 cxb5
29 axb5 ♕xb5
30 ♗d3

Now the bishop is forced to retreat but Black has a clear weakness on b7.

B

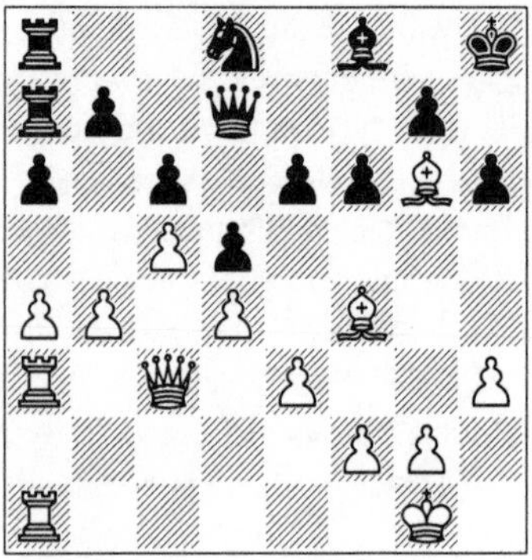

30 ... ♕e8
31 ♖xa5 ♖xa5
32 ♖xa5 ♖xa5
33 ♕xa5 e5 *(D)*

W

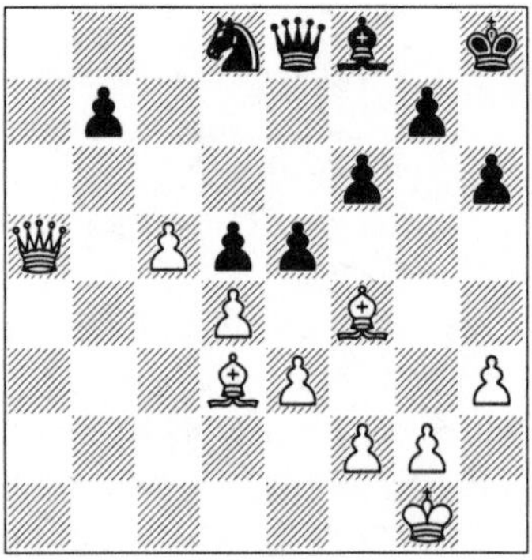

At last!

34 dxe5 fxe5

Black sets the trap 35 ♗xe5? ♘c6 winning a piece.

35 ♗g3 ♘e6

Through the thematic ...e5 Black has created a weakness on c5 at the cost of opening the position advantageously for the white bishops.

36 ♗b5 ♕c8

37 ♗xe5 ♕xc5
38 ♕a4

White has a clear advantage as in this type of position bishops rule!

38 ... ♘c7
39 ♗d3 ♗d6
40 ♗b2 ♕b4
41 ♕d7

Black's back-rank problems come back to haunt him.

41 ... ♗f8
42 ♗e5 ♕a3
43 ♗f5 ♘a6
44 ♕e6 1-0

There's not much to be done about the threat of ♕xh6+.

Black's Alternatives at Moves 3 and 4

Game 22
Behrmann – Anhalt
Regionalliga Niedersachsen 1990

1 d4 d5
2 ♘f3 ♘f6
3 e3 c5
4 dxc5 *(D)*

B

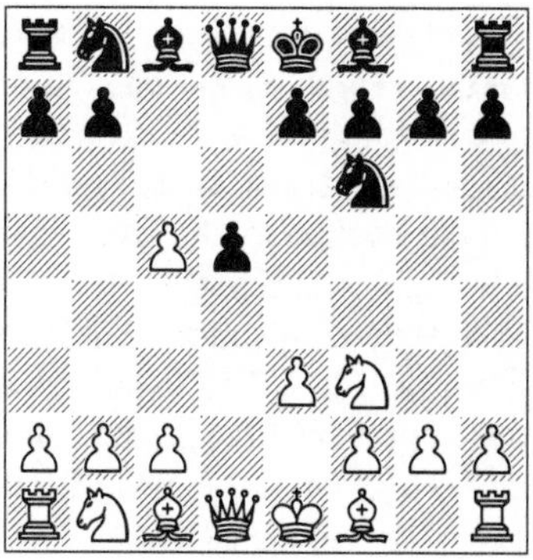

4 ... ♕a5+

Black has two alternatives, against which White has interesting ways to pose unusual problems:

a) 4...e6 (Black tries to be solid) 5 b4 (this is White's key idea: he hopes to create two passed pawns on the queenside) 5...a5 6 c3 (the idea for this variation came from one of Black's more ambitious defences to the Queen's Gambit: after 1 d4 d5 2 c4 c6 3 ♘f3 dxc4 4 e3 b5 5 a4 e6 we get a similar position with colours reversed; I believe the extra tempo gives White good chances for the advantage and certainly will throw Black upon his own resources) 6...axb4 7 cxb4 b6 8 ♗b5+ ♗d7 (8...♘bd7 9 c6 +–) 9 ♗xd7+ ♘bxd7 10 a4 bxc5 11 b5 *(D)*.

B

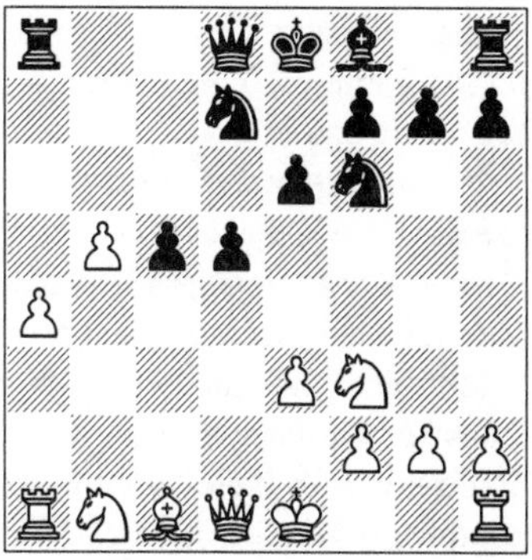

This is what White is aiming for out of the opening; a completely unbalanced pawn-structure where the player who understands the position better will triumph. The key points to remember are that ...e5 must be met by e4 and piece exchanges will generally favour White, as his outside passed pawns gain power the closer an endgame approaches. Of course if Black is kind enough to allow the pawns to advance free of charge, then you should be his guest! 11...♗d6 12 ♗b2 0-0 13 ♘bd2 ♗c7 14 0-0 e5 15 e4 (it is essential to prevent Black from achieving ...e5-e4, even at the cost of a pawn) 15...♘xe4 16 ♘xe4 dxe4 17 ♘d2 e3 (17...f5 18 ♘c4 is no improvement) 18 fxe3 ♕h4 19 e4 ♘f6 20 ♕e2 ♖fd8 21 ♗c3 (White prepares the advance of his a-pawn) 21...♘g4 22 ♘f3 ♕h5 23 h3 ♘f6 (Black has been unable to create any real problems on the kingside and White is now ready to press through his queenside pawns) 24 a5 ♕g6 25 b6 ♗b8 26 ♖fe1 ♘h5 27 ♘xe5 ♕g5 28 ♕g4 1-0 Vitor-Fancsy, Matinhos 1994. With his kingside initiative completely neutralized, Black called it a day.

b) 4...♘c6 (more aggressive – Black prepares ...e5; however, this move allows White to borrow ideas from another unusual defence) 5 c3 e6 (5...a5 6 ♗b5 e6 7 b4 transposes; or 5...e5 leads to similar positions to that of 5...e6 but with the e-pawn more vulnerable) 6 b4 a5 7 ♗b5 ♗d7 8 ♗b2 axb4 9 cxb4 b6 10 ♗xc6 ♗xc6 11 a4 bxc5 12 b5 *(D)*.

B

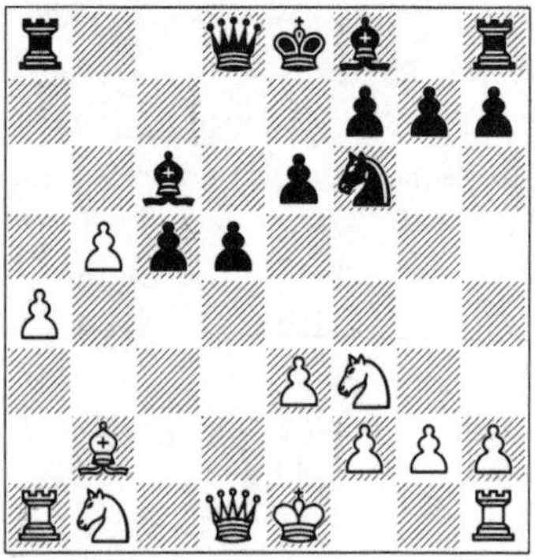

This position is a reversed Noteboom/Abrahams. White's extra tempo again means he has a good chance of an advantage. The strategic factors are very similar to those discussed in our previous variation, i.e. play for piece exchanges, look for opportunities to advance the queenside pawns and, perhaps most importantly, meet ...e5 by e4. Play could continue 12...♗b7 13 ♘bd2 ♗d6 14 0-0 0-0 15 ♕c2 ♖e8 16 ♖fe1 e5 17 e4 dxe4 (17...d4 18 ♘c4) 18 ♘g5 with a good position for White.

5 ♘bd2 *(D)*

B

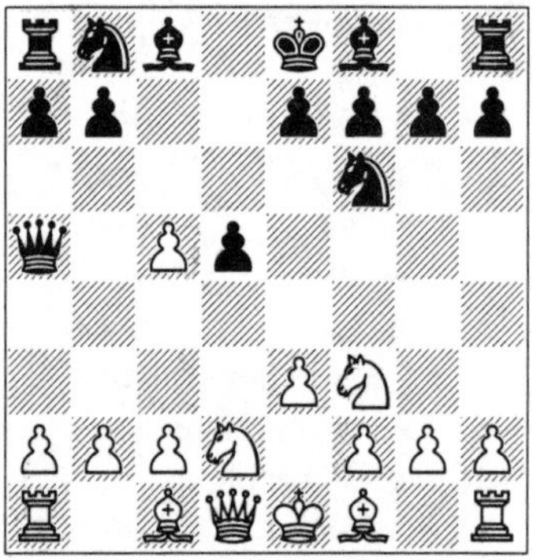

5 ... ♕xc5

The main alternative is 5...♘c6 6 a3 ♗g4 (Black decides upon classical development) 7 ♗e2 ♕xc5 8 b4 ♕b6 9 0-0 ♖d8 10 ♗b2 (White's play is very unpretentious – he simply completes development before undertaking active operations) 10...e6 11 ♘d4 ♗xe2 12 ♕xe2 ♗d6 13 c4 (this is a key part of White's armoury and already creates problems for Black due to the threat of c5) 13...♘e5? (Black has to be careful; he is also losing after 13...0-0? 14 c5 ♗xc5 15 ♘xc6 bxc6 16 ♗xf6 gxf6 17 bxc5 +–, but a better option is 13...dxc4 14 ♘xc4 ♕c7 15 ♘xd6+ ♕xd6, even though White is better, as the opening of the position favours his bishop and better developed pieces) 14 cxd5? (14 c5 ♗xc5 15 ♕b5+ ♕xb5 16 ♘xb5 wins a piece) 14...♘xd5 15 f4 ♘g6 16 ♘c4 ♕a6 17 f5 (Black is being driven back on both sides of the board) 17...♘e5 18 b5 ♕a4 19 ♘xd6+ ♖xd6 20 ♘xe6! (decisive) 20...♘c4 (20...fxe6 21 ♗xe5 +–) 21 ♘xg7+ ♔d7 22 ♗d4 ♖g8 23 f6 ♘cxe3 24 ♗xe3 ♕e4 25 ♖ae1 ♘xf6 26 ♗c5 ♖xg7 27 ♗xd6 1-0 Guimard-Wade, Barcelona 1946.

6 a3 **g6**
7 b4 **♕c3**
8 ♖b1 **♗g7**
9 ♗b2 **♕c7**
10 c4 **dxc4**
11 ♗xc4 **0-0**
12 ♖c1

White has a very active position and Black has had to lose a lot of time with his queen.

12 ... **♕d8**
13 ♕b3 **e6**
14 0-0 **♘bd7**
15 ♖fd1 *(D)*

B

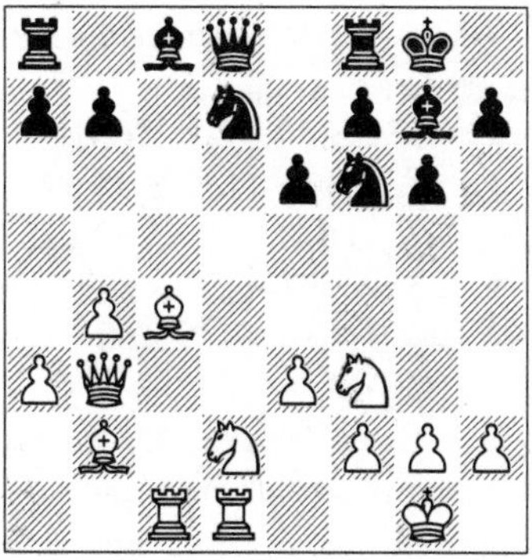

White has a large lead in development and the main problem is breaking through the black defences.

15 ... **♕e7**
16 ♕c2 **♘b6**
17 ♗b3 **♗d7**
18 ♗d4 **♖fc8**
19 ♕b2 **♗c6**
20 ♖c2

White prepares to take control of the c-file.

20 ... **♗d5**
21 ♖dc1 **♖xc2**
22 ♖xc2 **♗xb3**
23 ♘xb3 **♘bd5**
24 ♘a5 **h6**
25 ♕c1 **b6**
26 ♘c6 **♕e8?**

Black makes a fatal mistake. His position was still tenable after 26...♕d6.

27 ♘xa7 **♕a4**
28 ♖c8+ **♖xc8**
29 ♘xc8 **b5**

To his credit, Black tries to make it as hard as possible for White to realize his extra pawn.

30 ♘b6

White seeks piece exchanges to clarify the position.

30 ... ♘xb6
31 ♗xb6 ♘d5
32 ♗d4 ♕b3
33 ♗xg7 ♔xg7
34 ♘d4 ♕d3
35 h3 ♘c3?

The final mistake. 35...e5 would still keep Black in the game, at least temporarily.

36 ♕f1 ♕d2

The pure knight endgame is lost, so Black has to lose a second pawn.

37 ♘xb5 ♘e2+
38 ♔h2 ♘c1
39 ♘d4 ♘d3
40 ♔g1 e5
41 ♘f3 ♕c3
42 ♕b1 e4
43 ♘d4 ♕xa3
44 b5

This extra pawn decides the day in short order.

44 ... ♕a5
45 b6 ♕d2
46 b7 ♕xf2+
47 ♔h2 ♘e1
48 ♕xe4 1-0

Game 23
Kosashvili – Peker
Kfar Sava 1993

1 d4 d5
2 ♘f3 ♘f6
3 e3 g6

3...♘bd7 4 ♗d3 c5 5 b3 ♕c7 6 ♗b2 puts paid to any ideas of an early ...e5.

The 3...g6 system is a tough nut to crack and I feel the best approach is to carry on playing in the Colle-Zukertort style. (Please note that for the sake of convenience I have adjusted the move-order of the opening of this game, which actually went 1 d4 ♘f6 2 ♘f3 g6 3 b3 ♗g7 4 ♗b2 0-0 5 e3 d5).

4 b3 ♗g7
5 ♗b2 0-0 *(D)*

W

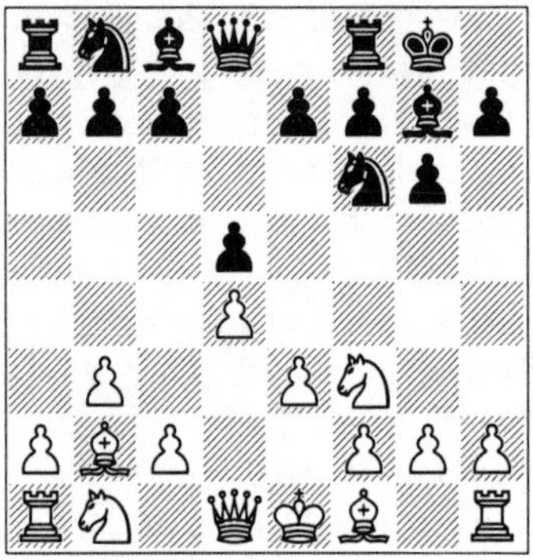

6 ♗e2

White's main decision is where to post his light-squared bishop. The other possibility is to put it on d3 via 6 ♘bd2 b6 7 ♗d3. However, this has two drawbacks. Firstly, the bishop bites on granite as Black's kingside fianchetto blunts its power; secondly, in some lines when Black plays ...c5 it may be useful to defend d4 with the queen or rook – then the bishop on d3 will get in the way. On the plus side, White's set-up makes it harder for Black to move his knight to e4. 7...♗a6 8 c4 (White is keen to keep his light-squared bishop; this move is also part of White's plan to attack Black's centre) 8...e6 9 0-0 ♘bd7 10 ♕e2 (White is ready to break in the centre with e4, so Black counterattacks) 10...c5 11 ♘e5 (if you have studied carefully the chapter on the Colle-Zukertort then you will be familiar with this move) 11...♘xe5 12 dxe5 ♘d7 13 f4 (White's attack is not as powerful as usual because Black already has a good defensive position on the kingside; on the other hand the g7-bishop is obstructed by White's pawn-chain and Black even suffers from some dark-squared weaknesses) 13...♗b7 14 cxd5 exd5 15 e4 ♕e7 (Black could pass with 15...d4 but after 16 ♘c4 the d6-square would be beckoning) 16 exd5 ♗xd5 17 ♖ae1 ♖fe8 18 ♘e4 (with an eye on d6 and f6) 18...♗xe4 (Black decides he cannot tolerate the knight, but giving up the bishop-pair is never an easy option) 19 ♕xe4 a6 20 a4 ♔h8 21 ♗c4 and White was better in Remling-Wapner, Budapest 1994.

6 ... c5

7 0-0 *(D)*

Presenting Black with a choice of either continuing to develop normally or to trying a dawn raid on the e4-square.

7 ... ♘e4

This is an attempt to take advantage of White's omission of ♗d3 and simultaneously to increase the pressure on d4.

Instead after 7...cxd4 (it is probably a little premature to relieve the tension in the centre) 8 exd4 ♘c6 9 ♘bd2 b6

B

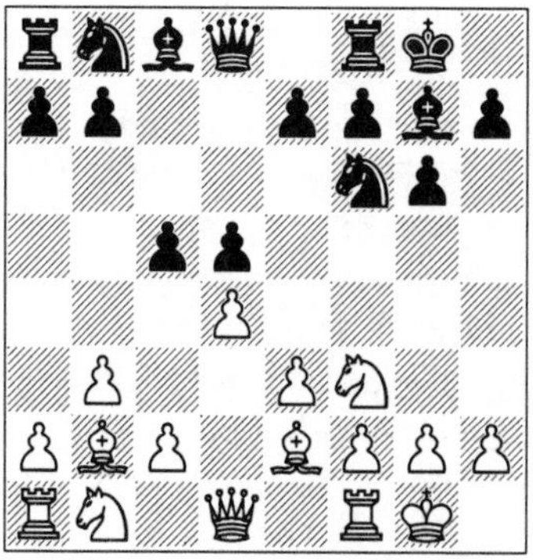

10 ♖e1 ♗b7 11 ♗b5 ♖c8 12 ♕e2 (White's build-up reveals one of the drawbacks of Black's set-up: if Black doesn't want to weaken his dark squares with ...e6 then he has to waste time passively defending his e-pawn) 12...♖e8 13 ♘e5 (White immediately takes advantage of the pin) 13...♘d7 14 ♘df3 ♘dxe5 15 ♘xe5 ♕d6 16 a4 White enjoyed a definite initiative in Van Riemsdijk-Kawano, São Paulo 1995.

8 c4 dxc4

9 bxc4 ♘c6

10 ♘a3

An unusual development of White's knight, but, with hanging pawns likely, White tries to avoid piece exchanges.

10 ... b6

11 h3 cxd4

12 exd4 ♗b7

13 ♘c2 ♖c8

14 ♘e3

The white knight is very well placed here as it exerts influence over both the centre and kingside as well as defending c4.

14 ... ♘a5
15 ♖c1 ♖c7
16 ♕a4 ♕a8
17 ♕a3 ♖fc8
18 d5

The aim of this thematic thrust is to remove a key defender of the black king and blunt the power of the queen and remaining bishop.

18 ... ♗xb2
19 ♕xb2 ♘d6

Black increases the pressure on the critical c4-square.

20 ♕d4 ♗a6
21 ♘d2

Fully securing the c4-point.

21 ... ♘ab7 *(D)*

W

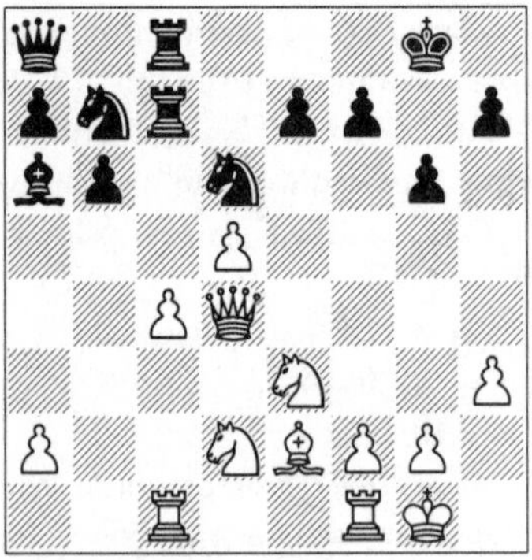

Black threatens ...b5.

22 ♖b1 ♘c5
23 h4

With the queenside covered for the moment, White logically takes action on the kingside.

23 ... ♘d7
24 h5 f6
25 f4

Otherwise ...♘e5 will be annoying.

25 ... ♖c5
26 hxg6 hxg6
27 ♗d3

The black king begins to feel the heat.

27 ... ♔f7
28 ♖f3 ♖h8
29 ♘g4 ♖h4
30 ♕e3 ♘f8
31 ♘e5+! *(D)*

B

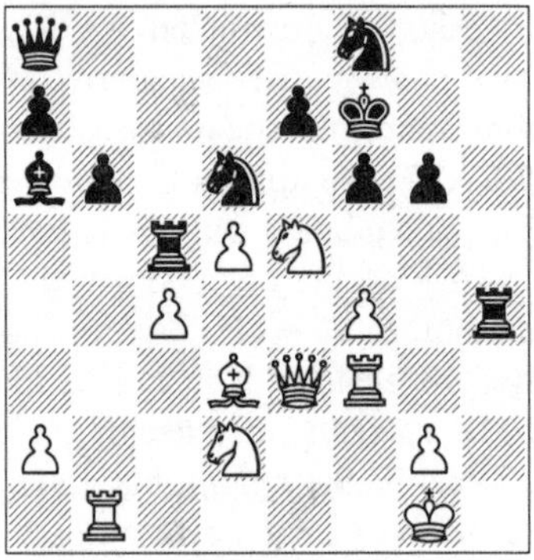

This knight offer begins the final assault on the black monarch.

31 ... ♔g7

The knight can't be taken: 31...fxe5 32 fxe5+ ♘f5 33 ♗xf5 gxf5 34 ♖xf5+ ♔e8 35 ♖xf8+ ♔xf8 36 ♕f2+ ♔e8 37 ♕xh4 +–.

32 ♘xg6 ♘xg6
33 ♖g3 ♖h6
34 ♕xe7+ ♘f7
35 ♘e4

The black position is in tatters as White's pieces come crashing through.

35 ... ♕d8
36 ♕xd8 ♘xd8

37 ♘xc5 bxc5
38 f5 1-0

White's material advantage will soon be overwhelming.

Game 24
Summerscale – A. Marić
Oakham jr 1990

1 ♘f3 d5
2 d4 ♘f6
3 e3 ♗g4

This is a more principled approach than 2...♗g4, as at least the white knight is pinned.

4 c4 *(D)*

B

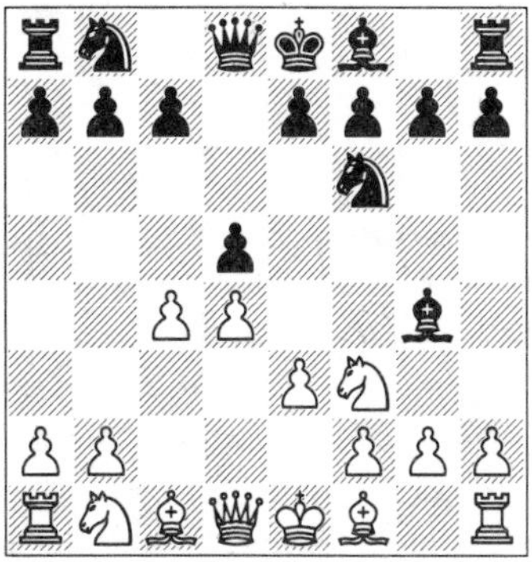

As usual White strikes back on the queenside.

4 ... e6

Other plausible moves are:

a) 4...♗xf3 (White should never fear this capture as the resulting positions are dynamically rich) 5 gxf3!? (perhaps surprising, but White has plans for his queen on the queenside) 5...c6 6 ♘c3 e6 7 ♕b3 and now:

a1) 7...♕b6 8 c5 ♕xb3 (8...♕c7 9 f4 ±) 9 axb3 ♘bd7 10 b4 a6 11 b5 ±.

a2) 7...♕c7 (7...♕c8 is similar) 8 ♗d2 ♘bd7 9 f4 (it is important for White to put the brakes on ...e5) 9...dxc4 10 ♗xc4 ♘b6 (10...c5 11 d5 favours White) 11 ♗d3 ♘bd5 12 a3 ♗e7 13 ♘e2 ♕b6 14 ♕c2 ♕d8 (this is a bit uninspired; Black should simply bite the bullet and castle) 15 f5 (played to weaken Black's grip in the centre) 15...exf5 16 ♗xf5 g6 17 ♗h3 (the bishop finds a new active diagonal) 17...0-0 18 0-0 ♘h5 19 e4 ♘c7 20 f4 (White's central pawn majority begins to make itself felt) 20...♗f6 21 e5 ♖e8 22 ♗g4 ♗g7 23 ♖f2 (the black knight isn't going anywhere, so White strengthens his kingside position) 23...♕h4 24 ♖g2 ♘d5 25 ♖f1 f5 26 ♗e1 ♕e7 27 ♗xh5 gxh5 28 ♘g3 ♖f8 29 ♘xf5 and White converted his material advantage in Lasker-Blackburne, London (4) 1892.

b) 4...dxc4 (this takes us into a line of the Queen's Gambit Accepted that is unfashionable for Black) 5 ♘bd2 (played in order to recapture with the knight on c4, giving it access to e5) 5...e6 6 ♘xc4 ♗b4+ (Black banks on speedy development) 7 ♗d2 ♗xd2+ 8 ♕xd2 ♘bd7 9 ♖c1 (the c-file is a key point of contention for both colours; White strives to prevent ...c5 by Black) 9...0-0 10 ♘fe5 ♘xe5 11 dxe5 *(D)* and now:

b1) 11...♕xd2+ 12 ♘xd2 and now 12...♘e8 is fairly grim for Black, but 12...♘d5 13 e4 ♘b4 14 f3 ♗h5 15 ♖xc7 ± is no better.

B

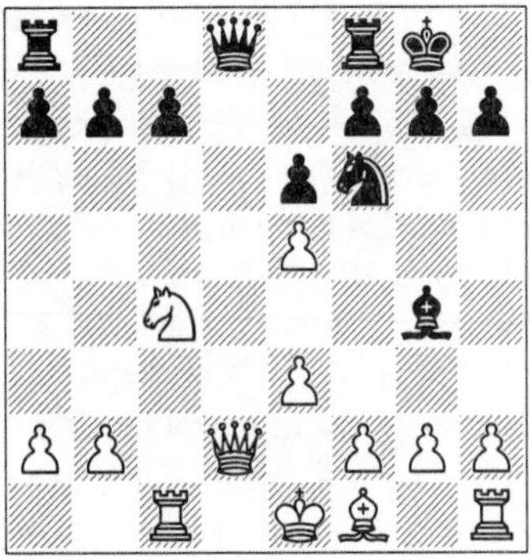

b2) 11...♘d7 12 ♕d4 ♗f5 13 g4 (Black's bishop serves as a target to enhance White's initiative) 13...c5 14 ♕f4 ♗g6 15 h4 h6 16 g5 h5 17 ♗g2 (the bishop is particularly effective along this diagonal...) 17...b5 (...so much so that Black is prepared to part with an exchange; if instead 17...♖b8 then 18 0-0 with the idea of ♖fd1) 18 ♘d6 ♕a5+ 19 b4! cxb4 (19...♕xb4+ allows White to take the black rook in safety: 20 ♕xb4 cxb4 21 ♗xa8 ♖xa8 ±) 20 0-0 ♖ab8 21 ♖fd1 ♘b6 22 ♗e4 (White still has a powerful kingside attack, despite castling on that side) 22...♘d5 23 ♖xd5 ♗xe4 (23...exd5 24 ♗xd5 leaves Black the exchange ahead but completely tied up) 24 ♘xe4 exd5 25 ♘f6+! ♔h8 (25...gxf6 26 gxf6 leads to a quick mate) 26 ♕f3 g6 27 ♘d7 (not just winning back the exchange but allowing White's attack to continue unabated) 27...b3 28 ♕f6+ ♔g8 29 e6 (White plays the attack with great energy; this is a standard pawn-break to lever open Black's defences) 29...♕b4 30 exf7+ ♔h7 31 ♘xf8+ ♖xf8 32 axb3 ♕g4+ 33 ♔f1 ♕xh4 34 ♖c6 ♕e4 35 ♖e6 ♕f5 36 ♕xf5 gxf5 37 b4 ♔g7 38 g6 ♖b8 (hastening the end, but Black was very tied up in any case) 39 ♖e8 1-0 Hebden-Matulović, Vrnjačka Banja 1991.

5 ♕b3 *(D)*

B

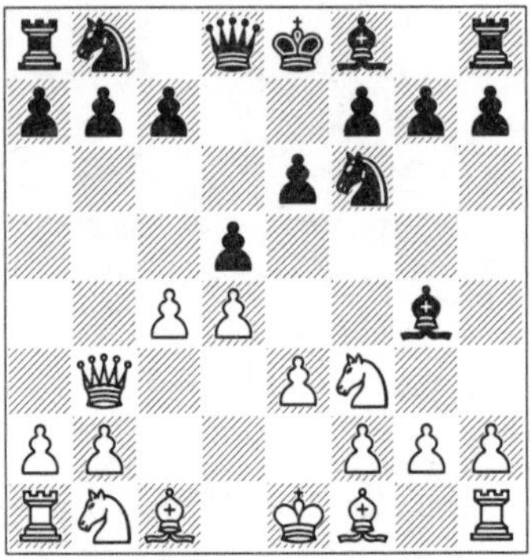

5 ... ♕c8

Again Black could consider the capture on f3. However, this now allows White some additional possibilities, for example 5...♗xf3 6 ♕xb7!? (White could of course simply recapture on f3 and play *à la* Lasker, but the move played is far more ambitious) 6...♘bd7 7 gxf3 ♖b8 8 ♕xa7 ♗b4+ 9 ♘c3 0-0 10 ♕a4 (the queen makes a dash for it with her booty) 10...c5 11 dxc5 ♘xc5 12 ♕c2 (Black has a large lead in development but greedy players will like White's position, and the onus is certainly on Black to prove he has compensation for the two-pawn deficit) 12...dxc4 13 ♗xc4 ♘d5 14 ♗d2 ♕f6 15 ♗e2 ♖fd8 (Black is now fully mobilized but White's position is quite resilient) 16 0-0 (bravely putting his head in the lion's mouth; the question is, does Black have a big enough bite?) 16...♕h4 17 ♖fd1 (good defence: White provides an escape route for the king, should it become necessary) 17...♗a5 (the problem for Black is he doesn't have any support for his lone attacker on the kingside and this move aims to remedy that situation; however, there is a tactical problem) 18 ♘xd5! (this looks risky, as it allows the black rook to enter the fray, but White has it all worked out) 18...♖xd5 19 ♗xa5 ♖g5+ 20 ♔h1 ♖h5 (20...♕xf2 21 ♖g1 defends) 21 ♗c7! (the key move to allow White to escape mate) 21...e5 22 ♗xe5 (another one bites the dust!) 22...♖xe5 23 f4 ♖e6 24 ♗c4 ♖h6 25 f3. The white queen is brought into the defence and with her introduction the black attack falters. White's large material advantage was eventually too much for Black in Iglesias-Perez, Havana 1970.

6 ♘c3 *(D)*

B

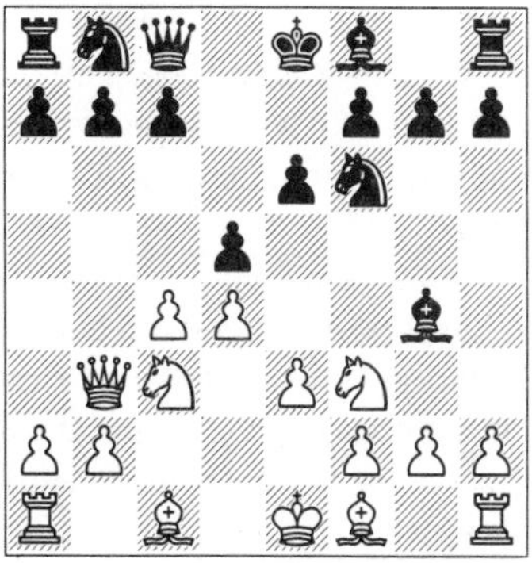

6 ... c6

Again the capture on f3 is a possibility but only has independent value if Black chooses to castle queenside, viz. 6...♗xf3 7 gxf3 dxc4 8 ♗xc4 ♘bd7 9 e4 (White pursues a policy of central expansion rather than weakening Black first with an early f4-f5) 9...♘b6 10 ♗e2 ♕d7 11 ♗e3 0-0-0. Although it may seem that the white king has nowhere safe to go, the same could be said of Black; if Black castles kingside his king will be subjected to an attack on the g-file with the white f- and h-pawns being used as battering rams, while on the queenside the semi-open c-file is a cause for concern. Meanwhile, White's central space advantage goes some way towards protecting his own king and gives White the manoeuvrability to attack on either wing. 12 ♘b5 ♔b8 13 a4 (the a-pawn is a useful part of the attacking process since if Black decides to kick White's knight with ...a6 at some stage, White can seriously consider just leaving his knight there in order to open the a-file against the black king) 13...♘c8 14 0-0 ♗e7 15 ♖fc1 (more and more pressure is brought to bear against Black's queenside; moreover, Black lacks space and as a result lacks a good way to prevent ♖xc7) 15...c6 16 ♗f4+ (winning a piece) 16...♘d6 17 ♗xd6+ ♗xd6 18 ♘xd6 ♕xd6 19 e5 ♕xd4 (19...♕d5 20 ♗c4) 20 exf6 ♕xf6 21 ♖d1 with a decisive material advantage for White, Green-Rex, Man vs Machine 1991.

7 ♗d2 ♘bd7

8 ♖c1 ♕b8
9 h3 ♗h5

As we have seen, exchanging on f3 is no picnic for Black, so instead she retreats, hoping for a solid game.

10 g4

Not a chance! I played this game when I was still young and fearless.

10 ... ♗g6
11 ♘h4 *(D)*

B

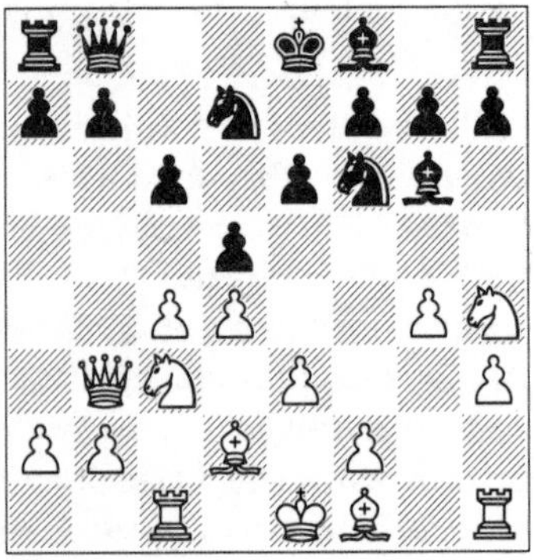

This move forms an important part of White's strategy, as it bags the bishop-pair, thus compensating for his weakened kingside.

11 ... ♗e7
12 ♘xg6 hxg6
13 ♗g2 ♘b6
14 cxd5 exd5
15 ♘a4 ♘xa4

Or 15...♘c4 16 ♗b4.

16 ♕xa4 0-0
17 b4 a6
18 ♕c2

18 ♕b3 is perhaps more accurate, but I wanted to keep an eye on the possibility of ...♘e4.

18 ... ♖e8
19 a4 ♕d6
20 ♕b1 *(D)*

B

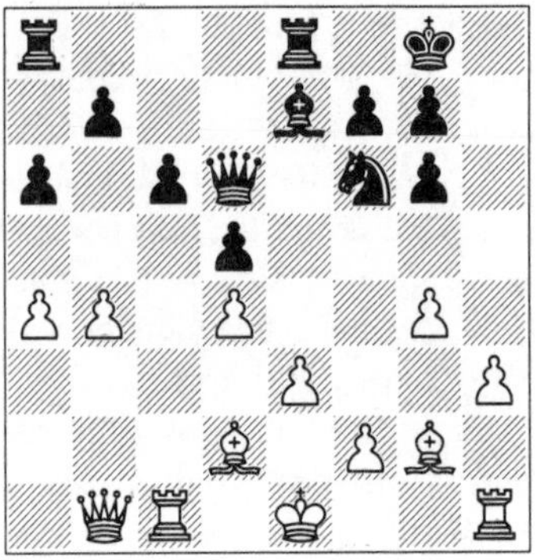

A case of too many queen moves; it would be better to castle and prepare a b5 break.

20 ... ♗d8
21 b5 cxb5
22 axb5 ♘e4
23 ♗b4 ♕b6
24 0-0

24 bxa6 ♕xa6 would have left my king in trouble, another reason why I should have castled earlier.

24 ... a5

24...♕xb5 is the acid test. In the cold light of day I have to admit White has insufficient compensation for the pawn.

25 ♕a2 ♕e6

Black was clearly worried about the pressure on the a- and b-files following a capture on b5 and all I can say is it was a real stroke of luck! Bluff is an essential part of any killer's repertoire.

26 ♗d2 ♗b6

27 ♖c2 ♕d7
28 ♖fc1 f5
29 ♗e1 ♔h7

It is clearly too risky to take on b5 now.

30 ♕b3 ♕f7
31 f3 ♘d6
32 ♗f2 ♖ad8
33 ♖c3 f4 *(D)*

W

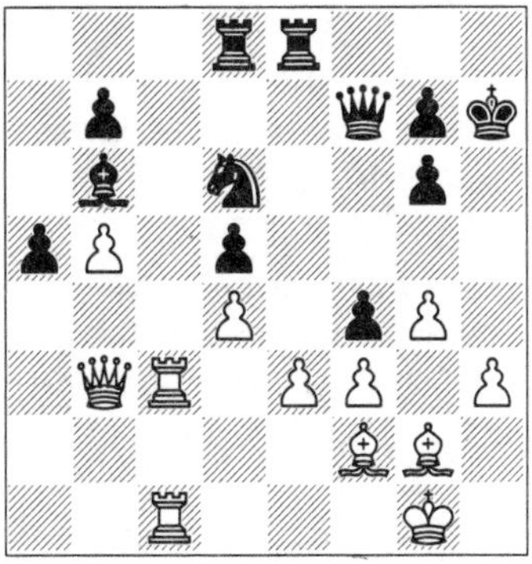

An excellent move, detonating my centre and giving Black attacking chances on the kingside. I must admit I began to feel I was being outplayed around here and decided to try to knuckle down to make things as difficult as possible for my higher rated opponent.

34 exf4 ♕xf4
35 ♖d1 ♘c4
36 ♕c2 ♗c7
37 h4

Trying to make the most of my chances on the kingside.

37 ... ♖e6
38 h5 ♖de8
39 hxg6+ ♔g8? *(D)*

39...♖xg6, despite the self-pin, leaves Black with a good grip on the position.

W

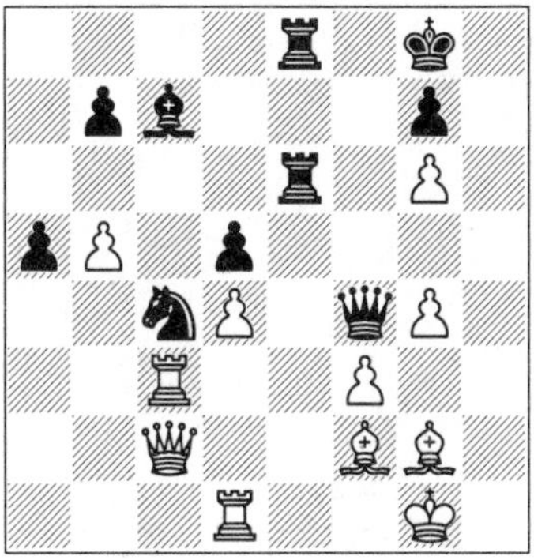

40 ♔f1 ♗d6
41 ♕f5

How quickly a position can change with one mistake! Although the move looks like a blunder, it is extremely clever (if I do say so myself!) and in the game Black was not up to the tactical task.

41 ... ♘d2+

This is far too optimistic. Black would still be doing well after the prudent 41...♕xf5 42 gxf5 ♖f6.

42 ♖xd2 ♕xd2
43 ♕f7+

Probably the move Black missed.

43 ... ♔h8
44 ♕xe6 *(D)*

This back-rank tactic must have been terribly embarrassing for my opponent, who had outplayed me for much of the game.

44 ... ♕d1+
45 ♗e1 ♕xe1+
46 ♕xe1 ♖xe1+

B

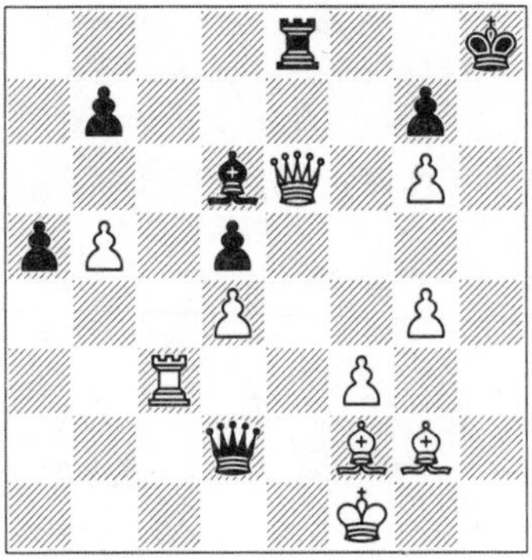

47	**♔xe1**	**♗b4**
48	**♔d2**	**a4**
49	**♔c2**	**1-0**

Game 25
Hebden – Summerscale
Upminster 1993

1	**d4**	**d5**
2	**♘f3**	**♘f6**
3	**e3**	**c6**

If 3...♗f5 then 4 c4 c6 with a transposition to Yusupov-Nikolić in the note to Black's 4th move.

4 c4 *(D)*

(1 d4 d5 2 c4 c6 3 ♘f3 ♘f6 4 e3 was the actual move-order but again I have adjusted it for our convenience.)

4 ... e6

This attempt to get an exciting Semi-Slav variation is neatly parried by White's clever move-order.

The main alternative is 4...♗f5 5 cxd5 cxd5 6 ♕b3 ♕c7 (6...♕b6 7 ♕xb6 axb6 8 ♘c3 is a bit better for White due to Black's weak doubled b-pawns) 7 ♘c3 e6 8 ♗d2 (White's

B

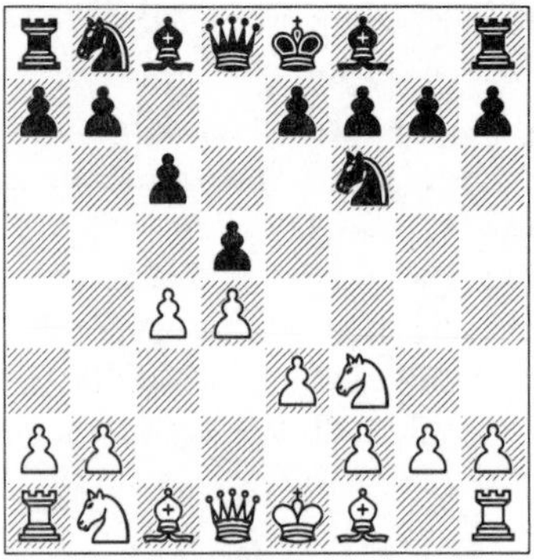

plan here is to develop quickly and pressurize Black along the open c-file) 8...♘c6 9 ♗b5 ♗e7 10 0-0 0-0 11 ♖fc1 intending ♘e5, Yusupov-P.Nikolić, Belgrade 1991. This is slightly better for White and certainly not very inspiring for the second player.

5 ♘bd2 ♘bd7

5...c5 is a principled way to fight back immediately against the white centre, although I suspect the concept of moving the c-pawn twice in the first five moves will be alien to most players. 6 cxd5 exd5 (6...♘xd5 allows White a nice space advantage after 7 e4 ♘f6 8 e5 ♘d5 9 dxc5 ♗xc5 10 ♘e4 followed by ♗d3 and attacking chances on the kingside to follow, Staniszewski-Jagodzinski, Polish Ch 1981) 7 b3 cxd4 8 ♘xd4 ♗b4 9 ♕c2 ♘c6 10 ♘xc6 bxc6 11 ♗d3 (White very sensibly declines the pawn offer, knowing that Black's structural weakness won't go away; not 11 ♕xc6+? ♗d7 12 ♕c2? ♖c8 ∓) 11...0-0 12 0-0 ♗d6 13 ♗b2 c5 (Black has the dynamic hanging pawns and White sets about breaking them up right away) 14 e4 ♘g4 (this early attack backfires on Black, who should have played either 14...dxe4 15 ♘xe4 ± or 14...d4 15 h3 ♗b7 16 ♘c4 ±) 15 h3 ♘h2 16 ♖fd1 ♕g5 17 e5! (taking the wind out of Black's sails) 17...♗xh3 18 g3 ♗g4 19 ♔xh2 ♗xd1 20 ♖xd1 f5 (Black pushes the self-destruct button but he was clearly worse in any case, e.g. 20...♗xe5 21 ♗xh7+ ♔h8 22 ♘f3 ♕h5+ 23 ♔g2 ♗xb2 24 ♖h1 ±) 21 exd6 f4 22 ♘f1 (three pieces for a rook is far too much) 22...♖ad8 23 ♕e2 ♕h6+ 24 ♔g1 f3 25 ♕e5 d4 26 b4 ♖xd6 27 ♘d2 cxb4 28 ♘xf3 ♖df6 29 ♗e4 1-0 Chernikov-Rapoport, Ceske Budejovice 1996.

6 b3 **♗d6**
7 ♗b2 **0-0**
8 ♗d3 **♕e7** *(D)*

This whole plan of preparing ...e5 is flawed, so Black would do better to play for ...b6 and ...c5 despite being a tempo down on normal Colle-Zukertort lines.

W

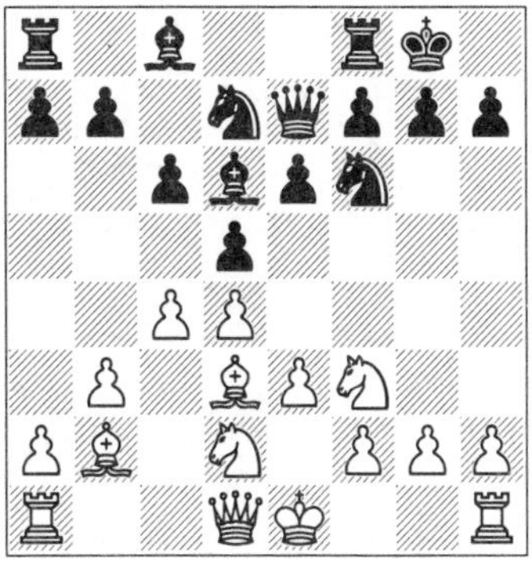

9 ♘e5 **dxc4**

Black chooses to relieve some of the central tension, which is no better or worse than maintaining it, for example 9...♖d8 10 0-0 ♘f8 11 ♕e2 ♘6d7 12 ♖ad1 a5 13 f4 a4 14 e4 (White has been able to build up an imposing central space advantage and already stands clearly better) 14...axb3 15 axb3 ♖a2 (the minor irritation of Black's rook infiltration in no way makes up for White's growing initiative and positional advantages) 16 ♘df3 f6 17 ♘xd7 ♗xd7 18 ♗b1 ♖aa8 19 e5 (further increasing White's command of space and opening the way for the b1-bishop to reach the kingside) 19...fxe5 20 fxe5 ♗a3 21 ♗c3 ♗b4? (somehow I knew my opponent would make this move, which draws away a key defender from his kingside) 22 ♗xb4 ♕xb4 23 ♘g5 *(D)*.

B

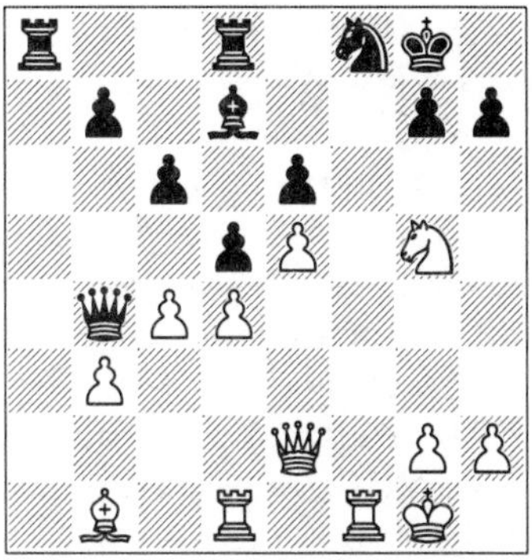

Black is now completely busted, as the following variations show:

a) 23...h6 24 ♘f7 ♖e8 25 ♘xh6+ gxh6 26 ♕g4+ ♔h8 27 ♖f7 +–.

b) 23...♕xb3 24 ♖xf8+ ♖xf8
(24...♔xf8 25 ♕f2+ ♔g8 26 ♗xh7+
♔h8 27 ♗c2 ♕xc4 28 ♕h4+ ♔g8 29
♕h7+ ♔f8 30 ♕h8+ ♔e7 31 ♕xg7+
♔e8 32 ♕f7#) 25 ♗xh7+ ♔h8 26
♗c2 ♕xc4 27 ♕h5+ ♔g8 28 ♕h7#.

c) 23...g6 24 ♘f7 ♖db8 25 ♘h6+
♔g7 (25...♔h8 26 ♖f7 ♕xb3 27 ♖df1
{threatening ♕f2-f6} 27...♕b6 28 ♕f2
♕d8 29 ♖xd7 ♕xd7 30 ♘f7+ ♔g8 31
♕f6 +–) 26 ♖f7+ ♔h8 (26...♔xh6 27
♕g4 +–) 27 ♕f3 +–.

d) The game continuation was no
better: 23...♗e8 24 ♖xf8+! (removing
the key defender of the kingside)
24...♕xf8 25 ♗xh7+ ♔h8 26 ♖f1 ♕e7
27 ♕g4 g6 28 ♕h3! (keeping an eye
on e6) 28...dxc4 29 ♕h6 ♗d7 30
♗xg6+ 1-0 Summerscale-Salo, Bratislava ECC 1996. 30...♔g8 31 ♗f7+ decides. I learnt the hard way the strengths
of White's position in the main game
against Hebden; in this game, six
years later, I was able to put the experience to good use.

10	♘exc4	♗c7
11	0-0	b5
12	♘e5	♘xe5
13	dxe5	♘d5
14	♕h5	h6
15	♘e4 *(D)*	

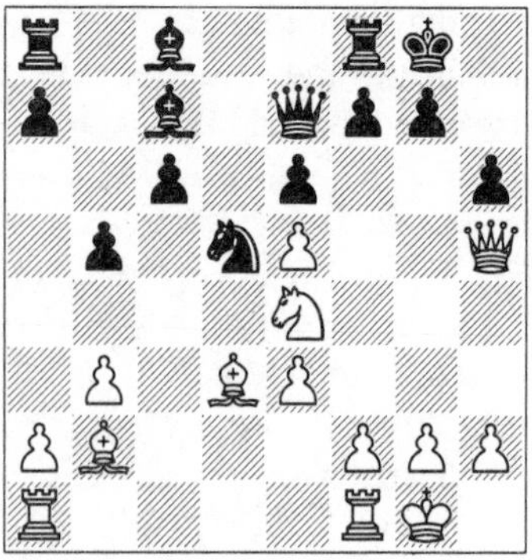

White's kingside initiative far outweighs Black's queenside pawn majority.

15	...	♖d8
16	♖ad1	♗b7
17	♕g4	♔f8
18	h4	♖ab8
19	♘d6	♗a8

For some reason that I couldn't
fathom at the time, I never seemed
able to take one of his pieces unless he
wanted me to! It's because Black just
has an terrible position.

| 20 | e4 | ♘b4 |
| 21 | f4 | |

The march of the f-pawn decides
the issue.

21	...	♖d7
22	f5	exf5
23	♖xf5	f6 *(D)*

| 24 | exf6 | ♕xd6 |
| 25 | fxg7+ | ♔g8 |

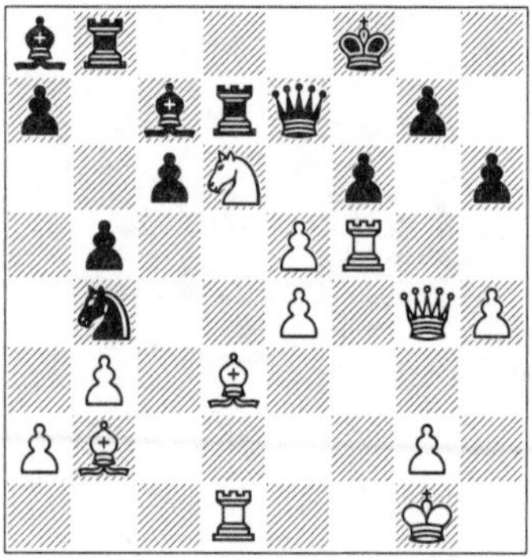

I had a faint glimmer of hope here, thinking he may have overreached himself until he played...

26 ♖f8+ 1-0

26...♖xf8 27 gxf8♕+ ♔xf8 28 ♖f1+ ♖f7 29 ♕g7+ is the end.

5 The Classical Queen's Indian

Introduction

Before we look at the variations relating to the Classical Queen's Indian, I would like to show you a game which will help to explain some of the problems White can have if he continues with the standard Colle-Zukertort set-up.

Game 26
Summerscale – Palkövi
Budapest 1990

1	**♘f3**	**♘f6**
2	**d4**	**e6**
3	**e3**	**c5**
4	**♗d3**	**b6**
5	**0-0**	**♗b7**
6	**♘bd2**	**♗e7**

One problem I found as a Colle-Zukertort player against Queen's Indian exponents was that their positions had so much flexibility. This was mainly due to the fact that they could delay ...d5 for as long as they wanted, thus making it harder to carry out the standard plan of ♘e5, f4, etc. In fact, I used to heave a sigh of relief as soon as they did play ...d5 (which wasn't very often). I think this game clearly illustrates the problems White can face because of Black's flexibility.

7	**b3**	**cxd4**
8	**exd4**	**♘c6**
9	**♗b2**	**♘b4**
10	**♗e2**	**♘bd5** *(D)*

W

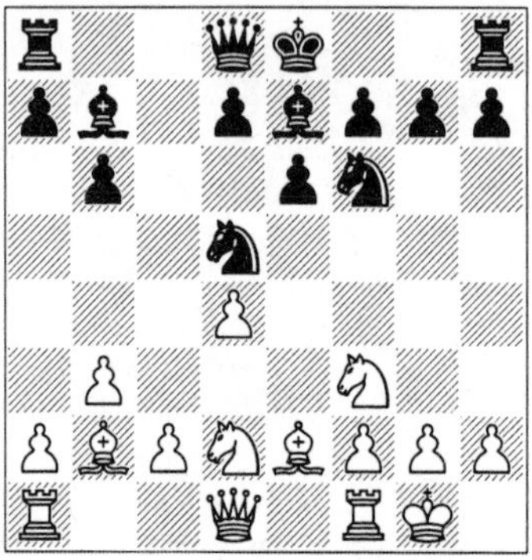

Black is playing the opening quite creatively and is making full use of the d5-square from an early stage. I had severe reservations about my next move but was loathe to allow the black knight into f4.

11 g3 ♗b4

The knight on d5 shows it also has eyes for my queenside and, not wanting to give up the bishop-pair, I was forced to make a grovelling retreat.

12 ♘b1 ♘e4

It felt as if the black knights were crawling all over my position.

13	**♕d3**	**f5**
14	**♘e5**	**♘g5**

Here Black sees a forcing continuation and goes for it, but with hindsight perhaps simply 14...0-0 would have kept the advantage.

15 ♖d1

Making an escape-square for my king, which lacks light-squared protection.

15 ... ♘h3+
16 ♔f1 ♘df4 *(D)*

W

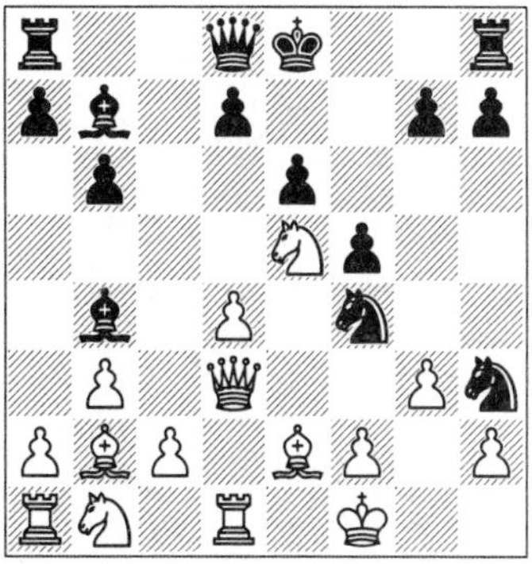

This is the idea Black was playing for, and to be honest I had completely missed it. Still, there was no use in worrying about it – I just had to knuckle down and take what was thrown at me. In retrospect, I now question Black's decision to win my queen and a pawn for three pieces, as I believe the material imbalance favours White.

17 gxf4 ♗g2+
18 ♔xg2 ♘xf4+
19 ♔f1 ♘xd3
20 ♖xd3 ♕h4
21 ♔g1 d6
22 ♘f3 ♕g4+
23 ♔f1 ♕h3+
24 ♔g1

I would have been very happy with a draw here as I was only an average international player while my opponent was a much higher rated international master. I knew the onus was on him to make something of the position.

24 ... ♕g4+
25 ♔f1 d5
26 c4 ♕h3+
27 ♔g1 ♕g4+
28 ♔f1 0-0
29 a3 ♕h3+
30 ♔g1 ♕g4+
31 ♔f1 ♗d6
32 ♘c3 ♕h3+
33 ♔g1 ♖f6 *(D)*

W

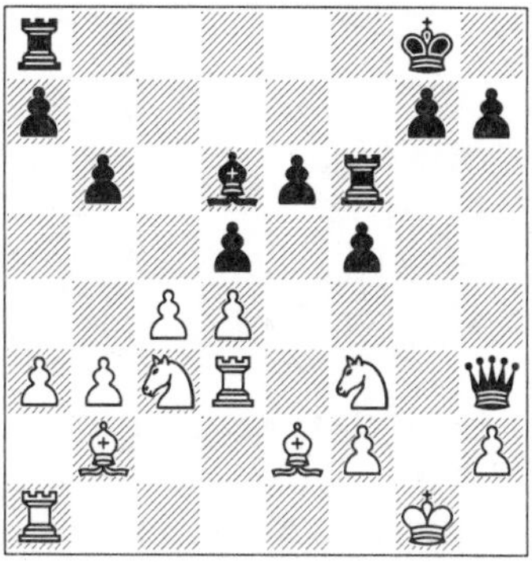

Finally Black makes an aggressive move towards my king.

34 ♘e5 ♖g6+
35 ♖g3 ♗xe5
36 dxe5 ♖xg3+
37 hxg3 f4!
38 ♗f1 ♕g4
39 ♘e2 fxg3
40 ♘xg3 ♖f8

We reached the time-control and it has to be said that over the next few moves my more experienced opponent outplayed me.

41 ♗e2 ♕f4
42 ♖f1 d4
43 ♔g2 d3
44 ♗d1 g6
45 ♗c3 h5
46 f3 h4
47 ♘e4 ♖f5 *(D)*

Things have begun to look very grim for White.

W

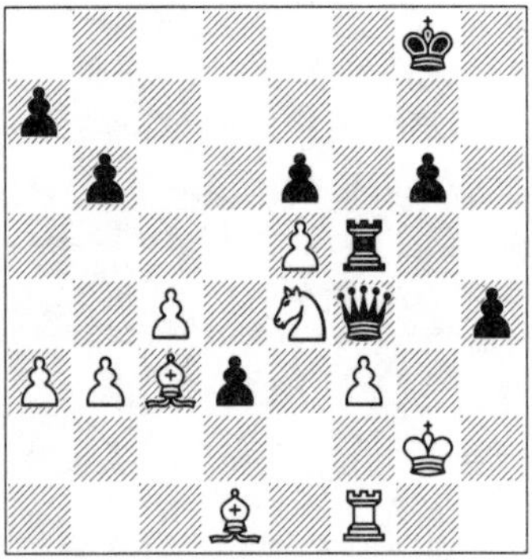

48 ♖g1 h3+
49 ♔h1 h2?

Too ambitious – he should have defended g6.

50 ♖xg6+ ♔h7
51 ♖g2 ♕c1

This was his masterstroke, which seems to create some difficult problems for White, but...

52 ♖xh2+ ♔g7
53 ♖g2+ *(D)*

The game was adjourned at this point and I was enormously grateful to

B

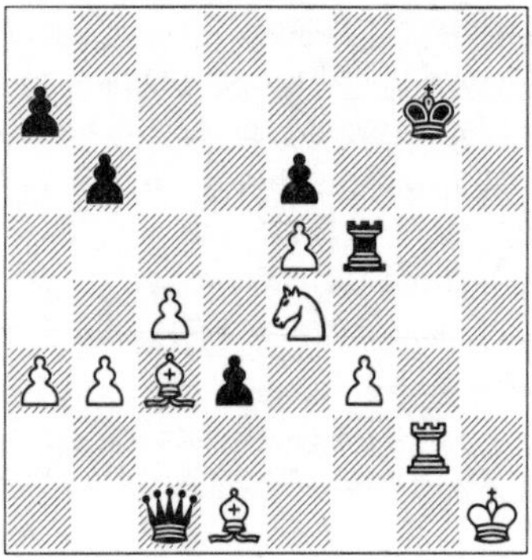

another English junior at the time, Gary Quillan, who spotted the way to trap Black's queen from this position.

53 ... ♔h8
54 ♖d2! ♖xf3

54...♕xa3 55 ♖xd3 is also fairly hopeless for Black.

55 ♗b2 ♖f1+
56 ♔g2 ♕xd2+
57 ♘xd2 ♖xd1
58 ♗c3

The position is now technically winning and I am still impressed with my technique in the game all these years on.

58...♖e1 59 ♔f3 ♖e2 60 ♘e4 ♔g8 61 ♗d2 ♔f7 62 a4 ♔e7 63 ♗e3 ♔d7 64 ♘d2 ♖h2 65 ♔e4 ♖h5 66 b4 ♖h1 67 ♗d4 ♖h3 68 c5 ♔c7 69 cxb6+ axb6 70 ♘c4 ♔c6 71 b5+ ♔b7 72 ♗e3 ♖h2 73 ♔xd3 ♖a2 74 ♘xb6 1-0

So it all turned out right in the end (apart from missing the plane home, but that's another story!). However, I don't think many players would take the white position by choice after move 12. A more aggressive system for White that keeps a firm eye on the crucial d5-square is the Classical Queen's Indian. By utilizing a Colle-Zukertort move-order, we take out some of Black's most significant options. Black can try to confuse the issue, as in the next game, but White keeps a clear head and rises to the occasion.

Game 27

Malaniuk – Merino Garcia

Linares 1996

1 d4 ♘f6
2 ♘f3 e6
3 c4

We could reach the diagram position by 3 e3 b6 4 ♗d3 ♗b7 5 0-0 c5 6 c4, which is significant as Black has not had the option of ...♗b4+. Note that ...d5 at any stage would let White transpose back to the Colle-Zukertort.

3 ... b6
4 e3 ♗b7
5 ♗d3 c5
6 0-0 *(D)*

B

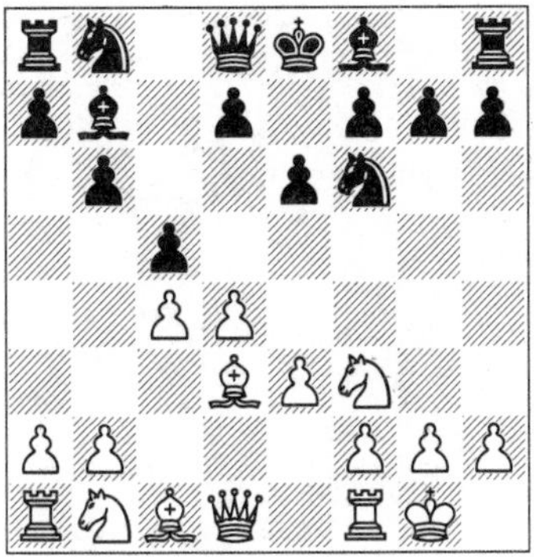

6 ... g6

6...♗e7 7 ♘c3 cxd4 8 exd4 d5 (or 8...d6 9 d5) 9 cxd5 ♘xd5 10 ♘e5 is the main line we consider later. Here Black plays more ambitiously, trying for a double fianchetto. In the main lines the most important decision for Black is whether he should allow the cramping d5 by White. If he doesn't want to, he must play ...d5 himself, after which White takes and we get an IQP position where White has attacking chances on the kingside.

7 ♘c3 ♗g7
8 e4

It makes sense to take the space in the centre that Black has so graciously offered.

8 ... cxd4
9 ♘xd4 d6
10 ♗e3 0-0
11 f3 a6

We have now reached a Hedgehog position. White's plan is to pressurize Black on the dark squares and keep a close eye on the black pawn-breaks, ...d5 and ...b5.

12 ♖e1 ♘bd7
13 ♗f1 ♕c7
14 ♖c1 ♖ac8
15 ♕d2 ♘e5
16 b3 ♖fd8
17 ♖ed1 ♗a8
18 ♔h1 ♕b7 *(D)*
19 ♗g5

The dark-squared attack begins.

19 ... ♕b8
20 ♕f4 ♘ed7

W

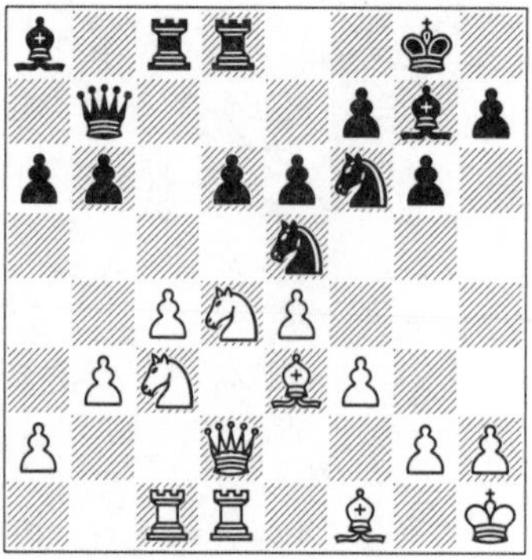

21 ♕h4 ♖e8
22 ♖c2

Stage two of White's plan is simple: attack the weak d6-pawn.

22 ... ♕a7

22...d5 immediately loses a pawn after 23 exd5 exd5 24 ♘xd5 ♘xd5 25 cxd5 ♗xd5 26 ♗xa6.

23 ♖cd2 d5

If Black thought he had prepared this well, he was mistaken.

24 exd5 exd5
25 ♘xd5 ♘xd5
26 cxd5 ♗xd5
27 ♘b5 *(D)*

B

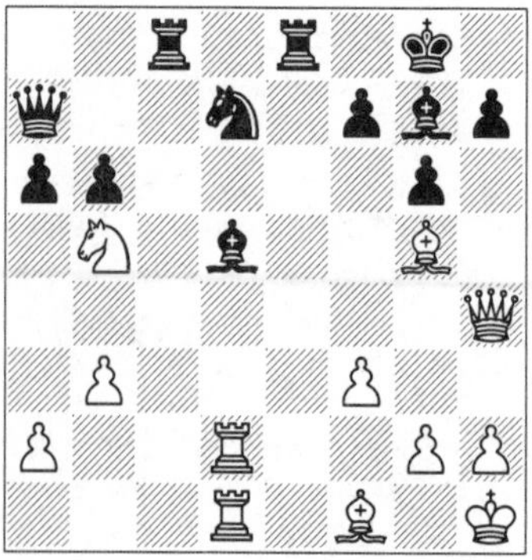

This key move sows the seeds of defeat for Black.

27 ... axb5
28 ♖xd5 ♘c5
29 ♗xb5 ♖e6
30 ♖d8+ ♖xd8
31 ♖xd8+ 1-0

It's forced mate as 31...♗f8 is met by 32 ♖xf8+ ♔xf8 33 ♗h6+ ♔g8 34 ♕d8+ ♖e8 35 ♕xe8#.

Black Omits ...d5

Game 28
Zsu. Polgar – Hraček
Stara Zagora Z 1990

1 d4 ♘f6
2 ♘f3 e6
3 e3 b6
4 ♗d3 ♗b7
5 0-0 c5
6 c4 ♗e7
7 ♘c3 *(D)*

B

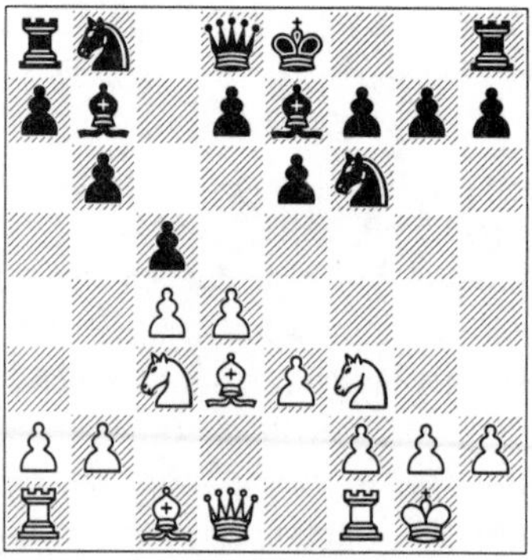

The main difference between the Classical Queen's Indian and the

Colle-Zukertort System we examined before is the positioning of White's queen's knight. This is more actively posted on c3 than on d2; indeed White often counts on this greater central influence to give him the advantage against inaccurate black responses.

7 ... cxd4

7...0-0? is a clear positional mistake as it allows White either a space advantage or a very strong attack against the black king after 8 d5! exd5 9 cxd5 *(D)*.

B

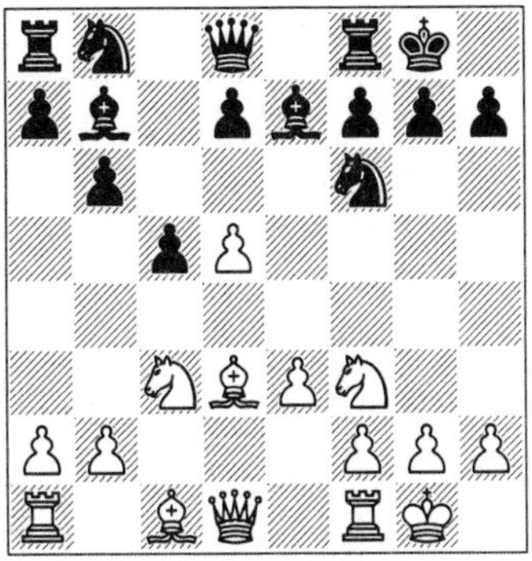

Black is faced with a difficult decision as to whether he should take the d-pawn.

a) 9...d6 (Black declines the proffered pawn but suffers from being stuck in a bad Benoni: both black bishops are ineffectively placed) 10 e4. As in the Benoni, the main hope of counterplay for Black lies in pushing his queenside pawn majority, but Black suffers here in that the bishop is getting in the way on b7; Black will have to lose at least two tempi if he is to achieve ...b6-b5 and this alone is enough to ensure that Black will never achieve full equality. Now:

a1) 10...♘a6 11 ♖e1 ♘c7 12 ♖b1 ♖e8 13 a3 ♘d7 14 ♗f4 ♖c8 15 ♕d2 a6 16 a4 ♘f8 17 b4 (a typical pawn lever in such positions, further restricting Black's possibilities on the queenside) 17...cxb4 18 ♖xb4 ± Bukić-Ljubojević, Bugojno 1978.

a2) 10...a6 11 a4 ♘bd7 12 ♗f4 ♘e8 13 ♕e2 ♗f6 14 ♖ab1 ♕e7 15 ♖fc1 (again White prepares the critical b4 break) 15...♘c7 16 b4 ♖ab8 17 ♘d1 ♖fc8 18 ♘e3 g6 19 bxc5 bxc5 20 ♘c4 (with the arrival of White's knight on its ideal outpost, White forces Black on the defensive and claims a large advantage) 20...♘e8 21 ♘a5 ♖c7 22 ♘d2 ♗g5 (the dark-squared bishop is usually Black's pride and joy in the Benoni but here it is fairly ineffective as there are no targets left on the h8-a1 diagonal) 23 ♗xg5 ♕xg5 24 ♘dc4 and White has achieved a dream Benoni position, Malaniuk-Polzin, Lyngby 1991.

b) 9...♘xd5 (this capture is playing with fire, but the alternatives are not much more promising, as we have already seen) 10 ♘xd5 ♗xd5 11 ♗xh7+ ♔xh7 12 ♕xd5 ± (Black suffers from an exposed king and weaknesses on the d-file) 12...♘c6 13 ♗d2 ♗f6 14 ♗c3 ♔g8 (14...♗xc3 15 ♕h5+ ♔g8 16 ♘g5 +–) 15 ♕h5 ♖e8 16 ♖ad1 (White now enjoys a definite initiative, being able to create threats with almost every move) 16...d6 17 ♖d5 (threatening ♘g5) 17...g6 18 ♕h6 (threatening ♖h5!) 18...♘e5 19 ♗xe5 ♗xe5 20 ♘g5 ♕f6 21 ♕h7+ ♔f8 22 f4 ♗xb2 23 f5! *(D)*.

B

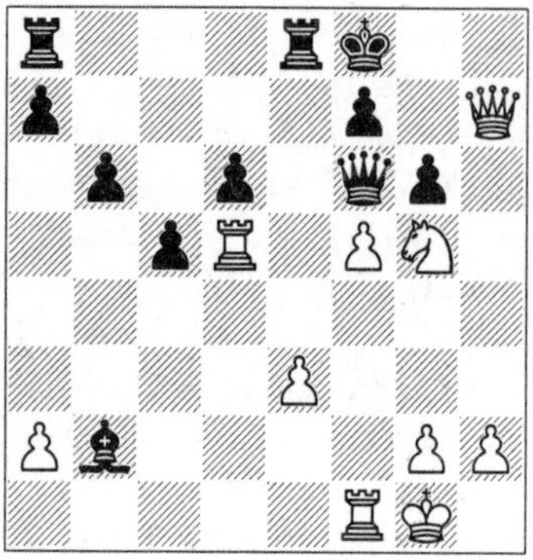

White just keeps on coming, with scant regard for material.

23...♕xg5 24 fxg6 ♕xe3+ 25 ♔h1 ♕f2! (a nice last-ditch try, but Black's position was beyond repair in any case) 26 ♖dd1! ♖e2 27 ♖xf2 ♖xf2 28 ♔g1 1-0 Dizdar-Plachetka, Slovakia-Croatia 1996.

8 exd4 *(D)*

B

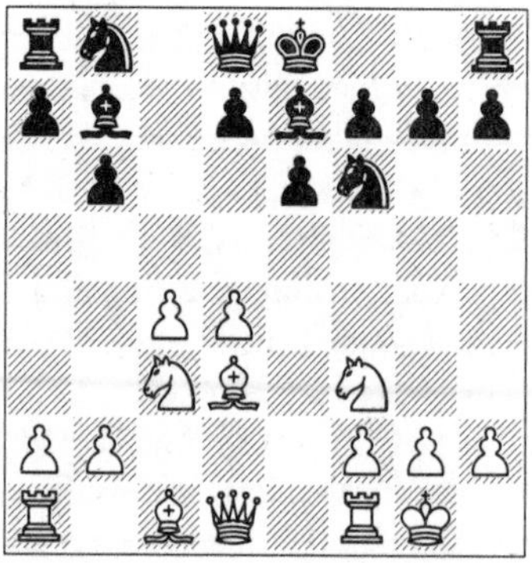

8 ... d6

8...d5 is dealt with in the next game.

8...0-0 9 d5 and now:

a) 9...h6 10 ♗c2 ♗b4 11 ♘e4 exd5 12 ♘xf6+ ♕xf6 13 cxd5 (White's central space advantage gives him greater mobility and hinders Black's development) 13...♗a6 14 ♗d3 ♗xd3 15 ♕xd3 a5 (Black finds a way to develop on the queenside but gives himself a weakness on b6) 16 a3 ♗d6 17 ♗e3 ♘a6 18 ♗d4 ♘c5 19 ♕b5 ♕g6 20 ♖ad1 a4 21 g3 ♕c2 22 ♘d2 ♖fb8 23 ♘c4 ♗c7 24 d6 ♗d8 25 ♖de1 and White has clearly the superior position, B.Lalić-Pliester, Isle of Man 1995.

b) 9...♘a6 10 ♗f4 d6 11 dxe6 fxe6 12 ♗g3 ♘c5 13 ♘d4 leaves White better as Black has three pawn islands to White's two, with the e6/d6 duo being particularly weak, Malaniuk-Tiviakov, Moscow 1992.

9 d5

This is the most incisive; I give the alternatives only as food for thought:

a) 9 a3 0-0 10 b4 ♘bd7 11 ♖e1 ♖c8 12 h3 ♖e8 13 ♗f4 ± Adler-Genov, Antwerp 1992.

b) 9 ♖e1 0-0 and now:

b1) 10 ♗g5 ♘bd7 11 ♕e2 ♖e8 12 ♖ad1 ♖c8 13 h3 ♕c7 14 ♕e3 ♕b8 15 d5 ± Lechtynsky-Mokry, Trenčianske Teplice 1985.

b2) 10 d5 e5 11 a3 a5 12 ♖b1 (White's plan should be becoming familiar by now: to expand on the queenside with b4 in order to create weaknesses there) 12...♘e8 13 ♕c2 g6 14 ♗h6 ♘g7 15 b4 ♘d7 16 ♕e2 ♗a6 17 ♖bc1 ♖c8 18 ♘a4 ♖e8 19 bxa5 bxa5

20 c5 ± Chekhov-Bareev, Kharkov 1985.

b3) 10 a3 ♘bd7 11 b4 ♖e8 12 ♗b2 ♗f8 13 d5 e5 14 ♘d2 g6 15 a4 ± Zsu.Polgar-Arnason, Budapest ECC 1989. White's plan is a5 followed by gradually increasing the pressure on the queenside, for example by doubling rooks on the a-file.

c) 9 b3 0-0 10 ♗b2 ♘bd7 11 ♖e1 a6 12 h3 (White begins an original plan of trebling major pieces on the e-file, hoping to land a tactical blow) 12...♖a7? (Black's play looks too slow here and he would do better to anticipate the danger on the kingside by ...♖e8 and ...♘f8) 13 ♖e3 ♕a8 14 ♕e2 b5 15 ♖e1 (White is very sensibly ignoring Black's queenside play and now begins to introduce some very nasty threats) 15...bxc4 16 bxc4 ♖e8 17 ♘g5 ♗f8 18 ♘xf7! (bang!) 18...♔xf7 19 ♖xe6 ♖b8? (after the more stubborn 19...g6, 20 d5 with the idea of e4 gives White an overwhelming attack) 20 ♖xf6+! 1-0 Yusupov-Teske, Bundesliga 1995/6.

Returning to the position after 9 d5 *(D)*:

9 ... e5

Black is well advised to keep the centre closed.

9...exd5 has turned out disastrously in practice: 10 cxd5 0-0 11 ♘d4 ♘bd7 12 ♘c6 (this is the problem; Black is more or less forced to give up his light-squared bishop and will have to contend with his light-squared weaknesses for the rest of the game)

B

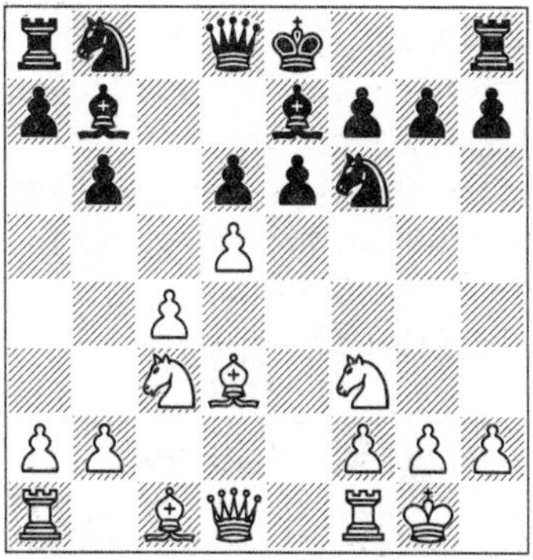

12...♗xc6 13 dxc6 ♘b8 (13...♘e5 14 ♗a6 ±; 13...♘c5 14 ♗f5 d5 15 b4 ♘e6 16 b5 ±) 14 ♕a4 (Black's biggest problem is his knight on b8: recently undeveloped, it has trouble getting into the game again) 14...d5 15 ♗f4 ♗d6 16 ♗g5 h6 17 ♗xf6 ♕xf6 18 ♖ae1 ♗c7 (Black jettisons his d-pawn, which is ultimately lost anyway; his biggest problem, however, remains the still undeveloped knight on b8, which interferes with the coordination of Black's pieces) 19 ♘xd5 ♕d6 20 ♘xc7 ♕xc7 21 ♖c1 a6 22 ♕e4 (with an extra passed pawn on the sixth rank, and the initiative, White's position is overwhelming) 22...g6 23 ♖c3 ♖a7 24 ♖fc1 ♖c8 25 ♕e3 h5 26 ♗e2 ♕d8 27 ♖d1 ♕e7 28 ♕xe7 ♖xe7 29 c7 ♖xe2 30 ♖d8+ ♔g7 31 ♔f1 1-0 Yakovich-Arkell, Hastings 1993/4.

10 ♘g5 *(D)*

10 ♖e1 is a more sedate positional approach, but after 10...♘bd7 11 ♖b1 White prepares to take advantage of Black's queenside weaknesses, and push his pawn majority, viz. 11...0-0

12 b4 ♖c8 13 ♘d2 a6 14 a4 ♘e8 15 ♘b3 f5 16 ♗f1 ♖f7 17 ♗d2 ♗f6 18 a5 (White has prepared well for this pawn lever, which gives him an outpost on a5 and isolates Black's a-pawn) 18...bxa5 19 ♘xa5 ± Malaniuk-Lysenko, Russia Cup (Ekaterinburg) 1997.

B

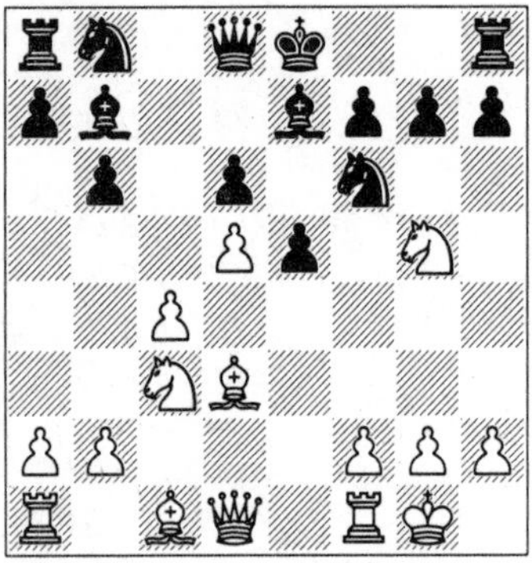

10 ... ♘bd7

Practice has also seen 10...0-0, which gets the king to relative safety and 10...h6, putting the immediate question to White's knight:

a) 10...0-0 11 f4 (this is an extremely desirable move, positionally speaking, as White introduces the ideas of either playing f5, making it harder for Black to push his kingside pawn majority, or as in the game opening the f-file, in order to attack the black king) 11...exf4? 12 ♗xf4 ♘bd7 13 ♕f3 ♖e8 14 ♕h3 ♘f8 15 ♖ae1 (White enjoys a clear advantage due to the superior mobility of his forces; at the same time his space advantage hampers the manoeuvrability of the black bishops) 15...a6 16 ♗d2 ♕c8 17 ♕h4 h6 18 ♘xf7! (with most of White's pieces pointing towards the black king, this sacrifice highlights the weaknesses in Black's position and the lack of harmony in the black camp) 18...♔xf7 19 ♗xh6! gxh6 20 ♖xe7+! 1-0 Høi-U.Nielsen, Gausdal 1990.

b) 10...h6 11 ♘ge4 ♘xe4 12 ♘xe4 and now:

b1) 12...g6 (this is an extremely ambitious approach, aiming to push the kingside pawns before completing development) 13 f4 f5 14 fxe5 dxe5 (14...fxe4 15 ♗xe4 gives White a huge initiative for the piece) 15 ♘g3 ♗c8 16 ♘xf5 ♗xf5 17 ♗xf5 gxf5 18 ♕h5+ ♔d7 19 ♖xf5 ♔c7 20 ♖xe5 with three pawns and an attack for the piece, Danner-Siegel, Swiss Cht 1993.

b2) 12...0-0 13 ♕h5 ♘d7 14 ♗xh6! *(D)*.

B

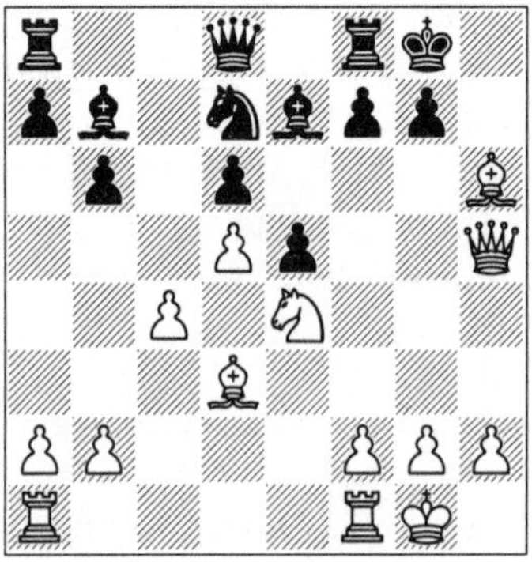

This intuitive piece sacrifice gives White a huge attack, with a perpetual check available as a 'safety net'. 14...gxh6 15 ♕xh6 f5 16 ♕g6+ ♔h8 17 f4 (White boldly goes for it, but this attempt to open lines gives Black just enough time to fend off the attack; 17 ♘g3 would be my suggested improvement as after 17...e4 18 ♘xf5 ♖xf5 19 ♗xe4 ♘f8 20 ♕h6+ ♔g8 21 ♗xf5 White has four pawns, a rook and an overwhelming position for two pieces) 17...fxe4 18 ♗xe4 ♘f6 19 ♕h6+ ♔g8 20 ♕g5+ ♔h8 21 ♕h6+ ♔g8 22 ♗g6 (White should have taken the perpetual check) 22...e4 23 f5 ♕c7 24 ♖f4 ♗d8 25 ♖h4 ♕g7 and Black has defended himself, K.Berg-Ward, London 1989.

11 f4 g6?

11...a6 is a more solid approach: 12 b3 ♕c7 13 a4 (White uses this standard push to dissuade Black from any ideas of ...b5 and to introduce the idea of ♗a3) 13...♕c5+ (this is too optimistic, but a more cautious approach such as 13...0-0 would allow White his normal plan of queenside expansion) 14 ♔h1 ♕d4 (this early queen sortie is easily repulsed and amounts to a clear loss of time) 15 ♕c2 ♘c5 16 ♗e2 e4 17 ♖d1 ♘d3 18 ♗xd3 exd3 19 ♖xd3 gave White a clear material and positional advantage in the game Kharkova-Litinskaya, Polish Cht (Lubniewice) 1994.

12 f5 h6

Black mistakenly kicks the white knight, assuming that it will retreat. 12...0-0 is a better option, although after 13 fxg6 hxg6 14 ♕e1, with the idea of ♕h4, White's attacking chances give him the edge.

13 ♘e6! *(D)*

B

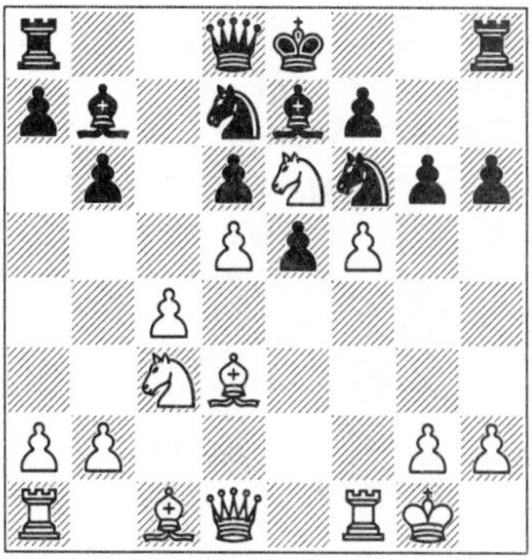

13 ... fxe6?

13...♕c8! 14 ♕a4 (with the idea of 15 fxg6 +−) 14...g5 15 ♘b5 fxe6 16 fxe6 ♘c5 17 ♘xd6++ *(D)* and now Polgar analysed:

B

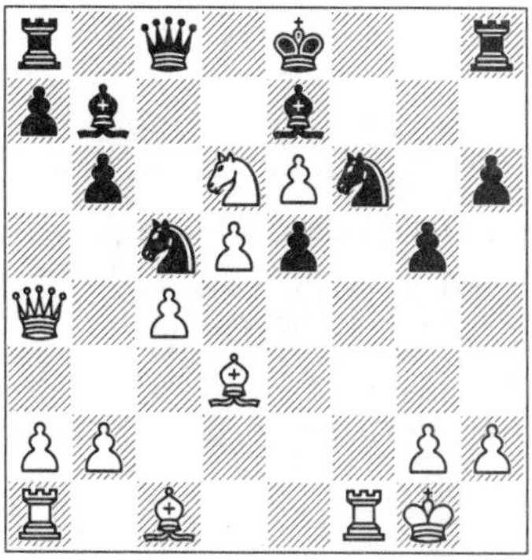

a) 17...♔f8 18 ♘xc8 ♘xa4 19 ♘xe7 ♔xe7 20 ♗c2 ♘c5 21 b4 ♘a6 (21...♘ce4? 22 ♗xe4 ♘xe4 23 ♖f7+ +−; 21...♘xe6 22 dxe6 ♔xe6 23 ♗b2 ±) 22 a3 ♖ac8 23 ♗b3 with the idea of 24 ♗b2 +−.

b) 17...♔d8 18 ♘f7+ ♔c7 19 ♕c2 ±.

14 fxe6 ♘f8

14...♘c5 15 ♗xg6+ ♔f8 16 b4 ♘a6 17 ♘e4 +–.

15 ♕a4+ **♘6d7**

16 c5! *(D)*

B

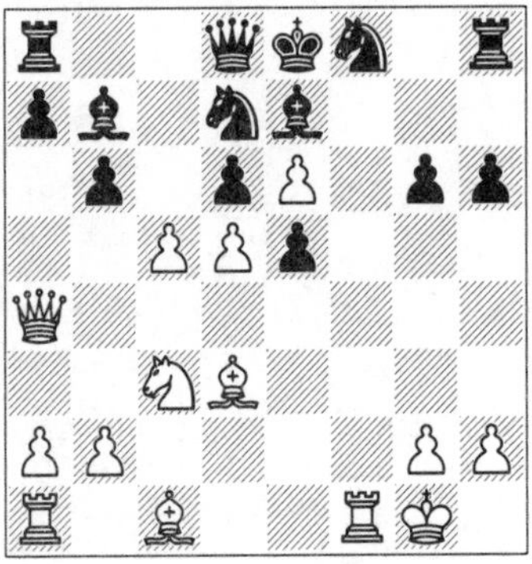

The light squares around the black king are a serious cause of concern.

16 ... **♗c8**

16...bxc5 17 exd7+ ♕xd7 (17...♘xd7 18 ♗xg6#) 18 ♗b5.

17 exd7+ **1-0**

White wins after 17...♗xd7 18 c6 ♗f5 19 c7+ ♕d7 20 ♗b5.

Classical Queen's Indian with ...d5

Game 29

Khalifman – Lobron

Groningen PCA qual 1993

1	**d4**	**♘f6**
2	**♘f3**	**e6**
3	**c4**	**b6**
4	**e3**	**♗b7**
5	**♗d3**	**c5**
6	**♘c3**	**♗e7**
7	**0-0**	**cxd4**
8	**exd4**	**d5** *(D)*

W

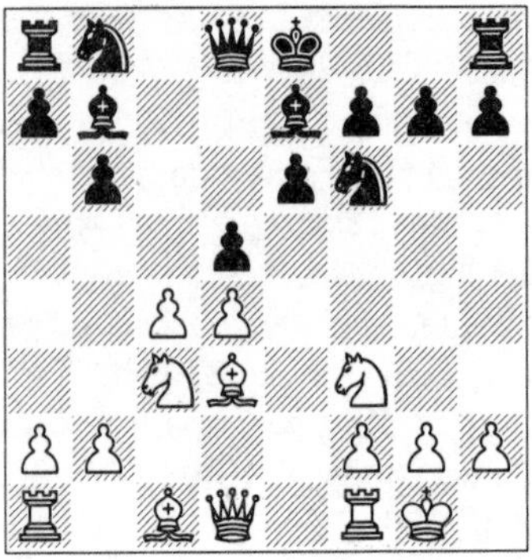

This is maybe Black's most classical approach to the position. Black grabs his share of central space, and in return White gets good attacking chances in the IQP positions that arise.

9 cxd5 **♘xd5**

9...exd5 keeps Black's share of space but leaves the b7-bishop poorly placed.

10 ♘e5

White introduces the threat of ♗b5+ and clears the path for White's queen to enter the fray.

10 ... **0-0**

11 ♕g4 **♘f6**

Black reintroduces a key defender of his kingside.

12 ♕h4 *(D)*

12 ♕h3!? is an untried suggestion by Keith Arkell.

12 ... **♘e4**

This very direct approach has scored reasonably for Black but I believe there is a way for White to gain the advantage. Black's main alternatives are:

B

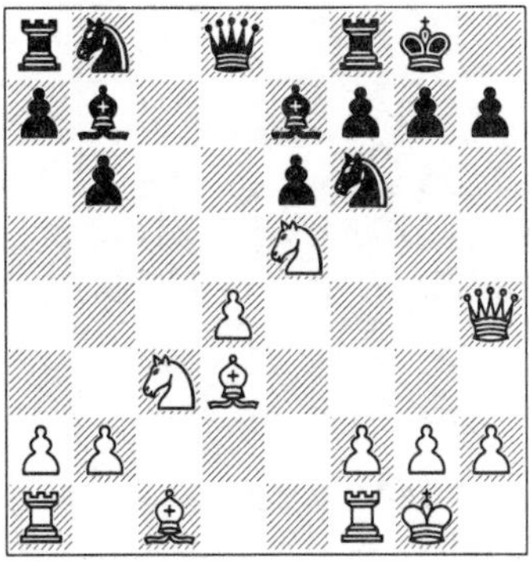

a) 12...♘bd7 (defensive; this is the most solid approach as long as Black continues to play that way!) 13 ♖d1 ♘e4? (13...♖e8 ± is better; then White will complete his development and play for a kingside attack) 14 ♕h3 ♘df6 (if Black thought he had the position firmly under control, he was rudely awaken by White's next) 15 d5! (this type of thematic central breakthrough shows why Black should keep the d4-pawn firmly blockaded) 15...♘xc3 16 bxc3 ♗xd5 17 ♗g5 and now:

a1) 17...h6 18 ♗xh6 gxh6 19 ♕xh6 (here the concealed attack of White's rook on d1 against the black queen on d8 makes defence almost impossible for Black) 19...♕c8 (or 19...♕e8; alternatively 19...♗d6 loses to 20 ♘g4 +−) 20 ♕g5+ ♔h8 21 ♘g4 ♘xg4 22 ♕h5+ ♔g7 23 ♕xg4+ ♔h8 24 ♕h5+ ♔g7 25 ♕h7+ ♔f6 26 ♕h6+ ♔e5 27 c4 ±.

a2) 17...g6 18 ♕h4! gives White a powerful attacking position as she threatens both c4 and ♘g4, Zsu.Polgar-Christiansen, San Francisco 1991.

b) 12...♘c6? (over-aggressive; this is a very careless, yet seemingly natural move, that an unsuspecting opponent might make without much thought) 13 ♗g5 (giving Black a choice of ways in which to lose) 13...g6 (13...♕xd4 14 ♘xc6 +−; 13...h6 14 ♗xf6 ♗xf6 15 ♕e4 +−; 13...♘xe5 14 ♗xf6 ♘xd3 15 ♗xe7 +−) 14 ♗a6! h6 (14...♗xa6 15 ♘xc6 +−; 14...♘xe5 15 ♗xb7 +−) 15 ♗xh6 ♘d5 16 ♕h3 (Black must lose at least the exchange) 16...♘xc3 17 ♗xb7 ♘e2+ 18 ♔h1 ♘cxd4 19 ♗xf8 ♗xf8 20 ♗xa8 ♕xa8 21 ♕e3 +− Plaskett-Arkell, London 1991.

13 ♕h3 ♕xd4 *(D)*

W

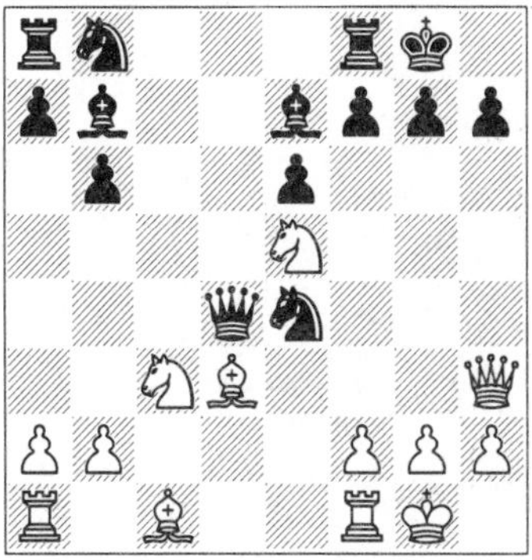

14 ♗f4

I recommend as an improvement 14 ♘xf7! ♖xf7 15 ♗xe4 ♗xe4 16 ♕g4 ♘c6 17 ♕xe4 ♕xe4 18 ♘xe4. At the end of the combination, which is mainly forced, White has a distinct endgame advantage due to the weak isolated pawn on e6 and his strong square on e4. Black has a long, arduous defence in front of him.

14	...	♘f6
15	♘e2	♕a4
16	b3	♕e8
17	♗g5	♘e4
18	♗f4	f5
19	♗c4	♗c5
20	b4	b5

½-½

White has some compensation for the pawn (but no more) in this murky position and I suspect both players were uncertain who was better.

6 Anti-Benoni

Introduction and Unusual Systems

Game 30

Hodgson – Martin Gonzalez

Seville 1987

1 d4 ♘f6

2 ♘f3 c5

With this move Black is trying to steer the game into a Benoni type of position. The problem for White is that there is no really good way to avoid this. What White can do, though, is enter a Benoni structure under his own terms and take a lot of the fun away from Black.

3 d5 *(D)*

B

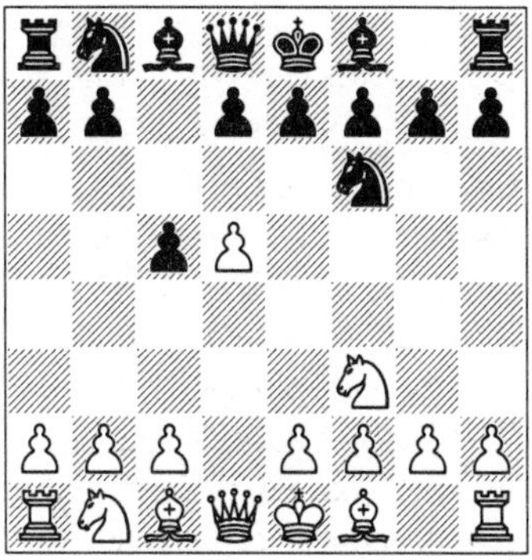

This forthright move, gaining space in the centre, is undoubtedly best. After 3 e3 g6 4 ♗d3 ♗g7 the benefits of Black's flexible development become apparent, as he has not yet committed himself to ...d5. White will have to choose between c3 and b3 at some stage but both moves will take us outside the scope of the repertoire. After 3 d5 Black is faced with a choice between direct central conflict and quiet development.

3 ... e6

This is the most direct move: Black challenges White to enter a Benoni with 4 c4. The Benoni is an extremely dangerous opening and play often becomes quite sharp. This is exactly what Benoni players want and I recommend a way of side-stepping the tactics.

One alternative is 3...c4, the so-called Hawk variation, which is a recommendation of Stefan Bücker. If White reacts sensibly it fails to impress. 4 ♘c3 ♕a5 5 ♗d2 (5 ♘d2 is the other theoretically approved way of getting the advantage, but the text-move is a lot less complex) 5...♘xd5 (more or less forced, else White will achieve a souped-up Benoni after e4) 6 e4 ♘xc3 7 ♗xc3 ♕c5 (after 7...♕c7 8 ♘d2 e6 9 ♗xc4 ♘c6 10 0-0 Black has problems unravelling his kingside) 8 ♕d4 ♕xd4 9 ♘xd4 a6 10 a4 b6 11 ♗xc4 (White has a large lead in development, which allows him to attack the black position) 11...♗b7 12 ♗d5 ♗xd5 13 exd5 e5 (Black drives away the strongly posted white knight; however, putting his pawns on dark squares only makes his bishop worse) 14 ♘f5 d6 15 ♔e2 ♔d7 16 ♘e3 ♔c7 (played in order to develop the queenside) 17 a5 b5 18 ♗d2 ♘d7 19 c4 (with a lead in development it is logical to open lines for your pieces to exploit) 19...bxc4 20 ♖hc1 ♔b7 21 ♖xc4 (the black kingside pieces are sitting idly by, but development is not easy) 21...♖c8 (21...♗e7 22 ♘f5) 22 ♖xc8 ♔xc8 23 ♖c1+ ♔b7 24 ♖c6 (targeting the weak points on a6 and d6) 24...♘f6 25 ♖b6+ ♔a7 26 ♗b4 ♗e7 27 ♗xd6 ♗xd6 28 ♖xd6 and White converted his material advantage in Høi-Liardet, Geneva 1991.

4 ♘c3 ♕a5

This attempt to hold up the e4 advance and prepare queenside counterplay falls short. Another possibility is 4...g6 5 e4 d6 (to prevent e5) 6 ♗b5+ ♗d7 7 dxe6 (highlighting the drawbacks in Black's move-order; 7 ♗xd7+ is also not bad, as after 7...♕xd7 8 0-0 ♗g7 9 dxe6 fxe6 10 ♗f4 e5 11 ♗g5 0-0 12 ♗xf6 ♗xf6 13 ♘d5 ♘c6 14 c3 White enjoyed a positional advantage in Vaisman-Nemirovski, France 1989) 7...fxe6 8 ♗g5 ♗xb5 9 e5!? (the simple 9 ♘xb5 ♕a5+ 10 ♕d2 ♕xb5 11 ♗xf6 is better for White, as Black has some work to do to get his king to safety, for example 11...♖g8 12 ♘g5 ♕d7 13 0-0-0 ±) 9...♗e7? (blundering away a piece; 9...♘bd7 is more stubborn) 10 exf6 ♗xf6 11 ♗xf6 ♕xf6 12 ♘xb5 +– ♘a6 13 ♘xd6+ ♔e7 14 ♘e4 ♕f4 15 ♕e2 ♖hf8 16 0-0 ♖ac8 17 ♖ad1 ♘b4 18 ♖fe1 e5 19 ♕b5 ♖c7 20 ♘xc5 1-0 Sukharisingh-Traut, Wiesbaden 1988.

5 ♗d2 *(D)*

B

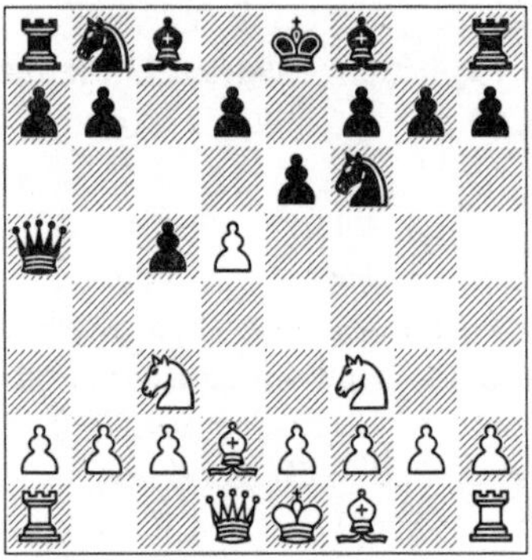

5 ... b5

The only sensible continuation. The alternative 5...♕b6 has been treated very roughly: 6 e4 g6 7 ♘e5 (with the idea of ♘c4) 7...♕c7 8 ♘c4 a6 9 ♕f3 (due to Black's time-wasting, White has been able to build a large initiative through simple moves) 9...♗g7 10 ♗f4 ♕d8 11 ♘d6+ ♔f8 12 ♗g5 exd5 13 ♘xd5 1-0 Morant-Jarvela, Finnish Cht 1986.

6 ♘e4 ♕d8

6...♕b6 keeps the queen active but allows White to weaken the black kingside: 7 ♘xf6+ gxf6 8 e4 ♖g8 (all other moves simply allow White a big advantage after c4 and ♗c3) 9 c4 bxc4 10 ♗c3 ♗b7 11 ♗xc4 (White sacrifices the g-pawn to accelerate his attack) 11...♖xg2 12 ♘h4 ♖g5 13 ♕e2 ♗e7 14 0-0-0 ♗a6 15 ♗xa6 ♕xa6 16 ♕f3 ♕xa2 17 e5! with a big initiative and full compensation for the sacrificed material, Åkesson-Hector, Malmö 1986.

7 ♘xf6+ ♕xf6
8 e4

The big problems for Black here are his severely misplaced queen and queenside pawn weaknesses.

8 ... ♕g6
9 ♕e2 ♗e7
10 0-0-0 0-0
11 ♘e5 ♕f6
12 ♘g4 ♕g6

This is Black's sixth queen move by move 12, a sure sign that the opening hasn't gone according to plan.

13 h4

White already has a large advantage and, to add insult to injury, the queen is now used as a target to start White's kingside attack.

13 ... exd5
14 exd5 ♕d6
15 g3 c4?

Black is fiddling while his position burns. It is no surprise that this attempt at a 'pawn-storm' fails with all the queenside pieces undeveloped.

16 ♗g2 ♗b7
17 ♗f4

Winning material or forcing mate!

17 ... ♕c5
18 d6 ♗xg2
19 dxe7 ♖e8
20 ♘f6+! *(D)*

A nice finishing touch.

B

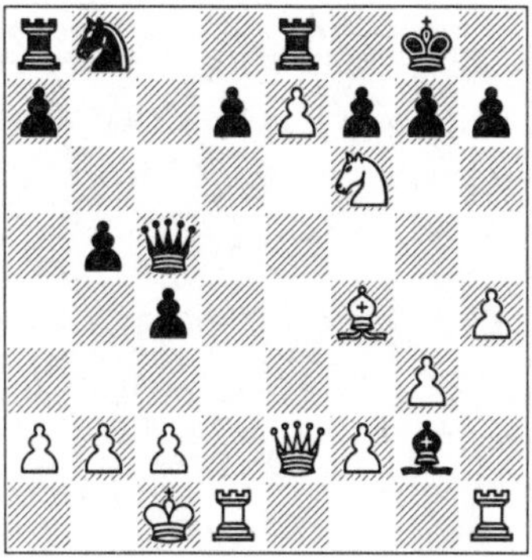

20 ... gxf6
21 ♕g4+ 1-0

21...♔h8 22 ♗h6 would be the humiliating end.

4...exd5

Game 31
Karpov – Topalov
Dos Hermanas 1994

1 d4 ♘f6
2 ♘f3 c5
3 d5 e6
4 ♘c3 ♘xd5
5 ♘xd5 exd5
6 ♕xd5 ♗e7
7 e4 0-0
8 ♗e2!? *(D)*

This is Karpov's new idea in this variation. Previously, only the more natural-looking 8 ♗c4 had been tried. This is still a viable alternative, but has the problem that White often has to lose time defending the bishop after Black plays a later ...♗e6. After the text-move this is not a problem.

B

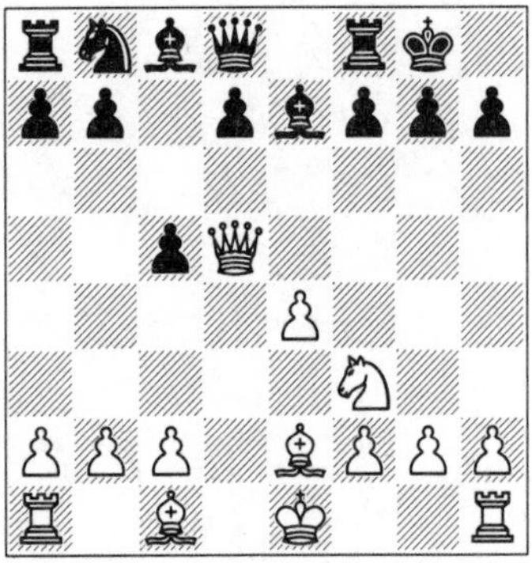

8 ... d6
9 0-0 ♘c6

9...♘d7 10 ♖d1 ♘f6 11 ♕d3 is a little better for White, who can intensify his bind on d5 by c4.

10 c3

The key to this variation for White is to keep a careful eye on Black's freeing ...d5 break, which, although difficult to prevent in the long run, must be discouraged at present. Here White prevents 10...♘b4 followed by ...d5.

10 ... ♗e6
11 ♕h5 h6!?

The immediate 11...d5 can be met by 12 ♖d1 d4 (forced) 13 e5!? with a space advantage and attacking chances on the kingside.

12 ♖d1 ♖e8
13 ♗f4 ♗f8!

Black is defending accurately and threatens to harass the white queen with ...g6.

14 ♘d2 *(D)*

To make space for the lady.

14 ... g6
15 ♕f3 d5

B

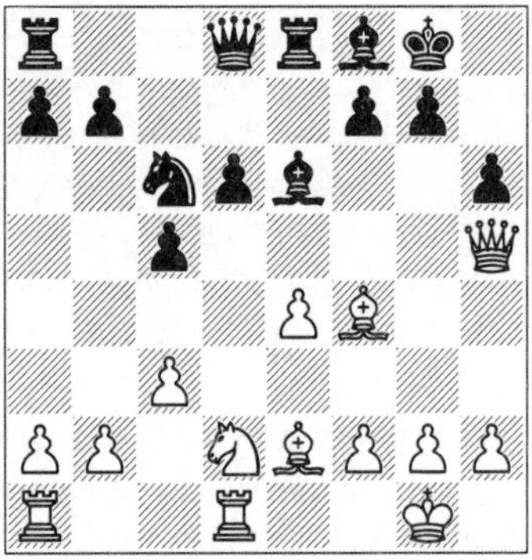

The only problem Black has to watch now is tactics on the d-file.

16 ♕g3 ♕e7
17 exd5 ♗xd5
18 ♗f1 ♕f6
19 ♘b3

This position seems completely equal, which makes it even more impressive how Karpov gradually creeps up on his top-class opponent.

19 ... ♖ad8
20 ♖d2

White's main idea for the moment is to try to gain control of the d-file without allowing too many simplifying exchanges.

20 ... ♗e6
21 ♗c7! *(D)*

This is a key component in wresting control of the d-file.

21 ... ♖xd2
22 ♘xd2 ♗f5
23 ♘c4 ♖e4
24 ♘e3 ♗c8
25 ♖d1

Mission accomplished! The d-file now belongs to White – thus the first

B

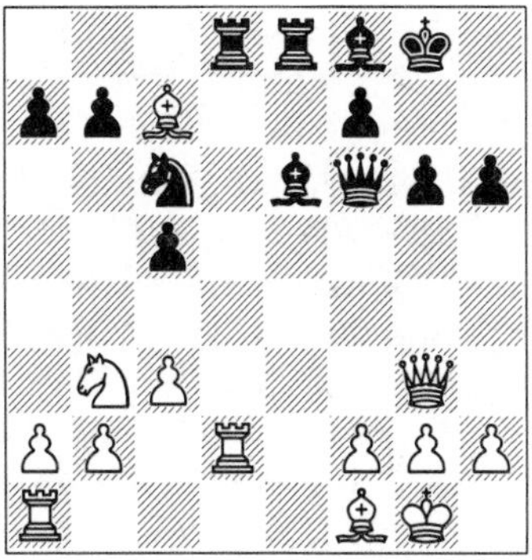

small advantage is accumulated. The knight on e3 is significant in reducing Black's possibilities on the e-file.

25 ... ♖e8
26 h3 ♕g5
27 ♕f3

Karpov sticks to his policy of keeping pieces on the board.

27 ... ♔g7
28 ♗f4

Suddenly the black queen is embarrassed for squares.

28 ... ♕e7

Alternatives are no better: 28...♕h4 29 g3 doesn't help, while 28...♕h5 29 ♕xh5 gxh5 is not the sort of endgame to play against the master of exploiting small advantages, and 28...♕f6 29 ♗xh6+ loses the queen.

29 ♘d5 ♕e4
30 ♘f6!! *(D)*

This wonderful mini-combination forces a gain of material.

30 ... ♔xf6

30...♕xf3 31 ♘xe8+ +–.

31 ♗e5++ ♔xe5
32 ♕xe4+ ♔xe4

B

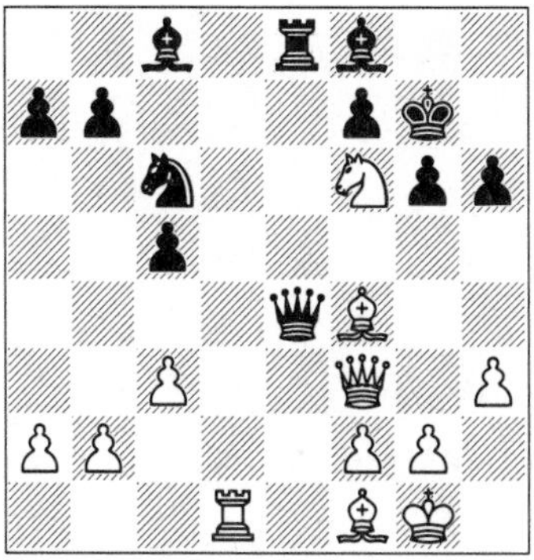

33 ♖e1+

This skewer followed by a fork of Black's two bishops was the fiendish idea behind White's 30th move.

33 ... ♔f5
34 ♖xe8 +– ♗e6
35 ♖xf8 ♗xa2
36 ♖c8 1-0

Black resigned, seeing no good answer to ♖c7 and not wanting an endgame lesson.

4...d6 5 e4: Alternatives to 5...exd5

Game 32
Speelman – Suba
Seville 1981

1 d4 ♘f6
2 ♘f3 c5
3 d5 e6
4 ♘c3 d6
5 e4 *(D)*

Black now has an important choice between exchanging on d5 (see the next game) and trying to retain some

B

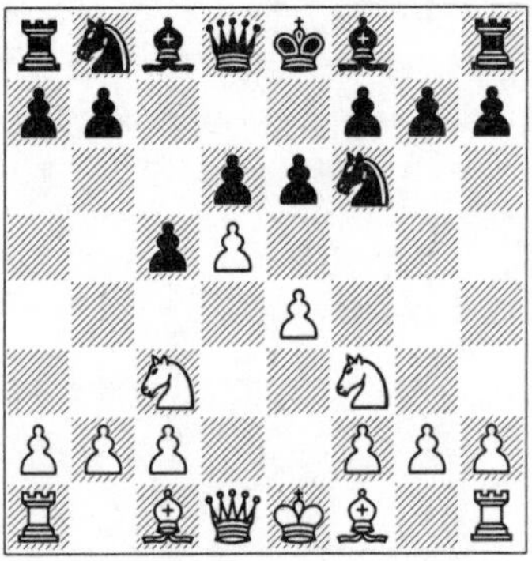

flexibility by delaying that exchange – we focus on the latter approach here.

5 ... a6

This is played to prevent the threat of ♗b5+. If 5...♗e7 then 6 ♗b5+ gives Black a choice of ways to reach an inferior position:

a) 6...♘bd7? (this is just plain bad) 7 dxe6 fxe6 8 ♘g5 (Black has no good way to prevent the knight's arrival on e6) 8...♕a5 9 ♘xe6 ♘xe4 (Black rests his meagre hopes on a counterattack but is helpless against the white onslaught) 10 ♘xg7+ ♔f7 11 ♕h5+ ♔xg7 12 ♗h6+ ♔f6 (12...♔g8 13 ♕d5#) 13 ♕f3+ 1-0 Machulsky-Rios, Philadelphia 1992. Black decided he'd had enough because after 13...♔g6 14 ♕xe4+ ♔xh6 15 ♕xe7 White will have recaptured the sacrificed material with interest and still have an awesome attack.

b) 6...♗d7 leads to a small endgame advantage for White after 7 dxe6 fxe6 8 e5 dxe5 9 ♘xe5 ♗xb5 10 ♕xd8+ ♗xd8 11 ♘xb5 0-0 12 ♗e3 (White is better on account of the weak isolated e-pawn; Black has a long, arduous defence in front of him) 12...♘a6 13 c3 ♘d5 14 ♗d2 ♖f5 15 ♘c4 ♗e7 16 0-0 ♖d8 17 ♘xa7 ♘ac7 18 a4 ♘f4 19 ♘b5 ♘cd5 20 ♖ae1 ♘f6 21 g3 ♘d3 22 ♖xe6 ♘xb2 23 ♘xb2 ♖xd2 24 ♘c4 ♖d7 25 ♘b6 1-0 Benjamin-Shaine, Boston 1988.

c) 6...♘fd7 7 dxe6 fxe6 8 ♘g5 ♗xg5 9 ♕h5+ g6 10 ♕xg5 ♕xg5 11 ♗xg5 ± Sharif-Luco, Cap d'Agde 1994. White enjoys the advantage of the two bishops and can target the weak d-pawn.

6 dxe6 ♗xe6

6...fxe6 7 e5 leads to a structural advantage for White.

7 ♘g5 b5

8 ♘xe6 fxe6

9 g3 *(D)*

B

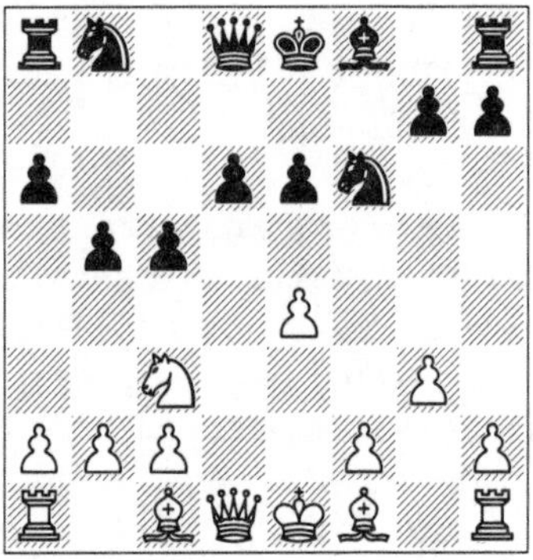

Tempting Black to win a pawn.

9 ... ♘c6

9...b4 10 ♘e2 ♘xe4 (Black wins a central pawn but falls behind in development with his king stuck in the centre) 11 ♗g2 d5 12 ♘f4 ♕f6 13 0-0

♖a7 (anticipating White's next) 14 ♘xd5! (White sacrifices anyway! – the black king's cover is ripped to shreds) 14...exd5 15 ♕xd5 ♘d6 16 ♗g5 +– (Black is defenceless against the onslaught) 16...♕d4 (16...♕f5 17 ♖fe1+ ♔d7 18 ♖e5 ♕g4 19 ♖d1 ♖c7 20 ♕f7+ ♔c8 21 ♖e8+ ♘xe8 22 ♕xe8#) 17 ♕e6+ ♖e7 18 ♗xe7 ♗xe7 19 ♖ad1 ♕f6 20 ♖xd6 1-0 Correa-Madeira, São Paulo 1991.

10 ♗g2 ♕c7

11 0-0

White is better due to his two bishops and his ability to target Black's vulnerable central pawns.

11 ... ♗e7

12 ♘e2 ♔f7

13 ♘f4 ♖he8

14 a4 b4

15 g4 *(D)*

B

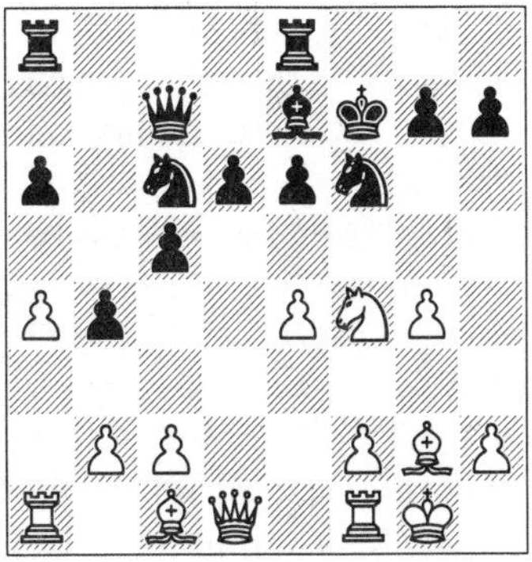

White's central space advantage allows him to attack on any part of the board at will, as indeed he has on the last three moves.

15 ... h6

16 h4

Threatening g5, which makes Black choose a radical solution...

16 ... g5

...but this creates a new target.

17 ♘h3 ♘h7

18 f4 *(D)*

B

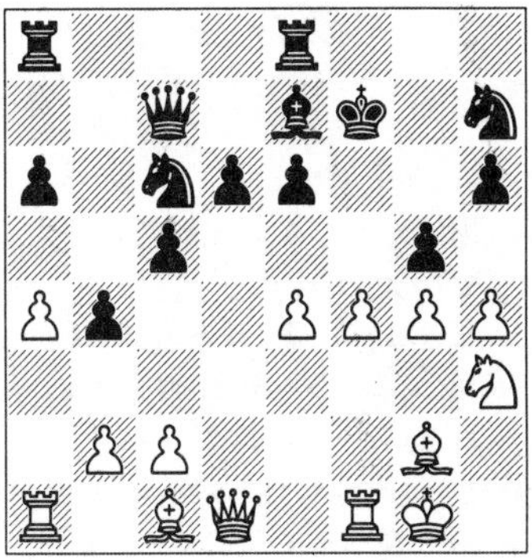

Blowing open the kingside. It may seem risky to play like this with White's king posted there but the g2-bishop defends White's monarch well – and creating chaos is a Speelman trademark.

18 ... ♔g7

19 hxg5 hxg5

20 fxg5 ♘e5

21 g6

White jettisons a pawn to give his pieces some breathing space and begin an attack on the dark squares.

21 ... ♘xg6

22 ♕d2 ♘hf8

23 ♘f4 ♘xf4

24 ♕xf4 ♗d8

25 e5

Grabbing some more dark squares.

25 ... d5
26 ♕h6+ ♔g8
27 ♖xf8+

A mini-combination to force a winning endgame.

27 ... ♖xf8
28 ♕xe6+ ♕f7
29 ♕xf7+ ♖xf7
30 ♗xd5 ♖c8
31 ♗e3 ♔g7
32 ♗xf7 ♔xf7
33 ♖f1+

Black could already resign with a clear conscience.

33...♔g7 34 ♔g2 ♗e7 35 e6 ♔g6 36 ♖f5 ♖c6 37 ♖e5 ♔f6 38 ♖e4 ♖d6

38...♖xe6 39 ♗g5+ ♔f7 40 ♖xe6 ♔xe6 41 ♗xe7 ♔xe7 is a won king and pawn endgame.

39 ♔f3 ♖d1

Seeking piece activity is a golden rule of most endgames but here Black has left himself with too steep a hill to climb.

40 b3 ♖d5 41 ♗f2 ♔g6 42 ♔e2 ♔g5 43 ♗g3 ♖d8 44 ♔f3 ♔g6 45 ♖f4 ♖d6 46 ♖f5 ♖d2 47 ♖f7 ♗f6 48 ♖f8 ♖xc2 49 ♗e5 ♗e7 50 ♖g8+ ♔h6 51 ♖e8 c4 52 ♖xe7 1-0

5...exd5 6 exd5

Game 33
Short – Eley
Rochdale 1977

1 d4 ♘f6
2 ♘c3 c5
3 d5 e6
4 e4 exd5
5 exd5

If given the chance I recommend White recaptures on d5 with the e-pawn.

5 ... d6
6 ♘f3 *(D)*

B

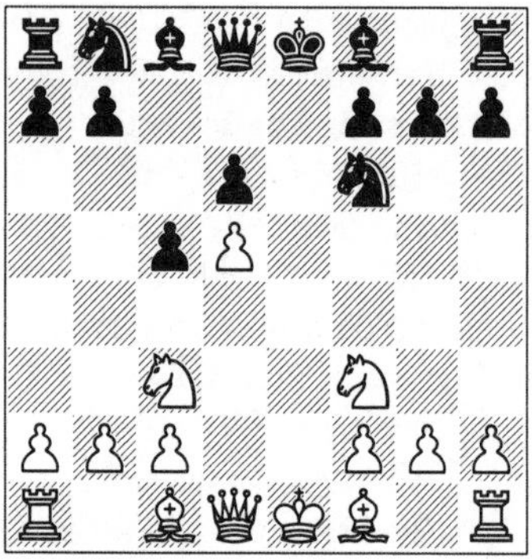

6 ... a6

The black systems in this section are by and large unambitious (6...♗g4 and 6...♗e7 lead to similar stodgy positions), the one exception being when Black attempts to fianchetto his dark-squared bishop, but this has its drawbacks, as we shall see. The basic plan for White is to develop sensibly and go for the b4 break on the queenside. I can't see the attraction of these lines for Black as he often is left with a dull, inferior position with hopes for a draw at best.

a) 6...♗g4 7 ♗e2 ♗e7 8 0-0 0-0 9 ♗f4 ♘a6 10 ♖e1 ♘c7 11 h3 ♗xf3 12 ♗xf3 ♖e8 13 a3 (White is now almost fully developed and can begin his queenside expansion) 13...♕d7 14 b4 cxb4 15 axb4 (if White can now achieve c4 he will have built up an impressive position; Black could seek to prevent this with ...b5 but then the a-pawn would be weak and White would try to exploit the hole on c6 – just imagine a white knight there) 15...♘b5 16 ♘e2 (White plans simply ♕d3 and c4) 16...♕f5 17 g4 (this is a very useful move, driving the black queen back and introducing the threat of g5) 17...♕c8 18 ♕d3 ♘c7 19 c4 ± (White has achieved all his goals and stands better) 19...♘a6 20 ♖ab1 ♗f8 21 ♖ec1 (Black is suffering from a lack of space, so White refuses to give Black the possibility of exchanging pieces at the moment) 21...♘d7 22 ♘d4 ♕d8 23 ♗g2 ♕f6 24 ♕d2 (the only source of counterplay for Black involves the e5-square, so White prepares to take that away from Black before proceeding with the main plan of advancing on the queenside) 24...h6 25 ♗g3 ♘e5 26 f4 ♘d7 27 ♗f2 ♘c7 28 ♘b3 ♖e7 29 c5 ± (with this next stage completed, White can claim a large advantage) 29...♖ae8 30 ♘d4 ♖e4 (this attempt to lash back inevitably fails, but Black was bound hand and foot in any case – it is not easy to sit back and wait for what slow torture your opponent has in mind for you next) 31 ♗xe4 ♖xe4 32 ♘f5 dxc5 33 bxc5 ♕a6 34 ♖a1 ♕b5 35 ♘d4 (trapping the black queen!) 35...♖xd4 36 ♕xd4 +– (White is two exchanges up – the rest only requires the barest technique) 36...♕b3 37 ♖c3 ♕b2 38 ♖d3 ♕c2 39 ♕c3 ♕xc3 40 ♖xc3 ♘xd5 (a mini-victory for Black: finally one of his minor pieces achieves what the others have only dreamt about – activity! Alas, it is not enough to save the game) 41 ♖c4 g5 42 ♖xa7 ♘xf4 43 ♖xb7 ♘e5 44 ♖xf4 gxf4 45 ♔g2 h5 46 gxh5 f6 47 ♖c7 ♗h6 48 c6 f3+ 49 ♔f1 1-0 Mohandesi-Pearson, Erevan OL 1996.

b) 6...♗e7 7 ♗e2 0-0 8 0-0 *(D)* and now:

B

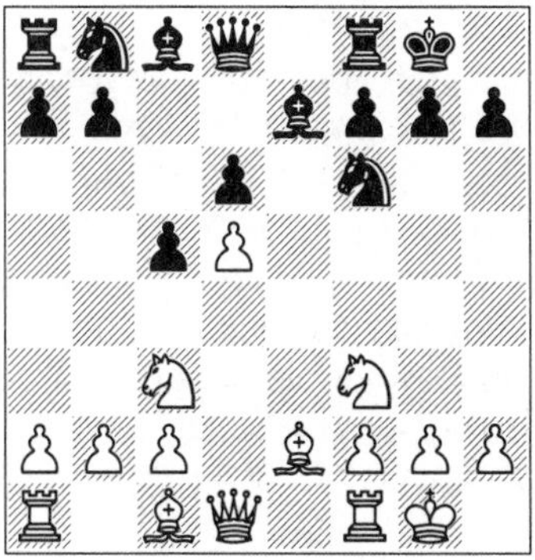

b1) 8...♘a6 (this should be met with similar treatment to that in line 'a') 9 ♖e1 ♘c7 10 a4 a6 11 ♖b1 ♗g4 12 b4 (again this is the key move) 12...♘d7 13 ♗f4 ♗xf3 14 ♗xf3 cxb4 15 ♘e4 (this clever move is designed to prevent Black's knight from reaching its ideal square on c5; the temporary loss of a pawn is of small importance) 15...♘f6 16 ♘g3 a5 17 c3 ♖e8 (17...bxc3 18 ♖xb7 leaves Black with a cramped position and no way, in the long term, to hang on to his c-pawn; nevertheless, this must be superior to the text-move, which leaves him with additional weakness on the queenside) 18 cxb4 ♗f8 19 ♖xe8 ♘cxe8 20 ♗d2 axb4 21 ♖xb4 ± (now to go with his space advantage and bishop-pair, White has a target on the b-file) 21...b6 22 ♗e3 ♘d7 23 ♗e2 ♘c5 24 ♗b5 ♘f6 25 ♗c6 (the bishop is ideally placed here in the heart of Black's position, combining attack with defence) 25...♖a7 26 ♕b1 ♘fd7 27 ♘f5 ♕f6 28 ♗d4 (the white pieces coordinate extremely effectively) 28...♕g6 29 ♘e3 ♘d3 30 ♗xb6 (White cashes in and picks up a material advantage in exchange for the bishop-pair) 30...♘xb6 31 ♖xb6 ♘c5 32 ♕xg6 fxg6 33 ♖b4 +– ♔f7 34 ♘c4 ♔e7 35 h4 ♔d8 36 ♖b8+ ♔e7 37 a5 (to add to Black's already significant problems, knights are particularly ineffective when dealing with passed rooks' pawns) 37...♔f7 38 ♗e8+ ♔e7 39 ♗b5 ♔f7 40 ♖b6 ♗e7 41 a6 ♔f6 42 ♘a5 ♗d8 43 ♖xd6+ 1-0 San Segundo-Cacho, Linares Z 1995.

b2) 8...b6?! (this move just looks slow) 9 ♖e1 ♘a6 10 ♗b5! (White threatens ♕e2 winning a piece; already Black's careless eighth move looks misjudged) 10...♘b8 (a pathetic retreat; however, 10...♘c7 11 ♗c6 ♖b8 12 ♕e2 wins the bishop on e7) 11 ♕e2 (this begins a forced variation which leads to an endgame advantage for White; it is also possible to play in the middlegame with the restraining 11 a4) 11...a6 12 ♕xe7 ♕xe7 13 ♖xe7 axb5 14 ♗g5 (threatening to take the knight followed by either ♘e4 or ♘b5) 14...♘bd7 (the only move) 15 ♘xb5 ♘xd5 16 ♘xd6! f6 (16...♘xe7 17 ♗xe7 ±) 17 ♘xc8 ♘xe7 18 ♘xe7+ ♔f7 19 ♘d5 fxg5 20 ♘xg5+ ♔g8 21 f3 (White has a clear advantage with two pawns and two dominating knights for the exchange) 21...♖ae8 22 ♖d1 (White creates a potential attack on the black knight and plans ♘e4) 22...♘f6!? (Black sacrifices another pawn in a bid to make his rooks active; 22...♖e2 23 ♘c3 reveals one of the points behind White's last move, viz. 23...♖e7 24 ♘ge4) 23 ♘xb6 ♖e2 24 ♖c1 ♖d8 25 ♘c4 ♖d4 (Chandler points out in *Informator* that 25...♘d5 loses to 26 ♔f1 ♘f4 27 ♘h3) 26 ♔f1 ♖e7 27 b3 h6 (or 27...♘d5 28 ♘e4) 28 ♘h3 ♘d5 29 ♘f2 ♘c3 (Black is doing his utmost to keep the white knight out of e4) 30 a4 (trying to tempt Black into a faulty combination and releasing the passed a-pawn at the same time) 30...♖h4 (Chandler gives 30...♘xa4 31 c3 ♖xc4 32 bxc4 ♘b6 33 ♘e4 with a winning endgame for White) 31 h3 ♘a2 32 ♖a1 ♘b4 33 c3 ♘c2 34 ♖c1 ♘e3+ 35 ♘xe3 ♖xe3 36 ♘e4 (the knight finally arrives on its most desirable square and White has a winning advantage) 36...c4 37 b4 ♖f4 38 ♘c5 ♖f5 39 a5 ♖d5 40 ♘e4 ♖ed3 41 ♔e2 ♖b5 42 ♖a1 ♖d7 43 a6 ♖a7 44 ♘c5 ♖b6 45 ♔e3 1-0 Chandler-Mi.Tseitlin, Palma de Mallorca 1989.

c) 6...g6 *(D)*.

This is inaccurate because Black doesn't have time to fianchetto and get his king to safety. 7 ♗b5+ ♘bd7 8 0-0

W

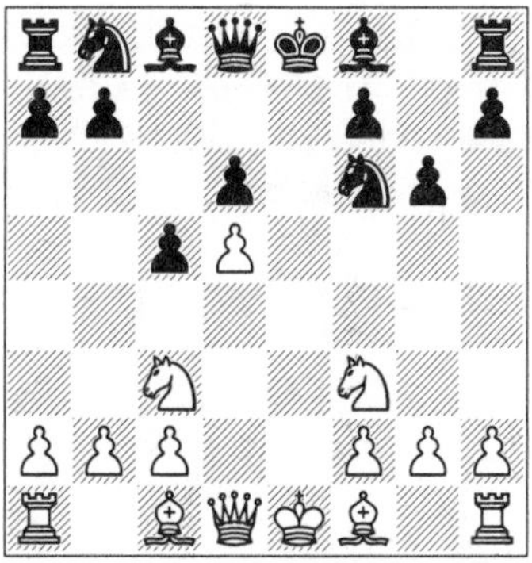

B

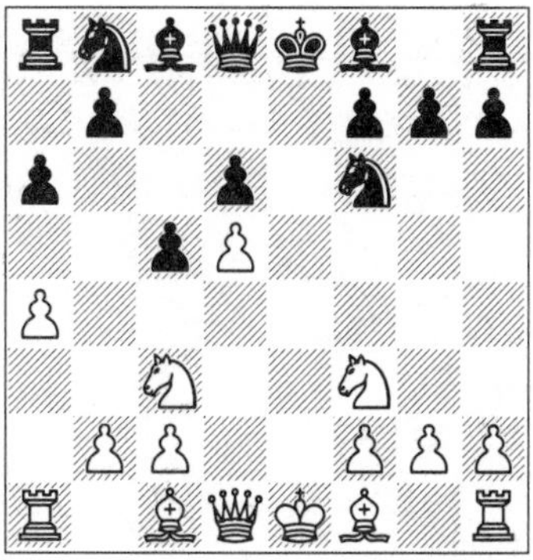

♗g7 9 ♖e1+ ♔f8 10 ♗f4 (the misplaced black king already gives White a large advantage) 10...♕c7 11 ♕e2 ♔g8 12 ♘g5 ♘b6 13 ♘ge4 (Black is in no position to defend his weak d6-pawn with both rooks still out of play) 13...♘xe4 14 ♘xe4 ♘xd5 (Black holds on to material equality for the moment, but the opening of another central file hugely favours White's better developed forces; 14...♗f8 15 ♘f6+ ♔g7 16 ♘e8+) 15 ♗xd6 ♕d8 16 ♖ad1 ♗e6 17 ♗c4 ♘c7 18 ♘xc5 ♗xc4 19 ♕xc4 ♘e8 20 ♗g3 ♕f6 21 ♘d7 ♕c6 22 ♕xc6 bxc6 23 ♘b8! 1-0 Kharitonov-Gutierrez, Bayamo 1989. Black is helpless against a back-rank invasion.

7 a4 *(D)*

7 ... ♗g4

7...g6 8 ♗f4! (this move casts doubt on Black's entire strategy of fianchettoing his dark-squared bishop) 8...♗g7 9 ♕e2+ ♔f8 (9...♕e7 10 ♗xd6 wins a clear pawn) 10 h3 ♘h5 11 ♗e3 ♘d7 12 ♕d2 ♘e5 13 ♗e2 ♘xf3+ 14 ♗xf3 f5 (Black makes some *luft* for his king but weakens his position at the same time) 15 ♗xh5 gxh5 16 0-0 ± ♗d7 17 ♖fe1 b5 18 axb5 axb5 19 ♗g5 ♕c8 20 ♗e7+ (again the poor positioning of the black king leads to a material disadvantage and his majesty's early retirement) 20...♔g8 21 ♖xa8 ♕xa8 22 ♗xd6 b4 23 ♖e7 h6 24 ♖xd7 bxc3 25 bxc3 ♕a1+ 26 ♔h2 ♕xc3 27 ♕e2 1-0 Chuchelov-Evers, Goch 1991.

8 ♗e2 ♗xf3

9 ♗xf3 ♘bd7

10 0-0 ♗e7

This more passive development of Black's bishop makes his position a lot harder to crack.

11 ♗f4 0-0

12 ♕d2 ♖e8

13 ♖fe1 ♘f8

14 ♘e4 *(D)*

Rather than going for the more ambitious plan of b4, White is content to exchange pieces and rely on the power of the two bishops.

14 ... ♘xe4

15 ♗xe4 ♗f6

16 c3 ♕d7

17 ♕d3 ♕c7

B

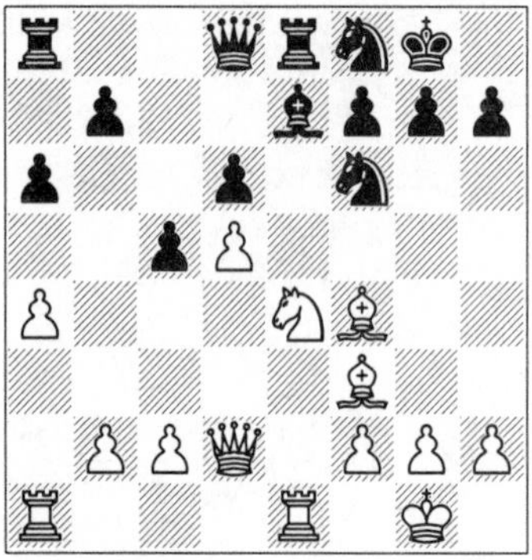

18 ♗f5 g6
19 ♗h3 ♖e7
20 ♖xe7 ♕xe7
21 ♔f1 ♖e8
22 ♕d2

White prepares to trade pieces on the e-file and enter an advantageous endgame.

22 ... ♕e4?

Black counterattacks and insists on piece activity but perhaps underestimated the power of White's passed d-pawn.

23 ♗xd6 ♕c4+
24 ♔g1 ♖e2
25 ♕f4 ♕xf4
26 ♗xf4 ♖xb2
27 d6 ♘e6
28 ♗xe6 fxe6
29 ♖d1

Despite material equality White has a winning advantage, as the d-pawn is a monster.

29 ... ♔f7
30 d7 ♗d8
31 h4

Black has to lose a piece.

31...h6 32 ♗xh6 b5 33 ♗g5 ♗a5 34 axb5 axb5 35 d8♕ ♗xd8 36 ♖xd8 b4 37 cxb4 cxb4 38 ♖b8 e5 39 g4 b3 40 h5 gxh5 41 gxh5 e4 42 ♖b7+ 1-0

Black delays ...d6

Game 34
Khuzman – Minasian
Pula Echt 1997

1 d4 ♘f6
2 ♘f3 c5
3 d5 g6
4 ♘c3 ♗g7
5 e4 0-0? *(D)*

This provocative move seeks to keep maximum flexibility in the black position. Black avoids 5...d6 6 ♗b5+ and may sometimes try to do without ...d6 altogether. My recommendation is that you allow yourself to be provoked!

W

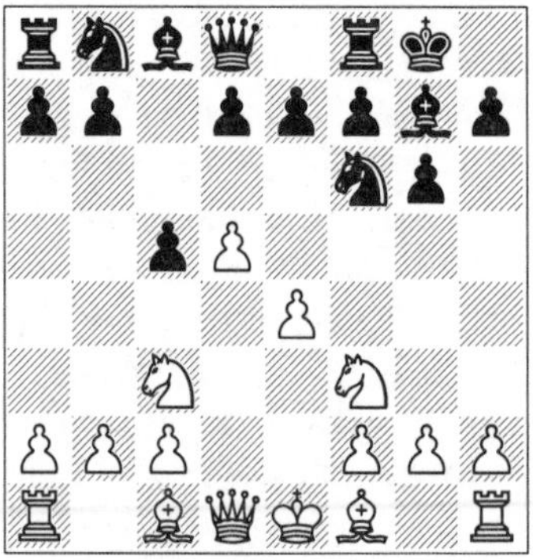

6 e5!

White goes for it! The way to refute Black's ambitious opening is to attack full steam ahead.

6 ... ♘g4

It was originally thought that the white pawns were overextended and this, together with Black's lead in development, would give Black at least an equal game. However, White's next move, which was a suggestion of Yermolinsky, puts that assessment into question.

The alternative, 6...♘e8, fares no better, as White can launch a powerful kingside attack by 7 h4! d6 8 e6! (this sacrifice plays an essential part in weakening Black's kingside pawn-structure) 8...fxe6 9 h5 (White goes all-out for the kill) and now *(D)*:

B

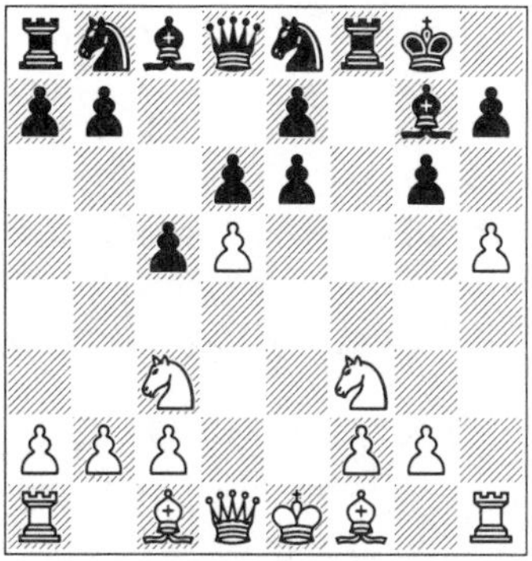

a) 9...gxh5!? 10 dxe6! ♘f6 (or 10...♗xe6 11 ♘g5 with a huge attack) 11 ♘g5 with a wonderful attacking position for White.

b) 9...exd5 10 hxg6 hxg6 11 ♕xd5+ e6 12 ♕d3 (White targets the 'weakie' on g6 created by his 8th and 9th moves) 12...♖f5 13 ♘h4 (forcing Black to give up material to relieve his beleaguered king) 13...♘c6 (13...♖h5? 14 ♕xg6 ± leaves White with an investment-free attack) 14 ♘xf5 gxf5 15 ♗h6 (it is normal practice to try to remove as many defenders from the enemy king as possible) 15...♘e5 16 ♕d2 ♕f6 17 ♗b5 ♗d7 18 ♗xd7 ♘xd7 19 ♗xg7 ♔xg7 20 0-0-0 (White is now fully developed and ready to start the next wave of his attack) 20...♘e5 21 ♖h3 ♘f7 22 ♘e2 ♔f8 (22...e5 {to stop ♘f4} would be met by 23 ♘c3, taking advantage of the newly weakened d5-square) 23 ♘f4 ♖d8 24 ♖e1 ♘g7 25 ♖h7 (gradually White begins to pile on the pressure) 25...♘g5 26 ♖xg7 ♕xg7 (26...♔xg7?? 27 ♘h5+) 27 ♖xe6 with a very big plus for White due to Black's weak king. Yermolinsky-Khmelnitsky, USA Ch (Modesto) 1995 finished 27...♘f7 28 ♘g6+ ♔g8 29 ♘e7+ ♔f8 30 ♘g6+ ♔g8 31 f4! ♕h7 32 b3! d5 33 ♕c3 d4 34 ♕xc5 ♕h1+ 35 ♔b2 d3 36 ♘e7+ ♔g7 37 ♘xf5+ ♔h7 38 ♕e7 ♕h5 39 ♖h6+ ♕xh6 40 ♕xf7+ 1-0.

7 ♘g5! *(D)*

B

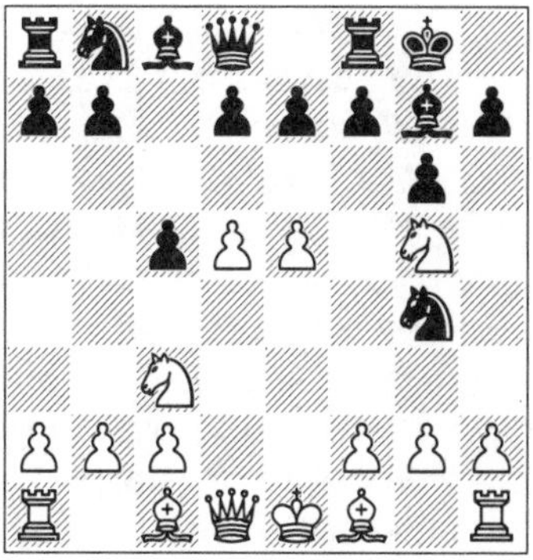

This new idea presents severe difficulties for Black.

7 ... ♘h6

7...♘xe5 leaves the knight stranded and after 8 f4 f6 (forced; 8...h6 9 ♘h3 wins a piece for White) 9 ♘xh7! ♔xh7 10 fxe5 fxe5 11 ♗d3 White threatens a very nasty check on h5.

7...h5 weakens the kingside. Then 8 f4 (intending h3 and g4) 8...d6 9 e6 gives White an interesting attacking position.

8 h4

Sounding the charge.

8 ... f6

8...♗xe5 (a very greedy move) 9 h5 gives White a murderous attack, as Baburin has analysed: 9...♘f5 (forced; 9...♗g7 10 ♘xh7! ♔xh7 11 hxg6+ fxg6 12 ♗xh6 ♗xh6 13 ♕d2 g5 14 ♕xg5 ♖f6 15 ♗d3+ +–) 10 ♘xh7!! ♔xh7 11 hxg6+ ♔g7 12 ♖h7+ ♔g8 13 ♕h5 fxg6 14 ♕xg6+ ♗g7 15 ♗h6 ♖f7 16 ♗d3 +–.

9 ♘ge4 ♘f7

After 9...fxe5 White just ploughs on with 10 h5 ♘f5 11 hxg6 hxg6 12 d6!, creating chaos in the black camp.

10 h5!

By now it should be becoming clear that White values his kingside attack (quite rightly) as more important than his e-pawn.

10 ... f5

After 10...♘xe5 11 hxg6 hxg6 12 f4 ♘f7 13 ♕g4 Black is in deep trouble, while 10...fxe5 11 hxg6 hxg6 12 ♕g4 leaves White with an imposing position.

11 ♘g5 ♘xg5

As Baburin has analysed, both captures on e5 lead to mate:

a) 11...♘xe5 12 ♘xh7! ♔xh7 13 hxg6+ ♔g8 14 ♕h5 ♖e8 15 ♕h7+ ♔f8 16 ♗h6 +–.

b) 11...♗xe5 12 ♘xh7! *(D)* and now:

B

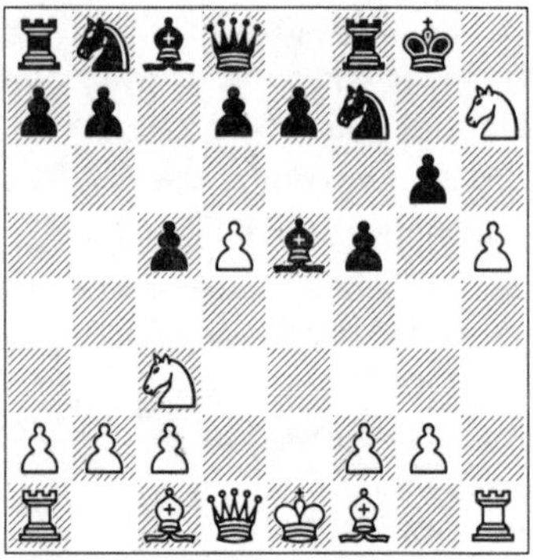

b1) 12...♔xh7 13 hxg6++ ♔xg6 14 ♕h5+ ♔f6 15 ♕h4+ ♔g6 16 ♕h7+ ♔f6 17 ♗g5+! ♔xg5 18 ♖h5+ ♔f6 19 ♖xf5#.

b2) 12...♗xc3+ 13 bxc3 ♔xh7 14 hxg6++ ♔xg6 (the complications are in White's favour – he enjoys a great lead in development and his attack is irresistible) 15 ♕h5+ ♔f6 16 ♕h4+ and here:

b21) 16...♔g6 17 ♖h3 +–.

b22) 16...♔e5 17 ♗f4+! ♔xd5 18 ♗b5! e5 19 0-0-0+ ♔e6 20 ♗c4+ d5 21 ♗xd5+ ♕xd5 22 ♖xd5 ♔xd5 23 ♕e7 +–.

b23) 16...♔g7 17 ♗h6+ ♘xh6 18 ♕xh6+ ♔f7 19 ♕h7+ ♔f6 20 ♖h6+ ♔e5 21 ♕g7+ ♖f6 22 ♖h8 +–.

12 ♗xg5 ♗xe5

12...h6 is also analysed by Baburin. White has a very attractive way to continue: 13 hxg6! hxg5 14 ♖h8+!! ♗xh8 15 ♕h5 ♖f7 (forced) 16 gxf7+ ♔g7 17 ♗d3 e6 18 0-0-0 with a winning attack due to the threat of ♖h1. White's pieces coordinate amazingly well, while Black's queenside remains asleep until the end of the game.

13 hxg6 hxg6

14 d6!

White introduces the idea of an attack on the a2-g8 diagonal.

14 ... ♗f6

15 ♗xf6 ♖xf6

After 15...exf6 (Baburin) White would have continued by 16 ♕d2 with a very strong attack.

16 ♗c4+ e6

16...♔g7 is met by 17 ♕d2, transferring the attack to the dark squares.

17 ♕d2 ♕f8

18 ♘d5! *(D)*

B

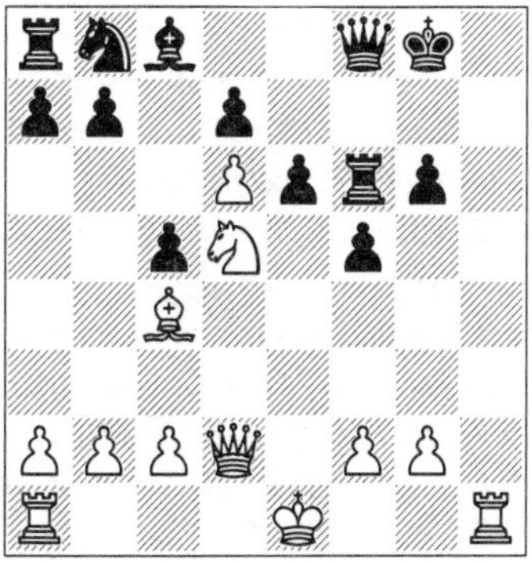

White insists that his bishop is invited to the party.

18 ... exd5

18...♖f7 19 ♘c7 +–.

19 ♗xd5+ ♖e6+

19...♖f7 is well met by 20 ♕g5 ♔g7 21 ♗xf7 ♔xf7 22 ♖h7+ ♔e6 23 ♕e7+! ♕xe7 24 dxe7 +–.

20 ♗xe6+ dxe6

21 ♕g5

The powerful passed d-pawn and White's monstrous initiative are too much for Black to cope with.

21 ... ♗d7

22 0-0-0 ♗e8

This allows White to tie Black up completely but even the more natural-looking 22...♘c6 doesn't stave off defeat after 23 ♖h6 ♗e8 24 d7 ♗f7 25 ♕h4! ♕g7 26 d8♕+ ♖xd8 27 ♖xd8+ ♘xd8 28 ♕xd8+ ♕f8 29 ♖h8+ ♔xh8 30 ♕xf8+.

23 ♕d8! 1-0

Black is helpless against the threat of d7.

Black delays or omits ...e6

Game 35

Speelman – Djurhuus

Copenhagen 1996

1 d4 ♘f6

2 ♘f3 c5

3 d5 g6

4 ♘c3 ♗g7

5 e4 d6

6 ♗b5+ *(D)*

The idea behind this check is to interfere with what has proved to be

B

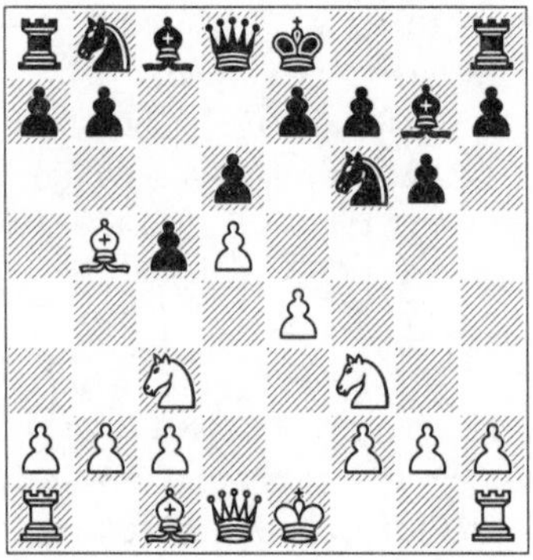

Black's most popular plan, namely to castle, play ...♘a6-c7 and perhaps ...♗g4. White hopes the check will disrupt this approach and force Black onto his own resources. Black has countered in three different ways in practice.

6 ... ♗d7

This is the best way for Black to block the check, but the alternatives also deserve attention:

a) 6...♘fd7 (perhaps the worst way of getting out of check with the exception of the ridiculous 6...♔f8; for no apparent reason, Black interferes with his own development) 7 a4! (again adopting a policy of making it difficult for Black to carry out his most likely plan; this move is directed against Black's expansion on the queenside by ...a6 and ...b5) 7...0-0 8 0-0 ♘a6 9 ♖e1 ♘c7 10 ♗c4 b6 11 ♗f4 (White's play is of course not solely concerned with limiting his opponent's possibilities; here he prepares e5, a major idea in this variation – White must open some lines in order to attack successfully) 11...♗a6 12 ♗xa6 ♘xa6 13 ♕e2 ♘c7 14 e5 (this is the thematic pawn-break, but I would prefer the preparatory ♖ad1 first) 14...dxe5 15 ♘xe5 ♘xe5 16 ♗xe5 *(D)* and now:

B

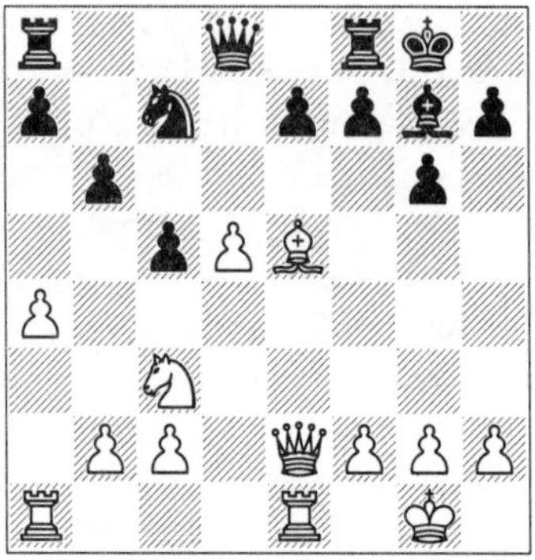

a1) 16...♗xe5? 17 ♕xe5 ♖e8 18 ♖ad1 (this is the position White would have aimed for with the more accurate 14 ♖ad1) 18...♕d7 19 ♘e4 ± (Black has no good way to prevent the crushing d6) 19...♖ad8 20 d6 f5 21 dxc7 ♕xd1 22 ♕e6+ 1-0 Pira-San Marco, Paris 1993.

a2) 16...♘xd5 is a good try for equality, e.g. 17 ♖ad1 (17 ♗xg7 ♔xg7 18 ♕e5+ ♘f6 19 ♕xe7 ♖e8) 17...♘xc3 18 ♗xc3 ♕c7 19 ♗xg7 ♔xg7 20 ♕xe7 ♕xe7 21 ♖xe7 ♖fe8 with fairly level chances.

b) 6...♘bd7 (this is more logical, but Black has some difficulties unravelling his queenside) 7 a4 0-0 8 0-0 a6 9 ♗e2 b6 10 ♗f4 ♘e8 11 ♕d2 ♘e5 (Black tries to keep e5 under lock and key) 12 ♗h6 ♘xf3+ (Black has to give ground in the centre, as White is ready to exchange both the knight on e5 and the bishop on g7 followed by f4, for example 12...♗d7 13 ♘xe5 dxe5 14 ♗xg7 ♔xg7 15 f4 ±) 13 ♗xf3 ♗xh6 14 ♕xh6 ♗d7 15 ♗e2 (White nevertheless prepares f4 followed by a central breakthrough) 15...♘f6 16 f4 ♕c7 17 ♕g5 ♔g7 18 e5 (at last!) 18...♘g8 19 exd6 exd6 20 f5 (the pawn exchanges have significantly weakened the squares around the black king – a fact that White is quick to exploit) 20...♘f6 21 ♖f4 h6 22 ♕g3 ♖ae8 23 ♖af1 ♗c8 24 h4 (White has built up his kingside attack patiently and now starts the second wave of attack) 24...♖e5 25 fxg6 fxg6 26 ♗d3 g5 (a painful move to have to make) 27 hxg5 hxg5 28 ♗f5 ♘h7 29 ♗xh7 ♖xf4 30 ♖xf4 ♔xh7 31 ♖f8 (the decisive infiltration) 31...♗f5 32 ♖xf5 ♖xf5 33 ♕d3 1-0 Züger-Bischoff, Altensteig 1993.

7 a4 0-0

7...♗xb5 is an anti-positional move that just serves to give White extra pressure along the a-file.

8 0-0 ♘a6

8...♗g4!? is an unpretentious way to play the position, but the tempo lost (...♗c8-d7-g4) is enough to ensure White a small advantage: 9 ♖e1 ♘bd7 10 h3 ♗xf3 11 ♕xf3 ♘e8 12 ♗f1 (the bishop is safely tucked away) 12...e5 (Black resorts to drastic measures to counter White's long-term plan of f4 and e5) 13 dxe6 fxe6 14 ♕e2 ♕e7 15 ♗e3 a6 and Black's central pawn weaknesses gave White the advantage in D.Gurevich-Mortazavi, London 1994.

9 ♖e1 ♘c7
10 ♗f1 ♗g4
11 h3 ♗xf3
12 ♕xf3 e6!? *(D)*

W

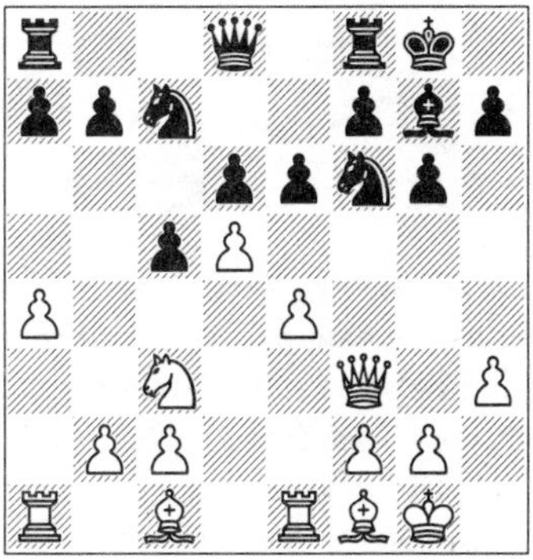

Again we see Black deciding to take action in the centre before White can organize a breakthrough himself.

13 ♗g5 h6
14 ♗h4 e5

After 14...exd5 15 exd5 ♖e8 16 ♖xe8+ ♘cxe8 17 ♗b5 ♕e7 18 ♔f1 White has the advantage in view of his bishop-pair and Black's inability to contest the e-file.

15 a5 ♘ce8

If 15...a6 to prevent White's next, then 16 ♖eb1 preparing b4 gives White the edge.

16 a6 *(D)*

16 ... ♖b8

Black decides he can't bear the pawn to remain on a6 and puts his hopes in counterplay along the b-file. 16...b6 17 ♗b5 gives White a nice

B

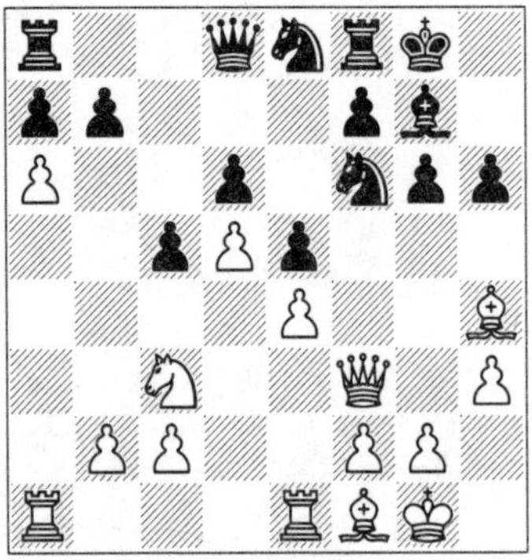

bind on the queenside and the possibility of organizing a pawn-break with either b4 or f4 at his leisure.

17 axb7 ♖xb7

18 ♘b5

The black a-pawn is a serious weakness.

18 ... ♕b8

19 c4 ♘h7

20 ♕a3 f5

In view of his positional problems, Black has to go for counterplay.

21 exf5 gxf5

22 ♘xa7 ♘g5

After 22...♖xb2 the black queen becomes overloaded: 23 ♘c6 ♕b7 24 ♘e7+ ♔f7 (24...♔h8 25 ♘g6+ +−) 25 ♘xf5 +−.

23 ♘c6 ♕c7

24 ♕g3 f4

25 ♕d3 *(D)*

Black's light-squared weaknesses become a crucial factor, enabling White to part with the exchange.

25 ... f3?!

After 25...e4 26 ♖xe4 ♘xe4 27 ♕xe4 the threats of ♗d3 and ♘e7+

B

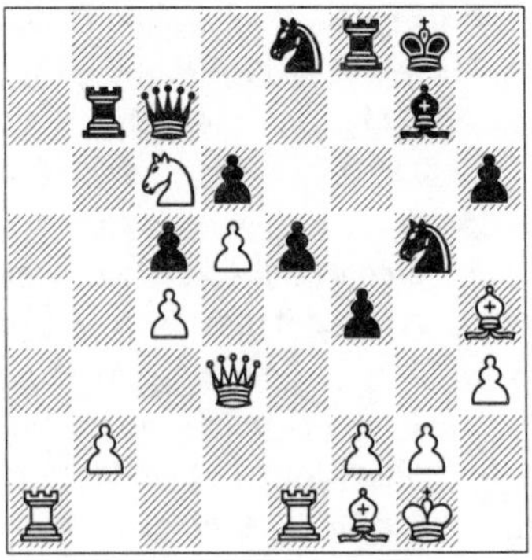

give White an overwhelming position.

26 ♗xg5

Threatening ♘e7+.

26 ... hxg5

27 g3!

White takes away one of Black's sources of counterplay.

27 ... ♘f6

27...♖xb2 can be met by 28 ♕g6 targeting g5 and introducing the idea of ♗d3-f5-e6.

28 ♕xf3 ♕d7! *(D)*

W

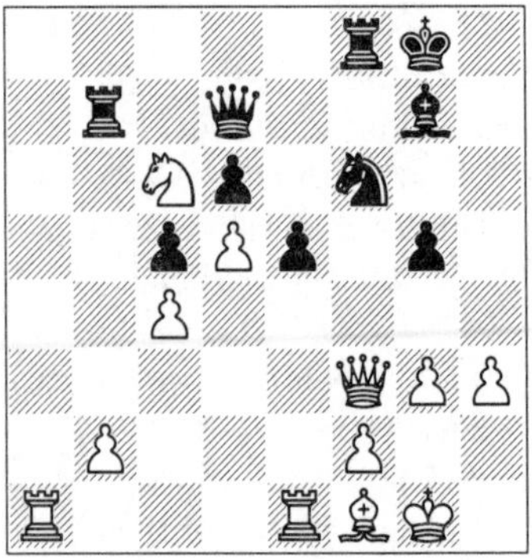

29 ♕e2

White is two pawns ahead and the rest is just a matter of restricting Black's counterplay.

29 ... ♕f5
30 ♗g2 g4
31 h4 ♗h6
32 ♖a7!

It's always a good idea to exchange pieces when material ahead.

32...♖xa7 33 ♘xa7 e4 34 ♕c2 ♖e8 35 ♘b5 ♕e5 36 ♘c3 ♔g7 37 ♘xe4 +– ♕d4 38 ♖e2 ♘xe4 39 ♖xe4 ♖xe4 40 ♕xe4!? 1-0

Black resigned since, even with opposite-coloured bishops, his material deficit is just too large.

The aggressive 3...b5

Game 36
Khalifman – Fominykh
Russian Ch 1995

1 d4 ♘f6
2 ♘f3 c5
3 d5 b5

This is possibly the most ambitious try for Black, striking out and gaining space on the queenside.

4 ♗g5 *(D)*

This Trompowsky-like response is the theoretically recommended one.

4 ... ♗b7

Black has quite a large choice of alternatives here:

a) 4...♕a5+ (this looks almost like a beginner's check but it is designed to disrupt White's natural development; it was played by an ex-world champion

B

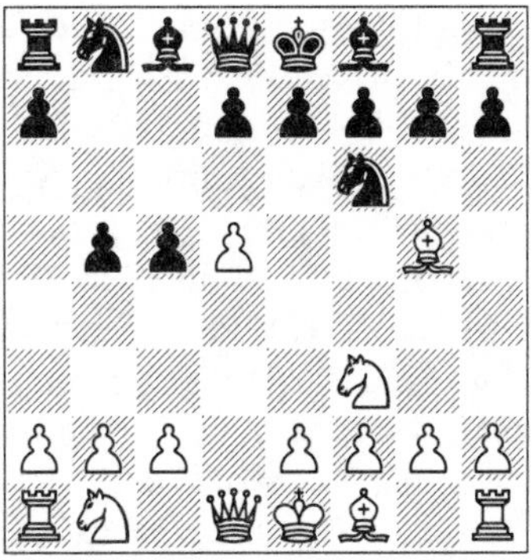

so deserves some respect) 5 c3 ♘e4 6 ♘bd2 (White could consider 6 ♗h4, but decided the lead in development outweighed giving up the bishop-pair) 6...♘xg5 7 ♘xg5 h6 8 ♘gf3 d6 9 e4 ♘d7 10 a4 (this is a typical pawn-lever in this variation, seeking to exploit the weaknesses left by Black's third move) 10...bxa4 (10...b4 11 ♘c4 gives White's knight a wonderful outpost although it has to be said the text-move does the same thing) 11 ♖xa4 ♕c7 12 ♕a1 (the weakness of the black a-pawn clearly outweighs White's slightly backward b-pawn) 12...♘b6 13 ♗b5+! (White aims to exchange off the light-squared bishops to strengthen his control of the queenside light squares) 13...♗d7 14 ♗xd7+ ♕xd7 15 ♖a6 ♘c8 16 0-0 (White enjoys a clear advantage, with a lead in development and targets on the queenside) 16...e5 (to stop White playing e5) 17 dxe6 fxe6 18 ♘h4 (White now skilfully opens up a second attacking front on the kingside; Black's inactive pieces are poorly placed to counter this) 18...♔f7 19 f4 ♕d8 (the natural-looking 19...♗e7 loses after 20 f5! ♗xh4 21 fxe6+ ♔xe6 22 ♕a2+ ♔e7 23 ♖f7+) 20 ♘hf3 ♕e8 21 f5 (the winning breakthrough) 21...exf5 22 ♕a2+ ♕e6 23 ♘e5+! (White exploits all the pins masterfully) 23...♔e7 24 ♘c6+ ♔d7 25 ♕a4 ♔e8 26 exf5 ♕e3+ 27 ♔h1 1-0 Ståhlberg-Petrosian, Budapest 1952. Black will shortly be mated after 27...♕xd2 28 ♘e5+.

b) 4...♘e4 (putting the question to the g5-bishop) 5 ♗f4 *(D)* and now Black normally chooses to challenge d5 in one of two ways:

B

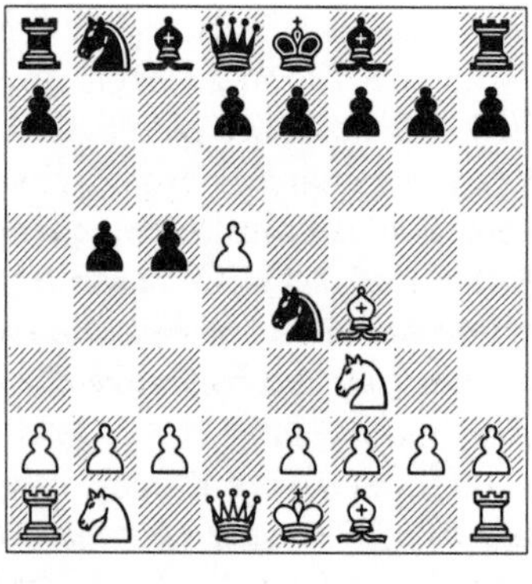

b1) 5...♗b7 6 a4 (White fights for control of c4) 6...♕a5+ 7 ♘bd2! (quick development is more important than hanging on to the d5-pawn) 7...♗xd5 8 axb5 ♕b6 (8...♕xb5 9 c4 +–) 9 ♘xe4 ♗xe4 10 ♘d2 ♗b7 11 e4. The pawn on b5 is a major thorn in Black's side, as it hinders the development of his queenside. The vulnerable position of Black's queen will enable White to develop his initiative with tempo. Black has tried two possibilities here:

b11) 11...♕f6?! (a pawn-grabbing mission which proves totally counterproductive) 12 ♗e3 ♕xb2 13 ♗xc5 ♕c3 (Black has been wasting time with queen moves {this is the fifth} and retribution is not long in coming) 14 ♗c4 ♗xe4 15 ♖a3 ♕e5 16 ♖e3 f5 (16...♕xc5 is no better: 17 ♘xe4 ♕b4+ {17...♕xc4 18 ♘d6+ +–} 18 c3 ♕a3 19 ♘d6+ ♔d8 20 ♘xf7+ +–) 17 ♘xe4 fxe4 18 ♕d5 ♕xd5 (18...♕a1+ 19 ♔d2 ♕xh1 20 ♕xa8 ♕xh2 21 ♗xa7 +–) 19 ♗xd5 e6 20 ♗xa8 ♗xc5 21 ♖xe4 gave White a winning endgame advantage in Stohl-Votava, Prague 1992.

b12) 11...d6 12 ♘c4 ♕d8 13 e5 dxe5 (13...d5 14 ♘a5 is very unappetizing for Black) 14 ♕xd8+ ♔xd8 15 ♘xe5 ♔e8 16 ♗c4 (16 b6, with the idea of ♗b5+, is interesting) 16...e6 17 0-0-0 ♗e7 18 ♖he1 (White is preparing a surprising sacrificial attack; Black would love to castle, but of course can't) 18...g5 19 ♗g3 a6 20 b6 h5 (20...♘c6 walks into the same tactic after 21 ♘xf7 ♔xf7 22 ♗xe6+ ♔e8 23 ♖d7 ♗c8 24 b7 ♗xb7 25 ♖xb7 +–) 21 ♘xf7 ♔xf7 22 ♖xe6 ♖d8 23 ♖de1 1-0 Stohl-Blodshtein, Pardubice 1992. Black must lose one of his bishops to 24 ♖e7.

b2) 5...e6 6 e3 ♗b7 7 a4 ♗xd5 (7...b4 allows White to keep his grip on d5 with ♗c4) 8 axb5 ♗e7 9 ♗d3 a6 (Black sacrifices a pawn to free his queenside) 10 ♖a4 f5 11 bxa6 ♕b6 12 ♗xb8! (White undogmatically gives up the bishop-pair to maintain his passed a-pawn) 12...♕xb8 13 b3 ♗c6 14 ♖a2

0-0 15 0-0 d5 16 c4 ♗d6 17 ♕c2 and Black had insufficient compensation for his pawn deficit in Arkell-Collas, Cappelle la Grande 1991.

c) 4...♕b6 (Black ensures he can avoid doubled pawns but he loses time in the process) 5 ♗xf6 ♕xf6 6 c3 g6 7 e4 *(D)*.

B

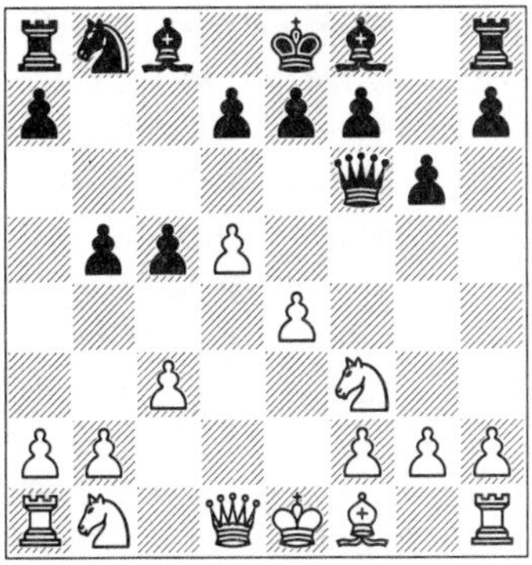

White threatens ♗xb5 and e5, forcing the queen to move yet again. Black has tried two options:

c1) 7...b4 8 e5 ♕f4 (the queen is in for a tough ride wherever she goes but she is particularly vulnerable here; better is 8...♕b6 9 ♘bd2 ♗b7 10 ♘c4 with a small edge for White) 9 ♘bd2 ♗g7 10 g3 ♕f5 11 ♘c4 (White is ready to continue gaining time by ♗d3 so the black queen tries to fight her way out of trouble) 11...♕e4+ 12 ♕e2 ♕xd5 13 ♖d1 ♕e6 (13...♕c6 14 ♘d6+ exd6 15 exd6+ ♔f8 16 ♕e7+ ♔g8 17 ♘g5 +–) 14 ♘g5 ♕f5 15 f4 (with the awesome threat of ♗h3 winning the queen) 15...♗xe5 (this saves the queen at the cost of a piece but, not surprisingly with no other pieces yet developed against White's well-mobilized force, Black is completely lost) 16 ♘xe5 0-0 17 ♗h3 ♕f6 18 ♘g4 ♕g7 19 ♕xe7 ♗b7 20 0-0 f6 21 ♕xg7+ ♔xg7 22 ♘f3 ♖e8 23 ♖d6 ♖e6 24 ♖xe6 dxe6 25 ♗g2 ♘a6 26 ♖d1 ♗d5 27 c4 ♗c6 28 ♘g5 1-0 Engqvist-Kallgren, Stockholm Rilton Cup 1996/7.

c2) 7...♕b6 is a more sensible approach, getting the queen away from the danger area, but it is difficult to imagine that Black could achieve equality after so many queen moves. 8 ♘bd2 d6 9 a4 (again Black has problems holding his queenside together) 9...bxa4 10 ♘c4 ♕c7 11 ♕xa4+ ♘d7 (11...♗d7 avoids the problems of the game, but leaves White better after the simple 12 ♕a5) 12 ♕c6 (highlighting Black's light-squared weaknesses) 12...♕b7 (exchanging queens is disastrous for Black: 12...♕xc6 13 dxc6 ♘f6 14 ♘b6 ♖b8 15 ♘xc8 ♖xc8 16 ♖xa7 ♘xe4 17 ♗a6 +–) 13 e5 (the thematic central breakthrough) 13...♗g7 (13...dxe5 14 ♘fxe5 ♕xc6 15 ♘xc6 is very pleasant for White) 14 exd6 e6 15 ♕xb7 ♗xb7 16 dxe6 fxe6 17 ♘g5 (White has a decisive material advantage) 17...♗d5 18 ♘e3 ♖b8 19 ♗c4 ♖xb2 20 0-0 ♗xc4 21 ♘xc4 ♖b7 22 ♖ae1 ♗f6 23 ♖xe6+ ♔f8 24 f4 h6 25 ♘e5 hxg5 26 ♘xd7+ ♖xd7 27 fxg5 ♖f7 28 gxf6 1-0 Razuvaev-Vaganian, Kislovodsk 1982.

d) 4...d6 (challenging White to carry out his positional threat of doubling Black's pawns) 5 ♗xf6 (it is desirable to damage Black's pawn-structure) 5...exf6 6 e4 a6 7 a4 (business as usual) 7...b4 8 ♗d3 g6 9 ♘bd2 ♗g7 10 0-0 0-0 11 ♘c4 (White has a small edge due to his space advantage and the difficulties Black has in achieving meaningful counterplay) 11...a5 12 ♘fd2 ♕c7 13 f4 ♘d7 14 ♕e1 ♗a6 15 ♕h4 ♖fe8 16 f5 (an excellent move, entombing the dark-squared bishop and preparing a kingside attack) 16...♖ad8 17 ♖f3 ♗c8 18 ♖af1 ♘f8 (Black has been forced into utter passivity and must await his fate) 19 ♘e3 ♗d7 20 b3 h5 (played so the g7-bishop can find some activity, but unfortunately weakening the kingside at the same time) 21 ♘dc4 ♗c8 22 g4 (opening the kingside for the final assault) 22...♗h6 23 gxh5 ♗xe3+ 24 ♘xe3 g5 (this is only a temporary closing of the kingside) 25 ♕f2 ♔h8 26 ♘g4 ♘d7 27 ♖g3 ♖e7 28 h4 and White had a winning attack in the game Kasparov-Nenashev, Geneva 1996.

5 ♗xf6 exf6

6 e4 *(D)*

B

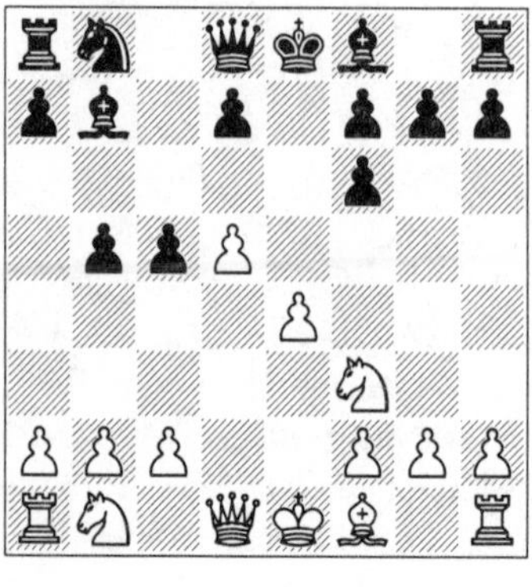

6 ... c4

Black has several other options:

a) 6...♕b6 (to avoid the loss of the b5-pawn) 7 ♗e2 ♗d6 8 0-0 0-0 9 a4 bxa4 10 ♘bd2 ♗a6 11 ♗xa6 ♕xa6 12 b3 ♖e8 13 ♖xa4 ♕b7 14 ♖e1 ♗f8 15 ♘c4 led to the usual advantage for White in Soln-Pinter, Ljubljana 1994.

b) 6...a6 (likewise securing b5) 7 a4 b4 8 ♗c4 d6 9 a5 (to take the b6-square) 9...♘d7 10 c3 bxc3 11 bxc3 ♗e7 12 0-0 0-0 13 ♕d3 ♕c7 14 ♘bd2 ♖fb8 15 g3 ♗c8 16 ♖a2 (White can afford to manoeuvre patiently because Black lacks counterplay) 16...g6 17 ♔g2 ♘f8 18 ♖e1 ♗d7 19 ♘f1 h5 20 ♘e3 ♖b7 21 ♘d2 ♗b5 22 f4 ♘d7 23 ♖h1 ± Zsu.Polgar-Andruet, Val Maubuée 1988. White is ready to expand on the kingside.

c) 6...♕e7 (trying for counterplay in the centre) 7 ♘bd2 b4 (7...♗xd5 8 ♗xb5 ♗xe4 9 0-0 gives White the initiative) 8 ♗c4 g6 9 0-0 ♗g7 10 a3 (Black's unusual move-order gives White this extra option of opening lines on the queenside) 10...0-0 11 axb4 cxb4 12 ♘b3 (a pawn sacrifice to try to exploit White's lead in development) 12...♕xe4 13 ♘a5 ♗a6 14 ♖e1 ♕f4 15 ♕d3 ♕d6 16 ♗xa6 ♕xa6 17 ♘c4 ♕b7 18 ♖a4 f5 19 ♖ea1 a6 20 ♕e2 a5 21 ♖xa5 ♖xa5 22 ♖xa5 ♘a6 23 b3 ± Khuzman-Rashkovsky, Kuibyshev 1986.

7 ♗e2

White concentrates on getting his king to safety before commencing active operations.

7 ... ♗c5

Black plays very dynamically but White can achieve an advantage by attacking the weak queenside pawns.

8 0-0 a6

9 a4 ♕b6 *(D)*

W

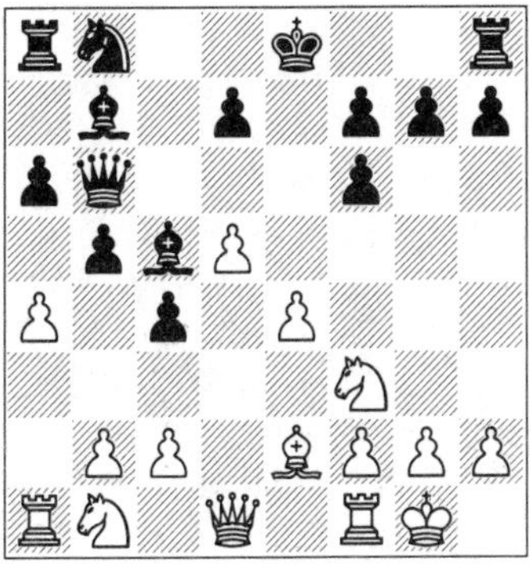

10 c3!?

An unusual approach, but by no means bad. The alternative 10 axb5 is much more direct; after 10...axb5 11 ♖xa8 ♗xa8 12 ♘c3 0-0, 13 b3 is perhaps the most principled way to take advantage of Black's queenside pawn advances. After 13...cxb3 14 cxb3 Black has been unsuccessful from this position:

a) 14...♖e8 15 ♕d3! ♗b7 (15...b4 16 ♘a4 ♕a5 17 ♘xc5 ♕xc5 leaves Black with no compensation for his structural weaknesses) 16 ♕xb5 ♗a6 17 ♕a4 ♗xe2 18 ♘xe2 ♘a6 19 ♕xd7 ♖xe4 20 ♘c3 ♖b4 21 d6 1-0 Piket-Brenninkmeijer, Groningen jr Ech 1986. Black is faced with back-rank mate, the threat of ♘d5 and the continuation 21...♕b8 22 ♖e1!.

b) 14...f5 (a radical way to get rid of the weakness, but a pawn is a pawn!) 15 exf5 b4 16 ♘a4 ♕a5 17 ♘xc5 ♕xc5 18 ♗c4 d6 19 f6! ♘d7 (19...gxf6 horribly weakens the kingside: 20 ♖e1 ±) 20 fxg7 ♖e8 21 ♘g5 ♘f6 22 ♕a1 ♘g4 23 ♕b1 ♘f6 24 ♕a1 ♘g4 25 ♕a4 ♘f6 26 ♘h3 ♗xd5 27 ♗xd5 ♕xd5 28 ♕xb4 ± Browne-Quinteros, Buenos Aires 1979.

10 ... 0-0

11 ♘d4 ♖e8

11...♗xd4 12 cxd4 ± leaves Black without compensation for his inferior pawn-structure.

12 ♗f3 d6

13 axb5 axb5

14 ♖xa8 ♗xa8

15 b4 cxb3

16 ♕xb3 ♗xd4

Not 16...b4? 17 ♕a4 forking a8 and e8.

17 cxd4 *(D)*

B

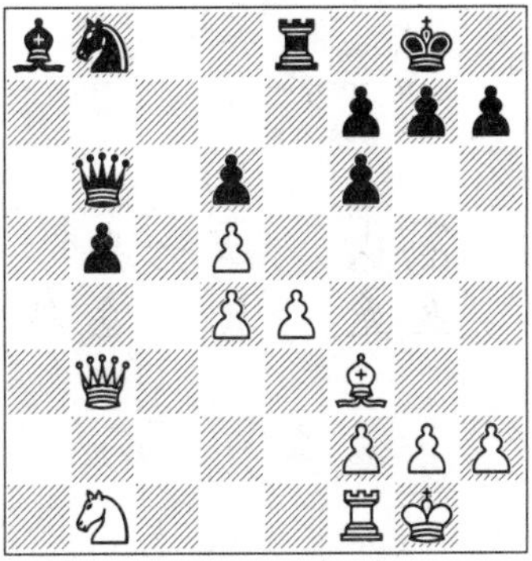

The trio of white pawns control many important central squares.

17 ... ♘a6

17...♕xd4 18 ♕xb5 is not a favourable exchange for Black.

18 ♘a3 ♖b8
19 ♖d1 g6
20 ♘c2 ♗b7
21 ♗e2 ♗c8

White's advantage lies in his imposing centre, which severely limits Black's counterplay.

22 h3 ♗d7
23 ♖a1 ♖a8
24 ♕b2 ♘c7
25 ♖xa8+ ♘xa8
26 ♕a1 ♘c7
27 ♘b4

Black is by and large reduced to moving to and fro.

27 ... h5
28 ♗d3 ♔f8
29 ♔f1 ♗c8
30 ♔e2 ♗b7
31 f3 ♔g7 *(D)*

W

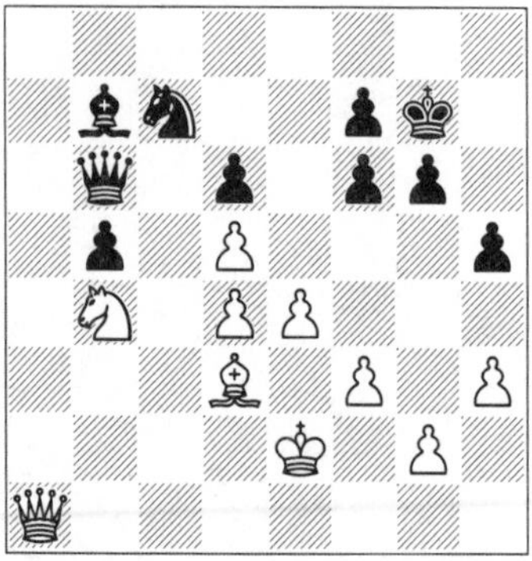

32 g4! h4
33 ♔e3 ♘a6

The exchange of knights is a minor success for Black but does not take away his fundamental problem – lack of space.

34 ♘xa6 ♗xa6
35 ♕c3 ♗b7

35...b4 36 ♕c6.

36 ♕b4 ♗a6
37 f4 g5 *(D)*

W

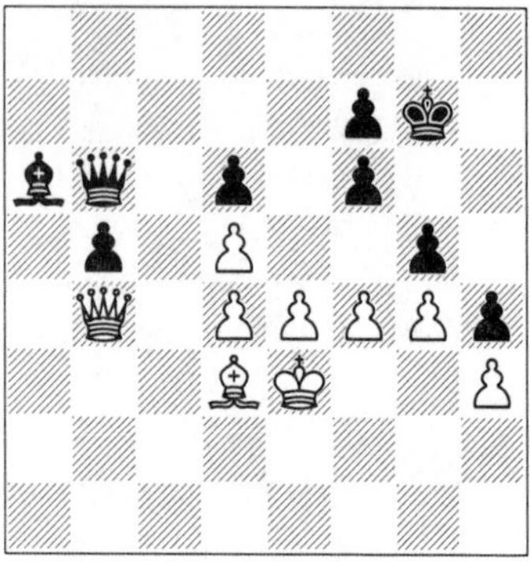

38 f5! ♔f8
39 ♕c3 ♗b7
40 ♕b4 ♗a6
41 ♔d2 ♔e8
42 ♔c2 ♔d7
43 ♔b2 ♔c8
44 e5! *(D)*

B

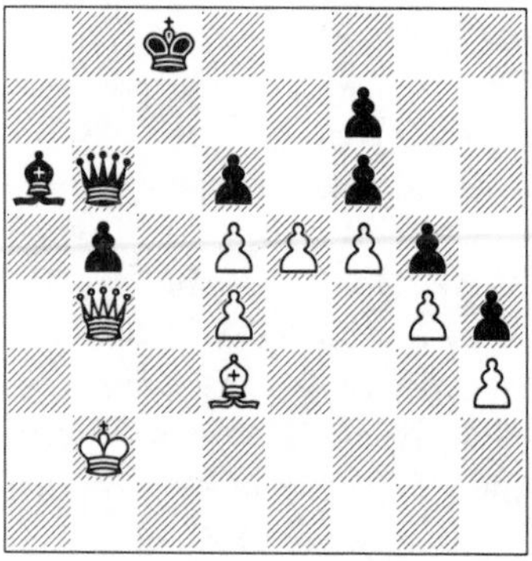

This decisive breakthrough leaves Black defenceless.

44	**...**	**fxe5**
45	**dxe5**	**♔d8**

45...dxe5 46 ♕f8+.

46	**e6**	**f6**
47	**♕c3**	**♔e7** *(D)*
48	**♕c6!**	**♕b7**
49	**♔b3**	**♕c8**
50	**♔b4**	**♗b7**
51	**♕xc8**	**♗xc8**
52	**♔xb5**	**♗b7**
53	**♗c4**	**1-0**

An excellent example of complete domination by a top-class grandmaster.

W

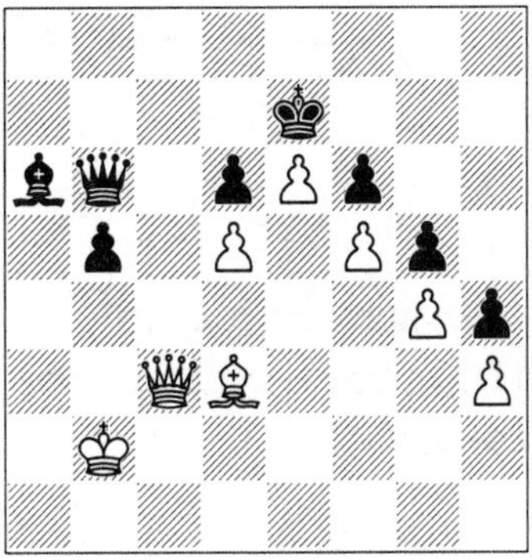

The endgame is lost for Black, as either his bishop will be trapped or the e-pawn will promote.

7 The Anti-Dutch 2 ♗g5

Introduction and Unusual Second moves for Black

Dutch specialists tend to be quite uncompromising, creative types. They often know their pet lines very well and make no secret of their aggressive intentions. I have used the 2 ♗g5 Anti-Dutch successfully for a number of years. Very few players I have encountered have felt comfortable on the black side. Even fewer have been able to find their way to a playable game. For this reason many Stonewall Dutch enthusiasts play 1...e6 followed by 2..f5 but as we shall see White can cause problems with the unusual move 3 d5!?. The main theme running through both these systems is that White is looking for an advantageous time to play the e4 pawn-break, which often ruins the black pawn-structure.

Game 37
Rowson – Preuss
Copenhagen 1996

1 d4 f5
2 ♗g5 *(D)*

In the Dutch Defence it is very difficult for Black to organize himself satisfactorily without moving his g8-knight

B

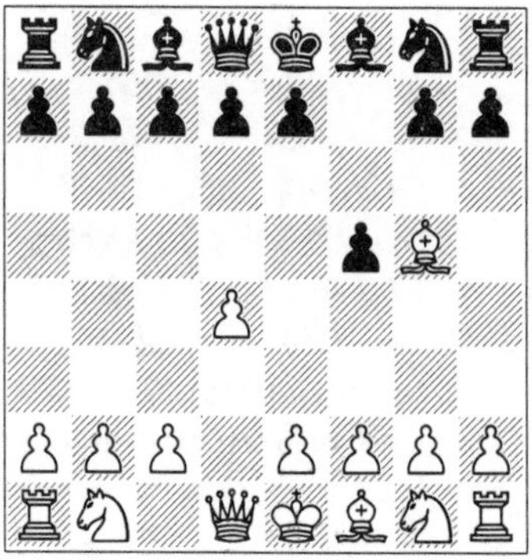

or his e7-pawn. White's last move is a direct attempt to take advantage of this very problem. Here we look at options for Black where he tries to side-step the issue or mistakenly challenges White to prove his strategy. We will concentrate in this game on divergences from the main lines (2...g6 and 2..h6 3 ♗h4 g5).

2 ... d6

Alternatively Black has:

a) 2...c5 (striking back at the centre) 3 dxc5 ♘a6 4 e4 (this is a fundamental attacking move in the ♗g5 Anti-Dutch, by which White levers open the centre for his pieces to come flying out) 4...fxe4 5 ♘c3 ♘xc5 6 ♗e3 ♘e6 (6...e6 loses a piece to 7 ♗xc5 ♗xc5 8 ♕h5+; what is not so obvious is that 6...b6 also loses material – I believe it was Chris Ward who first pointed out that 7 ♗xc5 bxc5 8 ♕h5+ g6 9 ♕d5 ♖b8 10 ♕e5 arrives at an extremely unusual situation where the white queen is forking both black rooks!) 7 ♘xe4 ♘f6 8 ♗d3 g6 9 h4 ♗g7 10 ♘xf6+ exf6 11 ♘f3 b6 12 ♕e2 ♗b7 13 0-0-0 ♕c7 14 h5 0-0-0 15 ♖h4 and White had a nice initiative to go with his structural advantage in Miles-Meulders, Amsterdam 1978.

b) 2...c6 (making a bolt-hole for Black's queen) 3 c4 ♕b6 (3...h6 4 ♗e3 with the idea of f3, ♗f2, and play similar to note 'b1' to Black's 4th move) 4 ♕d2 *(D)* and now Black can continue to ignore White's dark-squared bishop or chase it away:

B

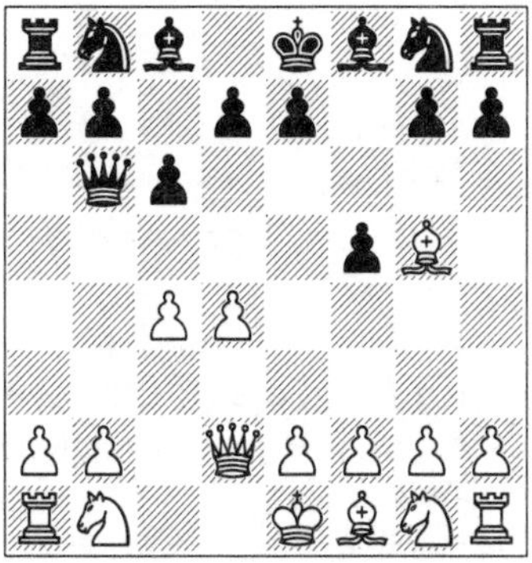

b1) 4...h6 5 ♗e3 d6 6 ♘c3 ♘f6 7 f3 g5 8 ♗f2 ♗g7 9 e3 (White builds up patiently because 9 e4 would leave White vulnerable to ...♘g4 after a capture on e4) 9...♘a6 10 ♘ge2 ♗d7 11 ♘g3 0-0-0 12 ♗d3 (giving Black a problem about how to defend f5) 12...f4 (12...e6 13 d5 ±) 13 exf4 gxf4 14 ♘ge2 ♘h5 15 a3 ♕c7 16 ♗g6 and White had won a pawn in Atalik-Panagiotopoulos, Ano Liosia 1996.

b2) 4...d6 5 ♘c3 ♘d7 6 e4 fxe4 7 ♘xe4 ♘gf6 8 ♘xf6+ (White takes a very no-nonsense approach in this game and simply completes development as quickly as possible, and then puts the semi-open e-file to good use) 8...♘xf6 9 ♗d3 e5 10 ♘e2 ♗e6 11 0-0 ♗e7 12 dxe5 dxe5 13 ♕c2 g6 14 ♖fe1 (White has a clear advantage thanks to Black's weak isolated e-pawn, so rather than subject himself to a long, painful defence Black stakes everything on a desperate attack) 14...♘g4 15 ♘f4 ♘xf2 16 c5 ♗xc5 17 ♘xe6 ♘h3+ 18 ♔f1 ♘xg5 19 ♘xc5 0-0-0 20 ♖xe5 ♖hf8+ 21 ♔g1 (the pin on White's knight looks awkward but Black has no way to exploit it and White simply remains a piece up) 21...♘f7 22 ♖e3 ♖d5 23 ♖c1 ♘e5 24 ♗e2 ♖f5 25 ♖c3 h5 (25...♘d7 26 ♗g4) 26 ♔h1 ♕d8 27 ♘e4 ♖d4 28 ♖e3 ♖f4 29 ♖e1 h4 30 h3 g5 31 ♘c5 ♕a5 32 b4 ♖xb4 33 ♖xe5 ♖be4 34 ♗g4+ 1-0 Cebalo-Miton, Biel 1997.

c) 2...♘f6 (immediately challenging White to carry out his strategy and give up the bishop-pair; however, this is simply misguided, as White gets a much better version of a Trompowsky where Black has additional kingside weaknesses) 3 ♗xf6 exf6 4 e3 d5 5 c4 *(D)* with an unappetizing choice for Black:

c1) 5...c6 6 ♘c3 ♗e6 7 cxd5 cxd5 8 ♕b3 ♕d7 9 ♘ge2 g5 (9...♗d6 10 ♘b5 ♗e7 11 ♘f4 ±) 10 g3 ♘c6 11

B

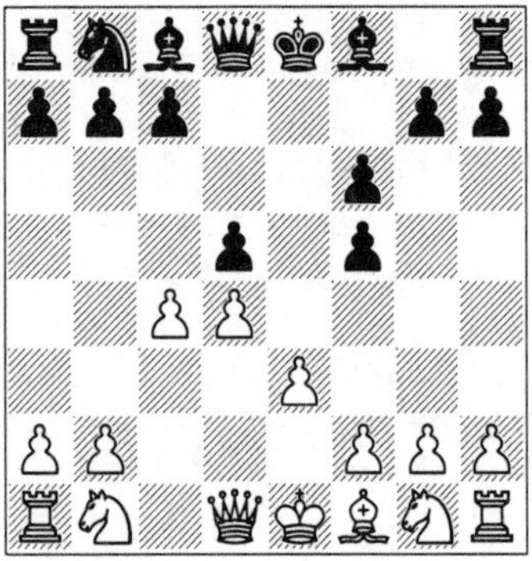

♗g2 ♖d8 12 ♖c1 with a clear advantage to White because of the weak d5-pawn, Ricardi-An.Rodriguez, Villa Martelli 1997.

c2) 5...♗b4+ 6 ♘c3 0-0 7 ♕b3 ♗xc3+ 8 bxc3 ♘c6 (this temporarily loses a pawn but Black is also worse after 8...dxc4 9 ♗xc4+ ♔h8 10 ♘e2, when he has no compensation for his structural defects) 9 cxd5 ♘a5 10 ♕b5 b6 11 ♗e2 ♗b7 12 ♗f3 a6 13 ♕d3 ♕d7 14 c4 b5 15 cxb5 axb5 16 ♘e2 ♗xd5 17 ♗xd5+ ♕xd5 18 0-0 is a little better for White, although a draw was agreed in Fominykh-Guliev, Russian Cht (Kazan) 1995.

c3) 5...♗e6 6 cxd5 ♕xd5 (6...♗xd5 7 ♘c3 ♗f7 8 ♕f3 ♕c8 9 ♗d3 g6 10 ♘ge2 ♘d7 11 h4 h5 12 0-0 c6 13 e4 ± Danielian-Yilmaz, Moscow 1992) 7 ♘c3 ♗b4 8 ♘ge2 g5? (losing, but the alternatives leave White with a very pleasant position, e.g. 8...♗f7 9 ♕a4+ ♘c6 10 0-0-0 ♗xc3 11 ♘xc3 ±) 9 ♕a4+ ♘c6 10 0-0-0 (it is a measure of the drawbacks of the black position that White forces the win of a piece by simply developing!) 10...♕a5 11 d5 ♕xa4 12 ♘xa4 ♘e5 13 dxe6 ♘g4 14 ♖d7 ♘xf2 15 ♖g1 ♘g4 16 ♘g3 ♘xe3 17 ♘h5 0-0 18 e7 1-0 Wells-Musson, Iraklion ECC 1997.

3 ♘c3 h6

A very committal decision, as now Black suffers in nearly all the tactics as a result of his weak kingside light squares.

4 ♗d2 *(D)*

B

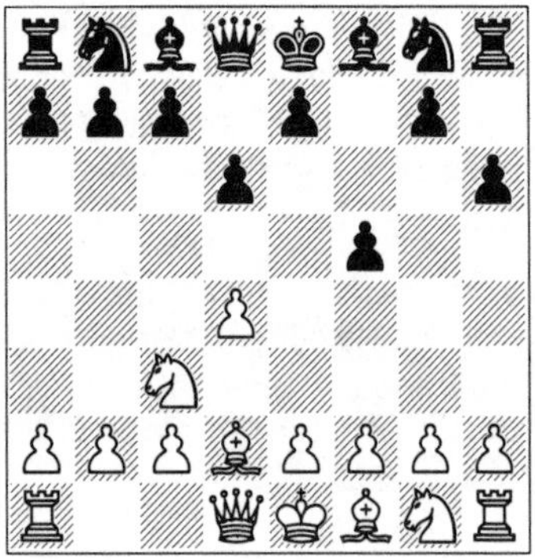

4 ... ♘f6

4...d5? 5 e4 dxe4 (5...fxe4 6 ♕h5+ ♔d7 7 ♕xd5+ +–) 6 ♕h5+ ♔d7 7 ♕xf5+ +–.

5 e4 fxe4

6 ♘xe4 ♗f5

6...♘xe4 7 ♕h5+ ♔d7 8 ♕f5+ e6 9 ♕xe4 ±.

7 ♘g3 ♗h7

8 ♘f3 ♘bd7

9 ♗c4 d5

10 ♗d3 *(D)*

White shows good understanding. Swapping off light-squared bishops highlights Black's kingside weaknesses

B

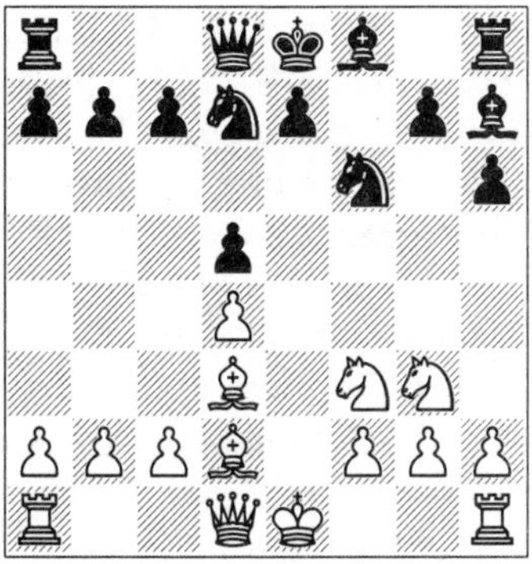

and is of far greater relevance than White's doubled d-pawns.

10 ... ♗xd3
11 cxd3 c6
12 0-0 ♕b6
13 b4 g5

Black is asking too much of his position. As unsavoury as it may be, he had to castle queenside and hope to brave it out.

14 ♗c3 e6
15 ♕e2 *(D)*

B

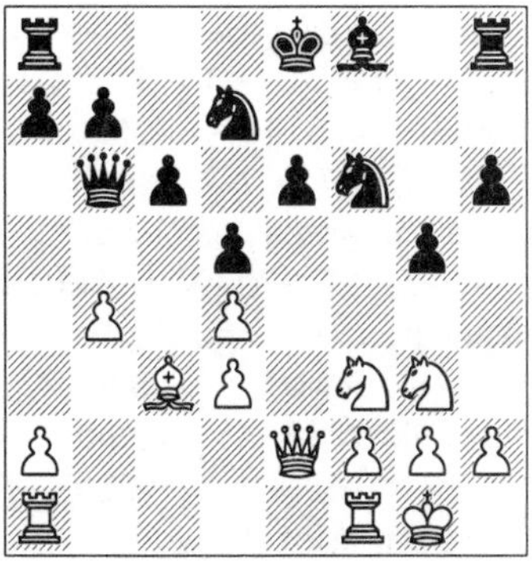

15 ... ♔f7

Now the end is swift.

16 ♘e5+ ♘xe5
17 dxe5 ♘d7
18 ♕h5+ ♔g7
19 ♘f5+ exf5
20 e6+ 1-0

There's not much to be done about ♕f7+.

Main Line: 2...g6

Game 38
Summerscale – G. Wall
London 1994

1 d4 f5
2 ♗g5 g6

This could be considered the main line of the ♗g5 Anti-Dutch.

3 ♘d2 *(D)*

B

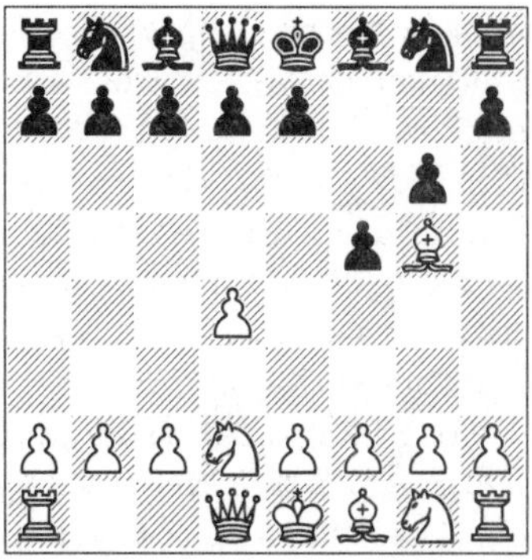

The point behind putting the knight here rather than c3 is that, as in the main game, White retains the option of c4 should Black play ...d5.

3 ... d5

Black has a major and popular alternative in the form of 3...♗g7, which

White should meet with the central advance 4 e4:

a) 4...♗xd4?! (this is the only way for Black to try to exploit White's move-order but it allows White a huge initiative) 5 exf5 ♗xb2 6 fxg6 and now:

a1) 6...♗xa1 7 ♕xa1 ♘f6 8 ♘e4 0-0 9 gxh7+ ♔h8 (9...♔xh7 10 ♗d3 with a huge attack) 10 ♗h6 ±.

a2) 6...hxg6 7 ♖b1 (7 ♗d3 is dangerous {for both sides} and for those who want to go all-out) 7...♗g7 8 ♗d3 and for the price of a pawn White has a dream attacking position.

b) 4...fxe4 5 ♘xe4 d5 6 ♘c5 *(D)* and now:

B

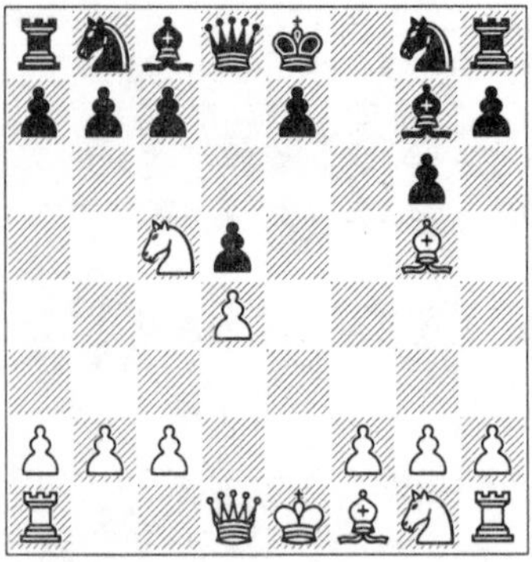

b1) 6...♕d6 7 ♘f3 with two main possibilities:

b11) 7...e5 (this asks too much of the black position, which is not well enough developed to support such a thrust) 8 ♘xe5 ♗xe5 9 ♕e2 ♘c6 10 ♘b3 ♘xd4 (this allows Black to keep hold of his important dark-squared bishop) 11 ♘xd4 ♔f7 12 ♘b5 ♕e6 13 f4 ♗d6 (13...♗xb2 14 ♖b1 is no better for Black) 14 0-0-0 h6 15 ♕xe6+ ♔xe6 16 ♘xd6 ♔xd6 17 ♗h4 and White was better because of his bishop-pair and the exposed black king in Hodgson-Lim Hoon Cheng, Manila OL 1992.

b12) 7...♘f6 8 ♘d3 0-0 9 ♗f4 (White is keeping a careful eye on Black's possible pawn-breaks, ...e5 and ...c5) 9...♕b6 10 c3 ♗f5 11 ♕b3 c6 12 ♗e2 ♘bd7 13 0-0 ♘e4 14 ♖fe1 ♖ae8 15 ♘fe5 ♘df6 16 f3 ♘d6 17 ♕xb6 axb6 and now rather than the over-ambitious 18 g4 of Chekhov-Vyzhmanavin, Moscow 1992, 18 ♗f1 would have kept White's advantage due to his firm grip on e5 and the backward black e-pawn.

b2) 6...b6 7 ♘b3 ♘f6 (7...♘h6 turned out very badly when played by a future super-GM: 8 h4 ♘f7 9 ♘h3 ♕d6 10 ♕d2 e5 11 0-0-0 ♘xg5 12 hxg5 e4 13 ♕f4 ♗f8 14 g3 c6 15 f3 ♗xh3 16 ♗xh3 ♕xf4+ 17 gxf4 ♗d6 18 f5 ♗f4+ 19 ♔b1 gxf5 20 ♗xf5 e3 21 ♖dg1 ♔f8 22 g6 1-0 Nalbandian-Topalov, Biel 1993) 8 ♘f3 0-0 9 ♗e2 ♘e4 (9...c5 allows White the better pawn-structure after 10 c4 ♗e6 11 cxd5 ♗xd5 12 dxc5 bxc5 13 0-0 ± Glek-Bronstein, Minsk 1983) 10 ♗e3 ♕d6 (Black very sensibly goes about completing his development before trying to break out; however, it is still not enough for full equality) 11 0-0 ♘d7 12 ♘bd2 ♗b7 13 ♘xe4 dxe4 14 ♗c4+ ♗d5 15 ♘d2 ♗xc4 16 ♘xc4 ♕d5 17 ♕e2 e5 18 dxe5 ♘xe5 19

♘xe5 ♕xe5 20 ♕c4+ ♔h8 21 c3 ± Miles-Van Mil, Isle of Man 1995. White has the better chances due to his plan of attacking the weak e-pawn.

4 c4 **c6**
5 e3 **♗g7**
6 ♕b3 **h6**
7 ♗h4 **♘f6**
8 cxd5

It is important to exchange now, before Black has a chance to play ...e6.

8 ... **cxd5**
9 ♗b5+ **♘c6**
10 ♖c1 *(D)*

B

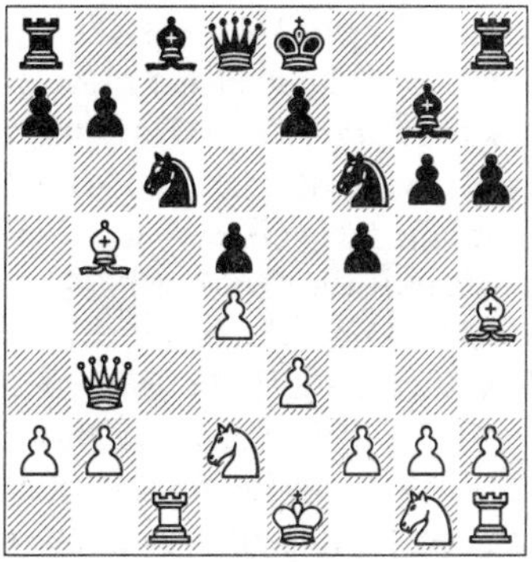

10 ... **g5**

10...♕d6 was the only way to avoid material loss although White retains a clear edge after 11 ♗g3 ♕e6 12 ♘gf3.

11 ♖xc6

The move Black missed.

11 ... **bxc6**
12 ♗xc6+ **♗d7**
13 ♗xa8 **♕xa8**
14 ♗g3

White is a clear pawn up.

14 ... **0-0**
15 ♘e2 **h5** *(D)*

B

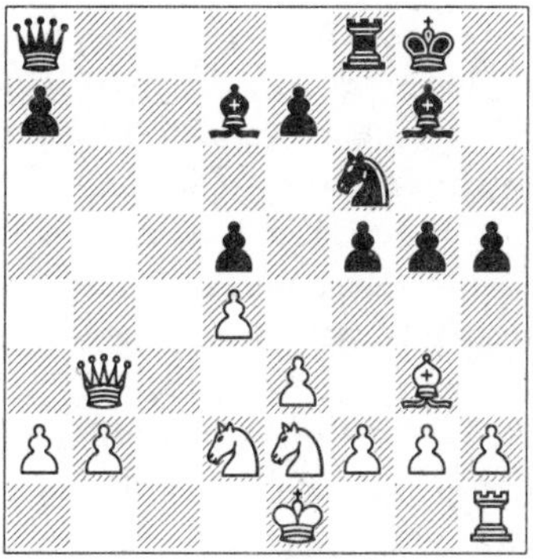

Black may as well try this, as with normal play he is completely lost.

16 ♗e5 **h4**
17 0-0 **h3**
18 ♖c1 **♗c6**
19 ♘f3 **♗h6**
20 ♘g3 **♘d7**
21 ♕c2 **f4**
22 ♕g6+ **1-0**

2...h6 3 ♗h4 g5 4 e4!

Game 39
Summerscale – Santo-Roman
Montpellier 1994

1 d4 **f5**
2 ♗g5 **h6**

2...d5 is inaccurate when White hasn't blocked his c-pawn. In practice, this has been roughly treated, with White getting a favourable version of the Queen's Gambit, e.g. 3 e3 c6 4 c4 ♕b6 5 ♕c2 e6 6 ♘c3 ♘d7 7 cxd5 cxd5 8 ♗d3 ♘df6 9 ♘f3 ♘e4 10

♗b5+ ♗d7 11 ♗xd7+ ♔xd7 12 ♘e5+ 1-0 Cohen-Curran, Lyons 1993.

3 ♗h4 g5

This is the most testing response to White's opening: Black launches an attack on the kingside using White's bishop as a target. To do so without first developing entails some risk, as you might expect.

4 e4! *(D)*

Note that most other black third moves here are equally well met this way.

B

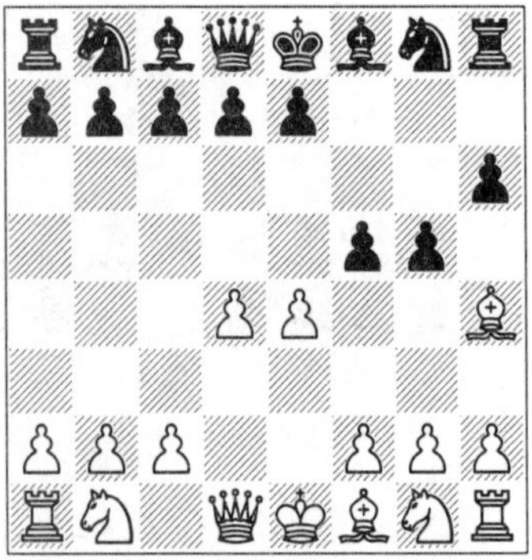

This is the key idea: White rips open the centre and offers a piece should Black want to take it.

4 ... ♗g7

The alternatives are:

a) 4...gxh4?? 5 ♕h5#.

b) 4...d5 5 ♕h5+ ♔d7 6 ♗xg5 dxe4 7 ♗h4 ±.

c) 4...♘f6 5 e5 e6 6 exf6 ♕xf6 7 ♗g3 f4 8 ♘f3 ♘c6 9 c3 b6 10 ♗b5! ♗b7 11 ♗xc6 dxc6! (11...♗xc6?! 12 ♘e5 0-0-0 13 ♘xc6 dxc6 14 ♕f3 e5 15 h3 ♕e7! 16 ♗h2 exd4+ 17 ♕e2 ±) 12 ♘bd2 gives White an edge thanks to his better pawn-structure, Prié – Santo-Roman, French Ch 1997.

5 ♗g3 fxe4

5...f4 allows White to reveal his main idea: after 6 ♗xf4 gxf4 7 ♕h5+ ♔f8 8 ♕f5+ Black is faring badly whichever way he plays now, for example:

a) 8...♔e8 9 ♗e2 ♘f6 (9...h5 10 ♗xh5+ ♖xh5 11 ♕xh5+ ♔f8 12 ♕f5+ ♔e8 13 ♘f3 gives White a clear advantage with a rook and soon three pawns for two pieces with Black having lost castling rights) 10 e5 e6 11 ♕g6+? (11 ♕xf4 leaves White a pawn up, as the f6-knight can't move on account of ♗h5+) 11...♔f8 12 exf6 ♕xf6 13 ♕xf6+ ♗xf6 14 c3 and White's inaccuracy had clouded the issue in Wachtel-Sloan, Chicago 1994.

b) 8...♘f6 9 e5 d6 10 ♕xf4 dxe5 11 dxe5 ♘c6 12 ♘f3 ♕d7 13 exf6 ♗xf6 14 ♘c3 and in Summerscale-Bauer, Montpellier 1995, I converted my extra pawn, which set me up nicely for my first GM norm.

6 ♘c3 ♘f6

7 f3 exf3

8 ♘xf3 *(D)*

White has now got a much better version of the Staunton Gambit since Black has significantly weakened his kingside. White's plan is simply to try to play on these weaknesses as much as possible.

8 ... d6

9 ♗c4 ♘bd7

10 ♕d3

B

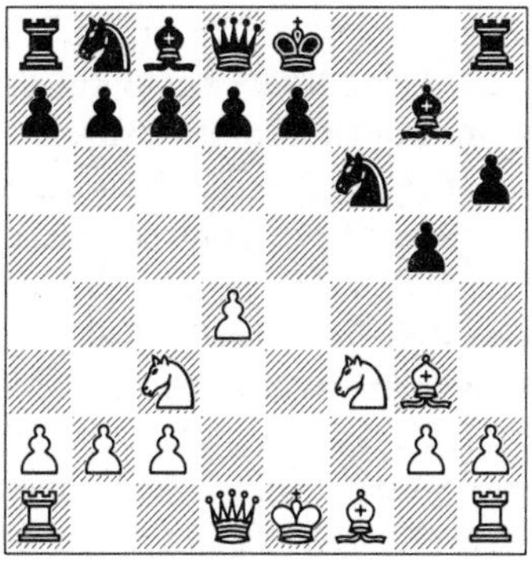

10 ♘e5 is also an interesting possibility.

10 ... ♘f8
11 d5

By grabbing more space I more or less obliged Black to open the centre for my better developed pieces.

11 ... e5
12 dxe6 ♗xe6
13 ♗xe6 ♘xe6
14 0-0-0 ♕d7 *(D)*

W

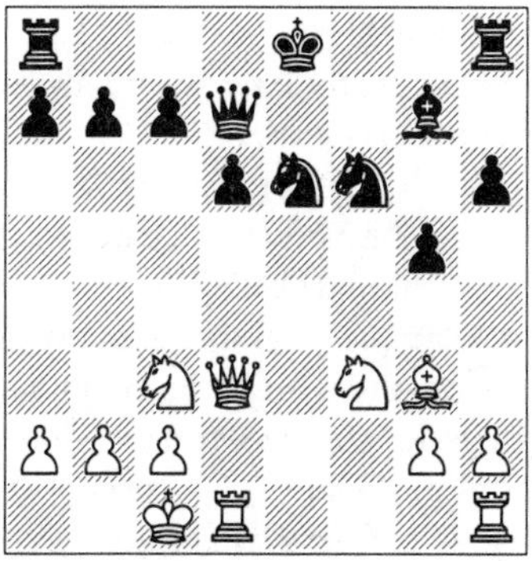

15 ♕c4! 0-0-0?

Black cracks under the pressure but it is easy to understand why he didn't want to castle kingside: 15...0-0 16 ♖he1 ♖ae8 17 h4 g4 18 ♘e5 ♕c8 19 ♘g6 ♖f7 20 ♗xd6 ±.

16 ♖xd6 ♕xd6
17 ♗xd6 ♖xd6
18 ♘b5 ♖b6
19 ♘fd4 1-0

1 d4 e6 2 ♘f3 f5

Game 40
Cifuentes – Bricard
Andorra 1991

1 d4 e6
2 ♘f3 f5
3 d5 *(D)*

B

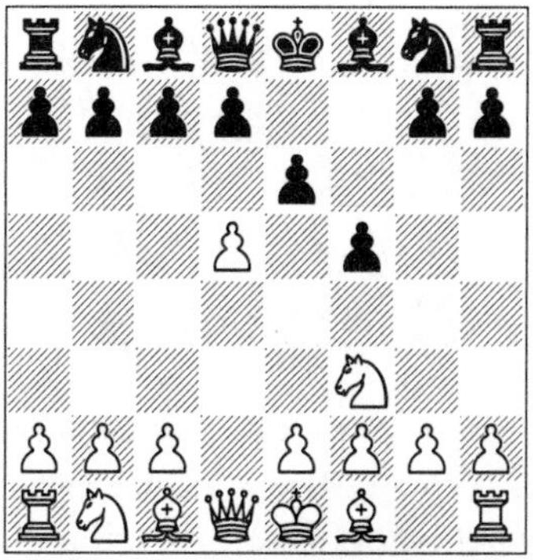

This move aims to disrupt Black's normal flow in the Dutch and will be especially effective against Stonewall players, who will be at a bit of a loss now. The aim is to gain a small safe advantage but there are sharper options along the way too.

3 ... d6

Alternatives are:

a) 3...♘f6 4 dxe6 dxe6 5 ♕xd8+ ♔xd8 6 ♘c3 ♗b4 7 ♗d2 c6 8 e4 (this move seeks to leave Black with a permanent weakness on e6) 8...fxe4 9 ♘xe4 ♗xd2+ 10 ♘exd2 and, having achieved his objective, White enjoyed a small advantage in Cifuentes-D.Parr, Hastings 1994/5.

b) 3...exd5 4 ♕xd5 d6 *(D)* and now White has two choices; the first is solid but aggressive, while the second is highly materialistic yet hard to refute:

W

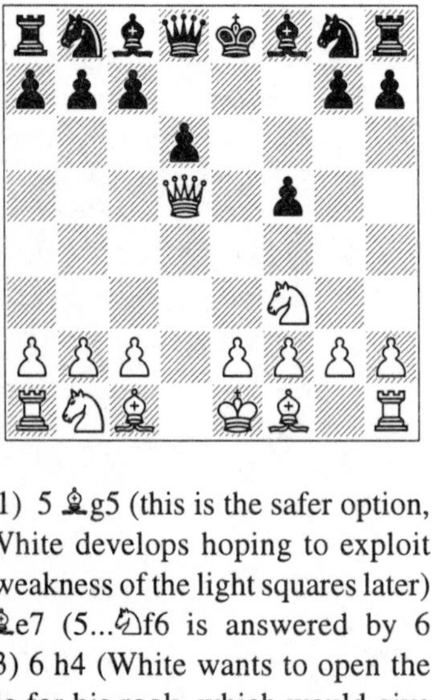

b1) 5 ♗g5 (this is the safer option, as White develops hoping to exploit the weakness of the light squares later) 5...♗e7 (5...♘f6 is answered by 6 ♕b3) 6 h4 (White wants to open the h-file for his rook, which would give him some interesting tactical possibilities as we shall see) 6...♘f6 7 ♕b3 (White is hoping for ...h6, which would further weaken Black's light squares on the kingside) 7...♘e4 8 ♘bd2 ♘c6 9 ♘xe4 fxe4 10 ♘d2 ♗xg5 11 hxg5 d5 12 c4 (White rightly goes about undermining Black's big pawn-centre) 12...♘d4 13 ♕c3 ♘e6 14 g6 (this is one of the tactical drawbacks of the exchange on g5 for Black, as the pawn becomes a real thorn in his side) 14...h6 15 ♕e5 dxc4 16 e3 ♕g5 17 ♕xe4 0-0 18 ♗xc4 (White has an attack and an extra pawn to boot) 18...♔h8? (18...♖e8 is better) 19 ♗xe6 ♖e8 20 ♕d5! (White holds on to his extra piece) 20...♕f6 21 ♗xc8 ♖axc8 22 ♕f7 ♕g5 23 ♘f3 ♖xe3+ 1-0 Granados Gomez-Sorroche, Olot 1994.

b2) 5 ♘g5 (this is a very sharp option that wins material at the expense of White's development; this game shows some of White's possibilities, but my gut feeling would be to leave this one alone) 5...♕e7 6 ♘xh7 c6 7 ♕b3 ♗e6 8 ♕g3 ♖xh7 9 ♕g6+ ♕f7 10 ♕xh7 ♗e7 11 ♘d2 ♘d7 12 ♘f3 ♘f8 13 ♕h3 f4 14 g4 0-0-0 15 ♕h5 g6 16 ♕a5 ♗xg4 17 ♕xa7 ♘d7 18 ♗d2 ♕c4 19 ♕d4 1-0 Hauchard-Bricard, Belfort 1992.

c) 3...♗d6 4 dxe6 dxe6 5 ♘c3 ♘f6 6 e4 (again this is the critical pawn-break for White) 6...♗b4 7 ♕xd8+ ♔xd8 8 ♗d2 fxe4 9 ♘xe4 ♗xd2+ 10 ♘exd2 and again White is better, as he has a simple plan of developing and pressurizing Black's weak e-pawn, Ortega-Kovačević, Formia 1995.

4 dxe6 ♗xe6

5 ♘g5 *(D)*

White tries to drive the bishop from its best diagonal and prepares the way for e4.

5 ... ♕d7

B

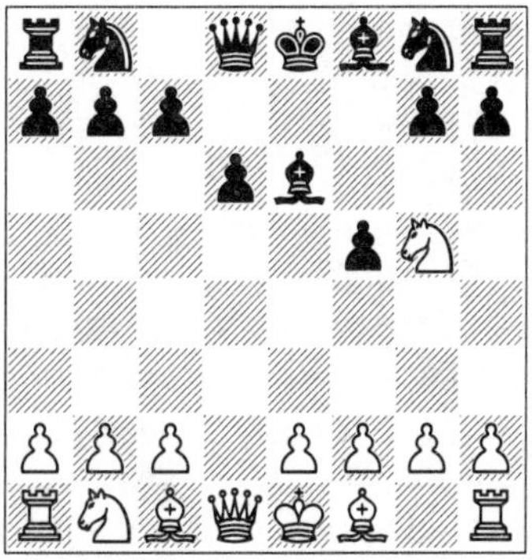

6 ♘c3 ♘f6
7 g3

7 e4 is also interesting here.

7 ... c6
8 ♘xe6 ♕xe6
9 ♗h3 d5
10 0-0 ♘bd7
11 ♕d3 g6
12 ♕e3 ♘e4
13 ♘xe4 dxe4
14 ♕c3 ♖g8
15 ♗e3 0-0-0
16 ♖fd1 *(D)*

B

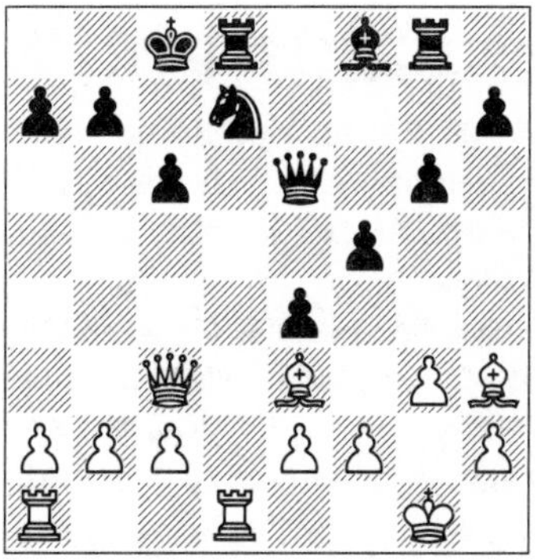

White is slightly better here in view of his bishop-pair. Against a normal move like 16...a6 he should continue with a4 and b4, with a queenside attack. Black, perhaps lulled into a false sense of security by the closed nature of the position, blundered with:

16 ... ♔b8??
17 ♗xa7+ 1-0

The bishop is immune from capture on account of ♕a5+ winning the rook on d8. Black, probably disgusted with himself, called it a day.

8 Odds and Ends

Here I will examine the various irregular systems that Black tries from time to time. The key is to keep your cool when faced with these openings. Just develop sensibly and use the space advantage you are invariably given. Above all, don't expect too much and don't underestimate your opponent just because he plays a few funny-looking moves in the opening. I used to make a living in intermediate tournaments off opponents who did exactly that!

Game 41
Summerscale – Basman
British Ch (Plymouth) 1992

1 d4 *(D)*

B

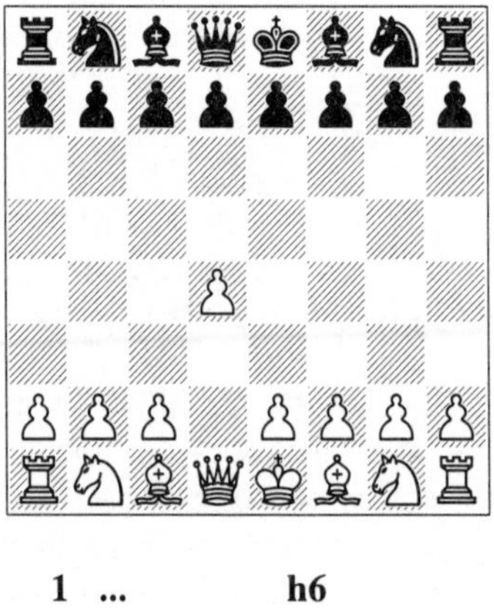

1 ... h6

This is perhaps the most irregular of all the openings we cover. The other attempts to confuse White are:

a) 1...e6 (1...b6 will come to the same thing) 2 ♘f3 b6 (Owen's Defence is the only variation after 1...e6 that takes us outside the scope of those already analysed) 3 e4 ♗b7 4 ♗d3 (the best way to meet unusual variations is to play simply – and the clearest plan in this position is to complete development, protect the pawn-centre and then expand on the queenside) 4...c5 5 c3 ♘f6 6 ♘bd2 ♘c6 7 a3 ♗e7 8 0-0 d6 9 b4 cxd4 10 cxd4 ♖c8 11 ♗b2. White has completed all his objectives and stands better.

b) 1...b5 (the St George) 2 e4 ♗b7 3 ♗d3 e6 4 ♘f3 a6 (the St George used to be in my repertoire and I found it most difficult when White simply played to keep the central tension) 5 ♘bd2 ♘f6 6 0-0 c5 7 c3 ♘c6 8 ♖e1 cxd4 (8...♕b6 9 e5 ♘d5 10 dxc5 ♗xc5 11 ♘e4 ♗e7 12 ♗g5) 9 cxd4 ♖c8 10 a3 *(D)*.

Again, this idea of queenside expansion is quite effective. 10...♘a5 11 ♕e2 ♕b6 12 b4 ♘c4 (Black has overlooked a tactic; instead he should swallow his pride and retreat) 13 ♗xc4 bxc4 14 ♘xc4 ♕c6 (Black hits c4 and e4) 15 ♘a5! ♕c7 (15...♕xe4

B

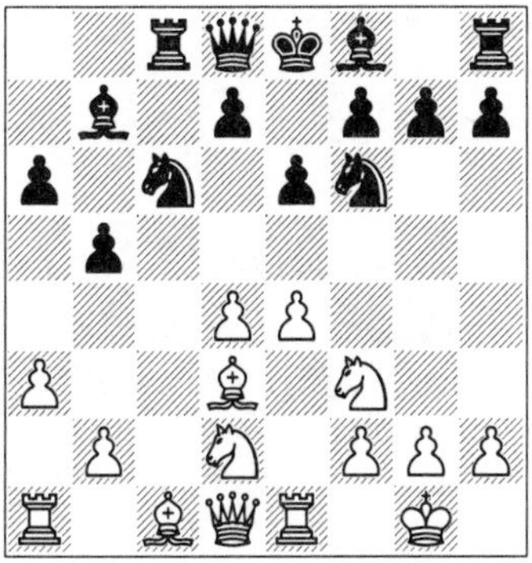

loses a piece to 16 ♕f1 ♕d5 17 ♖e5) 16 d5 ♗a8 (this loses a second pawn, but Black's position was pretty disgusting in any case) 17 ♕xa6 1-0 Torre-Winants, Brussels 1986.

c) 1...c5 2 d5 f5 is the so-called Clarendon Court – an opening with which I have a 100% score as Black, including a victory over Mark Hebden, but I suspect it is because nobody has played 3 e4! fxe4 4 ♘c3 ♘f6 5 g4 (White threatens g5, more or less forcing Black's response) 5...h6 (this is a serious weakening of the black kingside) 6 ♗g2 d6 7 h3 ♘bd7 8 ♘ge2, when White has every reason to look to the future with confidence. He can recapture on e4 at will and then set about probing those light-squared weaknesses.

d) 1...♘c6 2 ♘f3 d5 transposes to the Anti-Chigorin line already discussed in Game 20.

e) 1...e5 is the Englund Gambit, which used to be a favourite of my old club president at Fulham, Mr Bill Jenkins. Unfortunately it is still as bad as when he used to play it. However, I owe a huge debt of gratitude to Bill, for if he hadn't ferried me around for away club matches I wouldn't be where I am today. 2 dxe5 ♘c6 3 ♘f3 ♕e7 4 ♘c3 ♘xe5 5 e4 (a very sensible approach, not attempting a direct refutation but keeping hold of a space and development advantage) 5...c6 6 ♗e2 ♘xf3+ 7 ♗xf3 d6 8 0-0 ♗e6 9 ♖e1 ♕d7 10 ♗f4 ♗e7 11 ♕d2 ♘f6 12 ♖ad1 gave White a clear advantage in Timman-Hendricks, simul 1987.

f) 1...d5 2 ♘f3 c6 3 c4 e6 4 e3 (the only way for Black to create problems within our repertoire is if he plays...) 4...f5 (a delayed Stonewall; however, an effective response was played against me in the European Club Cup) 5 ♘c3 ♘f6 6 ♗d3 ♗d6 7 h3 0-0 8 g4 *(D)*.

B

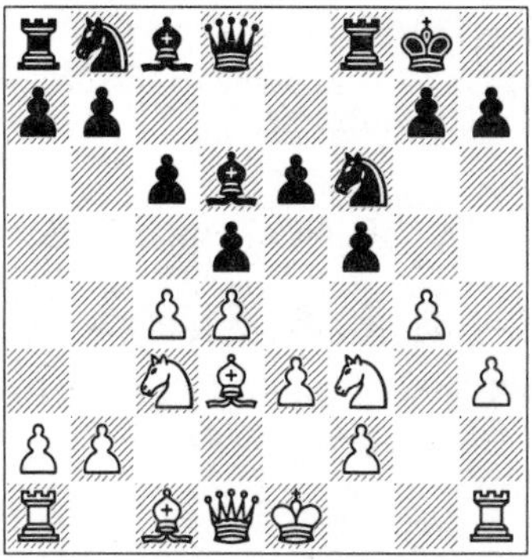

This is the big idea. Black would be foolish to take on g4 and open the h-file and so must find a way to defend against gxf5. 8...♘e4 (this is the most natural move but it does not solve all of Black's problems) 9 gxf5 exf5 10 cxd5 ♘xc3 11 bxc3 cxd5 12 ♕b3 ♗e7 13 ♗a3 ♗xa3 14 ♕xa3 ♘c6 15 0-0-0 ♗e6 16 ♖hg1 ♔h8 17 ♖g2 ♖c8 18 ♖dg1 (the white king is surprisingly safe, whilst the g7-pawn is targeted; ...g6 will just encourage the h-pawn to advance, so I defended passively) 18...♖c7 19 ♔b2 ♖f6 20 ♔a1 (White sensibly tucks his king away from the danger zone) 20...♗g8 21 ♖g5 ♕c8 22 ♘h4 g6 23 ♗xf5 (I had overlooked this little combination, which forces a favourable material imbalance for White) 23...gxf5 24 ♖xg8+ ♕xg8 25 ♖xg8+ ♔xg8 26 ♕c5 (two rooks are normally worth at least a queen but here, with the black pawns split on the kingside and in the centre, the white queen and knight form a lethal combination) 26...♖d7 27 ♘g2 a6 28 ♘f4 ♖fd6 29 c4 ♘e7 30 cxd5 ♘xd5 31 ♕c8+ ♔f7 32 ♘d3 ♔g7 33 ♘e5 ♘e7 34 ♕c4 1-0 A.Shneider-Summerscale, Bratislava ECC 1996.

2 e4

This game was a bit of a daunting experience for me, as I was up against the guru of unusual opening lines. At least I was forewarned and therefore expecting the unexpected!

2	**...**	**c5**
3	**c3**	**cxd4**
4	**cxd4**	**d6**
5	**♘c3**	**g5**

Black is playing a strange kind of c3 Sicilian with ...h6 and ...g5 thrown in voluntarily. Needless to say, this idea hasn't really caught on!

6	**♗c4**	**♘c6**
7	**♘ge2**	**♘f6**
8	**♕b3**	**♖h7** *(D)*

W

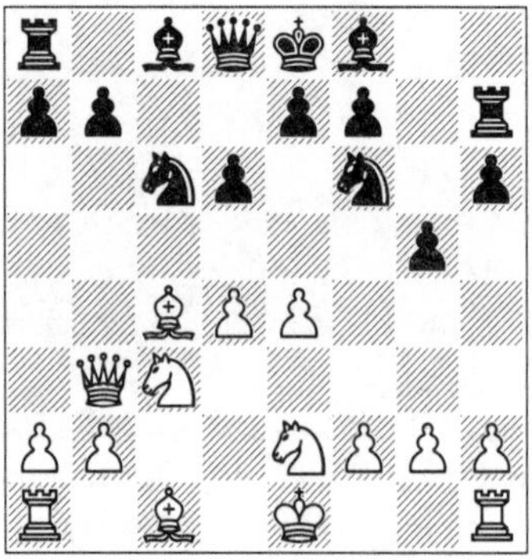

Black defends creatively, but his pieces begin to look a little awkwardly placed.

9	**0-0**	**a6**
10	**♗d3**	**♖g7**
11	**♗e3**	**♘g4** *(D)*

W

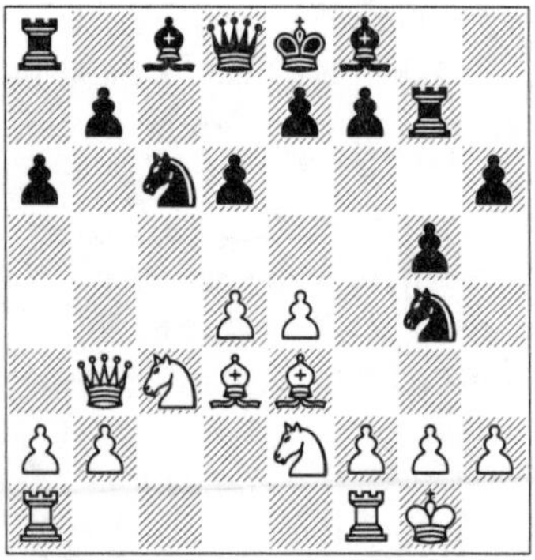

Having more or less completed my development it was time for action.

12	**♘d5**	**e6**
13	**♘b6**	**♖b8**

14 ♖ac1

Threatening d5, so Black prevents this.

14 ... d5

15 exd5

Of course White wants to open the centre as the black king is stranded.

15 ... ♘b4 *(D)*

W

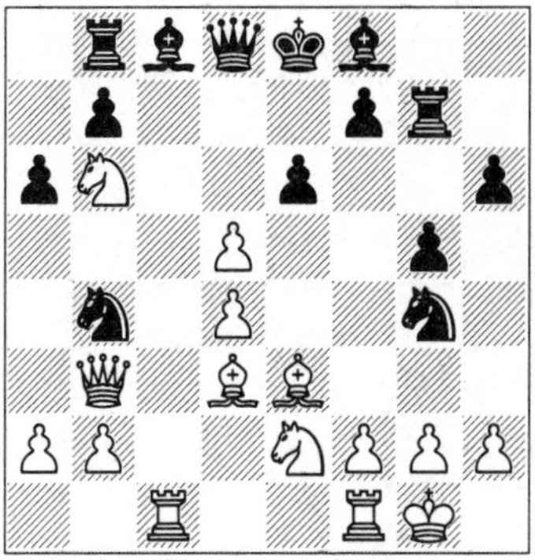

I took a glance at Black's position and noted its rather ridiculous appearance. Therefore I started looking for a forced win.

16	**♘xc8**	**♖xc8**
17	**♕a4+**	**b5**
18	**♗xb5+!**	**♔e7**
19	**♕xb4+**	**♔f6**
20	**♖xc8**	**♕xc8**
21	**♗xa6**	**♕c7**
22	**d6**	**♗xd6**
23	**♕b7**	**1-0**

Index of Variations

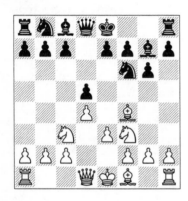

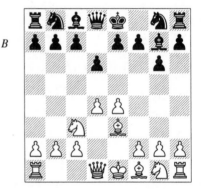

IN HER day, Lin's mother Kim had been quite the heralded beauty. The moment she turned sixteen, her family had suitors from all the neighboring villages doing their best to bid for her hand in courtship. They brought gifts by the armful—cured meats, sugary confections, all the gold trinkets they could scrape up. It reached a point where jealous whispers started circulating among the neighbors, and Kim's family had to start distributing the wealth just to appease them.

Not that any of it mattered. In her red silk bower, Kim turned up her nose at all the would-be wooers. She had no use for any of them—nor for the life of a farmer's wife. She had higher goals, dreams of celluloid stardom in the Hong Kong cinema. As soon as she could, she would be on the first boat to Kowloon and away from the banality of village life.

Of course, nothing turned out the way Kim had planned. When she turned seventeen, her parents betrothed her to a small merchant in a neighboring village. All the tears in the world couldn't change her parents' minds; times were hard, and a beautiful daughter was a valuable commodity—there simply was no other way.

The night before her wedding, Kim had one last chance to escape. Her friend May's brother was going to Kowloon; all she had to do was steal out of her house under the cover of night and join him. So she packed her bags, wrote her note, and got ready. And yet, when the time came, she couldn't do it. All of a sudden, faced with the prospect of an uncertain future, Kim did what she swore she would never do—she chose the safe and steady road over the unknown.

The years that followed the wedding were hard ones. Financially, times were tough. Kim's new husband soon lost his business, and they had to scrape around doing odd tasks to make ends meet. But that was nothing compared to the mental toll; married to a man she barely knew and haunted by what could have been, Kim grew bitter and sullen. Years later, even after they had immigrated to America and had attained a level of middle-class prosperity, she l these resentments. She eventually grew to care for but there was no mistaking what her first love was. r all this. Kim didn't believe in hiding things. She told everything in the hopes of teaching her important life lessons: that she must have ambition, drive, and financial independence to do whatever she wanted if she planned to have a better life. Lin was a quick student, but there was one lesson she took to heart that Kim never counted on: to throw caution to the wind and forsake the safe path, lest she spend the rest of her life caged by regrets.

IF THERE was one thing that Drew Black most definitely was not, it was safe. Then again, none of the guys Lin worked with were.

"So then this guy Mike at work was telling a group of guys at the table how he 'didn't see daylight' with some blonde in the Hamptons," Lin recounted to M.J. and Alex as they nursed drinks at the Oriental Palace Restaurant in Koreatown. It was Monday night, and after a down day at the stock market, a vent session with her girls was just what Lin needed.

"I told you that brokers were pigs," Alex said. "I don't know how you deal with all these jackasses every day. No wonder you want to move to the London office."

Lin smiled wistfully. While it would be nice to get away from some of the jerks in her office, that wasn't her driving force for wanting to move to London. Like New York, London was a major player in the world of big-time finance. It was inevitable that she would want to try her hand, to see if she was up for the challenge. But London was no easy proposition; aside from the difficulty of getting a job there, Lin was also well aware of what she'd be giving up. She had a good life in New York: friends, family, a job where she was respected and well-liked. London was a crapshoot, and she wasn't sure if she was ready for it.

"Yeah, well," Lin shrugged, "who knows when I'd be able to get to London. In the meantime, I'll just have to deal with the guys at work as best as I can."

"That blows," M.J. said. "I know it's hard to work with a lot of men, but for them to be discussing that shit at work is bogus."

"Well, one good thing happened at work last week," Lin said, changing the topic. "This new guy Drew started, and he's great. Cute, charming." She carefully tucked a stray strand of hair back into her immaculately styled upsweep. "Did I mention cute?"

"Ahh." M.J. nodded slowly. "So you want to jump him or what?"

"He's very sexy," Lin conceded, her expression dreamy as she thought of Drew's hypnotic green eyes. "But he's not ready to settle down, that's for sure. I'm totally on to him." She took a sip of her Malibu pineapple and muttered under her breath, "I'm definitely on to him."

"Forget about Drew for now." M.J. leaned forward. "How about doing something fun tonight?"

"What did you have in mind?" Alex asked.

"Karaoke!"

Karaoke had been one of M.J.'s favorite activities to do with the girls when they were teenagers and had sneaked a few drinks on a Saturday night out in the city. Their favorite pastime was sneaking into other people's private rooms at the famous Jeung Color OK Karaoke house and pretending they were part of the party group—all the easier to make fun of the "singers."

"Uhh . . . singing?" Lin wrinkled her nose. "I don't think so, J. Go with Jagger and you two can sing your hearts out."

Alex burst out laughing as M.J. adopted a mock-offended look. "Well, I know M.J. thinks she's the next American Idol and all, but maybe it could be fun. We never do crazy stuff like that anymore." She rubbed her chin. "Lin, what do you say?"

"I can't believe you two are serious! Alex—I think I liked it more when you weren't so into crazy stuff!" Lin exclaimed. "But okay, fine. Just don't expect me to get up on stage!"

M.J. didn't need any further prodding. After she hailed the waiter, they paid the check and departed from the Oriental Palace. Ten minutes later, they were sailing through the doors of the Jeung Color OK Karaoke house, a dimly lit lounge with disco lights and vinyl booths. To pacify Lin, M.J. requested a private room for the three of them so that no one else would witness Lin singing.

"I'm feeling a bit tipsy," M.J. said, weaving as she walked. "I'm going to sing some Celine Dion and really belt it out."

Alex and Lin both rolled their eyes.

"And, as usual, we'll laugh at you." Alex grinned. "Hey, speaking of Ms. Dion, I think I hear someone singing 'A New Day' right now in the main room."

"I do, too," Lin agreed. "Let's go watch."

As the three girls walked into the main singing room, they all caught a glimpse of the performer on stage and had the same reaction—sheer and utter shock.

"Oh my God!" Alex grabbed M.J.'s wrist. "Is that—?"

"Stephen!" M.J. screamed.

Sure enough, on stage for all the world to see, was Lin's ex-boyfriend Stephen. And he wasn't just on stage. He was swaying and shaking his hips and belting out the lyrics to Celine Dion's hit song—"Hush, now I see the light in the sky . . ."

Alex and M.J. both turned to look at Lin, who had been stunned into silence.

This couldn't be right, Lin thought. This wasn't the Stephen she knew—the uptight doctor whose craziest maneuver consisted of wearing stripes with solids. He didn't know anything about singers, and he certainly didn't know anything about singing.

"You okay, Lin?" M.J. grinned.

"I am . . . I mean . . . ," Lin stammered. "I just can't believe that he's up there—and singing to Celine Dion!"

"I know!" M.J. said gleefully. "And you dated him!"

"Yeah," Alex chuckled. "Who would believe that was Lin Cho's boyfriend?"

As her friends laughed and high-fived each other, Lin could only cover her face and cringe. Sure, Stephen was free to do as he pleased, and if he wanted to sing karaoke, what say did she have in it? Yet, Lin couldn't help wondering what people would think if they knew that was her ex-boyfriend up on stage. . . .

Just then, Stephen finished his song. He turned, caught sight of the girls, did a double take—and headed straight toward them.

"Lin?" Stephen broke into a grin. Lin, who'd been trying to nudge M.J. and Alex away, froze.

"Uh, Stephen?" She forced a smile. "Hi, how are you?"

"I'm good." He paused, looking a little confused. "What are you doing here? I never figured you for the karaoke type."

"Well . . . J here wanted to sing," Lin said quickly. "It's kind of a girls' night out."

"Very nice." He nodded at her friends. "Hi, Alex. M.J., it's good to see you again."

M.J. grinned. "Same here."

"Hey, why don't you guys come and join us at our table?" He smiled at Alex and M.J. "I don't know if you heard, but I just belted out a tune."

M.J. grinned from ear to ear as Alex flashed him a thumbs-up.

"Oh, was that you singing Celine Dion? I almost didn't recognize you up there," Lin said.

Stephen chuckled. "I guess I've been trying a lot of crazy things ever since I turned thirty. I've always wanted to sing karaoke, so I figured I'd give it a shot." He clasped his hands. "And you know what? I actually had a blast up there, just me and the microphone."

Alex and M.J. looked at each other and grinned. As for Lin, all she could do was stare at him in disbelief. Her friends were right—how could an ex-boyfriend of hers enjoy singing karaoke?

"Right," she said, deciding to humor him. "Well, I'm glad you enjoyed yourself. We actually have to go because we reserved a private room. But good running into you!"

"You, too." He smiled. "It was really nice seeing you. And remember," he winked, "a new day will come and you'll be touched by an angel."

M.J. yelped and high-fived Stephen as Alex guffawed.

"Well, we better get going," Lin said loudly, ushering her friends away. "See you later, Stephen!"

As they headed toward their private karaoke room, Lin shook

her head. She couldn't believe she'd dated someone so dorky. And Celine Dion? What had she been thinking?

THE NEXT morning, Lin still didn't know the answer. But there was one thing she was sure of: Drew would never have looked so uncool. Sitting in her office, Lin decided that she would stick to the stock market and Drew from now on. Just as she had that thought though, Lin glanced down at her computer screen and gasped.

"Aaarggh!" she screamed. Drew rushed in.

"What's wrong?" he asked.

"Tyco just went down three points in the last four hours! George Levin—our biggest client—is going to flip. I told him we'd be okay last week."

"That's not good." Drew rubbed his temples. "He's not exactly a happy camper. In fact, he's pretty much the greediest old man I know."

"Just like everybody else," Lin said. "Everyone wants to be rich by the time they're old."

"Well, the man's got a point," he replied. "Money does make a man . . . or a woman."

Lin shook her head. "There are a lot of people in this world who are smarter than us, but who make less money." Lin thought about her mother, who was, without a doubt, one of the most enterprising people she had ever known. Having come to the United States with absolutely nothing, Kim had worked three jobs, shopped at Goodwill, and scraped together every cent so she could give her daughters a better life. Even though Lin now made several times what her mother had made at the height of her earning power, she wished she had even an ounce of the shrewdness that Kim had.

"That's true, but with money comes power." Drew pointed to Lin's pocketbook on her desk. "Look at you with your Louis Vuitton bag. Or me in my Armani suit. People are drawn to anything that exudes wealth."

Lin shrugged as she focused on her computer monitor. There was no way Drew could understand. He'd never had to wear hand-me-downs; he'd never known what it was like to be in a foreign country where he didn't speak the language; he probably didn't even know what Spam tasted like.

"Well, then, what are you doing here if not for the money?" Drew persisted.

"I happen to like what I do. Not for the payout itself, but for the . . . pursuit of it. I like helping my clients . . . make money." She cleared her throat.

It was a strange contradiction, to say the least. While Drew didn't understand that Lin's family didn't have the luxury of wealth, he wasn't completely wrong about Lin's infatuation with it. After all, how could she not be obsessed? Growing up, Lin had seen her family evolve from barely eking out a living as immigrants to being firmly entrenched in the American middle class. This progression would never have happened if the Chos weren't preoccupied with money; it was only by counting every last cent that they had gotten to where they were now. So what if they talked incessantly about incomes and vacations? So what if they were constantly comparing cars and houses and TVs? Her family had worked hard to get to where they were, and Lin didn't think there was anything wrong with their being a little materialistic if they wanted to be.

"Wow, that was touching," Drew said. "It sort of turns me on."

"Be quiet." Lin crinkled her nose. "Do you always have to act like a chauvinistic male?"

Drew grinned. "Only when I can get a reaction like that out of you. You're pretty opinionated for an Asian chick."

She glared at him as her phone rang. It was their boss, Rob.

"Lin, I need you guys to get the fiscal report from Mike on my desk by eight A.M. Monday morning. Just so you know, I'll be out of the office the rest of the week."

"You got it, Rob," Lin said. She hurriedly hung up the phone.

"So I heard the boss is going to Martha's Vineyard for the

Memorial weekend." Drew came over and sat on the edge of her desk. "What about you? Any plans?"

"Not much. I'm meeting with my parents for dinner at Shun Lee, then I'll probably just go out with my girls," she replied. "What about you?"

"Well, I'm volunteering tomorrow at the Y, but after that I'm actually moving into my new place. I have my very own bachelor pad now. You should come check it out sometime," Drew said, winking at Lin.

Lin started to smile then paused, struck by Drew's words. "You volunteer?" she asked.

"Yeah, I've been tutoring these fifth graders in math for the past two years."

"Wow," she said slowly, "I'm . . . speechless."

"I bet that doesn't happen very often," Drew said lightly. "So you think you can stop by this weekend?"

It was moments like these that always got Lin in trouble—when she would somehow get sucked in by a guy like Drew even though the whole situation reeked of trouble.

"Well—" She smiled flirtatiously. "—we'll see."

EVEN THOUGH there was a part of Lin that was tempted by the prospect of seeing Drew, she had more pressing weekend plans—like taking her mother and father to dinner. One of the perks of making a good salary was that Lin could afford to take her parents out to the nicest restaurants in New York City. Like Shun Lee, an exquisite, ultra-expensive, haute-Chinese restaurant on the Upper East Side. The emerald shrimp dumplings were a particular favorite of the Cho family. Unfortunately, this time, the appetizers came with an extra item.

"Lin?" Drew suddenly appeared at their table. "How are you? What are you doing?"

"Drew?" Lin gasped. "I should be asking you the same question."

"I just had dinner with my aunt and uncle," he said. "A friend of mine thinks this is a great place for a family dinner."

She shot him a look, but he beamed innocently. As she fidgeted with the linen napkin on her lap, her mother gave him a frown of disapproval. Lin knew her mother wasn't going to be happy about her socializing with Drew.

"Hey, Drew," Lin said nervously, "this is my mom, Kim, and my dad, Harry."

Drew flashed them one of his trademark smiles. "Hi, Mr. and Mrs. Cho. It's nice to meet you."

Kim forced a smile. Harry managed a pleasant "Hi, how are you?"

"Drew works with me," Lin said brightly. "He's actually one of the partners from our team."

"Partners?" her mom asked skeptically.

"Yes," Lin explained, "we work together on several mutual funds projects. He's one of the best traders in the business."

Kim ignored Lin. "So are you married?"

Lin couldn't believe her ears. What was her mother up to?

"No, I'm not married," Drew said, "but I'm still young and looking for the right woman." He looked pointedly at Lin, who flushed and stared down at her plate.

"Are you interested in my daughter?" Kim asked.

Lin almost passed out from embarrassment. She knew that her mother was old-fashioned and pretty much crazy when it came to Lin and guys, but this was too much. "Um, Mom," she interrupted, "you're so funny. Drew works with me, Mom. *Works* with me!"

Of course, Drew Black was no dummy.

"No, Mrs. Cho," he said very seriously. "Lin is a lovely lady, but we're nothing but friends. We work together. That wouldn't be right."

"I see." Kim nodded. "Good."

"Mom." Lin gritted her teeth. "Would you like another Tsingtao beer?"

"I like five right now," Kim said coldly.

"I'll get the waiter right away. Drew, it was good seeing you. Have a lovely evening."

He took the hint. "Have a pleasant dinner, Mr. and Mrs. Cho. It was very nice to meet you both. Take care."

The minute Drew was out of earshot, Lin confronted her mother. "Mom, how could you do that to me?" Her voice rose. "You can't embarrass me like that in front of my friends."

"He is white," Kim lectured. "I want you to find someone like Stephen again and stop fooling around with these playboys. They only want one thing. The fortune-teller warned you."

"Ugh!" Lin groaned as she turned to her food. Would she ever get through an entire meal without her mother criticizing and second-guessing her?

As soon as dinner was over, Lin's parents dropped her off at her apartment on the Upper West Side. She immediately whipped out her cell phone to call Drew.

"I'm so sorry about what happened at the restaurant," Lin apologized as she walked into her living room.

"No worries, Lin." He laughed. "Believe me, I understand. I have a Jewish mother. She's pulled shit like that before."

"Thanks." Lin broke into a smile. Not only was Drew gorgeous, but he was understanding as well! The fortune-teller had it half right—she was lucky. "She has some crazy idea that I'm going to go back to China with her and marry some farmer from Canton."

"That's funny." Drew chuckled. "Who would ever imagine Lin Cho with a farmer from China. . . . By the way," he added, "will you be at the office party on Friday?"

"Nowhere else."

"Good! I'll have to keep my eye on you. Everyone adores you."

Lin dropped down on a chair, kicked off her Jimmy Choos, and wriggled her toes. "Everyone?"

twenty-one

COMPANY PARTIES at Merrill Lynch were a lot like the Oscars. Leggy, beautiful women, sleazy old men, young dashing bucks, and a lot of free-flowing booze. At Lin's office Friday night, the branch's annual party was in full swing. The gunners were schmoozing, the ladies were glowing, and the air was thick with money. There couldn't be more fertile grounds for an office romance if one tried.

Dressed in a dazzling red spaghetti tube dress with sparkling bling all over, Lin ordered herself another glass of Cristal.

"Do you know how many of these guys have come up to me to tell me that I'm the luckiest man in the world because I work with the hottest woman in the office?" Drew walked over and whispered into Lin's ear.

Lin laughed. "Well, thank you. I must say you're not looking bad yourself."

Ding! Ding! Ding! Everyone turned toward the president of the branch, Henry Greenberg, who was poised to give a toast.

"If I could have your attention please." Greenberg raised his glass. "I'd just like to thank each and every one here for your hard work and dedication. With such determination and talent, our branch has managed to increase its revenue by thirty percent this year. Congratulations!"

The room roared as everyone applauded and turned back to the bar. At that moment, Rob walked over to Drew and Lin.

"I just want to say a few words to my team over here," Rob said as he raised his whiskey, obviously a bit tipsy.

Drew and Lin looked at each other and tried to suppress smiles.

"Mr. Black, with your addition, I have no doubt that our team will do even better this year. And Ms. Cho, without you, there wouldn't even be a team. You two kids are doing a tremendous job and have put an old guy like me to shame," Rob slurred.

Drew flashed a smile at Lin, a striking figure in his black Versace suit, midnight blue shirt, and silver tie. Lin had to resist the temptation to stare.

"Thank you for your kind words, Rob. I just want to say that I've never worked with such a good group before. Rob, with your guidance and wisdom, and . . . and with Lin's talent and intelligence, I feel privileged to be a part of this team. Thank you. Cheers!" Drew winked at Lin as they clinked glasses.

"God bless you two," Rob mumbled. "Hopefully, there will be many more years of success to come. Now if you'll excuse me, I think I'm going to grab some nuts."

Lin and Drew both laughed as Rob stumbled off.

"I was touched by your speech," Lin remarked. "Here's to you sucking up."

Drew smiled. "Oh, is that what you thought I was doing?"

"Most definitely," Lin said, taking a sip of her Cristal. "You're the kind of guy who always knows just what to say."

"Well, they don't call me Badass Drew for nothing." Drew snagged another glass of champagne from a passing waiter.

"Who's 'they'?" Lin chuckled.

"My boys from college," he said, taking a swig of his drink. "That was my name because I charmed all the girls."

"Oh, really?" Lin smirked. "Does that charm still work?"

"You tell me," Drew said as he turned toward her, his expression suddenly turning serious. "You know, I have a confession to make. I've been trying to think of an excuse to get you alone since the first time I laid eyes on you. But I didn't think I had a chance."

"Why not?" Lin looked into his eyes and felt her heart leap.

"Because you're so amazingly beautiful. And smart and a damn good broker. I figured you were out of my league." He leaned forward. "But maybe my confidence has grown because I think I have a chance."

"With who?" Lin looked innocently around the room.

But Drew was not to be sidetracked. He gazed at Lin very seriously. "I lied to your mom that time we met," he confessed. "I think you're absolutely breathtaking, and my interest in you is definitely not platonic. What do you say we go back to my place and have a few drinks?"

At that moment, Lin's radar kicked up. What was she doing? Yes, she loved flirting with men, but this was more than just flirting. Drew was sexy and charming and she liked him despite his ego. The only problem was that they worked together. But then again, taking risks was part of her everyday job.

"I think I'm going to head home," she said. "It's getting late, and I've already had way too many drinks."

"Are you sure?" he asked, his intent gaze making Lin feel light-headed. "Do you want me to take you home?"

Lin suddenly felt paralyzed, presented with such an oh-so-tantalizing prospect. There was a part of her that was doing somersaults, exulting that the wonderful Drew Black wanted her. Then there was the part of her that whispered that this was a terrible idea, that she was getting herself into a mess she might never be able to extricate herself from, that she was opening herself up to heartbreak.

"I'm afraid," Lin said slowly, "that if you take me home, you'll try to take advantage of me."

Drew pretended to look offended. "I would never do something like that, Lin. Come on, what do you say? We'll have a few drinks and I'll show you my new pad." He gave her his most seductive smile.

In the end, there was really no other choice for Lin. She wasn't her mother Kim. She wasn't going to settle for safe and steady. She wouldn't spend her life obsessed with what-ifs. And she would never stop reaching for the brass ring.

So she succumbed to the inevitable. "All right, all right. But I can't stay long."

IN LIN'S world, the stock market was a never-ending roller coaster. People could feel like king of the world one day or like shit the next. It could be a high on Monday, exhilaration Tuesday, and complete misery the rest of the week.

Lin was having one of those exhilarating days. It was the morning after the company party, and there was an extra skip in her step as she basked in the sunlight on her way to the Rickshaw Dumpling Bar. Was it because Nabisco had risen a few points or was it because she had finally merged assets with Drew Black?

"Hi, girls!" Lin beamed as she got in line behind M.J. and Alex. "How are you this morning? Isn't this place great?"

M.J. and Alex gave each other looks.

"What up?" M.J. said. "You certainly seem happy today."

"Oh, nothing." Lin looked up at the menu. "Isn't today just a beautiful day? I think I'll get the Peking duck dumplings and maybe the chocolate soup dumplings for dessert."

"That's it?" M.J. asked. "I heard the owner here has forty dumplings at a time. I'm going to have the chicken thai basil, szechuan chicken, shrimp, and classic pork and chive. Ten each for me!" she announced.

Lin stared at M.J., wondering how her friend wasn't eight hundred pounds. "Does Jagger know you eat like this?"

"Trust me," M.J. assured her, "Jagger would be getting forty dumplings himself if he were here."

"Fine," Alex said, "I'll order for us and make sure they know that the forty dumplings are for the oinker in the Adidas warm-ups."

"Thanks, Alex." M.J. shot her a pretend-outraged look as she and Lin laid claim to an empty table.

The minute Alex walked away, Lin turned to M.J. and relayed her big news. "Okay, you know I don't normally say these things, but he was so good in bed," Lin gushed.

"Shut up! You never say shit like that," M.J. exclaimed. "Was he even better than the guy you interned with years ago at Paine Webber?"

"Oh, him." Lin laughed. "But, um . . . yeah, I would have to say so. He's such a great kisser. He has such soft lips, and he definitely knows what he's doing."

Lin smiled. She was glad that she told J first. Not only was she more sympathetic to matters of the heart these days with her new-found coupledom, but she was also less likely to be judgmental than Alex.

M.J. saluted her with her fork. "I'm excited for you, Lin. I want to meet him!"

"I want you and Alex both to meet him." Lin twirled her wooden chopsticks. "He's great. And it's not just the sex. He treats me like a goddess. He just makes me feel . . . so special."

She tore her chopsticks apart gleefully. At that moment, Alex walked back over with their orders. M.J. quickly got up to help.

"So, what's all the commotion about? What did I miss?" Alex asked as she set the food down on the table.

"You missed a lot. Our girl Lin here just had the hottest night in her life with Drew Black," M.J. said, passing out their drinks.

"Drew Black?" Alex dropped down onto the chair across from Lin. "You mean the guy you work with?"

"Yes, that Drew. We went back to his place after the company party last night and it just sort of happened. We were up all night talking, and then one thing led to another . . . the next thing you know, all of our clothes were on the floor." Lin smiled at the memory as she took a bite out of her dumpling.

Alex's chopsticks clattered to the ground. "Lin!" she exclaimed. "What are you thinking? This isn't just some guy you met on a setup date. Haven't you heard all the warnings about dipping your pen in the company inkwell?"

Lin raised an eyebrow at Alex. "And you're completely immune to office romances, I assume?"

"All I'm saying is that these things have a way of ending up ugly," Alex responded. "You've got to be sure this isn't going to affect you at work."

Lin stared down at her tea. If there was one thing about her world that she would toss right out the window, it would be the rules. Without them, she would be able to make all the trades that she wanted and be a millionaire by age thirty. Who made up the rules anyway?

"Alex, I'll be fine," Lin said. "I'm a big girl."

. . .

DESPITE HER blasé attitude, Lin was more bothered by Alex's reaction than she let on. Alex just didn't seem to get it that she was happy because of Drew. Okay, so part of it was her fault, considering the way she'd first described him to her friends. But since then, things had changed. The two weeks following the company party had been pure bliss for Lin; they had spent almost every waking moment—and nonwaking moment—together. Drew was everything she had hoped for: romantic, fun, and surprisingly tender. He surprised her with long-stemmed roses and intimate weekend getaways to the Hamptons. And when they went out, he always managed to get them into the poshest restaurants and the most exclusive clubs. Above all, he treated her like a princess, constantly telling her how she was the most beautiful woman he knew. Drew could have had any woman he wanted, but he'd chosen her . . . it was almost enough to make her believe she was as wonderful as he said she was.

Now that Lin had gotten to know the real Drew, she wanted her friends to get to know him, too. So she invited Alex out to drinks on Thursday night at Le Colonial, a sleek, sultry French colonial restaurant and lounge where the clientele mingled under palm fronds. Lin knew she had been neglecting the girls the past two weeks, and this seemed like a perfect way to kill two birds with one stone: be with Drew and hang out with Alex all at once. The prospect of showing Alex, her biggest skeptic and closest pseudo–family member, that Drew was someone special was an added bonus. This could even be a test run for his official meeting with Lin's family at their house.

"Alex, I'm so glad you came tonight," Lin gushed as the girls sipped bamboo martinis in the upstairs lounge.

"Not as glad as I am to be out of work." Alex sighed happily as she leaned back in her chair. "But I should probably be grateful I don't have to travel—I bet M.J.'s bored out of her mind in Detroit."

"I know." Lin shook her head. "Poor J. When is she supposed to get back?"

"Tomorrow night, I think." Alex sipped her martini and glanced around the room. "So this is where the brokers hang out, huh?"

"Yes," Lin said distractedly, checking her phone. "I wonder what's keeping Drew."

"Is that him over there?" Alex asked.

Lin looked up in the direction that Alex was pointing. That was when she saw Drew and the rest of the guys from work at the bar chatting with Lana and the admin girls.

"Oh, yeah," Lin exclaimed, "there he is!"

"He looks awfully chummy with those women."

For a moment, Lin felt a stab of concern. But she brushed the thought aside, determined not to give in to her insecurities. "Oh," she waved it off, "those are just some of the secretaries." She got up and waved to Drew. "Drew! Over here!"

Drew looked up and nodded toward Lin. He ambled over to the girls. "Well, hey there." Drew grinned at Alex. "You must be Alex."

Alex smiled. "That would be me."

"You're everything Lin said you were." Drew winked at Lin, who giggled.

"Thanks," Alex said slowly.

"So—" Drew dropped down beside Lin. "—Lin says you're a lawyer."

Alex nodded. "That I am."

"Well, I'm glad to finally meet you," Drew said. "Before, when Lin said she had a friend who was a lawyer, I was picturing some ugly old broad, not a looker like you. Then again, I should have known that Lin's friends would be beautiful."

He leaned over and nudged Lin. She laughed a little and looked at Alex. Her face was expressionless—not a good sign.

"So," Drew continued, "did Lin tell you about our big score today?"

"No." Alex's eyes narrowed. "But I'm sure you're going to tell me about it."

"Oh, yeah." He turned to order a drink from a passing waiter.

"See, there's this rich asshole named Jankowski who we've been trying to land for a while. He's got a billion-dollar portfolio, and we've been trying to steal him from Smith Barney for a year. Anyway, we finally got him into the office today, but he was totally stonewalling us and even started to walk out. Which is when our lovely Lin came to the rescue!"

Lin's eyes widened. "Um, honey, I don't think Alex would be interested in hearing about this."

"Are you kidding me?" Drew exclaimed. "This is a great story." He turned eagerly to Alex. "I told Lin to put on the shortest skirt she had in the office, then drop her pen in front of Jankowski and lean over to pick it up. You should have seen the look on Jankowski's face! We signed him five minutes later!"

Lin bit her lip and stole a glance at her friend. Alex's eyes were steely.

"Isn't that great?" Drew said gleefully. "I'd like to see those bastards at Smith Barney try to match that!"

"Ingenious," Alex said coolly.

"You know," he continued, "you should try what Lin did. I bet you'd win more cases!"

"I'll have to keep that in mind," Alex said, looking utterly disgusted. She downed the rest of her drink and got up. "If you'll excuse me now, I forgot to send something out at work. I guess I'll have to take a raincheck on tonight."

"Oh, okay," Drew said. "It was nice meeting you, Alex."

Alex didn't even respond as she turned on her heel and stalked off. Lin jumped up out of her seat. "I'm just going to walk Alex out," she told Drew as she ran after her friend. Lin caught up with her on the sidewalk outside of Le Colonial.

"Alex, wait!" she called.

Alex turned around, hands on her hips.

"Look, Alex," Lin began, "I know what you're thinking—"

"I hope not," she snapped, "because then you would know what an asshole I think Drew is. Lin, you could do so much better than this! I expected a lot more from you."

"You don't understand," Lin pleaded. "I know Drew can come off as a jerk at first, but deep down, he's a good guy. Besides, you, of all people, should know what it's like to date a coworker."

"Lin!" Alex yelled. "That's completely different. First of all, Brady and I are just hanging out. Second, I would castrate him if he even suggested I do something like that. This guy Drew has you flashing your underwear to land an account! This from the woman who was the top moneymaker at Merrill Lynch last year. Don't you think there's something wrong with that?"

There was a part of Lin that knew Alex was right, that this behavior with Drew was wrong in about a million ways. But then there was the other part of Lin—the stubborn part—that didn't want to think about the ramifications of her relationship with Drew.

Lin's eyes welled up. "Look," she said, "you don't understand. You don't know what it's like between us. When it's just him and me, he's different. We're different. And I think I might be falling for him."

Lin wiped away her tears and glanced up at Alex. She knew her friend didn't understand. All her life, Alex had everything come easily to her. She went to the best schools, became a big-time lawyer, earned several times what her peers were making. While Lin herself earned a decent living, she didn't come close to Alex in terms of credentials. Most important, Alex had parents who adored her and believed she could do no wrong. She didn't have a mother like Kim, who never hesitated to tell Lin all the ways she had erred.

Her friend looked away as a long pause stretched between them. Then Alex glanced back toward Lin. "I'm sorry," Alex said finally. "You're right. I don't know what it's like between you two." She took a deep breath. "Just don't change yourself for this guy. You have to . . . be careful, okay?"

Lin nodded slowly. Alex leaned over and gave her a brief hug. Then she walked off as Lin silently watched her go.

Closing Bell

twenty-two

LIKE EVERYTHING else in life, the market was a gamble. Some people refused to sell their shares when they rose. Instead, they got greedy and invested more and more—until they hit the wall. In Lin's world, love and stocks paralleled each other perfectly.

Continuing to see Drew raised a glaring red flag in Lin's mind, but like those investors, she wanted to push the limits to see how far she could get. She saw the warning signs and the roadblocks, but she was determined to keep stepping on the pedal. She had come this far, and there was no turning back.

Dressed in a sharp navy blue power suit, Drew sauntered into Lin's office on Tuesday morning. He closed the door behind him, locking it afterward. Lin's face lit up. It had been several weeks since the company party, but her stomach still did a somersault every time she saw him.

"Hey, gorgeous." He smiled as he leaned in to kiss her. "How's my favorite girl?"

Lin blushed as they moved onto her couch. Drew always had a way of making her feel like the most beautiful woman in the world.

He was unbuttoning her blouse when her phone rang.

"Let's not get that," Lin whispered in Drew's ear as she continued to kiss him.

"You have to get that," he whispered back. "It could be important."

"Okay, okay." She got up and straightened her skirt. "Hello, Lin Cho."

"Hi, Lin," Lana said, "I have a package for you up by the front desk."

"Thanks, Lana." Lin fumbled to hang up the phone.

"Where were we?" she whispered to Drew as she threw his tie on the floor.

"Right here." Drew smiled as he nuzzled her neck. "You know, Lin," he said huskily. "I think we have the best business meetings in the world."

Lin smiled. "Oh really?"

"And you haven't seen the best yet," Drew said as he pulled her down onto the couch.

As they made love in Lin's corner office, someone knocked.

"Lin?" Rob called from the other side of the door.

Drew and Lin stared at each other in horror. Jumping up from the couch, they rushed frantically to get dressed and straighten themselves out. Lin helped fix Drew's tie, while Drew zipped up Lin's skirt. As Drew made his way over to the windowsill, Lin smoothed down her blouse. Her heart was pounding like a jackhammer, and she suddenly felt on the verge of hyperventilating. How could she have let this happen? This was her worst nightmare come true—her boss and mentor discovering the two of them *in flagrante delicto* in her office. She had to put a stop to this. She just prayed that she wasn't going to lose her job.

Silently cursing herself for being so stupid, she slowly unlocked the door. "Come in," Lin chirped in an overly bright tone.

"Hey, kids," Rob said upon entering. "Private meeting?"

Lin flushed and looked away. Fortunately, Rob didn't seem to notice.

"Drew, I've been looking all over for you. We need to sit down and talk. I got word from our headquarters that we'll be making some changes with management here. That means a couple of things, but most importantly, it affects our team. There'll be some different strategies and plans to discuss. How about we meet on Thursday?"

"Great!" Drew and Lin said in unison. Rob gave the two of them a curious look.

"Since when did you two begin sharing a brain?" he demanded. "But you know what—I like it! Just means that our team is in sync. Go team, go! Gotta run, but let's talk Thursday."

Rob closed the door behind him as Drew and Lin both exhaled.

"Boy, was that a close one!" Drew shook his head.

"Tell me about it," Lin said. "This is so wrong. I've never had sex in the office before." And she'd never do it again. She just hoped she'd have the resolve if or when that time came to say no. "Look," she began, "Drew, I think this wasn't such a good idea—omigosh!" she screamed, seeing the shattered remains of her bamboo plant on the floor.

"Oops." He spared a glance over as he fiddled with his tie. "I guess that must have gotten knocked over during our . . . activities." He snickered a little.

Lin was not amused. "This isn't funny," she snapped. "You've messed up all the feng shui in my office."

Drew frowned. "What do you mean?"

"I had someone come and take a look at my office when I moved in." Lin grabbed a small dustpan from her drawer and carefully swept up the mess. "I had to make sure the feng shui was good, and that included having a bamboo plant here."

"I see," Drew said, though he clearly did not, "is that why you have that weird thing hanging up there?" He gestured toward a concave mirror attached to one of the top corners of the window behind her.

"Uh, yeah." She reddened a little. "There's a church across the street, which is supposed to be bad luck. The mirror is supposed to combat that."

He nodded slowly. "Well, that's really cute, your little Chinese superstitions."

Lin frowned. "It's not supposed to be cute," she said a little testily.

"Sure, sure, whatever you say." He smiled as he slipped his arms around her. Despite herself, Lin felt her resolve weaken.

"Pick me up at eight tonight," she whispered as she kissed him lightly on the lips. "Now go! I have work to do."

The moment he left her office, Lin collapsed into her chair. That had been close—too close. She hid her face in her hands. She would never have done something so reckless when she was with Stephen. What was it about Drew that made her lose all control of her senses?

She knew exactly what it was: He was dangerous, but he was also exciting. Just being around him was intoxicating, an addictive mixture of thrills and the forbidden. When she was with him, Lin felt invincible as well. Which was why, despite her misgivings, she couldn't help but fall under his spell again.

BY THE end of the day, the close call with Rob had become a distant, distinctly less alarming memory. Lin couldn't stop smiling as she strolled down the hallway after her afternoon Starbucks run. She'd had a number of good flings in her life but never like this. Who said that you couldn't mix business with pleasure?

"Lin, how are you?" Krishan called out from the copy machine as she walked down the hall toward her office.

Lin broke into a grin and strolled over to him. "How's the market doing today?"

"It's doing great," he replied. "Green on my screen."

"Excellent!" she applauded.

"What's with the cheeriness?" he asked. "Looks like you're having a good day."

"I am." Lin smiled. "Things are great."

"Really?" Krishan asked. "New man?"

"Sort of," she giggled.

"Details, I need details. You can't leave your captain hanging like that."

"Carry on," Lin said as she walked away. "So long, Krishan."

He called after her. "Hey, how can you sell out on a fellow alum like that?"

Lin chuckled. Krishan always knew what to say and he always seemed to know what was going on—which was why she had to steer clear of him. At least for now. Just as that thought crossed her mind, she almost tripped on the carpet outside her office. Quickly composing herself, she turned around to see Krishan looking at her curiously.

"Later!" she said with fake cheer before she quickly closed the door.

FORTUNATELY, THE rest of the week didn't bring any further threats of discovery. By the time Lin met up with Alex and M.J. that weekend at the Chelsea Wine Vault, she had all but forgotten her near-brush with disaster.

"This is so exciting," Lin exclaimed. "I've always wanted to do a wine tasting!"

"Me, too," M.J. said, looking around the spacious red-brick winery. "I might not know the difference between a ten-dollar bottle and one of these expensive wines, but I still like to drink it!"

"Well, then it's time to start your education," Alex said. "Here, try this."

"Mmm," M.J. took a sip of the white wine Alex handed her, "tastes like apricots—what's it called? Fal-and-geena?" She frowned at the label of the bottle.

"Falanghina," Alex corrected her. "It's an ancient Italian grape. This wine is made by the Ocones in Campania, and it's really excellent. Soft, dry, no oak and just a touch of vanilla."

"I couldn't have said it better," M.J. said, downing the rest of the glass. "I was just going to say it's delicious! You chose a great place, Alex."

"M.J.'s right," Lin agreed. "We've talked about this for years. Thanks for finally organizing."

Alex waved it off. "It was easy. They do a wine tasting every month."

"Well, I think this is great," Lin said. "In fact, I'm going to bring Drew here! He's a big wine guy, so he'll be really impressed."

M.J. and Alex exchanged knowing glances.

"I think Lin might be in love," M.J. teased. "She's stuck in happy world."

"Hush, guys." Lin took a sip of her Syrah. "What's wrong with being happy? Drew treats me like a princess. Last night, he cooked me dinner, and we watched *Casablanca*. Then we had amazing sex."

"Hmm," Alex said noncommittally, "so what else is new with Drew?"

Lin giggled, feeling her face flush as she did. "Actually, we made love in the office the other day—"

"You're kidding me!" Alex said, appalled. "Weren't there other people there?"

"It was in my office; we locked the door, of course. Our boss walked in right after that, but we were fine," Lin said, refusing to admit how scared she'd been at the time. "It was sort of kinky."

"Ohmigosh!" M.J. covered her mouth. "You're that girl in the office. You're that boiler room girl people talk about!"

"Lin," Alex said, "this behavior is really crazy. You better be careful. News gets out quickly."

Lin swallowed. She knew Alex would have this reaction. And even though she'd been having the same thoughts herself, she wasn't willing to sit and hear her friend voice them.

"Look, Alex, I know you don't like Drew. But it's all great, really. He and I both promised we would never say anything." Lin looked at her watch. "Actually, I have to go now."

Her friends stared at her.

"You're leaving?" M.J. asked, mid-sip. "But . . . we're not done here."

"Yeah, we've only tasted two wines," Alex pointed out. "We've got five more to go."

"I know," Lin said. "I'm sorry. But I told Drew I would meet him at four. We're going shopping for something nice to wear to Auntie Betty's barbecue at the end of the month."

"Your aunt Betty's? Doesn't that mean your parents are going to be there?" M.J. asked. "They hate him."

"I know, but they have to accept the fact that Stephen and I are over and that Drew is in my life now." Lin put down her glass. "Look, I'll talk to you guys later, okay?"

As Lin sailed out of the winery, Alex looked after her with a frown. "I can't believe she just left. This is the fourth time she's bailed because of Drew."

"She's in love," M.J. said weakly.

"Yeah," Alex scowled, "in love with a jerk. Stop making excuses for her, J. Lin knows better than to ditch her girlfriends."

LIN DIDN'T think about ditching her girlfriends. The truth was, she didn't think about her friends, period. Her thoughts were completely occupied with Drew, and there was no room for anyone or anything else.

The last straw came several weeks later on the night that they were supposed to celebrate M.J.'s long-awaited interview with the legendary Michael Jordan. Caught up in sunbathing with Drew on his roof deck, Lin didn't remember the dinner until the last second. By the time she arrived, the girls were already finishing up their meals.

"I'm so sorry," Lin apologized as she ran into the restaurant. "I know I'm really late."

"Let me guess," Alex said tartly, "you were too busy having sex with Drew to remember?"

Lin blanched, taken aback by the anger in Alex's voice. M.J. bit her lip.

"Look," Lin retorted, "I know you're angry, Alex, but it's not Drew's fault."

"Why not?" Alex demanded. "You never ditched your friends

until you met him. You never acted like this when you were with Stephen."

M.J. stepped in. "Let's just simmer down for a second, girls."

Lin swallowed, feeling a sudden pressure in her chest. "That's not fair, Alex," she protested. "Drew is the best thing that's happened to me in a long time, and I would think that my friends would understand."

"Understand what?" Alex snapped. "This is a huge night for M.J. Remember M.J., your best friend? You know she's been waiting all her life for this interview, and she finally got it. You're telling me that you can't drag yourself away from this guy for one evening to help her celebrate?"

"Alex, it's okay, really—," M.J. said quickly.

"No, it's not okay," Alex interrupted, "and don't try to let her off, M.J. Lin, do you know how upset J was because you weren't here? And it's not just tonight. It's pretty much every single time we're supposed to go out nowadays. Either you're going out with Drew, or Drew needs you to do something for him, or it's something else having to do with Drew. If this guy is as great as you think he is, he can deal with you hanging out with your friends once in a while. He should want what's best for you." Alex looked Lin in the eye. "Then again, if he's hooking up with you in the office, maybe he's got his own interests in mind."

For a moment, there was nothing but silence. Then Lin whirled around toward M.J. "Is that what you think, too, J?"

M.J. dropped her gaze. After a moment, she nodded reluctantly.

Lin's face crumpled as she drew back from her friends. "You're wrong about Drew—both of you. He's sweet and romantic and supports me like no other guy ever has. He doesn't treat me like an idiot or tell me about the ten million things that are wrong with me. He makes me feel beautiful. Special. He could have any girl in the world—but he wants me. Don't you guys know what that means to me?" she cried. "Why can't you just be happy for me?"

And without waiting for a response, she turned around and fled the restaurant.

twenty-three

LIN FELT awful after her fight with the girls. So awful that she sent a much-too-expensive, overly extravagant, congratulatory bouquet of roses to M.J.'s office the next morning. And yet, she still couldn't bring herself to pick up the phone, call them, and admit that she was wrong. Because that was what this boiled down to essentially. It didn't matter that her friends were looking out for her or that they spoke with the best of intentions. All she knew was that she didn't want to believe that they could be right about Drew. She'd staked her reputation and her pride on him, and she was determined to back this pony to the finish line.

So a week passed and Lin still didn't call her friends. Even when she was aching to pick up the phone and tell them how sorry she was, she resisted the impulse. Instead, she focused her energies on Drew and occupied herself with planning his momentous introduction to her family at Aunt Betty's barbecue potluck on Thursday night.

Auntie Betty was Lin's favorite relative. She threw the best parties and made the greatest sticky rice with chicken wrapped in bamboo leaf. And for dessert, Lin could eat bowls of her famous tofu-fa, pudding made out of tofu topped with sugar cane syrup, followed by helpings of red bean with sweet lotus seed tong shui. Lin couldn't wait to introduce Drew to the sugary concoctions.

More than anything, though, Lin couldn't wait to introduce her family to Drew. A few months ago, she would never have imagined this, but now that she and Drew were a real, honest-to-goodness couple, she was finally ready to be an adult. Which is how they ended up at her aunt's doorstep on Thursday—he dashing in his Ralph Lauren jacket and she resplendent in her Pucci halter dress.

"Auntie Betty!" Lin hugged her aunt at the door. "So good to see you."

Auntie Betty was one of the most gorgeous Asian women Lin had ever known. She was fifty-three, hip, sassy, and "in" with the program. Formerly a fashion designer in Hong Kong who used to dress celebrities like Jet Li and Michelle Yeoh before they made it big, she'd quit the business when her *low-gung*, her husband, died in a car accident. These days, she depended on her mah-jong pals to keep herself occupied.

"Lin—" Her aunt embraced her. "—you get more beautiful every day."

"Thanks, Auntie." Lin beamed. "I have someone I want you to meet."

Drew walked up from behind. "Hi, I'm Drew. It's nice to meet you."

Auntie Betty hesitated for a moment then smiled. "Hello. Welcome."

As the three of them walked inside the house together, Aunt Betty pulled Lin aside and whispered, "He's very good-looking, but your mother is going to have a heart attack."

Lin smiled nervously. "You think so? I mean, I know Ma is never satisfied with anything I do, but I think she would like Drew if she got to know him. At any rate," she took a deep breath, "I guess it's time that I grow up and face the drama."

"Your ma will be okay," Auntie Betty reassured her. "She just wants to make sure you're happy and that you receive the love you deserve. Maybe she thinks you can find that with an Asian man. She's just looking out for you, you know."

"I know." Lin sighed. "It's just that I can look out for myself now."

"Understandable." Her aunt nodded and wrapped her arm around Lin. "Now let's go in and have some barbecue!"

Meanwhile, Drew was standing in the middle of the living

room, surrounded by Lin's relatives, who were all giving him death glares of disapproval. Lin caught up with him. "My parents are in the kitchen," she warned. "Just be cool, and things will be okay."

"Things will be fine, sweetie." He smiled. "Just relax and go grab yourself a burger."

Lin kissed him lightly on the lips—then froze as a tall, familiar figure strolled toward them. "Stephen!" Lin squeaked. "Wha . . . what are you doing here?"

"Hi, Lin," Stephen greeted her with a warm smile. "I was visiting my folks and ran into Aunt Betty. She mentioned you were coming home, so I thought I'd drop by. It's been a while since karaoke."

Lin turned and shot Aunt Betty an accusing look. Her aunt had the grace to appear sheepish, but she still seemed to find the whole thing more amusing than anything else.

"You guys were at karaoke?" Drew asked.

Lin blushed. "Oh, the girls and I went the other night and ran into Stephen," she said quickly.

He stuck his hand out. "I'm Stephen."

"Oh," Lin said hastily, "this is Drew, my—" She stopped, not knowing how to proceed, given the awkwardness of the situation.

Stephen shook Drew's hand. "Nice to meet you."

"So," Drew said slowly, "you're Stephen. I've heard about you."

Lin groaned. Drew was doing that thing she hated—deliberately saying something to assert his supremacy. It was one thing to do this in the workplace, but to pull this kind of thing here . . .

Fortunately, Stephen seemed unfazed. "So," he said cheerfully, "have you sampled Lin's grandmother's fried dumplings yet—"

Lin exhaled inwardly. Thank goodness for Stephen. She could always count on him to bail her out of tough situations. Certainly, considering how much Lin's family adored him, Stephen could have made an already awkward situation infinitely worse. Instead, he was actually smoothing things over for all of them. Maybe this wouldn't be a complete disaster. . . . Then Kim walked into the room with a skinny Asian man Lin didn't recognize, who was wearing a bow tie, horn-rimmed glasses, and pants that were much too short for him. Behind Kim, she could see her sister Sarah gesturing wildly at her, but Lin had no idea what she was trying to convey.

"Lin!" her mother said excitedly when she caught sight of her daughter. "Guess who made it to dinner tonight? This is Larry—"

Larry? Her supposed setup from a few months ago? Of all the ridiculous coincidences! Not to mention horrendous timing. How could she deal with Stephen, Drew, and her fresh-off-the-boat blind date all at the same time? Lin gaped at her would-be suitor. He seemed nice enough, but he wasn't Lin's type at all. Certainly, he could not have been more different from Drew, if he tried. Or Stephen . . .

Meanwhile, Kim had finally caught sight of Drew. Stopping abruptly, her animated smile immediately flattened out into a thin line. She planted her fists on her hips. "What is going on?" she demanded.

"Nothing, Mom." Lin smiled cheerily. "Are you enjoying Aunt Betty's fried fish balls?"

"Yes, I am." Kim pointed at Drew, undeterred. "But what is going on with you and him?"

"Hi, Mrs. Cho." Drew came over and gave her his sweetest, most sincere smile. "How are you? Good to see you again."

Kim frowned. "So you two dating?"

Lin and Drew looked at each other. This was the moment of truth.

"Mom," Lin began, "I know how you feel about me dating someone who's not Chinese, but I really like Drew and he really likes me, so yes, we're dating."

Kim looked stunned. Poor Larry had a what-have-I-gotten-myself-into expression on his face. Suddenly, Lin had a flashback to when her mother had taken her and her friends to the fortune-teller. Kim had been so worried that Lin would end up with a "white devil"—apparently, her fears had come true.

Meanwhile, in the background was Lin's great-grandmother Ling. Once she caught sight of Drew, she dropped her porcelain spoon and immediately started screaming in Chinese, *"Ah-Yah . . . bok gwai ah!"*

Stephen hurried over to Lin's grandmother to try to calm her down. Drew looked around like he had just walked into some alternate dimension. Lin turned to Aunt Betty, pleading with her to make Ling stop screaming "Oh my goodness, there's a white man!" At the same time, Sarah hastened over to help Stephen, while Larry stood off to one side, looking like he wished he could disappear. In short, it was chaos.

Meanwhile, the rest of the relatives burst into excited Cantonese chatter.

"Who is the white devil?"

"Why did Lin bring him home? What was she thinking?"

"She is a bad daughter. How could she do this to Kim?"

"Is he her boyfriend?"

"Of course not. He is a white devil. He can't be her boyfriend."

"White devils only want one thing—to corrupt good Chinese girls."

Fortunately, Drew didn't understand what they were saying. Unfortunately for Lin, she understood every word. How could her relatives say such awful things? She felt like screaming, lashing out, telling them that they were wrong. But she couldn't. Once again, she had shown herself to be a disappointment, yet another example of how she would never live up to her mother's expectations. . . .

Kim turned to frown at Lin. "Look at the mess you made."

Lin's eyes began to well up.

"I'm sorry to disrupt your family," Drew said. "If you want me to go, I'll go."

"Stop it," Lin cried. "You're not going anywhere. It's about time that my family learns to deal with reality. I'm not going to let them tell me how to live my life. You're with me, and I want everyone to know it."

Unfortunately, Kim did not share her daughter's views. Turning Lin toward her, she snapped, "How could you, Lin? You bring white guy home and scare your *pau pau.*"

"Mom!" Lin screamed. "Look, the last thing I want to do is to come here and cause trouble, but you all have to understand that I really like Drew. Just because he's not Asian doesn't mean that he's evil."

"Lin," Drew interrupted, "I'm going to go. I shouldn't be here. I'll call you later. You need to straighten things out with your family."

He gave her a quick kiss on the forehead and left. Lin watched him leave as tears rolled down her cheeks.

AFTER THE fiasco with her family, Lin dreaded seeing Drew. She was sure that he was horrified by the whole scene, convinced that she came from a family of lunatics. He would probably tell her he never wanted to see her again, while she would burst into an embarrassing display of tears.

As it turned out, she didn't have to worry. Because she didn't see Drew the next day or the day after that. Apparently, their office was a lot larger than she realized because he was nowhere to be found. And he didn't even e-mail or call or leave a voice mail.

Finally, he showed up on her doorstep Sunday night. He smiled at her, and when he took her into his arms, Lin couldn't bring herself to say anything about the "incident." They never did speak about it. And while a part of Lin was relieved, the other part of her wondered why.

She was still wondering hours later, as they were lying in her bed in silence. Why couldn't they talk about the episode with her family? With Stephen, her family had been an ever-present topic; if anything, it was Lin who had tried to deflect the conversation away from them, tried to create space between them and the overpowering presence of Kim.

She looked across the pillow at Drew, and for the first time, she noticed that they never really had anything to say to each other in moments like these. It was as if they had both expended all the conversation they had in them to get to this moment, and once they did, there was nothing left.

It didn't matter, Lin decided. He was with her, and that was good enough. Now she just had to get her parents to speak to her again.

A WEEK later, Lin finally had a talk with her parents about Drew over dim sum at the Gum Fung restaurant in Flushing. Taking a deep breath, she calmly sat down with them and told her parents they needed to accept that she was making decisions for her own life.

"I knew that Drew man would be trouble first time I saw him!" Kim declared. "He has shifty look in his eyes—"

"Mom!" Lin threw up her hands. "Have you heard a word I said? I know you don't approve of Drew, but it's my life, and I want to be with him!"

Her parents stared at her, momentarily silenced by her outburst.

"I just love you," Kim said, lowering her voice, "don't want to see my daughter hurt. You know white men like to divorce. . . . I don't want you to go through that."

"I know, Mom," Lin said, "but I can look out for myself. I know you want me to be with someone like Stephen, but I'm an adult now and you have to let me make my own decisions."

Lin's dad, Harry, had always been the quiet father, who no doubt developed this self-defense mechanism after years of marriage to Kim. Although he never said much, Lin always thought of him as the voice of reason in their family.

"Forget it," Harry spoke up. "Just eat some more turnip cakes and finish this dish of chicken feet."

"You're the best, dad." Lin hugged him. "I'm glad that everything is okay."

Lin glanced over at her mother, but Kim was mute.

. . .

"HENRY, IT'S been a rough few weeks," Lin said on the phone to her client, a surgeon at Bellevue. It was the day after dim sum with her parents, and Lin was having one of those no-time-for-coffee kind of mornings. "The market should be fine in the next couple of days. No worries, okay?"

As Lin hung up the phone, Rob knocked on her door.

"Hey, Rob, come on in," she said. "Have a seat. What can I do for you?"

"Not much," he said as he closed the door. "Have a few minutes? I want to talk to you about a couple of things."

"Sure," she said slowly, "something wrong?"

"Well, I guess I should tell you this before we meet with Drew later on," Rob began.

"Okay." Lin nodded uncertainly.

"Lin, I know that since you first started here, you've always expressed an interest in the international development of our company. Well, one of the changes that we're making is that we're trying to give some traders here the chance to work overseas. So I'm offering you a position in London for six months at the headquarters there. It would be a great opportunity for you," he explained.

Lin's mouth dropped open. "Wow, thank you so much for the offer. I don't know what to say. I'm honored, but I don't think I can give you an answer just yet. I mean, this is so sudden."

And yet, even as she babbled on, Lin felt the excitement bubble up inside her. All her life, she'd dreamt of two things: being a millionaire by the time she was thirty—and living in London. She'd always loved London. The tradition, the history, the unique old-world charm so different from the strip malls that she grew up with. She was sixteen when she first visited, and it was still the most exhilarating experience of her life. Besides that, this was her chance to finally see how she measured up against the competition.

"You don't have to decide anything immediately. The offer is there, and I've told my colleagues all about you. When you feel you're ready, please give them a call," Rob said, handing her a piece of paper. "By the way, I'm not going to mention anything to Drew because this should be something that's between us until you make your decision."

"Agreed." She nodded. "Thank you so much, Rob. I'm really grateful about this . . ." She trailed off as she noticed Drew chatting with Lana, the admin girl, outside her office.

Noticing Lin's preoccupation, Rob glanced behind him and chuckled. "He's quite the charmer, that Drew."

Her face froze. "Oh, really?" she asked.

"You must have noticed," Rob remarked. "You two spend a lot of time together."

"Actually, I didn't notice . . . ," she began when Drew entered her office.

"I hope I'm not interrupting this party," he said blithely, oblivious to Lin's frown. "How is everyone today?"

"Great, Drew. I was just saying how popular you've been lately." Rob looked pointedly at Lana outside the office.

Drew chuckled. "Well, I guess I'm just a popular guy. Right, Lin?"

Lin blinked. What kind of a line was that?

"Let me know how it goes." Rob shot Drew a wink. "Anyway, catch you all later and thanks again, Lin."

"Thank you," she responded automatically.

Drew closed the door behind Rob. "Hey, cutie," he said, reaching for her hand. "What's going on?"

"Nothing." She pulled her hand away. "Why don't you go talk to Lana out there?"

"What? What are you talking about?" Drew opened his eyes wide.

"I'm not invisible, you know. I was right here when you practically gloated to Rob about being Mr. Popularity with the ladies."

"Look, I can't help what other people think. You and I are together, but no one can know. You know that. I have to play it as cool as possible." Drew leaned forward. "Look, guys check you out all the time, but I don't give a shit because I know in the end, I have you."

On any other day, Lin might have let the comment slide by. But she couldn't get Rob's words out of her head. "Have me? Am I some kind of prize?" she demanded, her voice rising.

Drew jerked away. He was used to the flirty Lin, the sweet Lin—not this angry woman finding fault with him.

"Where is this coming from, Lin? I don't need this from you first thing in the morning." He scowled. "I'll see you later."

Lin watched miserably as he stormed out of her office.

THE REST of the day was unmitigated torture. Lin tried to focus on her work, but it was a futile task. The thought that she might have lost Drew—she didn't even want to contemplate the possibility. All her life, she'd wanted someone like him—handsome, successful, and most of all, confident. Drew believed he was better than anyone else—and when Lin was with him, she felt like she was better than anyone else, too. Not like she felt when she was with her mother, who never failed to point out how she was lacking in one respect or another.

The worst part, though, was she had absolutely no one to talk to about this—after all, she wasn't exactly on the top of M.J. or Alex's favorites list at the moment.

Still, after a sleepless night tossing and turning, Lin picked up the phone and called the person most likely to forgive her. "J?" she said tentatively. "It's Lin."

There was a pause. "Hey, Lin! What's up?"

Lin exhaled as she heard M.J.'s cheerful voice. Fortunately, M.J. was much more willing than Alex to let bygones be bygones. After a few awkward moments, they were talking like old times, and Lin had poured out the whole story about Drew.

"I don't think I'm a jealous person," Lin said to M.J. as she stared out her window at the city skyline.

"You're not, chickie," M.J. said soothingly. "He just overreacted and didn't know what to do. Men avoid confrontation. You need to talk to him."

"You're right." Lin sighed. "I do. I just think I'm used to talking everything out like I did with Stephen. Deep down, I feel like I don't know how things stand anymore. I think I want a commitment from Drew, but I'm trying to talk myself out of one because I don't want to deal with anything."

"Of course you feel that way, honey. You just got into a fight with a guy you really care about, and you don't want to get hurt."

"Well, it's not just that." Lin hesitated. "I just feel . . . an emptiness in my life right now. I mean, I know I have a good job, and I have a really good life, but still . . ." She took a deep breath. "J, you know how I used to dream about working overseas?"

"How could I not? That was all you could ever talk about for a while. I was going to smack you over the head and buy you a plane ticket to Europe myself." M.J. laughed.

"Well," Lin paused, "I've been offered a job in London, but I haven't made my decision yet."

"Are you serious?" M.J. gasped. "That's amazing! Congratulations! What's holding you back? Drew?"

"No. Well, yes and no. I mean, all of that stuff about Europe was just talk. Now that it's finally happening, I'm not sure what to do . . . I love New York. I love my friends. I love my job. I love my family. And now I have Drew. How can I just leave him without giving him a chance . . . without seeing if we have something together?"

"I understand." M.J.'s tone was sympathetic. "Look, whatever you decide, I know you'll make the right decision."

"Thanks, hon." Lin sighed. "I'm sorry I haven't been in touch. I know you and Alex are annoyed with me."

"It's okay," M.J. replied. "And Alex will be fine. We're just worried about you. Even though we'd really miss you if you went to London, we'll support you one hundred percent, no matter what you decide to do."

Lin smiled. "I know. You're the best friend a girl could have. And I promise I'll make more of an effort to see you guys." She took a deep breath. "I think I'm going to tell Drew about the job offer tonight. I haven't spoken to him all day, and I've been ignoring his phone calls."

"Just talk to him," M.J. urged her. "Everything needs to be out in the open. That's what a real relationship is—well, that's what I'm learning it's all about anyway."

"You're right. Normally, I wouldn't hesitate, but we work together so it makes things a bit tricky. . . ."

LIN ALWAYS thought that the worst thing about a fight with a boyfriend was the waiting. Was there going to be another screaming match? Was it over? Or would there be kissing and making up? As she sat in her office Wednesday morning, she couldn't help wondering. Then there was no more time to ponder as she heard a knock on her door.

"Come in," Lin called as she typed in a trade.

"Hi." Drew appeared in the doorway.

She looked up. "Hi."

Drew closed the door behind him. He walked over to Lin and handed her a rose, which she accepted slowly. "Lin, I acted like an ass, and I'm sorry."

She bit her lip. "You're sorry, huh?"

"Yes." Drew gave her a remorseful look. "I shouldn't have blown up at you like that the other day . . . but you do have to admit that you were acting pretty jealous."

"Well, I have the right to be when my boyfriend is flirting with other women in front of my face," Lin shot back.

"Okay, okay." Drew held up his hands in surrender as he leaned over to give her a light kiss on the lips. "How about we go out for some drinks with people here tonight, then go back to my place and make up?"

"Hmm . . . sounds like a plan, but what's with tonight's gig?" Lin wrinkled her forehead.

"Everyone's going to grab some drinks at Victor's Café for Rick's going-away party. I want you to be there," Drew said.

"I'm swamped, but I'll stop by, I promise." She licked her lips. "I also want to talk to you about something important tonight. It's about my meeting with Rob."

"Okay, no problem. Speaking of which, I have to talk to him now, too." He headed for the door. "I'll catch you later."

As Lin watched him walk out of her office, she relaxed into a smile. That was definitely better than she'd expected it to be. As she smelled her red rose, someone knocked on her door again. A moment later, Krishan poked his head in.

"Hey, Krishan." She smiled. "What's up?"

"Just wanted to let you know that you have a package outside by reception." He nodded toward the flower. "Nice rose, by the way. Did you steal that from Mary Klein's office? Her husband sent her a dozen roses for their anniversary, and she's missing a few."

Lin looked momentarily confused. "Um, no, someone gave this to me."

"Ahhhh . . ." Krishan smiled. "The boyfriend, huh? Very nice. Very nice." He waved good-bye. "All right, I'll catch you later."

AFTER KRISHAN left, Lin sat at her desk for a long while. It was strange, this feeling she had. She should have been thrilled, ecstatic, basking in happiness because all was well with Drew again. Instead, all she felt was a quiet unease. . . .

Stop it! Lin told herself sternly. *Stop looking for trouble, Lin.* She took a deep breath, determined to combat this bout of insecurity. After all, didn't Auntie Lee say she would find love? Well, she definitely loved Drew, and he clearly loved her since he still wanted to be with her after the fiasco with her family and her little meltdown.

Resolve strengthened, she called M.J. to gush about the positive turn of events.

"Well, that's cool," M.J. said, "it's great that you guys patched things up."

"I think I just blew the whole thing out of proportion," Lin sighed. "I was overwhelmed and tired and I just lost it. It's not his fault that all these women flirt with him. Considering how crazy I acted, he was really very understanding. And he was so sweet when we made up!"

"Mm-hmm," M.J. said.

Lin paused. "What's wrong?"

"What do you mean?" her friend asked.

"Because you sound like Alex."

"It's nothing," M.J. said quickly. "It just . . . sounds like you're making excuses for him."

Lin frowned. "Don't be ridiculous. I'm just being supportive. J, you should know that's a huge part of every relationship."

"Right," M.J. said neutrally.

"Look, Drew is a great guy, despite what everyone says. You'll see." And she would do whatever it took to make things work, Lin vowed to herself. Including not going to London.

"SO, DREW, where's Lin and Rob?" Krishan took a sip of his Belvedere on the rocks.

"Rob isn't going to make it, and I think Lin's coming in a little while. Nice tie, by the way." Drew flipped over Krishan's tie to check out the brand.

Krishan swatted his hand away. "Excellent. How is her new boyfriend, by the way?"

Drew jerked to attention as he looked at Krishan strangely. "New boyfriend? What are you talking about?"

"Don't play dumb with me, Mr. Charming. It's not a secret anymore. I know all about it. Lin and I went to college together, and she hasn't been this happy in years. You should have seen her the other day when she came out of her office. She was glowing," Krishan smiled. "By the way, every guy in this office is so envious of you. You get to spend every moment with her."

Drew was stunned but played it cool. How could she have told Krishan? Now the entire office knew. He drained his beer in a single gulp. "How long have you known?" he asked calmly.

"For a few weeks." Krishan frowned as he quickly caught on to Drew's reaction. "What's wrong? You look like you're about to kill a small country."

Drew asked the bartender for two shots of tequila and downed them both. Then he ordered a couple more shots.

"I say we call Lin now," he shouted to all the boys after his fifth shot.

"You don't have to," Krishan said, "she's right here."

"Hey, guys!" Lin smiled as she walked in and gave them all a hug.

As she turned to hug Drew, he pushed her away roughly. Lin was confused but she just turned and ordered herself a drink without saying anything.

"What's wrong with you?" Lin asked him quietly a few minutes later. "Is everything okay?"

"Oh, everything is just dandy." Drew downed his sixth shot. "Actually, I was just telling the boys here how good you were in bed."

Her eyes widened. "What?"

Krishan and all the guys started laughing, thinking that Drew was clearly wasted.

"I don't know what he's talking about," she joked. "How many shots has Mr. Black had here?"

"Stop playing dumb!" he hollered. "How dare you tell everyone in the office about us!"

As his voice rose, conversation around them came to an immediate standstill.

Lin stared at him. She had no idea what had possessed Drew, why he seemed hell-bent on ruining everything. All she knew was that she had to get out of there—immediately.

"Listen, I don't know what kind of stunt you're trying to pull, but I'm leaving," she announced, turning toward the door.

"Hold it!" Drew said. "Before you go, I just want to let you know that no one does a 'meeting' like you do."

Lin froze. She couldn't believe her ears. Fighting back tears, she forced herself to turn around and face Drew as her whole office watched them.

"You know what, asshole?" she yelled. "I don't know what you've been drinking, but I never, and I repeat, never, told anyone about us. You, on the other hand, obviously can't keep your big mouth shut."

"Oh yeah? Then can you explain to me why Krishan knows about your new boyfriend?"

"He knows because I told him I had a new boyfriend, but I never told him that it was you. I'm not the one who's a moron," she said, silent tears rolling down her cheeks.

Drew stared at her, stunned. Unable to stand the whispers and glances around them anymore, Lin turned and fled.

Krishan walked up to Drew. "Man, you're a sack of shit. She never told me her new guy was you. And it was *you* who stole Mary Klein's roses, wasn't it?"

Drew's mouth opened but no words came out.

twenty-four

LIN COULDN'T breathe.

Somehow, she'd gotten herself home, slammed the door behind her, and collapsed in a heap on the floor. How could she have let this happen? How could she have been so wrong? Lin clutched her head in her hands and started rocking back and forth, her breath coming in short, ragged sobs.

"Oh my God," she whispered, "what have I done?"

She knew the answer, of course. She'd taken her wonderful life, her super-successful career, her supportive family and friends—and trashed them all for an obnoxious jerk.

There was only one thing to do. Lin reached into her bag and yanked out her cell phone.

"OPEN UP!" M.J. banged on the door. "I know you're in there!"

Lin opened the door in tears. "Leave me alone. I want to curl up and die right now."

"No, you don't." M.J. followed her into her apartment. "The Lin Cho I know is not going to let some asshole get her down."

"How could he humiliate me like that in front of everyone from work? And after all I've gone through to get my parents to accept him," she sobbed. "I will never understand."

At that moment, the doorbell rang. M.J. opened the door—it was Alex. Lin bit her lip. It had been weeks since they last spoke. . . .

Alex stepped in. "Oh, Lin," she said as she gave her friend a big hug. Lin's face cleared as she relaxed in her friend's embrace.

"Do you want me to kick his ass for you?" M.J. asked.

Lin smiled through her tears. "Oh, guys . . . I feel like such an idiot."

"Don't say that," Alex said. "You know that's not true."

"I have to," Lin cried. "You guys warned me—but did I listen? No—even though I knew what kind of guy Drew was." She wiped a tear from her eye. "I knew he was bad news. I knew—I knew he could be a jerk," she sniffled. "I saw all the signs, but I just . . . I guess I just didn't think he could be a jerk to me."

"Honey, honey." M.J. stroked her hair. "You were in love. We've all been there."

Lin shook her head. "This is different," she cried. "I took him home. I even ditched you guys for him!"

Alex put an arm around Lin. "Forget about that. It's in the past now. Look, what can we do to help?"

Lin looked up at her friends gratefully. After all she'd done, she wouldn't have blamed them for turning a deaf ear, and yet, here they were. That set her up for a new round of tears.

"I just want all of this to go away," Lin sobbed. "I don't want to be part of that world anymore."

"Then make a fresh start," M.J. said. "Take that job in London!"

"You got a job offer in London?" Alex exclaimed. "That's so awesome. You better take it before I do."

"Yeah, it's—it's a six-month gig. It would be amazing, but—"

"But what?" M.J. persisted. "But you can stay here and look at that asshole every day and have the whole office know about your sex life? You should go, explore the world, and see what's out there."

"Do you really think so?" Lin asked, her eyes moist.

"We both do," Alex said firmly. "Maybe something good can come out of all this."

"Maybe." Lin bit her lip. "I feel really awful about how I've been acting lately." She swallowed hard. "I know," she sniffled, "I know I've been a terrible friend. You guys were so patient with me, and I—I treated your friendship like it was nothing." She hung her head. "I'm so sorry," she whispered, "I just hope you guys can forgive me."

Her friends were silent. Lin stared down at the carpet, afraid to look up. She didn't blame her friends if they didn't want to have anything to do with her, but she was also terrified of losing them. She'd failed everyone: her friends, her family, but most of all herself. With that track record, she'd be lucky if they'd ever want her back.

Finally, after what seemed like an eternity, she looked up at them. All she saw was kindness.

"Don't cry—of course we forgive you." M.J. threw her arms around Lin and hugged her tightly.

"M.J.'s right." Alex put her arms around them both. "We'll always be here for you—no matter what."

Lin smiled. "Thanks, guys," she said tearfully. "What am I going to do without you in London?"

"You're going to have a great time," Alex said firmly. "And you're going to dazzle everyone over there with how great a stockbroker you are."

"That's right," M.J. added. "You've always got us, but this is a once-in-a-lifetime opportunity."

For the first time that day, Lin's face lit up. "Wow, me and London?" she mused. "It really could be something."

AS LIN set foot into the office two days later, she couldn't help but think of the times in college when she got really drunk, woke up in some guy's bed, and then had to face his roommates in the morning. At this very moment, Lin felt the same way about facing everyone at work and worst of all—Drew.

"Good morning, Lana." Lin forced a smile as she walked by reception.

"Good morning," Lana sneered, narrowing her eyes. "You don't look so good. Bad night?"

"I'm fine." Lin walked away quickly—and right smack into Tom Wexler.

"Hey, Lin." Tom leered. "I had no idea you were such a naughty girl."

"Shove it, Tom," she snapped as she strode off.

Behind her, she could feel his eyes boring into her back. Tom had always been a sleaze, but previously his innuendo had always been tinged with respect. The way he'd looked at her today, though . . . she could still feel him mentally undressing her without even the slight hint of pretense.

Get a grip, Lin thought as she made her way to her office. *Don't let them get to you.*

But no sooner did she have that thought than she turned the corner—and saw Mark Shin. He was busy looking at a sheaf of papers in his hand, but just as Lin started to tiptoe past him, he looked up and saw her.

She stopped, caught. "Uh, hi, Mark," she mumbled.

For a moment, he just stared at her, no doubt thinking how she had disgraced the Asian race by her affair with the "white devil." Then, without saying a word, he walked off.

It was strange, Lin thought. All that time when Mark was chasing after her, she had wanted nothing more than to be rid of him. But now . . . seeing him look at her as if she were last night's trash, Lin felt herself yearning for anything—a glance, an understanding smile—from him.

Still, that was nothing compared with her meeting with Rob. For the first five minutes she was in his office, he didn't even acknowledge her as he chatted on the phone and pounded out e-mails. Finally, after an eternity, he put the phone down.

"Rob—," Lin began. She'd practiced this speech ever since she'd called Rich Benjamin to accept the offer the day before, and yet, now that the time had come, the words died in her throat. What could she really say to make this better? They both knew this world they lived and worked in remained a male-dominated vat of misogyny. It wasn't enough for a woman to be successful and hard-working; the women who survived the boiler room knew that they had to be twice as tough, twice as good as their male counterparts. There was no room for error, no cushion for slipups—Lin knew this, and she'd always prided herself on being able to ride the top echelons with the boys. Rob had seen her ability, had rolled the dice on throwing his support behind a twenty-something Asian woman—and now, Lin had crushed both their hopes. With one slip of judgment, she had gone from top-flight, universally respected power broker to just another trader's floozy.

"I'm sorry, Rob," she said finally.

Rob didn't look at her as he shuffled the papers on his desk. "Rich Benjamin is one of my closest friends, and a really good guy. He'll take care of you there."

Lin nodded. She tried to think of something to say, anything to alleviate the awkward tension. . . .

"Thank you, Rob."

He looked up at last, and in his eyes, Lin saw disappointment and sadness. Rob held out his hand. "Have a safe flight, Lin."

Somehow, Lin managed to step forward and shake his hand limply. She escaped to the door and shut it gently behind her.

Standing there in the hallway, Lin felt herself start to tear up. She was hunched over sniveling when footsteps sounded behind her.

"Lin?"

She turned. Thankfully, it was Krishan.

Upon seeing her face, he quickly steered her into an empty office nearby. "Come on, Lin." He gave her a fierce hug. "Don't let those bastards get the best of you."

Lin sniffled. "I'm trying, but it's so hard, Krishan. It's bad enough that I have Lana looking at me like I'm trailer trash, and

Mark acting like he never knew me, but Rob—Krishan, you don't know what it was like with Rob. He could barely even look me in the eye!"

Krishan looked at her gently. "This whole thing sucks. It's not your fault that Drew can't keep his mouth shut."

"I can't even think about him," Lin cried. "Hopefully, I can leave this place without seeing him."

Krishan laid a hand on her shoulder. "Listen to me, Lin Cho. You are stronger than Drew Black. You are stronger than those jackasses out there. You are stronger than this whole office."

Lin wiped her eyes. "I don't know . . . this is the only job I've ever known. I'm not going to know anyone in London. It'll be like starting all over again."

"And you're going to love it," he declared. "You're going to show those Brits how it's done by the big boys. Or girls. And that's an order from your captain."

That finally got a smile out of Lin. "Thanks, Krishan."

GIVEN THE miserable day that she'd already had, Lin had only one wish: to get out of the office without seeing Drew.

After saying good-bye to Krishan, Lin headed to her office and closed the door behind her. Krishan had already packed up most of her stuff the day before after she told him she'd accepted the London offer, so she just had to make a quick check to be sure she wasn't leaving anything behind.

She found the note and the bouquet of roses on her chair. It read: "Dear Lin, I feel like such an asshole. I am so sorry for everything and hope that we can still talk things over. I miss you, Drew."

Lin suddenly felt tearful again. She took a deep breath and looked outside her window. She had to keep telling herself that she would be in London in no time. Then her heart started racing when she heard a knock on the door.

"Hi." Drew entered tentatively. "How are you?"

Lin forced a bright smile. "I'm doing great. Going to London."

"I know. I heard. Big decision, huh?"

Lin nodded wordlessly. There was an awkward moment of silence.

Then Drew closed the door. "Lin, I'm so sorry. I really am. I'm the biggest jerk in the world." He looked into her eyes. "I'm going to miss you so much. We really had something special."

"Look, Drew," she managed to say, "nobody is sadder than me about what happened. But we had nothing. You love the idea of me. You loved that everyone at work was jealous of you when you were with me. But you don't really care about me, because you never would have said such horrible things and embarrassed me the way that you did."

Drew swallowed. "Come on, Lin. That's not true. I had to have you the moment I saw you. It was love at first sight."

"No, Drew, it was lust at first sight. You had to have me, and once you did, there was nothing left." She blinked away the tears in her eyes. "I'm sorry, but I have to leave. I mean, do you honestly think that I could work here with all these people knowing about us?"

"Lin." Drew actually looked sorry. "How can I make you change your mind?"

Lin stared at him. Once upon a time, this would have been all she ever wanted: Drew willing to do anything to be with her. But as she looked at his handsome, familiar features, all she could hear were the words he'd said to her the night before—words so hurtful that just remembering them made her physically cringe.

"You can't," she whispered. "Good-bye, Drew."

She grabbed her purse and the box on her desk, then jetted out of her office without a backward glance.

SEEING DREW had been hard, just as Lin knew it would be. But it was even tougher telling her parents the next night.

"What?" Kim gasped. "You going to London?"

Lin took a deep breath. "I know this is a shock, but it's a big step up for me. Only a couple people get this opportunity. I can't turn it down."

"But you going to be alone in London!" Kim exclaimed.

"I'll be fine," Lin reassured her. "The company's found me a fantastic apartment, and I've already started researching all the London neighborhoods. You'll be happy—there's supposed to be a great supermarket right around the corner from my apartment."

Kim frowned. "That not enough."

"Look, I know you guys don't want me to go," Lin sighed, "but I wish you wouldn't make this more difficult for me. I have to go—I really have to go."

There was a long pause, then her dad spoke up. "Go, Lin," he said. "This wonderful honor. You accept it."

Lin smiled at her father gratefully. Somehow, he always came through for her. Which was why he wasn't the one who worried her. She turned to look at her mother. "Mom?"

Kim sat down heavily on a chair, suddenly looking old and tired. "London far away. Who take care of you there?"

Lin looked at her mother, and suddenly, it was like a veil had been lifted. For the past fifteen years, all Lin could see and hear were the lectures, the reprimands, the ceaseless murmuring. Now, for the first time, she realized her mother was scared—scared about what would happen to Lin and scared of losing her.

She reached down and hugged her mother tightly. "I'll be okay, Mom. I promise."

WHILE SAYING good-bye to her parents was hard, it was nothing compared with saying good-bye to her girls.

The evening before Lin's departure, M.J. and Alex took Lin out for a glamorous night on the town. They went to her favorite restaurant, Tao, and ended the evening with cocktails at Lotus.

For most of the evening, they gossiped and chattered away about anything and everything. Alex talked about some big case she and Brady were working on, M.J. told them about Jagger's clothing line being launched in some stores in the West Village. Even Ming dropped by to say good-bye.

"Just remember," he instructed before he left. "Stick with the fish and stay away from the Chinese food."

Lin smiled at him. Even though Ming had been M.J.'s friend first, he'd become like a surrogate brother to all of them over the years. "Aren't you going to tell me that this is what comes from being with white guys?"

Ming just hugged her. "You'll have a great time."

Later, as the evening drew on, and things started to come to their inevitable close, Lin felt increasingly tearful. "Oh, guys," she sighed, "maybe I shouldn't do this!"

Her friends stared at her.

"What are you talking about, Lin?" Alex touched her hand. "You have to do this!"

"You'll be living in a fabulous city," M.J. added. "You're going to have so much fun there!"

"But I won't be having fun with you guys," she said. "It won't be the same."

"Of course it will," Alex assured her. "We'll e-mail and talk on the phone all the time."

"Yeah," M.J. chimed in, "you can tell us about all your exploits and make us crazy with envy!"

Lin laughed despite herself. She knew that her friends were trying hard to make her feel better. And even though she had no doubt that they would write and call all the time, she also knew it wouldn't be the same. If she had a bad day, she wouldn't be able to complain to her friends over a drink. She couldn't count on getting the latest, up-to-the-minute scoop on whatever was going on in their lives. She wouldn't be able to join their dinners, late-night cocktails, their Saturday morning brunches. Lin felt as if a part of her was being severed, cut off forever.

"You're going to love London," M.J. declared. "You've always wanted to go there."

"Yeah, but there's a difference between wanting to do something and actually having to do it," Lin said sadly.

LIN KNEW it wasn't going to be easy.

As the moment of her departure drew near, she became increasingly conscious of how much she depended on her friends, her family, her mom. Even when she went to college, she could count on having M.J. there. Certainly, she'd relied on all of them now to get her through this ordeal—helping her pack, sublet her apartment, and take care of the myriad details that she would never have been able to handle in such a short time period. But now, there was going to be an entire span of ocean between her entire support network . . . and her.

The farewells at the airport were the hardest part. Lin's father patted her awkwardly then stood silently by her side as Kim alternated between lecturing, scolding, and crying. As for Alex and M.J., they managed to keep up a cheerful chatter until it was time for Lin to leave—at which point, they both looked suspiciously shiny-eyed as they hugged her good-bye at the security checkpoint. Standing there in her friends' embrace, all Lin could think about was how she'd be able to weather the next year without them.

Still, Lin felt a sense of relief as her plane lifted off and away from New York that night. She loved her city, but at that moment, it had Drew's imprint all over it—the restaurants where they'd shared candlelight dinners, the park trails they'd jogged, the stores where they'd spent huge chunks of their salaries. Leaving all that for a completely foreign city was exactly what she needed.

Seven hours later, the jet landed at Heathrow. Carrying a messenger bag and sporting a black blazer, jeans, and sneakers, Lin exited the plane and walked through customs. She smiled as she heard the accents in the airport, saw the policemen in their bobby hats, and experienced the familiar-yet-unfamiliar feel of London.

Once she was in the baggage claim, though, her smile faded. A mass of unfamiliar faces confronted her, smiling, calling out greetings, holding out welcome banners—but not for Lin.

"Are you Lin Cho?"

She looked up. A handsome, ruddy, reddish-blond-haired man was smiling at her.

"Um, yeah," she said. "And you are—?"

"Ned Stone." He held out a hand. "Your new colleague and current welcoming committee."

Lin smiled and shook his hand. "It's nice to meet you. Actually, it's really nice to meet you. I was just wondering how I was going to get myself to the apartment."

"Well, wonder no more. Rich Benjamin sent me to make sure we got you to corporate housing safe and sound. So, to that end . . . let's get your bags."

"Sounds good to me!" Lin followed Ned toward the baggage claim area.

"And once we get you to your place, we'll go lift a pint at this pub I know nearby and get to know each other," he added.

Lin hesitated. "Look, Ned," she said slowly, "I just want you to know right off the bat that I'm not really looking for any kind of involvement. . . ."

Ned looked at her, his brow furrowed. Then his forehead cleared. "Oh, wait," he chuckled, "you got it all wrong." He held up his left hand and wiggled the ring finger—where a bright gold band gleamed.

Lin covered her mouth. "Omigosh," she gasped, "I am so sorry. I am such an idiot—"

Ned laughed and put an arm around her. "Don't worry about it. In fact, you'll meet my wife at the pub. She's a broker, too, so you guys will have a lot in common."

Lin smiled. "I would really like that."

twenty-five

LIN LOVED London.

She loved that she could walk to work along the Thames in the mid-August haze. She loved that she could watch *Romeo and Juliet* on the floor of the Globe by moonlight. She loved that she could spend an entire Saturday exploring Harrods and never manage to see everything. More than anything, she loved that there was an entire ocean between her and Drew Black.

It wasn't until now that Lin realized how much he'd influenced her everyday life. Working with him and dating him at the same time had imposed an omnipresent strain on her that she hadn't noticed until it was gone. Not only did Lin have to deal with the pressures of work, but she was also constantly on edge about their romance being discovered. Not to mention her worries about keeping Drew interested and away from other girls.

In comparison, being in the London office was a relief. The only thing anyone there knew about her was her reputation as a stockbroker. Lin was able to walk the halls freely and not have to worry about whispers following her. Her new boss and colleagues accepted her readily, while e-mails from Alex and M.J. provided a welcome touchstone any time Lin felt a touch of uncertainty or self-doubt.

Now that the pressure was gone, Lin was amazed at how relaxed she felt, how clearly she was able to think without the specter of Drew around every corner.

"OKAY, I'LL take that in pink," Lin pointed to the cotton-candy-colored Kate Spade straw purse in the window. "And if you have the wallet that goes along with it, I'll take that, too."

It was Saturday, and Lin was spending it in her favorite way imaginable: shopping at Harrods. There was something comforting about the brightly lit display cases, the endless stream of chattering tourists, the confectionery-like array of consumer goods before her. It was exactly the kind of sensory overload Lin liked—the kind that distracted her enough so that she wouldn't have to think.

Because Lin had a lot of time to think in London. She had time to think as she trudged home alone after a tough day at work. She had time to think as she ate takeout fish and chips in her empty apartment. And she had time to think while having a cup of tea by herself in the corner café as she watched a group of girlfriends gossip together at the next table.

Mainly, she thought about how she'd gotten to this point: how she'd decided to pursue a romance that everyone in her life—her family, her best friends—had warned her about. She didn't know why Drew had been so irresistible—or why someone like Stephen had been so repulsive. Now that she was a million miles away from him, Lin found herself thinking about Stephen quite a bit. She thought about how he treated her like gold, better than she ever deserved. She thought about how he was always there when she needed him, whether it was to cater to some whim that Kim had or to pick up her laundry because she was stuck at work. More than anything, she thought about how she never had to worry whether she was good enough for him.

"Here you go." The sales clerk handed Lin a giant shopping bag.

Lin shifted her other two bags onto her left arm as she tried to juggle her latest purchase with the unwieldy hatbox at her right elbow. Even though her shopping habits weren't any less exorbitant back home, she always had one of her friends with her to help. M.J. might shy away from all the haute couture, but she was always willing to offer a hand with Lin's bags.

"Ma'am, is everything okay?" The salesclerk peered at her from behind the counter. "Will you be able to carry all of that by yourself?"

Lin steadied the box and bags in her arms. She took a deep breath and straightened herself. "Yeah," she said, "I've got to."

As she staggered her way to the exit, Lin flashed back to her visit to the fortune-teller. Auntie Lee might have been wrong about her finding love, but she'd been right about Lin being lucky. She was lucky that London had fallen in her lap and that Rob had still been willing to let her go. Lucky that her family was still talking to her even if they disapproved of some of her choices. And lucky that her friends were still willing to take her back even after she'd abandoned them. Lin knew that there weren't that many second chances in life, and she was determined to make the most of this one.

. . .

"HEY, LIN, want another Guinness?"

Lin glanced up. It had been three weeks since she arrived in London, and her new colleagues had convened for a little after-work get-together at the pub around the corner. Ned was at the bar, calling out to her and nodding toward the empty mug in his hand. Lin shook her head with a smile and pointed to her own half-full mug. She was glad to have met Ned. He was kind, sweet, and absolutely in love with his wife, who, by the way, was pretty great in her own right.

"Okay," Ned slid into the seat beside her, "I know you're on a hiatus from guys, but I think the bartender has a soft spot for you. You sure you couldn't chat him up for a few free pints?"

Lin just looked at him. "Ned."

He nodded. "I know, I know. And can I tell you again how impressed I am with how you've handled this whole situation?"

She blushed. "I was really worried you wouldn't respect me anymore after you found out what happened."

"Are you kidding me?" he demanded. "This job is hard enough. I'm just glad I'm not a woman who has to deal with the wankers of this profession—"

Before he could finish his sentence, Lin heard a noise. They both looked up to see a Burberry-clad blond Prince William lookalike smiling down at them.

"Ned, who's your lovely friend here?"

"Oh, Ian. Uh, Lin, Ian works in the funds department. Ian, Lin came over from New York—"

"I know who Lin is." Ian leaned down and took her hand in his. "I've had my eye on her since the first day she walked through our doors."

From the corner of her eye, Lin saw Ned looking at her, but all she did was smile politely at Ian. "It's nice to meet you."

"Not as nice as it is for me to meet you." Ian flashed her a charming smile. "So, tell me, what can I do to convince you to get out of here and go somewhere quiet with me?"

Lin raised an eyebrow. Next to her, Ned sighed.

"That's very flattering," she said, slowly withdrawing her hand, "but I'm actually about to head home soon."

Ian shrugged. "Okay, your loss."

As he strolled away, Lin turned to see Ned smiling at her.

"What?" she said, as she pulled on her coat.

"Nothing." Ned shook his head. "I just find it hard to believe you ever had a designer suit addiction."

Lin chuckled as she got up. "Good night, Ned." And with that, she headed home.

SUNDAYS WERE the loneliest.

Even though she'd sworn to make the most of this chance at redemption, it was still hard being by herself. Lin didn't realize until now how much she missed the Sunday schedule: dim sum with her friends and dinner with her parents. She was so used to it that she had come to take the whole tradition for granted. It had always been yet another burden imposed by Chinese tradition and the expectations of her family.

Once in London, though, Lin found herself yearning for those Chinese Sundays. She missed the easy comfort that came from being around her family—listening to her sister's chatter, her grandmother's stories, Kim's lecture of the day. She missed the expectation that she was supposed to be somewhere, and the knowledge that her absence would be felt and the topic of much discussion and concern. More than anything, she missed knowing that her Sunday would be filled with noise and activity and her family's unconditional love.

"Hi, Mom," Lin said into the receiver.

"Lin!" Kim's voice reverberated over the phone. "What going on with you? Why haven't you called this week?"

"I'm sorry," Lin apologized. "I've been really busy with work and settling in and figuring out where everything was—"

"No excuse," Kim interrupted her. "Are you eating? Are you getting enough sleep? Are you taking your vitamins? Those people in England have bad teeth. I see pictures. You make sure you drinking milk and eating your fruits and vegetables—"

As Kim's voice droned on, Lin leaned back against the wall and smiled.

Date: Thursday, November 15
To: M.J.; Alex
From: Lin

Hey girls!
London has been amazing. I can't believe it's been almost five months already! I wish you were sitting here with me in my office right now. The Tower of London is right across the river from me—can you believe it? It's the most breathtaking sight. The people here have been really nice, and I've made some good friends. My new coworkers are great (we go out to the pub all the time!), and my boss here, Rich Benjamin, has been a real mentor to me. Mostly though, I've been spending a lot of time on my own—sightseeing, going to the theater, taking walks along the Thames. It's actually kind of nice. Been thinking a lot about life and what I really want . . . mostly just trying to be happy with myself first. Until I do that, I don't think I'll be ready to be with someone else . . .

After doing a quick scan of the message, Lin took a deep breath and pressed SEND. Writing an e-mail wasn't even remotely close to satisfying, but until she could see her friends in person, this would have to do.

"Lin!" Ned knocked on the door. "You coming out with us to the pub tonight?"

"Not tonight," she replied, typing rapidly. "But have a pint for me."

"Okay," he said as he strolled off, "see you tomorrow."

As Lin shut down her computer, she looked outside and watched the lights turn on in the Tower of London. She smiled, a real smile from the inside. There would be no pub-crawling for her. She had a special visitor to see tonight.

. . .

AFTER RIDING the tube for half an hour, Lin was finally standing in Heathrow, craning her neck at the stream of disembarking passengers. Just as she was checking her watch, a familiar voice rang out above the crowd.

"Lin!"

Lin whirled around and saw a sight that brought a smile to her lips: her mother Kim making her way through the crowd, dragging three suitcases that probably weighed more than she did.

"Mom!" Lin ran over to give her a kiss and to help with her bags.

"Look at you—face pale, so skinny, hair like bird's nest. Good thing I bring you some ginseng tea. I need some myself—that was terrible flight," Kim complained. "Food bad, people noisy—"

As she launched into one of her patented rants about the plane and the terrible things she'd been forced to endure, Lin felt a sudden surge of affection for her mother. Kim would never be June Cleaver, but looking at her now, Lin realized just how much she'd missed having her mother fuss over her.

Leaning forward to hug Kim, she whispered, "I'm glad you're here, Mom."

"SO YOU like London?" Kim asked.

It was Friday night, and Lin and Kim were sitting in a little café near Picadilly Circus, fresh from spending the evening at the theater. Even though they hadn't had time to order any food, her mother had already managed to cover her feelings about the chilly weather and the exorbitant London prices in the short time since they were seated.

Lin sipped her water. "London is good. It's been really nice living here. But don't worry, Mom, I'm not planning on moving here permanently."

"Did I say anything?" she asked. "I just want you happy."

"I know." Lin studied her glass. "Mom, I have to tell you something. You were right about Drew. He was bad news. I just didn't want to see it."

As the words left her lips, she lowered her eyes and waited for her mother to launch into her triumphant I-told-you-so speech. To her shock, it never came.

"Lin." Kim gazed at her sadly. "I'm sad what happened with Drew. I don't like him, but you did. I didn't want you hurt. Do you understand?"

Lin nodded slowly. "I do now. I was just so determined to prove you wrong about him."

"Why?" Kim frowned.

"Because . . . because . . ." Lin couldn't quite bring herself to say it.

"Because what?" Kim asked.

Lin bit her lip. "Because, Mom, you tell me every minute of my life how I'm doing everything wrong."

Her mother stared at her for a moment. Then she did exactly what Lin knew she would do—she completely poohed-poohed the entire notion. "Don't be ridiculous." Kim waved the idea off. "I don't do that. I just look out for you."

"Yes," Lin said patiently, "you look out for me by telling me how I'm always doing something wrong."

Kim leaned forward. "When?" She squinted at Lin. "When do I do that?"

"All the time! Like with guys. Maybe if you weren't always pushing Stephen on me, I wouldn't have been so quick to get together with Drew."

"What's wrong with Stephen?" Her mother shook her head. "I never understand you, Lin. Stephen is a nice boy with good job and good manners. What's so wrong with that?"

Lin opened her mouth to argue and closed it. What indeed was wrong with that? Once upon a time, a nice boy with a good job and good manners was the last thing Lin wanted. She wanted excitement, a challenge, someone who wasn't tailor-made for her mother. But now, sitting here in London almost half a year after the whole Drew chapter of her life, Lin suddenly began to find the idea of a nice, normal boy pretty appealing.

"I don't know," she mumbled, staring down at her tea.

"Lin—" Her mother reached out to tip her chin up. "—did you not like Stephen because of me?"

Lin knew the answer, of course, had known it all her life. Because, like Rome, all roads led back to Kim. "Yes," she conceded finally.

"But why?" Kim looked genuinely confused. "Is so bad if I like him?"

Lin shook her head. "No, Mom, it's not. It's just that . . . I don't want to be you."

The moment the words left her lips, Lin winced. That had come out sounding terrible, all wrong, not at all the way it had sounded in her head.

Indeed, Kim was looking at her with a hurt that Lin had never seen in her before. "So," she said, "you don't want to be like me."

"No, that's not what I meant," Lin groaned. "I mean, it is, but . . ." She started again. "Mom, you've always told me the truth. You told me how when you were growing up, you wanted nothing more than to be a movie star in Hong Kong. But then you got married, even though you didn't want to do it."

Kim frowned. "And?"

Lin took a deep breath. "And you regretted it for the rest of your life."

There was a long moment of silence.

"This is why you get involved with that Drew?" Kim asked.

Lin hesitated then nodded slowly. "A little. I mean, I liked him for who he was, too, but maybe part of it was that he wasn't someone you would have chosen for me. Mom, I see how you get when you talk about what you could have been. I don't want to be like that. I don't want to look back years from now and wish I had lived my life differently."

"Stop!" Kim said. "Stop that. Who said I want my life to be different? I have good life, good daughters. Nothing wrong with that."

Lin rolled her eyes. "Oh, come on, Mom. You and I both know that if you could live your life over, you wouldn't have chosen this life. You wouldn't have chosen us."

And there it was—she'd said it. The thought that had haunted her all these years, that had informed her every decision, that had ruled how she lived her life . . .

After what seemed like an eternity, Lin looked up. "I'm sorry, Mom—"

"No, I sorry." Kim's gaze was filled with sadness. "I sorry because I failed you."

Lin creased her forehead. "What are you talking about—?"

"If I was a good mother," she said slowly, "you wouldn't think this."

This couldn't be her mom talking, Lin thought. She couldn't ever recall a time when Kim had admitted to being wrong.

"Maybe when I was girl, I wanted to be actress, but that was a long time ago. When you get older, you learn more—you see things differently," she explained. "I know what is important in life now. Not being a movie star. What important is my daughters—nothing else."

Lin looked at her mother, and suddenly saw herself. For so long, she'd felt like the prodigal child, convinced that she would never be good enough, would never be able to compensate for Kim's lost ambitions. It had never occurred to her that Kim had been young and naïve once, too, consumed with girlish fantasies. Like her, Lin, too, had learned what was important in life. It had taken a broken heart, a near-career-ending disaster, and a move across the Atlantic, but she could finally see what was real—and what was a mirage. Suddenly tearful, she reached over and hugged her mother.

Kim held her tightly. Then, suddenly she pulled back, cupped Lin's chin in her hand, and gazed at her intently. "You good, smart girl, Lin. I'm proud of you. Why you don't see that?"

Lin smiled through her tears. "I guess I just didn't want to be a failure," she admitted. "I didn't want to be another one of your disappointments."

Kim shook her head. "You could never be disappointment, Lin. That stuff about Hong Kong—your auntie Betty always say I talk too much nonsense. Yes, before, I wish I went to Hong Kong. But now I look at you and your sisters, and I know I did the right thing."

Lin glanced up, and for the first time she could remember, she suddenly felt free, light, as if a tremendous weight had been lifted off her shoulders.

EVEN THOUGH there were times when her stay in London seemed like an eternity, Lin found the end came sooner than she thought. After six months, her rotation was up, and it was time to return to the States. Her last week in London was consumed with furious, last-minute shopping for gifts at Harrods, one more show at the theater, and a visit to Wimbledon. Her coworkers threw her a going-away party her last night in London, and unlike that night at Victor's Café with Drew, this evening was filled only with happiness. As she stood there in the pub, hoisting one last pint with Ned and his wife, Lin suddenly realized that she really was going to miss London.

Saying good-bye was the hardest. Standing at Heathrow again with Ned, Lin couldn't help but shed a tear. "Thanks for everything, Ned," Lin said sincerely. "I was so nervous about being here by myself, but you and your wife really made me feel at home."

"It was our pleasure," Ned said warmly. "Come back and visit, okay?"

Lin smiled. "That's a promise."

As she boarded the plane, Lin thought about her time in London. Professionally, the experience had been invaluable. Not only was she now well-versed in foreign markets, but she was also on a first-name basis with countless London CEOs. Plus, she'd fulfilled her lifelong dream of matching wits with her English counterparts—and found that she measured up pretty well. But most important, she'd had time to evaluate her life, ponder her decisions, and figure out what exactly it was she wanted. It was only now that she felt healed, whole, and strong enough to face New York again.

. . .

WORKING AT the New York Stock Exchange and living in TriBeCa, Lin strolled down the street with a different attitude. It had been a month since she'd moved back to New York. Knowing that she could never go back to Merrill Lynch, she'd accepted an offer from the Exchange once her London rotation was up. Now, back in the same town that had once caused her so much heartbreak, she truly felt like she was living a whole new life. In a way, coming back to New York City was like living in a new city in Europe. In the end, Lin wasn't sure if the city itself was all that different—maybe it was just the way she saw it these days.

As she walked up Fifth Avenue and into Central Park to meet her girls for a little ice-skating, she hummed to herself, drinking in the snow-covered trees, the crisp, winter air, the laughing children building snowmen on the Great Lawn. Life was good.

That was when she saw an attractive, familiar-looking man standing near the entrance to Wollman Rink.

"Lin!" Drew beamed as he came up to her. "You're a hard woman to track down. I had to do a lot of calling around before I found out where you were."

Looking at him, Lin was flooded with a sudden torrent of emotion. All the old feelings came back in a rush. "Drew—" Lin's heart beat wildly. "I'm doing great. How are you? Oh my gosh, it's been over half a year."

"I know. You still look great, like you always did. What have you been up to?"

"I work at the Stock Exchange now," Lin said. "What are you doing?"

"That sounds awesome. I'm still at Merrill Lynch. But I'm assistant vice president at the branch now."

"Wow, good for you." Lin smiled. "You must be psyched."

"I am, I am . . . I can't believe it's really you. You know, I sent you a few e-mails when you were in London, but you never wrote me back," Drew said hesitantly.

Lin shrugged. "Well, you know how it is."

Drew's face fell. He stared at her, clearly stunned that Lin was not falling at his feet.

"Well," she said quickly, "it was really nice running into you. Take care of yourself, okay?"

"Lin, wait." Drew stared at her, still waiting for the inevitable invitation. "Don't . . . don't you think this is weird?"

"Weird?" she asked.

Drew sighed, his shoulders slumped. "Lin, don't you think it means anything that I went to all this trouble to find you?"

For a minute, Lin didn't know what to say. So she'd finally gotten him to cave first—but now what? He still looked wonderful—if anything, the passage of time had only served to make him more handsome, more sophisticated and mature. And there was still that old chemistry between them—even now, Lin couldn't deny the attraction. Part of her wanted to throw her arms around him, to throw caution to the wind. But then there was the rest of her telling her to stay strong, reminding her about that awful night at the bar, and forbidding her to undo all the hard work she'd done to get her life back on track. In the end, she did the only thing she could do.

"Look, Drew, I'm not going to lie to you. I still think about you a lot." She paused. "But our time together . . . our time together has passed."

Drew looked stunned. "Lin, I told you that I was truly sorry for everything. I don't know what else I can do."

"There isn't anything to do, Drew. Things are just different now. I'm different now. So are you. Maybe we just can't be different together anymore." Adjusting her bag on her shoulder, Lin took one last look into his eyes. "Take care of yourself, Drew."

And with that, Lin walked away from Drew and from her past. In the end, it turned out that the fortune-teller was wrong. She hadn't ended up with Drew. But she *was* lucky—lucky to have her friends and her self back.

Her girls were waiting for her at the rink.

Alex could tell immediately that something was up. "What?" she demanded. "What happened?"

Lin laughed. "I guess I really am an open book." She took a deep breath. "I just ran into Drew on the way over here."

Her friends both gasped. M.J. put a hand on Lin's arm. "You all right?" she asked, concern etched on her face.

Lin smiled at her friends. "Yeah," she said, "I really am."

And she was. Drew would always possess a small part of her heart, but she was ready for bigger and better things. She was ready for the rest of her life.

lunar new year

福

Gun Hai Fat Choi

Come one, come all!

You're cordially invited to the annual

Lunar New Year Festival on February 18th

at the Cho residence located on

88 Pond Lane, Syosset, New York 11030

As usual, festivities begin at noon so bring your ly sees (red envelopes), you married ones, and for all those single kids out there, wear something red with lots of pockets to collect all your pocket money!

Don't forget to bring your appetites and your recipes!

Please RSVP Pau Pau or Gung Gung as soon as possible! See you all there!

Epilogue

FOR EVERY time her grandmother made Lin cringe or wince or wish that she could shrivel up and die, there was a time when she felt blessed to have her dictating her every move. There was a certain comfort in being able to relinquish control of her seesaw life and retreat to the security of being a child in her *pau pau*'s eyes. Sitting in her family's kitchen, Lin couldn't help but feel content as she struggled to knead the perfect crescent for her grandmother's legendary shrimp and pork dumplings. She only wished she could keep up with the staccato commands of the elderly—but no less dominating—matriarch.

"*Bawk dee! Bawk dee!* Thinner! Thinner!" Ling exhorted her to attain that impossibly delicate, paper-thin shell for the savory meat mixture she was stirring in a nearby pot.

Lin wiped her brow and sneaked a peek at the clock above the kitchen sink. Thankfully, it was almost noon. She'd been at her grandmother's beck and call since six that morning. While she'd always loved being in her family's cluttered, warmly lit house—always so full of delicious delicacies and mah-jong thrills—she was starting to feel the effects of too much cooking and too little caffeine. Fortunately, her mother was slated to relieve her at noon. Lin's stomach growled as she took in the aroma of the last batch of piping hot dumplings—her favorite New Year delicacy—that her *pau pau* had set out on the counter to cool. Deciding that she'd earned herself a treat, Lin reached out to grab one.

"*Mai sic!* Don't eat!" Her grandmother swatted her and whisked the dumplings away.

Lin sighed, eyeing the heaping dishes of food around her wistfully—the fragrant black bean jai vegetarian dish, the succulent garlic and scallion lobster, the tantalizing red bean paste puffs. There was nothing worse than cooking on an empty stomach.

As Lin contemplated the feast before her, Kim came in and started smoothing Lin's hair. "The guests will arrive any minute. Put on something pretty for once!"

Lin made a face and tried to pull away, just as she did when she was five. Of course, Kim only took this as further incentive to start criticizing Lin's hair, shoes, the very tint of her lip gloss. Fortunately, at that moment, the doorbell rang. Lin was out of her chair like a shot.

"I'll get it!" she sang out as she sprinted to the door.

The first set of visitors to arrive was her father and her aunt Betty. Lin hugged them then quickly composed herself to impart the traditional New Year's greeting.

"Gung hai fat choi," she said. "Happy New Year," she repeated in English. "Where are my red envelopes?"

"Gung hai fat choi," her aunt responded as she pushed the requisite red envelopes into Lin's hand, "but you forgot *'Sun ty geen hong.'* Have good health."

Lin nodded dutifully and fingered the envelopes just as she'd always done as a kid. It was crazy how excited she still got about the twenty bucks, especially given her current salary. But there was nothing like the feel of the red paper and the telltale bulge within to get her as giddy as she'd been when she was a child.

"Lin!"

Lin turned around and broke into a smile when she saw M.J. and her mother, Esther, at the door, with Ming and his fiancée, May, just behind. Lin hurried over to give them hugs.

"Gung hai fat choi!" she greeted them.

"Yeah, yeah, Happy New Year," M.J. said as she sailed in, while Ming and May opted for more traditional New Year greetings. Esther took Lin's face in one hand while she pressed a red envelope into her palm.

"You being a good girl, Lin? Still making a lot of money?"

Lin nodded. Satisfied, Esther clucked something at M.J. before taking off to find Lin's mother and grandmother. Lin shot M.J. an apologetic look, but her friend brushed it off with a shake of her head.

"So where's your dad?" Lin asked as she took everyone's coats.

"Oh, he'll be by later," M.J. replied. "He had a crazy morning."

Lin raised an eyebrow. "How so?"

"M.J. brought the white guy home." Ming wiggled his eyebrows. "I think her dad is still recovering from the whole thing right now. Her mom only came with us so she could tell your mother all about it, Lin."

M.J. smacked his arm. "That's not what happened, Ming." She turned to Lin. "Jagger did meet my folks, but they were actually semi-okay with it. Basically, if I stay off 'Page Six,' they'll be willing to put up with everything else." She rubbed her chin. "In a strange way, he's the perfect person to deal with them because it doesn't matter what they say or do—nothing offends him. It's water off his back."

"You say that now," Ming said, "but wait until your mom gets you alone. Then you'll get it."

M.J. rolled her eyes.

May gave Ming a warning nudge. "Now, Ming," she said, "you promised to behave."

"That's right." M.J. jumped at the possibility of reinforcements. "That's the only reason I agreed to let you meet Jagger—because you swore to keep an open mind about him."

"Yeah, yeah," Ming said airily, "so where's the white boy anyway?"

"He'll be here in a bit." M.J. chewed her lower lip. "He said he had to go home and get his Jet Li T-shirt."

Ming's eyes widened. "That is exactly the kind of thing I'm talking about," he exclaimed. "The white man raping and pillaging the Asian culture—" Fortunately, May dragged Ming away to the dining room before he could say any more.

M.J. shook her head and turned back to Lin. "I hope introducing Drew to your family wasn't as bad as that."

Lin sighed. "Pretty much everything involving Drew was bad."

"Aw, Lin." M.J. slipped her arm around her friend. "You're so much better off without him, ya know. I mean, look at Kevin—Auntie Lee was totally right about him."

Lin nodded emphatically. "I know." Still, she couldn't help wondering when she'd meet her own Jagger.

"I know just what you need," M.J. declared, "a good, old-fashioned pigging-out. And we can start right now, with some of your grandmother's delicious red bean puffs." She reached out to grab one of the delicacies—and upended the entire plate. The bean puffs crashed and scattered onto the floor. M.J. and Lin both winced.

"Uh-oh," M.J. said, "I better grab the broom before your grandmother comes in—"

"No!" Lin gasped. "No brooms! It's Chinese New Year—brooms are bad luck, remember? My grandmother will say we're sweeping our good luck away!" And if there was one thing the fortune-teller had been right about, it was Lin's luck.

M.J. gazed at the mess. "I hope you're not suggesting that I eat what's on the floor."

"Don't be ridiculous." Lin knelt down and started picking up the pastry pieces with a napkin. "See, we don't need a broom—"

At that moment, the doorbell rang again. M.J. seized the opportunity to leave Lin to clean up and went to answer the door. This time, it was Alex and her folks. Lin finished disposing of the food and quickly got up, smiling. Her friend looked great—there was a glow to her cheeks, a certain lightness in her walk that had appeared in the past couple months. Lin was sure it had something to do with Brady, but of course, Alex would never admit to it.

"Alex!" M.J. and Lin both shouted.

Alex exhaled as her parents quickly went to join their friends. "Thank God!" She shook her head. "We just went to my aunt's house to wish her happy New Year, and she started telling me about these Asian 'love boats' where singles go on this cruise ship to meet a wife or husband—like the ones for college kids but older. As if I would ever go on one of these things! But you know what the worst thing was? My parents were totally in on it. The minute my aunt started talking, they were mysteriously nowhere to be found!"

Lin and M.J. chuckled.

"I told you," Lin said. "Your parents may be afraid to say anything to your face, but they are no different from any other Chinese parents."

Alex sighed. "I'm just grateful they haven't met the guy I'm actually involved with. Who knows what they would say then?"

"Well," Lin slyly slung an arm around M.J., "our girl J just did that this very morning. And now she's bringing him to his first family gathering—here, tonight, in this very house!"

M.J. blushed.

Alex stared at her incredulously. "You invited Jagger here?" she said. "Are you insane?"

"Well," M.J. shifted uncomfortably, "I—"

"This is going to be great!" Alex exclaimed. "I can't wait to sit back and watch the show. M.J., you have more guts than I ever gave you credit for—"

She was abruptly interrupted by the familiar ring of the doorbell. M.J. bit her lip. Shooting her a quick smile, Lin went to answer the door . . . and found herself face-to-face with a compact Billy Joe Armstrong look-alike in a Jet Li silk-screened T-shirt and bright red Skechers. Jagger.

"Lin, right?" he said. "I think we met a long time ago at Serafina's."

Behind Lin, Alex snorted. "You don't sound sure," she called over Lin's shoulder. "I guess we Asians all look alike."

Jagger chuckled. "Nice to see you again, too, Alex." He turned to Lin. "She's wrong, you know. I remember you. Besides, I would never confuse you with Alex—M.J. said you were the nice one."

"Hey!" Alex managed to look both offended and pleased at the comment.

Jagger laughed as he winked at M.J. "Hey, babe."

Alex turned away with a dismissive wave. "Better take care of your guest, Lin."

"That's 'guests,' " a voice behind Jagger rang out.

Jagger turned and they all peered around him to see—Brady. Studying the dapper newcomer closely, Lin couldn't help thinking that this was the unexpected man Auntie Lee had told Alex about.

Brady smiled rakishly at the girls and then at Alex. "Hey, Alexa."

"Brady?" Alex staggered back. "What—what are you doing here?"

"Oh, I called your parents' house earlier today, and they told me that you guys would all be here this afternoon, so I figured I'd come over and wish my favorite litigator a happy New Year."

Alex shook her head. "I can't believe it," she muttered. "First the love boat, and now my parents have sold me out to my partner."

Brady strolled over and slung an arm around her neck. "Alex, it's okay—you don't need to play hard to get anymore."

Alex made a face, but she didn't push him away. Lin observed all this with an interested eye, thinking that her friend was protesting just a little too much.

"So," Jagger said after giving M.J. a very boyfriendly kiss, "you're Alex's dude, huh?"

Brady turned toward him. "Yeah, I guess you could say that."

For a moment, the two of them just studied each other, Jagger in his tattered jeans and Brady in his crisply tailored blazer.

Finally, Brady held out his hand. "I'm Brady."

Jagger shook it. "Jagger."

Lin exhaled, not realizing until that moment that she'd been holding her breath. Alex and M.J. looked at each other and wiped their brows in mock relief.

"Well," Lin said gaily, "come on in—you guys are all welcome. Just leave your shoes by the door—"

"What? Now there's two of them?"

They all turned. Ming stood there, hands on his waist.

"All right, Ming," M.J. stepped forward, "before you get on your high horse—"

"Ming? Is that you?" Jagger asked.

Ming blinked. The girls stared as Jagger and Ming stepped forward—and embraced.

"Ming, man!" Jagger high-fived Ming exuberantly. "I haven't seen you since we got snowed in at the T-wolves game two years ago!"

"Don't remind me!" Ming chuckled. "We were stuck in that god-awful city for three whole days before we could get a flight out."

"Hey, you still have that cheesehead hat?"

"Somewhere probably. What about you?"

"Sitting in my office as we speak." Jagger turned to M.J. "This guy and I spent a lot of time in the Mall of America during those three days, and there was the coolest store that only sold cheeseheads—I guess because it's so close to Wisconsin."

M.J. stared at them, befuddled. "So you guys—know each other?"

"Oh, we go way back," Jagger assured her, "before you and I ever met, M.J." He turned back to Ming. "Hey, Ming, I want you to meet Brady. Brady, this is Ming Chan."

Ming shook Brady's hand. "Nice to meet you."

M.J. couldn't believe it. Who was this stranger? And what had he done to Ming?

"I read your column every day," Brady said.

Ming beamed. "Oh, yeah? What did you think of yesterday's?"

"It was right on. I've been saying for years that Floyd Greene is overrated—the Magic should just trade him while they can get someone decent."

"Thanks, man," Ming said. "Hey, why don't we go into the kitchen and grab a few beers? My fiancée's helping set the table right now, so there'll be plenty to eat soon."

Jagger clapped Ming on the shoulder. "You're a good man, Ming." And with that, all three guys strolled off toward the kitchen.

"Okay." M.J. rubbed her eyes. "Did I just hallucinate all of that or did we manage to get through the intros without any bloodshed?"

"Nope," Lin confirmed, "a miracle has happened."

"Well, I'm just glad that I won't be the only one introducing a white boy to her parents." M.J. slyly elbowed Alex.

Alex scowled. "My parents are in such big trouble."

"But I thought you said nothing happened in Vegas," Lin said innocently.

Alex looked heavenward. "Nothing did!"

"Well, I don't know about you," M.J. commented, "but my Vegas flings don't usually show up out of the blue at my Chinese New Year parties."

"That's true," Alex acknowledged. "Your fling just turns out to be Ming's long-lost Minneapolis buddy!"

Lin chuckled. "And here I thought Ming hated white guys."

The girls all burst into giggles.

"Yeah, all we need now is for Drew Black to show up," M.J. said slyly.

Lin shuddered. "Please, let's not ruin the New Year already. What do you say we go and do some toasting of our own?"

Alex grinned. "Sounds like a plan."

They headed for the kitchen, where they ran smack into Ming, Jagger, and Brady.

"Hey, girls," Jagger called out.

"Well, aren't you three a cozy trio," Alex remarked. "I guess this is what they call male bonding. What are you going to do now—watch hoops together?"

The guys exchanged looks. Then as one, they all headed toward the living room. M.J. and Alex glanced at each other—and hurried after them.

Watching them, Lin smiled as she pondered how Auntie Lee's

prophecies had come true for her friends. It was too bad hers had somehow gone awry, she thought as she went to check the refrigerator for any alcoholic beverage she could find.

"Lin?"

Lin glanced up and almost banged her head into the refrigerator door. Stephen?

"Lin," Stephen stepped forward, "it's so great to see you again."

"Same here," she managed as she hugged him, feeling a surprising flutter in her chest. "I have to admit—you caught me off guard."

"You mean you weren't expecting to see me in your kitchen?" Stephen joked. "Believe me, I'm really not stalking you. I ran into your grandmother yesterday when I was in Chinatown, and she invited me over."

Lin blushed. "I would never think you were stalking me, Stephen. I'm just . . . a little startled."

"So hey, we didn't really get a chance to talk at your aunt's house. How's your job?" Stephen asked. "Still raking in the money?"

Lin stared at him. Since when did Stephen become interested in her career?

"Yeah, work's good," she said casually. "How have you been?"

"Good," he responded. "I've actually been on a sabbatical of sorts—I spent three months traveling around Asia and Australia."

Lin clapped a hand to her mouth. "Omigosh! That sounds amazing! I've always wanted to spend some time over there."

"It was pretty cool." He nodded. "The best was when I was in Tibet—"

As Stephen went on to describe his travels, Lin took the opportunity to study him surreptitiously. Now that she wasn't so distracted by the karaoke, she noticed he looked surprisingly lean and wiry in his Diesel jeans and black Che Guevara T-shirt.

"—so anyway, some of the pictures I took are actually being shown at a gallery downtown," Stephen continued. "Maybe we can go see them sometime."

Lin smiled. "I would really like that."

"That reminds me," Lin interrupted. "I have a surprise for us. Guess where we're going tomorrow?"

"I CAN'T believe we're here again," M.J. said.

"I can't believe a whole year has passed already," Alex added.

"Well, believe it," Lin replied, "we said we would come back, so here we are."

The girls all gazed around at the familiar red incense-filled room of Auntie Lee's parlor. It looked exactly as it had a year ago—as if time itself stood still there.

"What do you think she'll tell us this time?" Alex wondered.

"Well, I gotta say she ended up being pretty right about me last year," M.J. said.

Lin fiddled with her diamond hoop earrings. "I just hope this year turns out to be smoother than last—"

"You've returned."

They looked up as Auntie Lee toddled into the room. Like her parlor, she looked exactly as she did the last time they saw her—tiny and inscrutable.

"Hello, Auntie Lee," Lin began. "We came—"

"I know why you come," the fortune-teller interrupted. "You wish to know your fates for the New Year. Let me look at your faces, children, and I will tell you all. . . ."

The girls just grinned at each other as they drew closer to Auntie Lee.